THE EUROPEAN COURT OF HUMAN RIGHTS
BETWEEN LAW AND POLITICS

The European Court of Human Rights between Law and Politics

Edited by

JONAS CHRISTOFFERSEN

and

MIKAEL RASK MADSEN

OXFORD
UNIVERSITY PRESS

OXFORD
UNIVERSITY PRESS

Great Clarendon Street, Oxford OX2 6DP

Oxford University Press is a department of the University of Oxford.
It furthers the University's objective of excellence in research, scholarship,
and education by publishing worldwide in

Oxford New York

Auckland Cape Town Dar es Salaam Hong Kong Karachi
Kuala Lumpur Madrid Melbourne Mexico City Nairobi
New Delhi Shanghai Taipei Toronto

With offices in

Argentina Austria Brazil Chile Czech Republic France Greece
Guatemala Hungary Italy Japan Poland Portugal Singapore
South Korea Switzerland Thailand Turkey Ukraine Vietnam

Oxford is a registered trade mark of Oxford University Press
in the UK and in certain other countries

Published in the United States
by Oxford University Press Inc., New York

British Library Cataloguing in Publication Data

Data available

Library of Congress Control Number:
2011924932

Typeset by SPI Publisher Services, Pondicherry, India
Printed in Great Britain
on acid-free paper by
CPI Antony Rowe, Chippenham, Wiltshire

ISBN 978–0–19–969449–5

1 3 5 7 9 10 8 6 4 2

In memory of A. W. Brian Simpson (1933–2011)

Preface

The 50th Anniversary of the European Court of Human Rights (ECtHR) was marked at the Copenhagen Conference on the European Court of Human Rights convened at the Ceremonial Hall of the University of Copenhagen on 21–22 March 2009. Rather than celebrating the accomplishments of the Court, we set out to discuss how and why the European Court developed into a unique European institution: What helped this Court to succeed and how can this particular trajectory be of use in understanding the significant challenges facing the ECtHR in years to come both in terms of law and institutional politics?

A series of leading international scholars, who have all carried out substantial empirical research on the ECtHR, either from a legal or social scientific perspective, participated at the Copenhagen Conference. We greatly appreciate the constructive and active interventions of all participants. We further acknowledge the support of the Centre of European Constitutionalization, particularly Professor Henning Koch, as well as the Centre for the Studies in Legal Culture, both at the Faculty of Law, University of Copenhagen. Also we would like to extend our gratitude to the University of Copenhagen's Research Initiative 'Europe in Transition' which generously sponsored the conference. Finally, we would like to thank Miriam Mckenna, now a PhD student at the Faculty of Law, University of Copenhagen, without whose assistance the editing of this book would still be ongoing.

Jonas Christoffersen
Mikael Rask Madsen

Copenhagen
February 2011

Contents

Table of European Cases

EUROPEAN COURT OF HUMAN RIGHTS

EUROPEAN COURT OF JUSTICE

List of Contributors

Ed Bates, Senior Lecturer, University of Southampton, School of Law, England.

Jonas Christoffersen, Director of the Danish Institute for Human Rights, formerly Associate Professor, Faculty of Law, University of Copenhagen, Denmark.

Rachel A. Cichowski, Associate Professor, Department of Political Science, Law, Societies and Justice Program, University of Washington, Seattle, Washington, U.S.A.

Robert Harmsen, Professor of Political Science at the University of Luxembourg, formerly Senior Lecturer in European Studies at Queen's University Belfast, Northern Ireland.

Stéphanie Hennette-Vauchez, Professor of Public Law, Université Paris Ouest Nanterre–La Défense, formerly Marie Curie Fellow at the European University Institute, Florence, Italy.

Anthony Lester, practising barrister QC and member of Blackstone Chambers, as well as a member of the House of Lords (Lord Lester of Herne Hill), Co-Founder and Hon President of Interights and a member of the Joint Parliamentary Committee on Human Rights.

Mikael Rask Madsen, Professor of European Law and Integration and Director of the Centre for Studies of Legal Culture at the Faculty of Law, University of Copenhagen, Denmark.

Laurent Scheeck, Counsellor, International Relations Unit of the Chamber of Deputies, Luxembourg, formerly Associate Professor at the Institut d'Etudes Européennes–Université Libre de Bruxelles, Belgium.

Erik Voeten, Peter F. Krogh Associate Professor of Geopolitics and Global Justice, Edmund A. Walsh School of Foreign Service and Government Department, Georgetown University, Washington, D.C., U.S.A.

Luzius Wildhaber, Professor Emeritus at the University of Basel, Switzerland, Visiting Professor at Yale Law School and former President of the European Court of Human Rights (1998–2007).

Note to the Reader

All abbreviations used in this work are defined in the individual chapters.

In December 2009 the European Court of Justice (ECJ) was renamed the Court of Justice of the European Union (CJEU). In accordance with academic practice we refer to the Court by its original name—the ECJ—unless otherwise specified.

1

Introduction: The European Court of Human Rights between Law and Politics

Jonas Christoffersen and Mikael Rask Madsen

When seen in a broader historical context, it is perhaps somewhat surprising that Europe was to take the lead in the international protection of human rights following the atrocities of the Second World War. European societies had undoubtedly played a decisive role in the original formulation of human rights at the advent of the French Revolution. Yet Europe, particularly through the subsequent rise of imperial European societies, was also clearly manipulating the very same notion, limiting its applicability to a select group of individuals and instrumentalizing human rights as part of their self-described 'mission civilisatrice' abroad.[1] Moreover, in the aftermath of the Second World War, Europe hardly stood out as the future torchbearer for human rights. No continent had been more severely impacted by the hostilities and atrocities of the war—and no continent was more responsible for the outbreak of the conflict.

What nevertheless made the European project of human rights possible was the closely linked initiative of integrating Europe also in terms of politics and economics. Among the 'Europeanists' who congregated at the Congress for Europe in The Hague in 1948—one of the decisive moments in the initiation of the plan for European integration—it is striking that many did not distinguish between Europe 'the market' and Europe as a mainstay of human rights. In 1949, when the negotiations leading to the European Convention on Human Rights (ECHR) were being intensified, many of the key players still envisaged the ECHR, in the words of Pierre-Henri Teitgen, as part of a broader 'generalisation of social democracy' in Europe.[2]

The master plan of many of these legal and political actors was that the ECHR, as upheld by the European Court of Human Rights (ECtHR), was to produce a common conscience for all of (Western) Europe.[3] As we know now, these plans for

---

[1] See eg A. L. Conklin, *A Mission to Civilize: The Republican Idea of Empire in France and West Africa, 1895–1930* (Stanford: Stanford University Press, 1997). For a more critical account, C. Douzinas, *Human Rights and Empire: The Political Philosophy of Cosmopolitanism* (New York: Routledge-Cavendish, 2007).

[2] As cited in J. G. Merrills and A. H. Robertson, *Human Rights in Europe: A Study of the European Convention on Human Rights* (Manchester: Manchester University Press, 2008), 8.

[3] See further Chapter 2 below.

a genuine European constitutionalization—a 'United States of Europe' in the words of Churchill—eventually disintegrated throughout the 1950s with the failure of a series of integration projects, most notably the European Defence Community (EDC), and the European Political Community (EPC), and with them fell the idea of a genuine European constitution. The two-pronged approach to European integration, which in practice emerged with the development of the two distinct institutions of the Council of Europe and the European Coal and Steel Community (ECSC), was to be further cemented with the Treaty of Rome (1957).[4]

Conversely, the idea of integrating Europe through human rights was to take its own, and in many ways unique, path. The post-war European system dedicated to the protection of human rights in Europe today stands out as one of the most far-reaching and successful attempts at an international human rights protection regime. It has even become the de facto model for developing human rights elsewhere. This raises the complex question of what has made the ECHR system develop in this fashion; what facilitated and impeded this process and, not least, how will this trajectory impact on the future development of the Court in light of its current legitimacy crisis?

These are also the questions we seek to answer. For that purpose, we deploy an interdisciplinary approach. This book generally contends that an understanding of the rise of the European Court necessitates an analysis of the interdependency between the evolution of European human rights law and the changing socio-political and institutional contexts in which this development is embedded. However, we equally maintain that it is imperative that the analysis does not diverge from the legal core of the ECHR system but provides contextual analysis which helps to further the legal and institutional understanding of European human rights law.

The structure of the book seeks to respond to these analytical and methodological challenges. More specifically we seek to capture the interdependency between the evolution of law and European and international society by analysing the rise of the ECtHR using a historical chronological approach, starting with the genesis of the ECHR and concluding with a view to the future of the Court using the insights of European legal history. Obviously, like any other analysis using history as a framework, this is a selective history of the ECtHR. We do, however, hope to have captured the most essential and emblematic characteristics of what, over the last 50 years, have made the ECtHR stand out as a unique institution, both in Europe and internationally.

I. The ECtHR as a European Court

As indicated in these opening paragraphs, the ECtHR cannot be understood as a static institution. For analytical purposes, one can identity at least three major

---

[4] Cf A. Cohen and M. R. Madsen, 'Cold War Law: Legal Entrepreneurs and the Emergence of a European Legal Field (1945–1965)' in V. Gessner and D. Nelken (eds), *European Ways of Law: Towards a European Sociology of Law* (Oxford: Hart Publishing, 2007).

phases which the ECtHR has undergone since its inauguration in 1959. In its initial phase, the European Court sought only very gradually to develop its institutional autonomy and jurisprudence. Due to the general uncertainties regarding the future of the Convention, particularly the reluctance of the Member States to accept the Court's full powers and individual petition, the development was somewhat inverted, as it became paradoxically the Court—not the Member States—that had to prove it had a sound understanding of European human rights.

However, in its second phase, beginning in the mid to late 1970s against the backdrop of a series of geopolitical and social changes, the Court embarked on the development of a more progressive jurisprudence, evoking notions such as 'living instrument', 'margin of appreciation', and 'practical and effective'. In its third phase, beginning in the post-Cold War era, the Court went from being the guarantor of human rights solely in Western Europe to becoming increasingly involved in the transition to democracy and the rule of law in Eastern Europe.

Becoming the protector of the human rights of some 800 million Europeans from 47 different countries, the European system is today once again deeply challenged by a massive caseload[5] as well as the Member States' increased reluctance towards the Court. In fact, the Court has arguably entered into a fourth phase, in around 2004, focusing increasingly on the effectiveness of the ECHR in domestic law and developing new methods to cope with the overwhelming caseload, emanating to a large extent from new Member States.[6] The pilot judgment procedure is perhaps the strongest indicator of the Court's new initiatives in this phase of development. At the same time, the reform of the Convention, most specifically the ongoing reform process prior to, alongside, and soon after Protocol No 14 is also an integral part of these current developments.

These seemingly insurmountable challenges should not, however, overshadow the rich history of institutional adaptation and creativity—legal and political—which is part of the recipe for success of the ECtHR. In the broader picture of the build-up of international legal institutions over the twentieth and twenty-first centuries, the ECtHR in many ways is an unparalleled success, perhaps only equalled by the European Court of Justice (ECJ).[7]

Yet, whereas the ECJ has for decades been the subject of analyses from a number of disciplines, the scholarly understanding of the ECtHR remains comparatively unexplored in law and particularly the social sciences. A brief view of the literature on the ECJ is revealing. After some 25 years of systematic inquiry into the ECJ, we now have a good understanding of the many ways the ECJ has influenced

---

[5] By 31 March 2010, some 124,650 allocated applications were pending before the Court. Of these, some 27.7 per cent came from Russia. See *European Court of Human Rights Statistics*, 1 January–31 December 2010.

[6] See eg J. Christoffersen, *Fair Balance: Proportionality, Subsidiarity and Primacy in the European Convention on Human Rights* (Leiden: Martinus Nijhoff, 2009), ch 4.

[7] Now the Court of Justice of the European Union (CJEU). In this introduction, we use ECJ and CJEU interchangeably.

European integration. These include, for example, its changing role as driver of and passenger on the European train, its interface with national courts, in particular national supreme courts, its role in establishing the supremacy of European law, and many other issues, including the fiercely debated question of whether the ECJ—deliberately or not—is constitutionalizing European law.[8]

The only area in which the scholarship on the ECtHR can compare to that of the ECJ is in the area of legal-institutional and doctrinal analysis where a very significant literature exists.[9] However, the rich scholarship on the ECJ focusing on the interplay of European law and its contexts has only rarely been replicated in respect of the ECtHR. Some attempts have, however, recently been made to address the legal culture of the ECtHR,[10] the legal identities of the judges of the ECtHR,[11] the levels of activism,[12] the history of the European Court and Convention of Human Rights,[13] and its interplay with civil society.[14] That said, a broader analysis of the role of the ECtHR in respect of European integration—which also considers comparatively its role and position in respect of the ECJ and emerging European legal space—is generally missing.[15] Moreover, an approach which somehow seeks to integrate these new insights has so far been absent, only adding to the sense of uncertainly regarding the past and future of the ECtHR.

This book sets out to remedy this gap in scholarly inquiry into the ECtHR by examining the original and contemporary legal, political, and institutional history of the ECtHR and the ways in which it has shaped its jurisprudence and

---

[8] See eg K. Alter, *Establishing the Supremacy of European Law: The Making of an International Rule of Law in Europe* (Oxford: Oxford University Press, 2001); A.-M. Burley and W. Mattli, 'Europe Before the Court: A Political Theory of Legal Integration', 47 *International Organization* (2001), 41; H. Rasmussen, *On Law and Policy in the European Court of Justice* (Dordrecht: Martinus Nijhoff, 2001); M. Rasmussen, 'The Origins of a Legal Revolution: The Early History of the European Court of Justice', 14(2) *Journal of European Integration History* (2008), 77; A. Stone Sweet, *The Judicial Construction of Europe* (Oxford: Oxford University Press, 2004); A. Vauchez, 'Une élite d'intermédiaires: Genèse d'un capital juridique européen (1950–1970)', *Actes de la recherche en sciences sociales* (2007); J. H. H. Weiler, 'A Quiet Revolution: The European Court of Justice and Its Interlocutors', 26(4) *Comparative Political Studies* (1994), 510.

[9] See eg S. Greer, *The European Convention on Human Rights: Achievements, Problems and Prospects* (Cambridge: Cambridge University Press, 2006); J. G. Merrills and A. H. Robertson, *Human Rights in Europe: A Study of the European Convention on Human Rights* (Manchester: Manchester University Press, 2001).

[10] N.-L. Arold, *The Legal Culture of the European Court of Human Rights* (Leiden: Martinus Nijhoff, 2007).

[11] F. Bruinsma, 'Judicial Identities in the European Court of Human Rights' in A. Van Hoek, A. M. Hol, O. Jansen, P. Rijpkema, and R. Widdershoven (eds), *Multilevel Governance in Enforcement and Adjudication* (Antwerp: Intersentia, 2006).

[12] E. Voeten, 'The Impartiality of International Judges: Evidence from the European Court of Human Rights', 102 *American Political Science Review* (2008), 417.

[13] E. Bates, *The Evolution of the European Convention on Human Rights: From Its Inception to the Creation of a Permanent Court of Human Rights* (Oxford: Oxford University Press, 2010); M. R. Madsen, 'From Cold War Instrument to Supreme European Court: The European Court of Human Rights at the Crossroads of International and National Law and Politics', 32(1) *Law & Social Inquiry* (2007), 137; A. W. B. Simpson, *Human Rights and the End of Empire: Britain and the Genesis of the European Convention* (Oxford: Oxford University Press, 2004).

[14] L. Hodson, *NGOs and the Struggle for Rights in Europe* (Oxford: Hart Publishing, 2011).

[15] See, however, A. Cohen and M. R. Madsen, above n 4.

current problems. Regardless of the Court's long and ongoing processes of institutional autonomization and juridification, it is close to impossible to debate its contemporary practices and challenges if a broader understanding of the institution is not advanced. This book is therefore based on the premise that an understanding of the rise of the European Court necessitates an analysis of the interdependency between the evolution of European human rights law and the changing socio-political and institutional contexts in which this development is embedded.

We seek to frame a more comprehensive analysis of the evolution of the ECtHR in terms of an interdisciplinary approach that details the legal, historical, and socio-political connections in order to further understand the legal core of the ECHR system and vice versa. The chapters examine precisely the double dynamic of the evolution of the European human rights system—that is, the underpinning interplay of socio-political and legal development shaping the system. As explained further below, we therefore go beyond the conventional definition of the object of study of European human rights as being the Court's jurisprudence, and instead make the common object of inquiry the evolution of the Court in terms of a European and international institution marked by both law and politics.

II. The Structure of the Book

The structure of the book is developed with the objective of responding to this challenge of providing a contextual analysis in order to further the legal, political, *and* institutional understanding of European human rights law. Divided into two parts on, respectively, the 'Politics and Institutionalization' and the 'Law and Legitimization' of the ECtHR, all chapters address a set of closely related issues concerning the evolution of the ECtHR.

In Part I, 'Politics and Institutionalization', we track the institutional evolution of the ECtHR from the genesis of the system to its current institutional set-up and challenges. The five chapters of Part I generally concur with the observation that the ECtHR has been largely influenced by a dialectics of crisis and institutional change. In other words, an understanding of the development of the institution and its jurisprudence necessitates a better understanding of the underlying political struggles over both the institutional architecture and its legal base.

In Part II, 'Law and Legitimization', the general argument put forward is that the effectiveness of European human rights law is—and has been—considerably determined by the Court's social and political legitimacy. This legitimacy, however, is ensured mainly through legal and doctrinal development, being the ECtHR's direct means of communication with the Member States and its citizens. With the objective of addressing the contemporary problems of both law and institutional legitimacy of the ECtHR, all five chapters in this part examine the various ways in which the Court, by means of law, has sought, and is seeking, to legitimize itself in its gradually transforming jurisdiction as a result of the significant changes in the Member States.

Part I: Politics and Institutionalization

The opening chapter (Chapter 2), written by Ed Bates, examines the drafting of the European Convention and outlines its original intent. Revisiting the post-war negotiations between European lawyers and politicians all seeking to prevent a recurrence of the atrocities of the war, Bates brings to light a number of important elements that still have a bearing on the ECtHR. The original objective was mainly to freeze the minimum level of protection by the Contracting States—a simple means to prevent the populations of Europe from slipping into the hands of politicians without respect for human rights and fundamental freedoms, be it fascists or communists. And although the negotiators soon agreed that these common minimum standards should be protected one way or another, the idea of international accountability before an international Commission and Court was not met with great enthusiasm. Some feared inroads into national sovereignty, while others had little faith in the effectiveness of international institutions. The result was, if anything, a compromise. The President of the Consultative Assembly of the Council of Europe, Paul-Henri Spaak, was not shy of showing his disappointment, noting, at the occasion of the signing of the Convention in 1950 at the Palazzo Barberini in Rome, 'It is not a very good Convention, but it is a lovely Palace'. Bates's analysis generally demonstrates how discussions of the ECtHR which today still find an echo have continuously revolved around a distinct set of issues: national sovereignty, international protection, federal control, domestic implementation, judicial activism, and the Court's constitutional role and position vis-à-vis national authorities. The fundamental issues are much alike, both now and then. However, as Ed Bates stresses, the importance of the ECHR was nevertheless that a number of European lawyers and politicians managed not only to draft the Convention but also to develop a common European legal vision of international human rights law.

In Chapter 3, Mikael Rask Madsen analyses the institutionalization of the Convention and how the Court subsequently went through an institutional and legal metamorphosis in the 1970s, paving the way for the progressive human rights jurisprudence which has become synonymous with the ECtHR in later years. The first part of the chapter highlights the double challenge the ECtHR faced during the first 20 years following the signing of the ECHR. As the key mechanisms of the ECHR system—the jurisdiction of the Court and individual petition—were made optional in the 1950 Convention, a central task of the system consisted in finding a way of convincing the larger European powers (in particular France and the UK) to accept the key optional clauses, whilst at the same time providing justice to the cases being brought before the Commission and Court by individuals from other Member States. This strategy of 'legal diplomacy' was successful in the sense that larger powers eventually became full members, yet the jurisprudence of the early Court was limited and even self-constraining. In the second half of the 1970s, the situation eventually changed when the ECtHR embarked on developing a set of legal notions, in particular the notion of the Convention being a 'living instrument', which not only took the Member States by surprise but also signalled a new beginning for European human rights. Madsen argues that this striking transformation of European human rights has to be explained as an effect of both the considerable changing context of human rights of the 1970s and the institutional legitimacy built up during the previous period. Thereby, the analysis inserts the rise of the ECtHR as a legal institution in the broader social and geopolitical transformations of the 1970s, as well as underlining the relative institutional continuity of the ECtHR.

In Chapter 4, Erik Voeten examines the internal politics of the Court, in particular the importance of appointment practices and individual opinions of ECtHR judges. In 1980, Judge Matscher dryly observed that the interpretation of legal texts may remain 'a matter of opinion'.[16] Likewise, in 1966, the International Law Commission noted that 'recourse to many of these principles is discretionary rather than obligatory and the interpretation of documents is to some extent an art, not an exact science'.[17] Erik Voeten makes a case for the view that judges are politically motivated actors, and personal preferences, therefore, impinge on the application of abstract human rights standards in specific cases. While national bias is important, it rarely influences the outcome of reported cases according to Voeten's analysis. Moreover, Voeten's study suggests that the independence of judges will be strengthened somewhat by Protocol No 14 as judges who are about to retire seem less likely to exhibit national bias. According to Voeten, a factor of greater significance is the potential activist role of judges from the former socialist countries, who seem to be especially sensitive to the impact of former socialist regimes on human rights. At the end of the day, the individual judges do not emerge as markedly different from ordinary judges in courts of appeal. They have differences of opinion, but the internal culture of the Court reduces the impact of personal preferences to an acceptable level. But the fundamentally human character of adjudication nonetheless begs the question of legitimacy and accountability. Voeten suggests that political influence by governments on the appointment procedure may well be desirable from the perspective of legitimacy, as the overall ideological direction of the Court is thus subject to political accountability.

In Chapter 5, Rachel Cichowski takes up a central, yet little explored, issue related to the problem of law and legitimacy, namely how the legitimacy of the ECtHR is very much dependent on its ability to provide justice to the many individuals launching complaints to the Court. The chapter explores how the activism of civil society groups has played a central role in expanding the Strasbourg human rights repertoire and, thus, has functioned as an engine in transforming the Court's jurisprudence. The analysis is twofold. In the first part Cichowski provides a historical overview which outlines the rules for NGO/activist participation in litigation before the ECtHR, highlighting how this has changed over time and the

---

[16] Partly dissenting opinion of Judge Matscher in *Guzzardi v Italy* judgment Series A no 39 (1980).
[17] International Law Commission: Reports of the Commission to the General Assembly, II *Yearbook of the International Law Commission* (1966), 218, para 4.

important role the Court itself has had in changing this interface with NGOs. Cichowski moreover suggests the ways in which NGO/activist participation has helped shape the jurisprudence of the ECtHR. In the second part of the analysis, a comparative case study of cases against Turkey and the UK in the area of minority rights over a 15-year time period is undertaken in order to examine in more detail the dynamics between institutional development and law and NGO participation. Cichowski generally argues that the evolution of the Convention system was and continues to be critically linked to a dynamic interaction between civil society and the ECtHR. The legitimacy of this process remains a fine balance between societal inclusion and domestic government support. In other words, the double challenge already observed in the previous chapter in terms of providing justice and balancing government support can be extended to explaining the dynamic of NGO participation before the ECtHR.

In the final chapter of the first part (Chapter 6), Lord Lester of Herne Hill QC revisits the key arguments supporting the further development of the Court in light of its history. By paying tribute to the diplomatic skills of the Commission's staff in the formative years of the system, Lord Lester reminds us of the fact that much could have developed very differently. Lord Lester vividly elucidates the fundamental nature of the challenges facing the Court and argues that many solutions to pending institutional and juridical problems can be provided by paying more attention to the Court's 50 years of institutional and legal experience. Hence, many questions and answers continue to revolve around issues such as improving user-friendliness, identification of urgent and essential cases, strengthening judicial independence, creation of a streamlined review system, reducing case-handling time, ring-fencing and increasing the budget, improving flexibility in amending procedural requirements by a statute of the Court, provision of reasons in all decisions, increasing staff support to judges, and strengthening the quality of the Court's output. As a lawyer and politician, Lord Lester warns that the political will of the Contracting Parties may not suffice to meet the demands of the strongest voices of human rights advocacy. However, as the analysis suggests, this does not reduce or change the actual challenges the system is facing.

Part II: Law and Legitimization

The focus of the second part of the book is less on the institutional level but rather on the legitimization of the ECtHR through law. In the first chapter (Chapter 7), Robert Harmsen links the two parts of the book by first observing that the institutionalization and legitimization of the Convention is, seemingly, a never-ending story: 'The language of imperative reforms has become something of a reassuring constant for those concerned with the Convention and its Court'. But Harmsen is concerned less with the nature and scope of reform and instead makes the reform processes a starting point for a better understanding of the wider evolution of the role of the Convention system. And Harmsen insists that the Court is not the system. Nonetheless, the discussions surrounding the reform enacted by Protocol No 11 were limited in scope and regarded the reform as a technical matter of improving the case-handling capacity of the Court. Harmsen suggests that this was due to the fact that the system itself had achieved a degree of political legitimacy that left the reform to technical, legal experts. The narrow focus on the Court brought little attention to the Court's relationship with national authorities and the Committee of Ministers. Only with the debate leading up to the adoption of Protocol No 14 was the nature and role of the ECtHR challenged: should the ECtHR remain a Court largely concerned with granting relief to individual applicants or should the Court emphasize its powers to develop legal principles of broader applicability? Harmsen points out that the Court is no longer seen as an isolated institution divided between 'constitutional' and 'individual' justice, but is placed in a wider framework of institutions, including the Council of Europe's Commissioner of Human Rights, as well as the Committee of Ministers. It is within this context that the central role of the Court should be considered with regards to, for example, improving the effectiveness of the system e.g. by developing and expanding the right to an effective remedy, as well as by the creation and renewal of the pilot judgment procedure and, thus, providing a legal platform for the resolution of human rights disputes at the national and international level.

In debates on the ECHR, the ECtHR most often takes centre stage and the role of national courts is frequently overlooked, or even ignored. However, in Chapter 8 Stéphanie Hennette-Vauchez argues that the predominant constitution-alist-individualist divide is ill-adapted to deal with the empirical reality of the Convention, which according to Hennette-Vauchez is, in fact, far more national than international. Hennette-Vauchez contests the existence of a singly European human rights law: in her analysis, ECHR law is made up of the sum of the various national versions of ECHR implementations. The plurality of national versions and the crucial role of national authorities make the notion of one body of ECHR law out of touch with legal reality. Hennette-Vauchez addresses the plurality of ECHR law by engaging the two striking cases of France and Italy, which have been exposed to different encounters with the international limb of the Convention system. These two major stakeholders have to this day considerably diverse attitudes towards the ECHR and, accordingly, to its status in national law. The developments are shaped partly by legal actors from different backgrounds, partly by the general backdrop of the link between national and international law in the States. Whichever perspective is adopted, the attempts at legitimizing European law through legal conceptual work, including by building on the views of inter-nationalists and constitutionalists, places the ECHR at risk of losing, or at least reducing, its legitimacy: the central focus for citizens remains the national legal system and, thus, the legitimization of the ECHR through law is as national as it is European.

The third chapter of the second part (Chapter 9), written by Laurent Scheeck, looks at another increasingly important legal interface of the ECtHR, namely how the gradual approximation between the ECtHR and the ECJ has influenced Strasbourg's legal practices and offered new forms of legitimization. Scheeck sees the role of the ECtHR in the EU as 'a paradoxical case of asymmetrical inter-institutional power relations in Europe'. Basically, Scheeck argues, the ECtHR, despite in many ways being the less powerful of the two European Courts, has managed to influence EU law significantly in the area of human rights. Scheeck analyses the interplay between the ECtHR and the ECJ by focusing on the ECtHR's 'diplomatic intrusions' into the EU legal order, for example through the ECtHR's well-known dialogue with EU judges and political actors. This dialogue has now existed for some 30 years and the impact of Strasbourg jurisprudence is, according to Scheeck, perhaps nowhere as significant as in the EU. While the positive reception of ECtHR jurisprudence in the EU legal order is of importance for the legitimacy of the ECtHR, the ECJ itself has also instrumentalized this relation with the objective of cementing its view on the primacy of EU law. In his analysis, Scheeck sees this interplay as a form of 'strategic interdependence' which has developed as the product of many forms of interaction and types of actors, including the largely unexpected effects of jurisprudential entanglements between the two Courts. In view of the previous chapter, it is striking how the axis of the ECtHR–ECJ has managed to build a relatively stable strategic partnership around human rights. However with the Lisbon Treaty now in force, it is still to be seen whether this balance of power can be sustained. Certainly, the implementation into national law of the ECHR in many European countries a decade or two ago challenged the hegemony of the ECtHR in terms of being the ultimate authority on human rights. A similar transformation is not unthinkable in respect of ECtHR–ECJ relations. However, as Scheeck points out, the previous solution has provided added legitimacy to both parties and it will take some courage to change that.

Chapter 10, written by Jonas Christoffersen, analyses the challenges to the legitimacy of the Court and the ECHR system more generally due to its increased inability to provide the individual remedies that constitute the core of the system. Christoffersen's chapter follows up some of the issues raised in the previous three chapters, namely how best to develop the ECHR system in light of its many current challenges. In particular, Christoffersen makes a case for reversing the dynamics of ECHR adjudication by decentralizing the ECHR system. The way forward is to consider the Member States as the central actors of the system. The Court ought to continue the development away from individual justice towards a greater emphasis on constitutional justice—that is, the development of standards and general elucidation of the substantive content of the ECHR. At the same time, States must regain their independence. Christoffersen argues, inter alia: 'States may and must, depending on the circumstances, deviate from the case law of the Court and independently strike a fair balance between opposing forces and provide their own answers to pertinent human rights issues. States need to provide answers that have higher legitimacy than those given by the Court.' This view is linked with an objective of re-legitimizing the ECtHR as the Court has become an increasingly restricted international human rights remedy. This solution is not a case of academic speculation but rather a generalization of a number of developments already taking place where the subsidiarity of the system has become fundamental for understanding how the central role of the Court and the decentralized role of States can interact for the benefit of more than 800 million individuals. Yet,

Christoffersen leaves open the question whether anyone is ready to meet the challenge and change the power balance of ECHR adjudication

In the book's final chapter (Chapter 11), former President of the ECtHR, Luzius Wildhaber, highlights how the ever-increasing case overload is challenging the legitimacy of the ECtHR. Wildhaber argues that it is close to impossible to have a generalized guarantee of individual review of each and every application. Wildhaber likewise admits that 'the lobby of NGOs, professors, and even judges who warn against what they consider to be restrictions on the rights of individual application has been noisy and effective, and that there is virtually no lobby advocating effective reform'. Wildhaber proposes rethinking the ECtHR beyond the many incremental adjustments with the goal of providing a greater degree of stability and honesty. Wildhaber suggests that the Court is well advised to stay on safe ground rather than to develop standards of protection too aggressively, just as the Court should stay within the facts of particular cases and seek to remedy general issues of the national legal orders. More generally, however, Wildhaber points out that the challenge of the current overload could be addressed more effectively 'if (and that is a big "if") the judges of the ECtHR could be persuaded that it is their responsibility not only to render the Convention guarantees effective and real, but also and just as much to make the ECHR system effective and real, too'. Wildhaber further points to the role of political actors who have 'underestimated the difficulties and overestimated the real possibilities of the ECtHR to change national judicial and political systems'. Political actors have thus failed to draw the consequences of the changed reality of the ECHR and of Europe. Wildhaber's solution comprises a focus on the most serious human rights violations, a departure from an unrestricted right of individual petition, and perhaps a Supreme European Court of Human Rights.

III. Future Perspectives

We have opted not to include a concluding chapter in this book because addressing the evolution of the ECtHR is indeed addressing a moving target and any attempt to provide a final analysis is, in practice, bound to fail. Over the last year alone while editing this book, noticeable developments have occurred, in particular in relation to the build-up to and outcome of the Interlaken conference in February 2010 and, even more importantly perhaps, the decision by Russia in January 2010 finally to ratify Protocol No 14. The latter allowed for the long called for streamlining of the system, although it is highly uncertain whether it will actually provide a real solution to the problem of, for instance, the ever-increasing caseload.

The High Level Conference on the Future of the European Court of Human Rights held at Interlaken in Switzerland in 2010 provides another important indication of the possible ways ahead for the ECtHR. The adopted Interlaken Declaration is essentially an Action Plan designed to provide political guidance for the process towards long-term effectiveness of the Convention system and as such identifies a number of short- and long-term measures thought necessary to secure the functioning of the Court.[18] It is obviously premature to assess the impact of the Declaration which in practice points in many directions. These include: (a) securing the right of individual petition; (b) improving implementation of the Convention at the national level; (c) reviewing the filtering mechanisms; (d) administering repetitive applications; (e) improving the Court and its functioning; (f) strengthening the supervision of execution of judgments; and (g) introducing a simplified procedure for amending the Convention. At the time of writing, it mostly appears that the debates in the Council of Europe focus on implementation at national level and, thus, a reorientation of European human rights towards the national level as a strategy of providing relief to the overburdened system.[19]

These and other recent developments should also not overshadow the fact that many of the issues facing the ECtHR have remained over time. Although different responses have been crafted in different time periods, the fundamental issues related to the creation of the ECtHR in terms of both law and legitimacy are permanent, at least as long as States remain the starting point for understanding law, both national and international. As we will argue in the following, the real problem for the Court in this respect is the caseload, an issue only exacerbated by the increase in Member States and particularly the many cases coming from single countries, such as Russia, which potentially disrupt the ability of the institution to adapt and thus calls for intergovernmental action.

Eastern Enlargement was by many assumed to cause major upheaval of the system, and the increase in the caseload post-enlargement has been seen as a sure indication of this. Alarmist voices from both within the Council of Europe and specialists of European human rights have pointed to the risk of the Court loosing its hard won 'legality' and the Council of Europe transforming itself from a 'club of democracies' to a 'training centre' for countries in transition to democracy.[20] On the more institutional level, some of these concerns should perhaps be taken with a pinch of salt. As argued in respect of the EU, enlargement has hardly caused the many political and institutional ills first assumed.[21] As concerns Strasbourg, the major overhaul of the ECHR system was initiated in the mid-1980s and eventually implemented with Protocol No 11 in 1998 and thus happened to provide the institutional framework for a new and permanent Court at the time of significant increase in Member States.[22]

One particular concern in this respect was obviously the influx of judges from the former Eastern bloc countries. Now, about half the judges at the ECtHR are nationals of the new Member States from Eastern Europe. In his contribution to

---

[18] A. Mowbray, 'The Interlaken Declaration—The Beginning of a New Era for the European Court of Human Rights?', 10(3) *Human Rights Law Review* (2010), 519.

[19] The obvious national embeddedness of the whole ECHR system is explored in L. R. Helfer, 'Redesigning the European Court of Human Rights: Embeddedness as a Deep Structural Principle of the European Human Rights Regime', 19(1) *European Journal of International Law* (2008), 125.

[20] R. Harmsen, 'The European Convention on Human Rights after Enlargement', 5(4) *International Journal of Human Rights* (2001), 20–1.

[21] M. Pollack, 'Europe United? The Impact of the EU's Eastern Enlargement, Five Years On', 8(2) *European View* (2009), 239.

[22] See further Chapter 7 below.

this book, Erik Voeten argues on the basis of his statistical assessment of judge behaviour at the ECtHR that 'East European judges are more likely to vote against their own government than are other judges'. Curiously this suggests the very opposite of what pessimistic voices argued prior to enlargement, namely that the new judges would have weak independence vis-à-vis their home countries. Moreover, earlier studies by Jean-François Flauss conclude that no 'Eastern bloc' can be found in voting behaviour.[23] Indeed, the voting patterns which can be observed are more generalized pan-European and not essentially different from the period prior to enlargement.

This analysis suggests two things. First, that political action is needed to address the question of case overload. This is now on the agenda after the Interlaken conference, although actual reforms are to be devised. Secondly, it suggests that the ECtHR in terms of an international institution has generally managed to integrate the many new issues and actors into the specific legal culture developed over the last 50 years, regardless of these significant challenges. But, the story of the ECtHR is hardly reducible to a single formula. As many of the chapters argue, this development is as much legal as it is political, just as it concerns a changing set of actors, including the Member States, individuals, NGOs, the EU, and international organizations. The survival of the ECtHR across politically varied contexts—from the Cold War to the current globalization and expansion of Europe—underscores above all the Court's striking ability to adapt to new challenges.

If one took a shot at capturing the most fundamental feature of the history of the ECtHR, it would probably be adaptability. The present challenges make further adaptations absolutely necessary. With this book we hope to have paved the way to a better understanding of the ECHR system and hence a better basis for choosing the direction of the next stage of development. Improved protection of human rights and fundamental freedoms requires real, effective, and sustainable reforms in several Member States. The ECtHR is hardly the weakest link in the ECHR system.

---

[23] As quoted in Harmsen, above n 20, at 23–4.

PART I

POLITICS AND INSTITUTIONALIZATION

2

The Birth of the European Convention on Human Rights—and the European Court of Human Rights

Ed Bates

As its title suggests, this chapter examines the origins of the European Convention on Human Rights (ECHR) and its Court. It is reflective in its approach, for it is impossible to provide a comprehensive account of the background to and the drafting of the Convention in one short chapter.[1]

The account that follows is in four sections, corresponding to different stages in the drafting of the Convention. First, we shall see that the first proposals for a European human rights guarantee go back to May 1948, and that the instrument and the Court that were then proposed were bound up with lofty ideas of European unity. Just over a year later, in July 1949, detailed plans were set out for the ECHR. What remains remarkable about the Convention as it was conceptualized at that stage was just how fundamental the human rights guarantee was envisaged to be.

Secondly, we consider the drafting of the Convention before the Council of Europe. We shall see that overall the Member States did not react to proposals for a Convention with great enthusiasm—far from it. The text itself was drafted in a remarkably short period of time in 1950, and in its final form the Convention was a very compromised agreement.

Thirdly, we examine how the Convention was viewed at the time of its birth. Far from being a cause for celebration, the text was the source of some acrimony in the

---

[1] The *travaux préparatoires* of the ECHR are reproduced in eight volumes: A. H. Robertson (ed), *Collected Edition of the 'Travaux Préparatoires' of the European Convention on Human Rights* (1975–85) (The Hague: Martinus Nijhoff, 1985) (hereinafter, 'TP'). For a detailed commentary on the background to and drafting of the Convention see A. W. B. Simpson, *Human Rights and the End of Empire* (Oxford: Oxford University Press, 2001) (mainly from the UK perspective) and E. Bates, *The Evolution of the European Convention on Human Rights* (Oxford: Oxford University Press, 2010); this chapter draws upon materials found in chapters 3–5 of this book. See also G. Marston, 'The United Kingdom's Part in the Preparation of the European Convention on Human Rights, 1950', 42 *International and Comparative Law Quarterly* (1993), 796; D. Nicol, 'Original Intent and the ECHR', *Public Law* (2005), 152; and P. H. Teitgen, 'Introduction to the European Convention on Human Rights' in R. Macdonald, F. Matscher, and H. Petzold (eds), *The European System for the Protection of Human Rights* (Dordrecht: Martinus Nijhoff, 1993).

Council of Europe, and it was seen by some both within and outside Strasbourg as a real disappointment. In 1950 it seemed probable that a Court might never even be established. The Convention's future was beclouded with doubt at this stage.

In the last section, we look at the form that the Convention took as it had been agreed in 1950. This will include a closer look at the arrangements made for the European Commission of Human Rights and the European Court.

I. The First Proposals for a European Human Rights Agreement

The Convention was opened for signature on 4 November 1950,[2] less than two years after the proclamation of the Universal Declaration of Human Rights (10 December 1948). With the Convention, the European nations sought to demonstrate that their commitment to human rights went further than a mere declaration; they sought, as the Convention's Preamble put it, 'to take the first steps for the collective enforcement of certain of the rights stated in the Universal Declaration'. What had prompted this greater resolve to protect human rights on the part of the Europeans? The short answer is that in the late 1940s there was much to galvanize the West European nations into action.

First, there had been the Second World War and the human rights horrors it had precipitated. This had provided the impetus for the United Nations to take the first steps towards the creation of a modern international law of human rights. However, the motivation for the Europeans to act more decisively in this field was clear. They had suffered enemy occupation (in most cases, at least); they had been personal witnesses to the horrors associated with despotic regimes and the evils that these might inflict on their own people, as well as those from neighbouring States.

Secondly, there was the political climate of post-war Europe. The European continent had been ravaged by war; its individual economies were in ruins. Yet in the late 1940s the prospect of a third global conflict between 'East' and 'West' appeared to loom large. Communist regimes were installed in Poland, Czechoslovakia, Hungary, Romania, and Bulgaria. An 'iron curtain' divided 'free' and 'communist' Europe, with 1948 alone witnessing civil war in Greece, the Prague coup, and the Berlin blockade. The first proposals for a Convention were dominated by the idea that Europe was in danger of being overrun by the communists. Indeed Paul-Henri Spaak, one-time President of the Council of Europe's Consultative Assembly, once joked that the person who did the most to create the Council of Europe was Joseph Stalin.[3]

The Convention therefore grew out of a period of great anxiety and uncertainty in European history. Indeed, its very origins are bound up with the belief held by

---

[2] The First Protocol was opened for signature on 10 March 1952. It entered into force on 18 May 1954.

[3] A. H. Robertson, *Human Rights in Europe* (1st edn, Manchester: Manchester University Press, 1963), 4.

some that the nations of free Europe had to unite together to survive and in order to protect what they stood for.

'Message to Europeans'—The Hague, May 1948

On 8 May 1948, ex Prime Minister Winston Churchill presided over a congress of movements that had gathered at The Hague for an intensive high-level study of the political and economic problems of a proposed European Union. More than 750 delegates attended at a gathering that has since been associated with the formation of the 'European Movement'.[4] This was an independent body, although among its membership were many eminent statesmen, including several former prime ministers and foreign ministers, and a number of ministers in office, as well as other leading professional figures from across Europe. The shared vision was that the surpassing of the nation State by some type of European federation would not only resolve the severe economic and psychological crisis facing contemporary Europe, but also guarantee peace across a continent that had seen two world wars in 30 years.

The gathering at The Hague culminated with a 'Message to Europeans'.[5] Europe, the Message stated, was 'threatened' and 'divided', and 'the greatest dangers come from her divisions'. An '[i]mpoverished' and disunited Europe was marching 'towards her end' by internal barriers that stifled economic potential and left her internal democratic framework vulnerable in the face of communist doctrines both from within her borders and in view of the growing tide of so-called 'people's democracies' to the East. 'Without a freely agreed union', it was proclaimed, 'our present anarchy will expose us tomorrow to forcible unification, whether by the intervention of a foreign empire or usurpation by a political party'. The 'Message to Europeans' accordingly urged that the 'hour ha[d] come to take action commensurate' with the danger, to 'build the greatest political formation and the greatest economic unit our age has seen'. Moreover, a union of Europe was also needed to maintain 'Europe's finest achievement', '[h]uman dignity' and to:

revive her inventive powers for the greater protection and respect of the rights and duties of the individual of which, in spite of all her mistakes, Europe is still the greatest exponent.

The Message called for a 'united Europe, throughout whose area the free movement of persons, ideas and goods is restored' and 'a European Assembly where the live forces of all our nations shall be represented'. It called not only for 'a *Charter of Human Rights* guaranteeing liberty of thought, assembly and expression as well as the right to form a political opposition', but also 'a *Court of Justice* with adequate sanctions for the implementation of this Charter'.[6]

---

[4] See European Movement, *The European Movement and the Council of Europe* (London: Hutchinson & Co, 1949).

[5] For the full text see ibid, 37.

[6] Emphasis added.

The European Movement's proposals for a European Convention on Human Rights

Just over a year later, in July 1949, the European Movement produced a 32-page publication simply entitled, 'European Convention on Human Rights'.[7] It contained a draft European Convention on Human Rights[8] (hereafter, the 'European Movement Convention'), a Draft Statute for a proposed European Court of Human Rights, and explanatory notes under the heading 'Examination of Criticisms'. The three authors were Pierre-Henri Teitgen, Sir David Maxwell Fyfe, and Fernand Dehousse.

As the explanatory notes put it, the proposed Convention aimed 'at the creation among the European democracies of a system of collective security against tyranny and oppression'. It was deemed 'essential' that 'without delay, joint measures should be taken to halt the spread of totalitarianism and maintain the area of freedom'. The view was that '[i]f the proposed Convention can help to consolidate and broaden the foundations of liberty and can secure the acceptance by the European democracies of a collective responsibility for the defence of human rights, it will be of immeasurable value'.[9] Thus, the Preamble to the European Movement Convention spoke of an intention to '*preserve* the moral values and democratic principles which [were] the common heritage'[10] of the European nations.

The European Movement Convention set out a list of fundamental rights[11] to be protected by each State. The scope of rights protection was similar to the final version of the Convention itself, albeit the rights were merely listed. Also included was a broader provision by which each State would pledge, 'faithfully to respect the fundamental principles of democracy', in particular by holding free and fair elections, and by taking 'no action which [would] interfere with the right of political criticism and the right to organise a political opposition'.[12] Articles 3 and 4 were general limitation clauses for the operation of the aforementioned rights.

Articles 5 and 6 were of particular note since they pointed to the longer and shorter term aspirations of the European Movement. Article 5 referred to a

---

[7] European Movement, *European Convention on Human Rights*, INF/5/E/R (1949).

[8] A copy of the text can be found in the Appendix to TP, n 1 above, vol I.

[9] Ibid, vol I, 16.

[10] Preamble, European Movement Convention, emphasis added.

[11] Art 1 European Movement Convention. The list covered:

> (a) Security of life and limb; (b) Freedom from arbitrary arrest, detention and exile; (c) Freedom from slavery and servitude and from compulsory labour of a discriminatory kind; (d) Freedom of speech and of expression of opinion generally; (e) Freedom of religious belief, practice and teaching; (f) Freedom of association and assembly; (g) The natural rights deriving from marriage and paternity and those pertaining to the family; (h) The sanctity of the home; (i) Equality before the law; (j) Freedom from discrimination on account of religion, race, national origin or political or other opinion; (k) Freedom from arbitrary deprivation of property.

[12] Art 2, European Movement Convention.

'Supplemental Agreement' to be concluded at a later date; as a first step, however, Art 6 would apply. By this provision each signatory would undertake to maintain intact the rights and liberties selected for protection under Art 1, 'to the extent that [they] were secured by the constitution, laws and administrative practice *existing in each country at the date of the signing of the Convention*'.[13] The commentary, as well as the reference to a Supplemental Agreement itself, suggested, somewhat vaguely, that the longer term plan was to create a much more substantial and detailed European human rights code of some type. But it was also recognized that that was an ambitious goal, one that might never be realized, so in the meantime the imperative was to protect the status quo—hence Art 6 as a type of 'freezing' provision.

The first ambition of the European Movement, then, was that there should be no step-by-step regression in human rights standards, as had occurred with Germany's slide into dictatorship in the 1930s. To that end, it was proposed that a 'European Human Rights Commission' should be set up to select 'proper cases' from individuals or from States, but at the centre of the enforcement regime was a 'European Court of Human Rights'.[14] Indeed, the secondary role envisaged for the Commission at this stage was suggested by the proposal that the Court itself was to choose the Commission's members.[15] As to the Court, it would be the conscience of free Europe, acting like an 'alarm bell' warning the other nations of democratic Europe that one of their number was going 'totalitarian'. At this stage, then, the European human rights guarantee was very minimalist in its ambition; the European Court to which individuals would have access (via the Commission) would exist to help to nip in the bud any State's slide into totalitarianism. This was surely the explanation for the Court's otherwise extraordinary powers; it would be able to 'demand the repeal, cancellation or amendment' of an offending 'act'.[16] Any State that failed to comply with a judgment of the Court might be 'referred to the Council of Europe for appropriate action'.[17] On this basis Teitgen, Maxwell Fyfe, and Dehousse were convinced the Court would be no threat to the sovereignty of the European nations. Enlightened 'by the tragic experience of recent years and stimulated by the dangers and pressures of the present sombre situation'[18] the draft Convention was a proud declaration—though backed by a means of enforcement—of the liberties that 'free' Europe stood for. This after an era in which the continued existence of Europe's humanist culture and democratic way of life had been challenged as never before, and again seemed to be under threat from external sources.

---

[13] Ibid, Art 6, emphasis added   [14] Ibid, Art 7(b).   [15] Ibid, Art 8.

[16] See ibid, Art 13(b). The relevant part of the text stated that the Court would have the power to '. . . either prescribe measures of reparation or it may require that the state concerned shall take such penal or administrative action in regard to the persons responsible for the infringement, or it may demand the repeal, cancellation or amendment of the act'.

[17] Ibid, Art 14.

[18] European Movement, n 7 above, at 18.

II. The Convention's Drafting at the Council of Europe

Detailed plans for a European Convention and Court had therefore been hatched within the auspices of a movement already convinced as to their need. In the summer of 1949 the question remained whether such plans would prove acceptable to the governments of free Europe. After all, those nations had failed to respond to the 'Message to Europeans', given that the Council of Europe, created in May 1949, had not emerged as an organization for European unity. Moreover, when the Committee of Ministers received a copy of the European Movement Convention it ignored the accompanying invitation that the new Consultative Assembly be granted permission to debate proposals for a Convention. The Assembly neverthe-less got its chance to debate the matter. A widely formulated request was sent to the Ministers, signed by Winston Churchill and over 50 other members of the Consultative Assembly, for permission to discuss matters relating to the protection of human rights.[19] No State was willing to be the one that denied permission.

This episode was an indicator of things to come. As Simpson puts it, '[t]he truth was that a majority [of the governments] in the Council of Europe were, whatever their pretensions in public, unenthusiastic at the prospect of international Europe-an human rights protection'.[20] Events in 1950 would evidence this. At the same time, however, the moral force and ideological appeal of 'human rights', together, no doubt, with the dire political circumstances of the day, created an almost unstoppable momentum in favour of creating some type of European human rights guarantee. It followed that the most reluctant States would be cajoled along in the negotiations; the price for unanimity, however, would be compromise, and disap-pointment for the idealists.

The Convention before the Consultative Assembly

Teitgen and Maxwell Fyfe were members of the Consultative Assembly of the Council of Europe for its inaugural session at the University of Strasbourg in August 1949. Teitgen's opportunity to put the European Movement's proposals for a human rights convention to the Assembly came on 19 August 1949. He delivered what must have been a rousing speech.[21] Making reference generally to the desperate state of the world, it set out the case as to why there was a burning need for a European Convention *immediately*. At this stage the fundamental nature of the guarantee being proposed remained obvious.[22]

Teitgen's speech was well received and the Assembly set about the task of reformulating the European Movement Convention with great energy. Only three weeks later its proposals were ready. The matter had first received the detailed

---

[19] TP, n 1 above, vol I, 14–20.
[20] Simpson, n 1 above, 667.
[21] TP, n 1 above, vol I, 38–50.
[22] Cf the text of the motion debated at ibid, vol I, 36.

attention of the Consultative Assembly's legal arm, comprising 24 European lawyers presided over by Maxwell Fyfe—its Committee on Legal and Administrative Questions.[23] The rapporteur of that Committee—Teitgen—then prepared a report,[24] the Teitgen Report, which was subsequently presented to the Assembly.[25] The proposals were debated by the chamber, amended, voted upon, and matters concluded by the adoption of a formal Consultative Assembly Recommendation, number 38, dated 9 September 1949 ('Recommendation 38'), addressed to the Committee of Ministers.[26] Incorporated into Recommendation 38 were specific details of the attributes of the Convention that the Assembly was proposing, but what was produced was by no means a full text. The Assembly's Recommendation merely provided the basic proposals, and the detailed features of the Convention would be left to the Committee of Ministers. But this assumed, of course, that the States would approve the idea of a convention in the first place.

The Consultative Assembly debates and the reports produced are all available in the Convention's *travaux préparatoires*. They provide some fascinating insights into the Convention's origins, but only the most basic of comments about them can be provided here. First, the scope of the substantive guarantee for the proposed Convention as suggested by the Consultative Assembly was very similar to the European Movement Convention. The separate clause on free elections and democracy was recounted[27] and the rights that were proposed for protection were largely the same,[28] although reference was now made to the corresponding provisions of the Universal Declaration of Human Rights (UDHR). Having said this, there was a heated debate about whether the rights to property ('the right to own property, in accordance with Article 17 [of the UDHR]')[29] and to education ('the prior right of parents to choose the kind of education to be given to their children, in accordance

---

[23] See ibid, vol I, 154.   [24] See ibid, vol I, 216.

[25] See ibid, vol I, 264.   [26] See ibid, vol I, 276.

[27] See text accompanying n 12 above.

[28] Art 2 of Recommendation 38 listed the rights for protection as:

1. Security of person in accordance with Articles 3, 5 and 8 of the United Nations Declaration;
2. Exemption from slavery and servitude, in accordance with Article 4 of the United Nations Declaration;
3. Freedom from arbitrary arrest, detention, exile, and other measures, in accordance with Articles 9, 10 and 11 of the United Nations Declaration;
4. Freedom from arbitrary interference in private and family life, home and correspondence, in accordance with Article 12 of the United Nations Declaration;
5. Freedom of thought, conscience and religion, in accordance with Article 18 of the United Nations Declaration;
6. Freedom of opinion and expression, in accordance with Article 19 of the United Nations Declaration;
7. Freedom of assembly, in accordance with Article 20 of the United Nations Declaration;
8. Freedom of association, in accordance with Article 20 (paragraphs 1 and 2) of the United Nations Declaration;
9. Freedom to unite in trade unions, in accordance with paragraph 4 of Article 23 of the United Nations Declaration;
10. The right to marry and found a family, in accordance with Article 16 of the United Nations Declaration.

[29] See the debates of the Assembly as recounted in TP, n 1 above, vol II.

with paragraph 3 [of the UDHR]') should be covered by the Convention. All agreed on the great value of these rights in principle, when seen in the context of their abuse during the war and on the other side of the Iron Curtain, but the problem came with the actual drafting. The fear was that a loosely drafted text would hand too much power to international institutions.

As to the right to education, for example, everyone readily agreed that the indoctrination of children at school, a hallmark of Nazism, was clearly irreconcilable with democratic ideals. But drafting a clause that prevented this, while permitting a legitimate place for religious or philosophical convictions, was a different matter.

There was a similar story as regards the right to own property. Considering its importance 'for the independence of the individual and of the family',[30] as well as the fact that one of the first acts of many totalitarian States was to deprive their political opponents of their property,[31] the majority of the members of the Committee on Legal and Administrative Questions had regarded this right as one that the Convention should protect. However, in the limited time available it simply proved impossible to draft a provision that outlawed the practice of arbitrary confiscation by totalitarian regimes but which clearly could not be used as a means to question the nationalization policies of socialist governments such as that of the UK.

The disagreement on the rights to education and property proved heated and intractable. For practical reasons, therefore, the two rights in question were left out of Recommendation 38. After pressure from the Assembly at a later stage, they were included in the First Protocol to the Convention.

What remains very clear is that the human rights guarantee being proposed at this stage was of a most basic nature. Teitgen summed up the proposed guarantee as:

a list of rights and fundamental freedoms, without which personal independence and a dignified way of life cannot be ensured; the fundamental principles of a democratic regime, that is, the obligation on the part of the Government to consult the nation and to govern with its support, and that all Governments be forbidden to interfere with free criticism and the natural and fundamental rights of opposition.[32]

As regards the particular rights and freedoms selected for protection, the Teitgen Report recounted that:

4. The Committee unanimously agreed that for the moment, only those essential rights and freedoms could be guaranteed which are, today, defined and accepted after long usage, by democratic regimes.

   These rights and freedoms are the common denominator of our political institutions, the first triumph of democracy, but also the necessary condition under which it operates. That is why they must be subject to the collective guarantee.

5. Certainly, 'professional' freedoms and 'social' rights, which have in themselves a fundamental value, must also, in the future, be defined and protected; *but everyone will understand that it is necessary to begin at the beginning and to guarantee political*

---

[30] TP, n 1 above, vol I, 220.
[31] See eg the comments of Sund, ibid, 70.
[32] Ibid, 272.

democracy in the European Union, and then to co-ordinate our economies, before under-
taking the generalisation of social democracy.[33]

In one important sense, however, the proposals for a convention had moved on a stage from the proposals of July 1949. The 'freezing' provision[34] found in the European Movement Convention had been jettisoned, as had talk of a Supplemental Agreement. The *travaux* provides no indication why this occurred, but it would seem that the two-stage process envisaged by the European Movement[35] had been dropped in favour of a proposal for a more comprehensive convention.

What, then, was the role of the Convention and Court to be? The alarm bell idea remained central, as was repeatedly made clear in various statements made by Teitgen and Maxwell Fyfe, and all in the Assembly could agree with this. Yet, as the emphasized part of the passage above indicates, blended into the proposals for a European human rights guarantee was the notion of a European Union. This subtle mixing of ideas was evident in an initial draft of the Teitgen Report. Explaining why the Committee on Legal and Administrative Questions had backed the proposal for a Convention it was stated:

this guarantee will demonstrate clearly the common desire of the Member States to build a European Union in accordance with the principles of natural law, of humanism and of democracy, it will contribute to the development of their solidarity; it will fulfil the longing for security among their peoples; it will allow Member States to prevent—before it is too late—any new member who might be threatened by the rebirth of totalitarianism from succumbing to the influence of evil, as has already happened in conditions of general apathy. Would fascism have triumphed in Italy if, after the assassination of Matteoti, this crime had been subjected to an international trial?[36]

In the final version of the Report[37] the passages concerning the prevention of totalitarianism were deleted.

The debates before the Assembly and the various other documentation of the process therefore illustrated some confusion on precisely what was being proposed. The reality, no doubt, was that the Convention meant different things to different people. Maxwell Fyfe, for example, consistently referred to the 'alarm bell' idea; the other founding father, Teitgen, did too, but also indicated that he saw the Convention's future alongside the European Union agenda. The mission of the Convention as proposed by the Assembly was therefore open to interpretation, but it evidently had the potential to become a type of European Bill of Rights for the European Union that some in Assembly hoped was imminent.

It was perhaps for that very reason, and because not all the Assembly were enthusiasts for a European federation, that the proposals for a Court proved controversial. A handful of speakers in the Assembly opposed the creation of such an institution.[38] It was said

---

[33] Ibid, 218, emphasis added.   [34] See text accompanying n 13 above.
[35] Ibid.   [36] TP, n 1 above, vol I, 192.   [37] Ibid, vol I, 216.
[38] See the amendment proposed by Rolin and Ungoed-Thomas at ibid, vol I, 242–4. Rolin became the 'Belgian' judge on the Court 1959–73, and its President 1968–71.

to be too ambitious,[39] and unnecessary for the European nations where human rights were already well protected. All that was required was a European Commission of Human Rights, especially if, as was contended, the aim of the Convention was simply to prevent a return of totalitarianism in Europe.[40] Others feared judicial activism, reference being made to the political stance adopted by the US Supreme Court in the 1930s and in the context of the 'New Deal'.[41]

The 'no Court' proposal was put to a vote, but it was defeated.[42] Teitgen, who was later a judge on the Court,[43] championed the cause of judicial supervision of human rights.[44] He insisted that there would be no rivalry or encroachment between the proposed European Court and the International Court of Justice, as one speaker had suggested. Further, a Strasbourg Court would not be superfluous. The European conscience that the Convention and Court would represent required the authority of a *judicial* decision in accordance with the Council of Europe's adherence to the 'rule of law'.[45] Past experience had shown that the publication of opinions by mere 'Commissions' could be ignored.[46] It was necessary 'to create a conscience in Europe which will sound the alarm', and it had to be 'a Court belonging to Europe itself'.[47] Teitgen insisted that the comments made about judicial activism and the 'New Deal', did 'not bear examination'.[48] He begged his colleagues 'not to exaggerate the extent of the Convention which we are asking the Member States to sign', pointing out that virtually all the rights and freedoms to be covered had been accepted by the Assembly without debate. As regards those rights:

What we are going to ask these States, is to undertake to respect these freedoms and they shall not be dragged—if I may use this vulgar expression—before a Commission or a Court, unless they have, in an obvious way, broken these fundamental, essential and restricted undertakings.[49]

Teitgen's comments here, like his other interventions on this matter, may have been somewhat exaggerated. Evidently they were intended to convince some of the sceptics in the Assembly that the Convention would be no threat to State sovereignty. Having said this, there were clear indications from other statements that Teitgen made that he harboured a grander vision for the Convention and the Court, consistent with the European Movement's longer term aspirations. One notes then that the Consultative Assembly proposed not only the creation of a European Commission of Human Rights, to filter human rights applications from

---

[39] TP, n 1 above, vol II, 156 (Rolin).

[40] Ibid, vol II, 152–4 (Rolin).

[41] See ibid, vol II, 168 (Ungoed-Thomas). Another UK delegate, Nally, warned of a Convention with potentially 'a thousand and one interpretations', ibid, vol II, 148.

[42] Ibid, vol II, 184 (details of the majority are not given in the *travaux*).

[43] Teitgen was the 'French' judge for the period 1976–80. For his perspective on the Convention as it had evolved by 1975, see P. H. Teitgen, 'The European Guarantee of Human Rights: A Political Assessment' in Council of Europe (ed), *Proceedings of the Fourth International Colloquy about the European Convention on Human Rights, held in Rome 1975* (Strasbourg: Council of Europe, 1976), 29. See also n 1 above.

[44] TP, n 1 above, vol II, 174.   [45] Ibid.   [46] Ibid.   [47] Ibid.

[48] Ibid, vol II, 180.   [49] Teitgen, n 43 above, and TP, n 1 above, vol II, 178.

individuals, but also a 'European Court of Justice'[50]—rather than a 'European Court of Human Rights'. As Teitgen explained, such an institution could interpret and apply not only the Convention, but also other treaties yet to be negotiated before the Council of Europe.[51] He spoke of the ideological appeal of such a Court for the European citizen: 'It is because he will see, this evening or tonight, the creation of a European Court, that he will also understand that Europe is born.' There was already a Committee of Ministers and an Assembly, 'and there will also be a Court', and it would be there for the future too as regards other legal problems confronting the would-be Union.[52]

The Assembly therefore proposed the creation of a Court and a Commission. But it was the former that remained central to the enforcement regime envisaged by the Assembly.[53]

The completion of the Convention by the Member States

Several weeks later, on 5 November 1949—almost exactly one year before the Convention was opened for signature—the Committee of Ministers considered Recommendation 38. It proposed the convening of a Committee of Legal Experts to address the question of a Convention *ab initio*.[54] This was a clear rebuff to the Assembly given the considerable work it had already undertaken. It was the first of several to come.

The Committee of Legal Experts met between 2 and 8 February and from 6–10 March 1950 in Strasbourg.[55] It must suffice to say that important work was done at these meetings. Above all, the Legal Experts endorsed the proposal for a Convention, so intensifying the political pressure on the States to do the same. Working from the framework provided by the Assembly in Recommendation 38, the Legal Experts also produced what were really the first proper Convention drafts.[56] It was obvious, however, that there were certain political questions that the Legal Experts were not in a position to resolve. It therefore became necessary for the Committee of Ministers to convene a 'Conference of high officials, under instructions from their Governments' with a mission 'to prepare the ground for the political decisions' to be taken by the Ministers thereafter.[57] It was at this Conference, held in

---

[50] Art 8(1) of Recommendation 38. The powers of the Court had been watered down, however, compared to the European Movement's proposals. Art 24 of Recommendation 38 stated:

> The jurisdiction of the Court shall extend to all violations of the obligations defined in the Convention, whether they result from legislative, executive or judicial acts. Nevertheless, where objection is taken to a judicial decision, that decision cannot be impugned unless it was finally given in disregard of the fundamental rights defined in Article 2 by reference to Articles 9, 10 and 11 of the United Nations Declaration.

[51] Teitgen, TP, n 1 above, vol I, 286. Cf the statement made by Rolin, vol II, 150.
[52] Teitgen, TP, n 1 above, vol II, 180. See also 178.
[53] See Arts 8–27 of Recommendation 38.
[54] See TP, n 1 above, vol II, 302–4.
[55] See ibid, vols III and IV.
[56] See ibid, vol IV, 2–82.
[57] See ibid, vol IV, 84 and 92–4.

Strasbourg over 8–17 June 1950,[58] that the text of the Convention of 1950 really started to take shape. Many issues of importance were discussed and concluded at this stage, for example it was agreed that the substantive text should be drafted in the more detailed form that we know today. There were no real arguments as to the scope of the guarantee—that is, which rights to protect, apart from the right to free elections, which was deleted at this point upon the insistence of the UK[59] (the 'right' would reappear in the First Protocol). By far the most controversial issue, however, was how the system of control might operate, and here an impasse was reached. The Conference Report revealed[60] that nine countries (Belgium, Denmark, France, Ireland, Italy, Luxembourg, Norway, Sweden, and Turkey) were prepared to include a right of individual petition within the proposed Convention. However, the delegates from Greece, Netherlands, and the UK were opposed. A clear majority of the States were against a Court, however. Seven countries (Denmark, Greece, Netherlands, Norway, Sweden, Turkey, and the UK) declared themselves against; only four were in favour (Belgium, France, Ireland, and Italy). Eight countries were prepared to accept the idea of an *optional* court (Belgium, France, Greece, Ireland, Italy, Luxembourg, Sweden, and Turkey), but this was not acceptable to the Netherlands or the UK. The idea of an optional court was proposed nevertheless.[61] However, as it was clear that only a few States might accept its jurisdiction, other arrangements were proposed as regards the system of enforcement. Accordingly, the Commission of Human Rights was given a more prominent role at this stage. Ultimately, however, it would only be able to provide an opinion on any human rights case before it, and it would have no independent power of publicity. This was because the Conference proposed that, in the absence of the Court, the Committee of Ministers would be the final decision-maker in accordance with arrangements that would duly be reflected in what would be Art 32 of the original Convention.

---

[58] See ibid, vol IV, 100–296.

[59] The UK remained a major colonial power at this stage.

[60] See Report of the Conference of Senior Officials reproduced at TP, n 1 above, vol IV, 242–94.

[61] See ibid, vol IV, 178. The rejection of the proposals for a compulsory court can be explained, at least in part, by the lack of desire to create a European Union, which was inevitably closely connected with the idea of setting up institutions of control such as a European Court of Justice. On this point the following comments may be noted: Patijn (Netherlands) had argued that '[t]he time had not yet come to set up a Court with authority to interfere in the internal affairs of States. That was too ambitious. At this stage the Council of Europe should concentrate on political and economic questions. The establishment of a Commission entitled to give advisory opinions would be sufficient', vol IV, 114. Hoare (UK) had argued that, '[t]here were no legal questions which the Commission was not capable of solving. There was therefore no sufficient reason for establishing the Court', vol IV, 116. Sund (Norway) agreed with both these statements, TP vol IV, 118. Palamas (Greece) expressed the view that for the moment his government considered it enough to establish a Commission but that experience of the Commission's working would make it possible to decide at a later stage whether or not to set up a Court, vol IV, 118. As regards the question of optional jurisdiction, the UK was initially against, vol IV, 124–6; Patijn (Netherlands) while reserving his government's position, thought it would not accept an optional Court—'At the present stage all powers should remain in the hands of governments. The transfer of powers involved in the establishment of the Court could only be the last chapter of European integration', vol IV, 128.

In August 1950, the Committee of Ministers convened to consider the outcomes of the Conference Report. The Court would be 'optional', so the key issue remaining was the right of individual petition. By now five States, led by the UK,[62] opposed this,[63] but the battle for a mandatory right of individual petition was only conceded after a series of compromise proposals had been tabled and rejected. The Irish government did their best to force the issue; its representative, Sean MacBride, exclaiming that a Convention that lacked the right of individual petition was 'not worth the paper it was written on'.[64] It became apparent, however, that this issue could be the rock upon which the Convention as a whole might founder. An optional right of individual petition was therefore finally voted upon, receiving 12 votes in its favour. The vote was carried when MacBride, complaining how a small minority coerced the majority, stated that he was prepared to allow his initial vote against to be recorded as an abstention in order to achieve a unanimous decision.[65] This was how the famous Art 25 of the original Convention was born.

Against this highly charged political background the Convention text was finalized. When the Ministers reconvened for their sixth session, in November 1950 in Rome, the decision was taken to expedite matters.[66] The governments of Belgium, Denmark, France, Germany, Iceland, Ireland, Italy, Luxembourg, the Netherlands, Norway, Saar,[67] Turkey, and the UK signed the Convention for the Protection of Human Rights and Fundamental Freedoms at the Palazzo Barberini in Rome on 4 November 1950.[68]

III. How the Convention was Viewed in 1950[69]

'It is not a very good Convention, but it is a lovely Palace'! This, apparently,[70] was how the Consultative Assembly's President (Paul-Henri Spaak) announced the signing ceremony for the Convention and its location. It seems, indeed, that many in the Consultative Assembly were angry, if not furious, at the way matters had been concluded, and regarded the Convention of 1950 as a major disappointment.

This was already apparent when, in mid-November 1950, the Chairman of the Committee of Ministers, Count Sforza, appeared before the Consultative

---

[62] The UK Cabinet had reacted strongly against the Convention by this stage, see Simpson, n 1 above, 726–46.

[63] Greece, the Netherlands, the UK, and Belgium (on the latter, see TP, n 1 above, vol V, 62). So far as the writer is aware, the identity of the fifth objector is not revealed in the TP, see vol V, 112.

[64] TP, n 1 above, vol V, 112.

[65] Ibid, vol V, 114.

[66] See ibid, vol VII, 22ff.

[67] Saarland signed and subsequently ratified the Convention in 1953, but on 1 January 1957 it was incorporated into the Federal Republic of Germany.

[68] The signatures of Greece and Sweden followed on 8 November 1950.

[69] See Bates, n 1 above, 105–7.

[70] Quoted from D. Maxwell Fyfe, Earl of Kilmuir, *Political Adventure: The Memoirs of the Earl of Kilmuir* (London: Weidenfeld & Nicolson, 1964), 183–4.

Assembly. He said that earlier in the month the decision had been taken to expedite signature of the Convention rather than ponder on further improvements, as the Consultative Assembly had wished. It was explained that the Member States had not been able to agree unanimously on key features such as the right of individual petition:

We were at deadlock; but the Committee of Ministers was at least unanimous on this: that it was politically more desirable and more valuable to sign the Convention as it stood, as this in no way prevented subsequent study which might make it possible to remove the existing differences.[71]

Sforza offered the prospect that a protocol could be added to the Convention to make up for some of its deficiencies, such as the absence of the right to education, the right to property, and to free elections to the legislature. However, this hardly placated the Assembly and the debate that immediately followed revealed more than a hint of acrimony between the two Council of Europe institutions.[72]

A chief reason for this was the way the Committee of Ministers had treated the Assembly at the later stage of the Convention's negotiation. A (near complete) draft of the Convention had been sent to it by the Committee of Ministers in August 1950 requesting its opinion. The Assembly gave careful attention to the draft, debating it at length. It reluctantly accepted that the Court would be optional; however, great concern was expressed on certain matters such as the suppression of an automatic right of individuals to petition the Commission.[73] Sensibly it was proposed that States be allowed to 'opt *out*' of the right of individual petition rather than 'opting in'. These and several other amendments were included in a Recommendation[74] to the Committee of Ministers, which was passed *unanimously* by 111 votes. Nevertheless, in their haste to ready the Convention for signature, the Committee of Ministers paid mere lip service to this Recommendation—in effect it was ignored.[75] The Assembly was made to look like a 'schoolboy Assembly', as one of its members later put it.[76]

It transpired that the First Protocol to the Convention, guaranteeing the right to education, the right to possessions, and to free elections to the legislature, did follow relatively soon after the main ECHR text. By then, of course, it was already established that a State could ratify the Convention without having to accept either the right of individual petition or the Court's jurisdiction. In these crucial respects it was a shadow of the instrument that had been proposed by the Assembly in 1949 and, as we note below, it seemed unlikely that there would be a Court. Yet there was a more profound criticism, too, as far as Teitgen was concerned. The Convention was regarded as a

---

[71] TP, n 1 above, vol VII, 92.

[72] See the debate set out at ibid, vol VII, 92ff.

[73] See eg Lord Layton's comments at ibid, vol V, 210; Maxwell Fyfe, ibid, vol V, 226; and Lannung, ibid, vol V, 236–8.

[74] Ibid, vol VI, 192 (Recommendation 24).

[75] See the comments made by Maxwell Fyfe on the eve of signature of the Convention, ibid, vol VII, 36–9.

[76] Ibid, vol VII, 100 (Mr O'Higgins).

major disappointment for him since it guaranteed a select number of civil and political rights, *not democracy as such*. Accordingly, as he saw it, one of the fundamental aims of the Convention had been undermined. He protested to the Assembly:

We are less concerned to set up a European juridical authority capable of righting isolated wrongs, isolated illegal acts committed in our countries, than to prevent, from the outset, the setting up in one or other of these countries of a regime of the Fascist or Nazi type. That is the essential element of our purpose. We are seeking an international procedure capable of active intervention right from the start. But what in fact happens in such a case? They begin by suppressing democratic institutions, by suppressing the secret ballot and universal suffrage, by suppressing elected Parliaments. Then when the dictatorship is firmly established, it suppresses one after the other, the freedoms defined by earlier laws.[77]

As Teitgen saw it, therefore, the Convention had lost the 'greater part of its political efficacy'.[78] The above quotation not only evidences that the Convention was viewed with disappointment in Strasbourg in 1950, but is further evidence of the fact that the primary aim of the Convention's drafters had been to create a human rights guarantee of a very fundamental nature. Although the Convention has since evolved into a type of European Bill of Rights, it is evident from the above quote that Teitgen hardly saw the Strasbourg system as a remedy for individuals. Instead, the purpose of the Convention system and its Court was to rule on cases that had a wider European public interest.[79] This point is worth mentioning in light of the debate that has ensued since the 2000s as to the place of the right of individual petition within the Convention system.[80]

Other views on the Convention

The impression is not exactly gained, then, that the Convention was, in 1950 at least, regarded as a moment of triumph for the Council of Europe! Perhaps this accounts for the remarkably low profile it seems to have had in the Council of Europe's own literature in the early 1950s. It was not even mentioned in a short speech delivered in 1954 by the President of the Consultative Assembly, François de Menthon, to mark the first five years of the Council of Europe.[81] A similar speech delivered by the chairman of the Committee of Ministers at the time, Georges Bidault, gave the Convention only a fleeting reference ('Lastly, [the Council of Europe] has adopted and implemented a Convention for the Protection of Human Rights and Fundamental Freedoms which reflects the desire of the European peoples for greater protection for the human personality')[82] and it received only a brief mention in a 20-page article entitled 'Le Conseil de l'Europe'

---

[77] Ibid, vol V, 294, emphasis added. See also ibid, vol VIII, 154.

[78] Ibid, vol V, 294. For his part, Maxwell Fyfe remained of the view that the Convention's 'alarm bell' role could still function, see ibid, vol V, 228.

[79] In this connection, see also Teitgen, n 43 above.

[80] See eg L. Wildhaber, 'A Constitutional Future for the European Court of Human Rights?', 23 *HRLJ* (2002), 161; Bates, n 1 above, 498–500.

[81] Council of Europe, *The First Five Years* (25–31) (Strasbourg: Council of Europe, 1954), 15.

[82] Ibid, 12.

published by Léon Marchal, the secretary of the Council of Europe, in the first ever edition of the *European Yearbook*.[83]

The example provided by the journal *International Organization* perhaps epitomizes the Convention's lowly status at this stage of its life. This was a US-based journal, but it took a keen interest in regional affairs at the European level. It made only passing reference to the Convention amongst the news of what was, or rather was not, being achieved before the Council of Europe in 1950 as squabbles relating to the future of that organization took prominence in the editions of the periodical.[84] The text of the Convention was not even considered important enough to include within the documentary section of the journal.

In the early 1950s there were just a handful of academic articles on the Convention published in the mainstream legal journals. Most pieces described the drafting process and the 'nuts and bolts' of the Convention machinery. Where expressed, views about the Convention were usually guarded and circumspect. Schapiro recognized that the Convention was an achievement in itself and represented a hope for the future.[85] The writer concluded that 'the first Court of Human Rights to be agreed on in principle in any Convention is modest and restricted in its jurisdiction', but it marked 'an important advance in the development of international law'.[86] The Court 'may yet prove an important influence and model for the protection of fundamental rights and liberties'. Similar views were expressed by Merle in an article published in *Revue du droit public et de la science politique*.[87]

A consistent criticism concerned the inadequacy of the substantive text as a free-standing bill of rights. With its many clawback clauses and other restrictions for the enjoyment of rights, the Convention's substantive text was described by one critic as one that 'abounds in escape clauses based on highly flexible notions of national security, public safety, and the economic well-being of the community'.[88] Unsurprisingly the other main point of criticism concerned the optional nature of key aspects of the enforcement machinery. In an article surveying efforts to create international human rights instruments in the two years following the UDHR, Martin was prepared to 'sum up' that:

in the crucial matter of enforcement, the Convention, as it now stands, fails to live up to the enthusiasm which the Strasbourg Assembly had shown in 1949; but even in its debilitated form, the draft deserves commendation for its loyalty to some, at least, of those fundamental principles of international implementation which the United Nations Commission on Human Rights has spectacularly failed to uphold.[89]

---

[83] L. Marchal, 'Le Conseil de l'Europe', 1 *European Yearbook* (1955), 25.

[84] Anon, 'Council of Europe', 5(1) *International Organization* (1951), 216.

[85] M. Schapiro, 'The European Court of Human Rights', II *University of Western Australia Annual Law Review* (1952–3), 79.

[86] Ibid, 79.

[87] M. Merle, 'La Convention Européenne des Droits de L'Homme et des Libertés Fondamentales', 57 *Revue du droit public et de la science politique* (1951), 705.

[88] A. Martin, 'Human Rights and World Politics', 5 *The Year Book of World Affairs* (1951), 53.

[89] Ibid, 55.

However, the acidic comments made by Green in 1951 remain a historical record of the genuine disappointment and scepticism directed towards the Convention by some at the time. He criticized the Convention from many angles, leaving the reader with the impression that the whole venture at Strasbourg between August 1949 and November 1950 had been little short of a farce. The last lines of his scathing article summed up his main heads of criticism and read:

In view of the wide exception clauses tending to negate the value of the Declaration of Rights, and the difficulties attaching to the inception of the Commission and the Court— difficulties which no State appears willing to overcome—and the unwillingness of the members of the Council of Europe to ratify the Convention one is tempted to apply to this document the words of Horace: '*parturiunt montes, nascetur ridiculus mus*'.[90]

The Latin phrase translates as 'the mountains are in labour; a ridiculous mouse will be born'.

IV. What Had Been Agreed?[91]

Green's comments seem extreme today. However, in 1950, after the exhaustive efforts of the UN Commission on Human Rights with respect to the international bill of rights, high hopes had rested on the European nations to set an example to the rest of the world and create an effective human rights guarantee. In the final analysis, however, they had failed to deliver in this regard, as we elaborate below. Moreover, the Convention's future looked far from bright at this stage. As the quotation from Green indicates, there were real doubts about the readiness of the States to accept it.[92] Ten ratifications were required for its entry into force, and, of course, these were achieved by 3 September 1953. Still, at the start of the 1950s it had been 'generally doubted' that there would 'ever' be enough States willing to make Art 46 declarations so as to trigger the creation of the Court.[93] The condition that there be eight such declarations was initially viewed as 'an indefinite postpone-ment'[94] of such a body. In the meantime Art 25 (now Art 34) in its original form made the right of individual petition optional; five States had to make declarations under this provision before the Commission would become competent to receive individual applications from those States. The Commission achieved this compe-tence in 1955.

---

[90] L. Green, 'The European Convention on Human Rights', V *World Affairs* (1951), 444.
[91] See Bates, n 1 above, ch 5. In the following section, references to Articles in the Convention will refer to the numbering used in the original Convention text. Where relevant, the current numbering will be in parenthesis.
[92] See also the comments made by Horvath, questioning whether the Convention would enter into force: B. Horvath, 'The European Court of Human Rights', 5 *Österreichische Zeitschrift für öffentliches Recht* (1953), 167.
[93] L. Sohn, 'Book Review', 57 *American Journal of International Law* (1963), 169.
[94] Robertson, n 3 above, 166.

The Convention in 1953

So how did the ECHR look at the time of its entry into force in 1953? As is well known, Section I provided for the protection of a number of civil and political rights, and this was soon supplemented by the First Protocol, for those States accepting it. Article 1 of the Convention stated that the Member States, 'shall secure to everyone within their jurisdiction' the rights and freedoms set out in the Convention. The obligation on States was, therefore, not to 'undertake'[95] to secure the rights, but to *immediately* secure them. This wording underlined the significance of the international legal obligations entered into by each State. As we note below, a State which ratified the Convention was required to ensure that its domestic law was consistent with the Convention's substantive obligations (unless it had made an appropriate reservation[96] to the Convention) and the wording of Art 1 (as well as Art 13 (effective national remedies)) reinforced this.

But what was the extent of those obligations? In contrast to the Assembly's original proposals, the rights protected by the final Convention had been drafted in some detail, as the examples of Arts 5 and 6 demonstrate. The detailed drafting approach had been at the insistence of a group of States, headed by the UK, which wanted the text to set out the full extent of the obligations to be created by the Convention in advance of ratification. It had been argued that, because international obligations were being created, States had to know the *precise* extent of their undertakings before they committed to them.[97] Unsurprisingly, the same group of States had opposed the need for a Court of Human Rights which, of course, might develop a European human rights jurisprudence.

Yet in many areas the final substantive text of the Convention was not precise. Inevitably it was full of general, imprecise notions, frequently referring to non-legal standards and values such as 'inhuman and degrading treatment' (Art 3), 'respect for private and family life' (Art 8), 'within a reasonable time' (Art 5(3)), 'in accordance with the law' (Art 8(2)), and 'necessary in a democratic society' (Arts 8(2) to 11(2)). It was no doubt for this reason that most of the substantive Articles of the Convention (other than Arts 3 and 4(1)) were crammed with, and in some cases, overloaded by restrictions and 'clawback' clauses. These attempted to set out in advance the possible justifications for interference with the rights 'protected'. At the same time, however, they had the effect of lessening the Convention's value as a free-standing instrument of human rights obligations capable of curtailing the arbitrary actions of States. The case for international organs of control was thereby enhanced.

It was in this last regard, however, that the Convention of the 1950s really disappointed, as we have already suggested. The perspective of 1953 was probably

---

[95] Cf the language of Art 2(1) of the International Covenant on Civil and Political Rights.
[96] On reservations, see Art 64 (now Art 57).
[97] See eg the comment made by Mr Hoare (UK) at the Senior Officials Conference, TP, n 1 above, vol IV, 106, and also of Mr Patijn (Netherlands) at 108 and Mr Sund (Norway) at 110–12.

that the Convention was regarded primarily as a system of human rights control operating at the 'State versus State' level, and one in which the system of control was subject to political considerations, or was at best quasi-judicial. We say this because when the Convention entered into force (1953), the only two institutions of control were the European Commission of Human Rights (instituted, in fact, in 1954) and the Committee of Ministers, and the only mandatory way of triggering the system of 'collective enforcement'[98] was via interstate cases (Art 24, now Art 33).

All cases would first go to the Commission, a body that was required to meet *in camera*,[99] and was clearly envisaged as a quasi-judicial, quasi-political institution (since 'Protocol 11' took effect, this institution has, of course, been abolished). It was telling, for example, that there were no qualifications for membership,[100] so Commissioners did not have to be highly qualified lawyers. Moreover, Commissioners would be elected by the Committee of Ministers alone,[101] although each member would sit 'in their individual capacity',[102] holding office for six-year periods.[103] As is well known, the Commission was charged with various tasks: it would receive applications, investigate them, and decide whether a case should be declared admissible (something which originally required the authority of *the whole* Commission). Thereafter there was a significant emphasis on efforts to achieve a conciliatory outcome based on respect for human rights. So, for example, every admissible case *had* to be addressed by a specially constituted sub-Commission, made up of seven Commissioners, including one chosen by each party.[104] As it was originally drafted, therefore, contentious matters only, that is, those not already resolved by way of friendly settlement, would receive the attention of the *full* Commission. If so, in accordance with Art 31, the Commission would 'draw up a report on the facts and state *its opinion* as to whether the facts disclose a breach by the State concerned of its obligations under the Convention'.[105] However, the Commission was given no independent power of publicity as regards this 'Article 31 Report'; it was obliged to relinquish jurisdiction to the Committee of Ministers for it to deliver a final decision on the matter (that is, unless the Court had been instituted, although even then the respondent State would have to have accepted the Court's jurisdiction, and the Commission, or an interested State, opted to refer the case to the Court[106]). The Committee of Ministers would *not* be bound by the Commission's Report.[107] Acting under Art 32, it would take conclusive decisions

---

[98] Although note Art 57 (now Art 52).

[99] Art 33 ECHR.

[100] This was changed by Protocol No 8, opened for signature in 1985 and entering into force in 1990.

[101] Art 21 ECHR (although the same provision required that election could only be made from a list drawn up by the Consultative Assembly).

[102] Art 23 ECHR.

[103] Ibid, Art 22(1).

[104] See ibid, Art 29 and generally Arts 28–30.

[105] Ibid, Art 31(1), emphasis added.

[106] See text accompanying n 119 below.

[107] The Senior Officials Conference Report had confirmed that the Committee of Ministers 'must be left entire freedom of decision', TP, n 1 above, vol IV, 256.

on the merits not by a simple majority, but 'by a majority of two-thirds of the members entitled to sit on the Committee'.[108] Accordingly, the odds were stacked in a respondent State's favour for, in the absence of such a majority, the Committee could take no action.

Individual petition

The arrangements just described reflected the fact that in 1950 most of the States that had been involved in the Convention's negotiation opposed the creation of a Court outright, while a minority had got their way by insisting that individual petition be an optional feature of the Convention. It was, of course, these two aspects of the Strasbourg system that were the seeds of the future transformation of the Convention.

Acceptance of the right of individual petition was important for the Convention to evolve beyond a limited conceptualization of it as an interstate, democratic 'alarm bell' for Europe. As Professor C. H. M. Waldock,[109] the first President of the European Commission put it:

If you regard the Convention as a constitutional instrument—as *a European Bill of Rights for the individual*—then it seems difficult to deny the importance of granting the individual a personal right to place his grievance before the Commission. If, on the other hand, the Convention is regarded rather as a pact for collective action to check the development of any totalitarian methods of government in member countries, then the individual's right of recourse to the Commission may seem less important than that of the Member States. *The Convention compromised on the point.*[110]

In effect, the President of the Commission acknowledged that the Convention of the 1950s was ambivalent in terms of its mission as either a 'pact for collective action' against totalitarianism or a 'European Bill of Rights'. But he was also saying that the future of the Convention lay in the hands of the Member States; in particular, it rested with their decisions to accept its key control feature: the right of individual petition. There was no doubt, however, as to how Waldock hoped to see things progress. His speech was introduced with the lines:

I propose to sketch for you a broad picture of the Convention as a European Bill of Rights— a Bill of Rights for free Europe. *It is that aspect of the Convention which is supremely important.*[111]

---

[108] Art 32(1) ECHR.

[109] C. M. H. Waldock, 'Address by C. M. H. Waldock' in Council of Europe, *Fifth Anniversary of the Coming into Force of the ECHR: Brussels Exhibition, 3 September 1958* (Strasbourg: Council of Europe, 1959), 19 (also published as C. M. H. Waldock, 'The European Convention for the Protection of Human Rights and Fundamental Freedoms', XXXIV *British Year Book of International Law* (1958), 356.

[110] Ibid, 359, emphasis added.

[111] Ibid, 356, emphasis added.

The Court

It was the Court, of course, that really had the capacity to bring the Convention to life and make it into a European Bill of Rights via the creation of 'Strasbourg' jurisprudence based on individual application cases. Yet, as we know, political attitudes towards the Court, plus the way that the system of international control had been designed, with its emphasis on the conciliatory Commission, made this an unlikely proposition.[112]

Provision had nevertheless been made for a Court within the Convention text of 1950, all the relevant Articles being found in Section IV of the treaty. There would be as many judges as there were Member States of the Council of Europe. So, when the Court was finally instituted in 1959, every Council of Europe State was entitled to be involved in the process for the nomination of a judge, whether or not they subscribed to the Court, indeed, whether or not they had ratified the Convention. As to the process of election, each Member State would draw up a list of three candidates, which had to include at least two of its nationals.[113] The Consultative Assembly would elect from those lists by a majority of the votes cast. Judges had to be 'of high moral character and ... either possess the qualification required for appointment to high judicial office or be jurisconsults of recognised competence'.[114]

Even if instituted, few cases were expected to reach the Court; Art 42, for example, provided that the judges be paid on the basis of 'each day of duty', rather than receiving an annual salary. The original Convention text stipulated that each judge would hold office for nine years and could be re-elected.[115] Article 45 stated that the Court's jurisdiction would extend to 'all cases concerning the interpretation and application of the present Convention'; Art 49 provided that, '[i]n the event of dispute as to whether the Court has jurisdiction, the matter shall be settled by the

---

[112] Note eg the comments made by Isi Foighel, a former 'Danish' judge on the Court. He reminisced about his time as a lecturer at the University of Copenhagen at around the time the Convention was concluded and, in particular, a conversation he had with Max Sørensen, who had been involved as a Danish representative in the negotiation of the Convention (and would later become president of the Commission, and a judge on the Court). Sørensen poured cold water on Foighel's excitement about the new Convention. Foighel explained:

> He [Sørensen] looked at me for a long time and then responded with amazing patience. 'Don't be naïve, Foighel,' he said, 'this Court will never function. No government will accept being dragged before an international court by its own citizens.' Painstakingly, Professor Sørensen explained that the rules had been made so as to allow compromises—friendly settlements—before cases ever came before the Court. There was no talk of jurisprudence here, my teacher said, only of politics. The only reason that governments had agreed to establish this court in the first place had to do with the end of the Second World War and their wish to enhance the importance of the individual now as opposed to the grandeur of the state. (I. Foighel, 'Reflections of a former Judge of the European Court of Human Rights' in S. Lagoutte et al (eds), *Human Rights in Turmoil* (Leiden: Brill, 2007), 276.)

[113] Art 39(1) ECHR (cf today's Art 22).
[114] Ibid, Art 39(3) (cf today's Art 21).
[115] Ibid, Art 40. Protocol No 14, now in force, establishes a single, nine-year term.

decision of the Court'. When hearing cases it was expected that a chamber of seven judges[116] would be convened, but nothing was said as to how a case would be conducted, except that the composition of the Court was to be determined by lot, and a State party to proceedings was entitled to have the judge of its nationality on the bench.[117] The Convention also included Articles providing, for example, that reasons should be given for the Court's judgments[118] and stating that the Court should appoint its own President.

Assuming the Court had jurisdiction, it had no choice as to which cases from the Commission it might hear. The judges were totally reliant on cases being referred *to them* and here Art 44 stipulated that only High Contracting Parties and the Commission 'shall have the right to bring a case before the Court'. Article 48 clarified matters further. Once the Commission had completed its Article 31 Report and sent it to the Committee of Ministers, within a three-month period only[119] the Court could receive cases via four referring sources:

(1) the Commission;
(2) the respondent State;
(3) the Member State which had referred the case to the Commission in the first place (that is, for an interstate case);
(4) the Member State whose national was alleged to be a victim.

It will be noted, then, that the individual applicant did not have the ability to refer a case to the Court.

As regards the Court's powers, and the procedures following the delivery of a judgment, these were set out in Arts 50 and 52 to 54. Article 50, providing for a discretionary power for the Court to award 'just satisfaction', remains very similar to today's Art 41. The first lines of the original version of this Article, which has since been slightly modified,[120] were the only ones in the Convention that made it clear that the Court's role was to *declare* whether there had been a breach of the Convention 'by a legal authority or any other authority'. Article 52 stated that '[t]he judgment of the Court shall be final';[121] Art 54 stated that the Court's judgment would be 'transmitted to the Committee of Ministers', and it was added that that body, 'shall supervise its execution'.[122]

---

[116] Ibid, Art 43. The Rules of the Court subsequently allowed for a Chamber to relinquish jurisdiction to the full Court in certain circumstances, eg if the case raised a serious question of interpretation.

[117] Ibid, Art 43 (cf today's Art 26(4)).

[118] Ibid, Art 51. The same provision stated that separate opinions could be attached to the judgment (cf today's Art 45).

[119] Cf ibid, Art 32(1).

[120] The text of what is now Art 41 was shorted by Protocol No 11. It now reads: 'If the Court finds that there has been a violation of the Convention or the protocols thereto, and if the internal law of the High Contracting Party concerned allows only partial reparation to be made, the Court shall, if necessary, afford just satisfaction to the injured party'.

[121] Cf today's Art 44(1) ECHR.

[122] Cf today's Art 46 ECHR.

Returning to Art 50 (now Art 41), this was derived from similar clauses that appeared in a number of early twentieth-century bilateral arbitration treaties.[123] The Article was a developed version of a draft introduced by the Committee of Legal Experts, which had rejected the suggestion[124] that the Court have power directly to influence domestic law by declaring certain acts invalid. According to the Legal Experts, Art 50 was:

in accordance with the actual international law relating to the violation of an obligation by a State. In this respect, jurisprudence of a European Court will never, therefore, introduce any new element or one contrary to existing international law. In particular, the Court will not have the power to declare null and void or amend Acts emanating from the public bodies of the signatory States.[125]

It was clear then that the Court was not intended to have powers similar to a constitutional court; all it could do would be to declare that a breach of the Convention had occurred on the facts of a case before it. Having said this, the potential indirect influence of a Court judgment on the domestic law of the State would have been apparent in 1950. Article 53 stated that the judgment was binding on the respondent State, while, as noted above, Art 1 referred to a State's duty to 'secure' Convention rights. It was clear in 1950 that a Court judgment finding that a State had breached the Convention would amount to that Court identifying that the State had committed an international wrongful act for which it was responsible at the level of international law.[126]

This would give rise to a customary internal law obligation to make reparation, which 'reparation must, as far as possible, wipe out the consequences of the illegal act and re-establish the situation which would, in all probability, have existed if that act had not been committed'.[127] How far that obligation might go on the facts of any case would have to be established. However, customary international law dictated that no State could plead its own domestic law as a defence to its non-application of an international legal obligation.[128]

V. Conclusions: The Future Significance of the ECtHR

In the above pages we have reviewed the circumstances in which the Convention was created and the Court was proposed. We have seen that the Convention was born against the backdrop of the Second World War, and was conceptualized by

---

[123] For an explanation see the Court's commentary in the *De Wilde, Ooms and Versyp v Belgium* judgment of 10 March 1972, Series A no 14 para 16.

[124] See text accompanying nn 16 (the European Movement's proposals) and 50 (Consultative Assembly) above.

[125] TP, n 1 above, vol IV, 44, emphasis added.

[126] *Chorzów Factory (Indemnity) (Merits) case* PCIJ A17, 29.

[127] Ibid.

[128] The principle has been confirmed frequently by the International Court of Justice, eg the *Wimbledon* case (1923) PCIJ A19 and the *Fisheries* case ICJ Reports 1951, 116 (132). See also Art 27 of the Vienna Convention on the Law of Treaties.

the European Movement as, initially, a type of collective pact against totalitarianism. That idea remained prevalent when the Convention was debated in 1949 within the Council of Europe, although at that stage too there was evidence of a broader agenda, reflecting the European Movement's aspirations for a European Union.

When it was drafted by the Member States of the Council of Europe, however, the general mood was against the immediate creation of a Court, if not the Convention itself. The sovereignty-conscious States insisted on procedures that would allow them to retain more control over the international system, hence the Commission and Committee of Ministers arrangements described above, as well as the famous 'optional clauses'. By the time the Convention entered into force on 3 September 1953, just three States (Denmark, Ireland, and Sweden) had accepted the right of individual petition and two (Denmark and Ireland) the jurisdiction of the Court. It seems that the general mood among observers at that stage was one of disappointment. There was a feeling that it was unlikely that there would ever be such a thing as a European Court of Human Rights.

While there may have been pessimism over the Court's future, it was appreciated at the time how significant an institution it could be. In 1951 Barna Horvath delivered a lecture entitled 'The European Court of Human Rights' to the New York School for Social Research. One of Horvath's aims was to dissipate negativity about the Convention's future by discussing its future prospects *if* States were prepared to overcome its key shortcomings, in particular regarding acceptance of the right of individual petition and the jurisdiction of the Court. The hope was expressed that, should the Court come into existence, its jurisprudence could remedy the many faults found with the substantive text, making the Convention a meaningful charter of rights and freedoms. The lecture concluded:

The student of international protection of human rights has reason to be modest in his expectations, when criticism reveals the enormous difficulties of drafting a satisfactory Convention and of establishing a smoothly running international adjudication. The difficulties include that of division of power between national and international authorities, different methods of protecting individual and social rights, the paramount difficulty of assessing the human rights aspect of human and legal rights, and lastly, the difficulties experienced in the comparative aspects of the impact on human rights of different parts, branches, and systems of positive law... [129]

For Horvath there was a 'reasonable hope that the European Court, once it starts adjudicating human rights, will solve the difficulties by trial and error, by developing precedents and principles'.

Lauterpacht's commentary on the (proposed[130]) Convention in his celebrated 1950 book, *International Law and Human Rights,* was equally prophetic, and it also

---

[129] See Sohn, n 93 above, 191.

[130] Lauterpacht completed his book (H. Lauterpacht, *International Law and Human Rights* (London: Stevens & Sons, 1950)) at the beginning of 1950, so his comments were directed to the proposals set out by the Assembly and were made before the completion of the Convention later that year. See ch 18 of his book ('The Proposed European Court of Human Rights').

provided a revealing insight into how one of the greatest international lawyers of his era viewed the Court at this earliest stage. Lauterpacht began by questioning whether an international human rights court was really necessary for Western Europe. This was because the democracies of those States had already proved themselves to be 'the faithful trustees of the rights of man'.[131] As Lauterpacht saw it, the chief merit of the Convention, therefore, was as a safety valve for when things went wrong, for '[e]ven in democratic countries, situations may arise in which the individual is in danger of being crushed under the impact of "reason of state"'. Here reference was made to the Dreyfus affair in France. Also quoted was a passage from Lord Atkin's famous dissent in *Liversidge v Anderson*,[132] Lauterpacht was implying that the issues raised by that case generally (internment during wartime) were ones which were worthy of being subject to the safeguard that international human rights organs could provide. So there was a justification for a European human rights guarantee:

even in countries in which the rule of law is an integral part of the national heritage and in which the courts have been the faithful guardians of the rights of the individual, there is room for a procedure which will put the imprimatur of international law upon the principle that the State is not the final judge of human rights.[133]

Even so, for Lauterpacht such issues were really more appropriate for consideration by a quasi-judicial body such as the proposed Commission of Human Rights. This was because, '[i]t is to be expected that a substantial number of cases brought before the Commission will be on the border-line where the apparently vital necessities of the State and the rights of man converge and conflict'.[134]

The explanation for Lauterpacht's hesitations about a European Court then was twofold. Seen from the perspective of 1950, the West Europeans already did a good job in protecting human rights. Moreover, the idea of a European Court was revolutionary in itself and indeed controversial given the highly charged nature of the cases likely to come before it. Such considerations pointed to the appropriateness of having a body such as the Commission before cases reached the Court.

However, and to be clear, Lauterpacht was *not* opposed to a European Court in principle. Writing in 1950, his concern was to point out what a serious proposition it would be. International judicial protection of human rights, Lauterpacht warned, was a serious step which required all concerned to appreciate that 'no achievements of substance can be brought about without actual sacrifices in sovereignty'.[135] Above all, the proposal for a Convention, and in particular a European Court of Human Rights, would entail that international agencies would have 'the power to investigate and review judicial decisions of the highest municipal tribunals', and it implied 'in effect the authority to review the legislative acts of sovereign parliaments'.[136] The idea of a European Court of Human Rights therefore implied the

---

[131] Ibid, 445.
[132] *Liversidge v Anderson* [1942] AC 206.
[133] Lauterpacht, n 130 above, 446.
[134] Ibid, 447 (citing Lord Atkinson's judgment in *R v Haliday* [1917] AC 260).
[135] Ibid, 453.   [136] Ibid.

surrender of a very significant amount of sovereignty. In some striking passages Lauterpacht then commented on the relevance that the Convention might have for the UK in particular,[137] adding that 'the range and number of decisions given every year' by the US Supreme Court was 'a reminder of the vast—and, to some, alarming—possibilities of international review'.[138] These possibilities had to be 'kept clearly in mind', for 'in a system of judicial review by international courts the decision of which are legally binding, a portion of national sovereignty will be vested in ... the European Court of Human Rights'.[139]

No doubt it was these very considerations that influenced the negotiating States' attitudes towards the Court in 1950. As we know, however, the completion of the Convention in 1950 was not the last word on its future, or that of the Court. Indeed, the Court would be instituted by the end of the decade, and, in the longer term, Lauterpacht's predictions that it might emulate to some extent the work of the US Supreme Court would prove to be most apposite.[140]

---

[137] He suggested that a Strasbourg Commission and Court would have jurisdiction to review:

> the practice embodied in the Control of Engagements Order and the legislation on which it is based; the executive and legislative regulations of the right of assembly, such as the local prohibition of processions; executive or judicial limitation of or interference with the right of a meeting; ... any alleged denial of justice by courts on political grounds—a plausible reason for appeal in trials for treason; any alleged arbitrary imprisonment—it [being] noted that the power of imprisonment for contempt by courts and Parliament is, in theory, arbitrary inasmuch as it is not subject to a judicial remedy. (Ibid at 453–4, footnotes omitted.)

Specific reference was made to the 1947 House of Lords case in *Christie v Leachinsky* [1947] AC 573 noting that it would have been subject to review at Strasbourg.

[138] Ibid, 454.
[139] Ibid, 455.
[140] On the subsequent evolution of the ECHR, see Bates, n 1 above, chs 5–12.

3

The Protracted Institutionalization of the Strasbourg Court: From Legal Diplomacy to Integrationist Jurisprudence

Mikael Rask Madsen

Some of the most decisive developments in European human rights law took place in the mid to late 1970s when the European Court of Human Rights (ECtHR) embarked on crafting what is now known as its dynamic human rights doctrine. Notions such as 'living instrument', 'practical and effective', as well as others, helped to develop an interpretative approach which was progressively to change the course of European human rights over the subsequent decades.[1] Moreover, the framework for a more effective and more European doctrine of human rights was also laid out which was to result in several high-profile clashes with a number of the top legal and political institutions of the Member States. While most observers today have come to view these dynamics as integral to the development of human rights protection in Europe, this however conceals the legal, as well as the historical, significance of these transformations. The starting point for appreciating the degree of change implied by the 1970s jurisprudence is obviously not contemporary European human rights jurisprudence, but the early, more uncertain, practices and jurisprudence of the ECtHR in its initial period of operation beginning in 1959. In this more historical light, the institutional and legal ramifications of the 1970s transformation are truly remarkable.

The original Convention had mainly sought to ensure liberal democracy in Europe.[2] As argued by Andrew Moravcsik, the goal of the 1950 European Convention of Human Rights (ECHR) was predominantly 'to lock in democratic governance against future opponents' and was by no means 'a conversion to moral altruism' of the

---

[1] Between particularly 1975 and 1979 the Court delivered a series of judgments which are still of considerable legal importance. These include most notably, *Golder v United Kingdom* Series A no 18 (1975), *National Union of Belgian Police v Belgium* Series A no 19 (1975), *Handyside v United Kingdom* Series A no 24 (1976), *Kjeldsen, Busk Madsen and Pedersen v Denmark* Series A no 23 (1976), *Ireland v United Kingdom* Series A no 25 (1978), *Tyrer v United Kingdom* Series A no 26 (1978), *König v Germany* Series A no 27 (1978), *Sunday Times v United Kingdom* Series A no 30 (1979), *Marckx v Belgium* Series A no 31 (1979), *Airey v Ireland* Series A no 32 (1979), and *Winterwerp v Netherlands* Series A no 33 (1979).

[2] Cf Chapter 2 above.

Member States.[3] Against the backdrop of these Cold War-inspired objectives, the initial institutionalization of the ECHR was, as will be argued in the first section of this chapter, a very delicate manoeuvre as it was somehow paradoxically in potential conflict with the very geopolitical objectives of establishing European human rights. Seen in this light, only the more severe violations of human rights in the Member States were as such relevant in terms of safeguarding free Europe and certainly not more technical issues. The latter, conversely, were seen as potentially counterproductive and even serving the interests of subversives with Soviet inclinations or the growing number of liberalization movements seeking to exhibit the European double standards of human rights as practised particularly by European imperial societies.[4] Consequently, the goal was hardly to alter substantially the protection of human rights in the Member States but collectively to guarantee against a return to totalitarianism in Western Europe. This left the Court (and Commission) in a rather complex role which called for both legal and diplomatic skills. The result was a very measured legal development over the first 15 years where the objective of providing justice to individuals was carefully balanced with both national and geopolitical interests. This phenomenon, I label 'legal diplomacy'.[5]

Against the background of an analysis of the initial development of European human rights as 'legal diplomacy', the second section of this chapter then raises the question of how the considerable change of the Court in the mid to late 1970s came about and what social, political, and legal conditions facilitated it. In order to address this question, the chapter looks into both the structure and agency of the ECtHR and their transformations over the time period 1959–79. In terms of agency, I analyse the judges of the changing Court in order to test the most often pronounced explanation for this change, namely that a new and different set of actors started occupying the Strasbourg bench beginning in the mid-1970s. Secondly, I explore the changing social and political conditions under which the ECtHR operated as a proxy for explaining the transformation of the Court and its jurisprudence. I finally challenge both explanations by suggesting an interpretative framework based on Bourdieusian reflexive sociology which argues for a relational and, thus, structural connection between the agency of the ECtHR and its surroundings as a framework for explaining the transformation of the Court.[6]

Using this approach, I conclude by situating the decisive transformation of the Court and its jurisprudence in what I term the European transformation, that is, the grand transformation of European society which occurred in the 1970s as both a product of geopolitical changes and the new social politics coming out of the late

---

[3] A. Moravcsik, 'The Origins of Human Rights Regimes: Democratic Delegation in Postwar Europe', 54 *International Organization* (2000), 248–9.

[4] A. W. B. Simpson, *Human Rights and the End of Empire: Britain and the Genesis of the European Convention* (Oxford: Oxford University Press, 2004).

[5] The notion is further developed in M. R. Madsen, 'Legal Diplomacy: Law, Politics and the Genesis of Postwar European Human Rights' in S.-L. Hoffmann (ed), *Human Rights in the Twentieth Century: A Critical History* (Cambridge: Cambridge University Press, 2011).

[6] For further details on the approach, see M. R. Madsen, 'Transnational Fields: Elements of a Reflexive Sociology of the Internationalisation of Law', 3 *Retfærd* (2006), 23.

1960s and early 1970s. It is these combined processes, the chapter argues, that both framed and facilitated the development of the dynamic human rights jurisprudence of the ECtHR. For the same reasons, the new approach of the ECtHR was not in conflict with the broader structural transformation of Western Europe of the period but rather deeply integrated in it. It was, indeed, a sophisticated legal expression of this very transformation as well as of what we today label European integration.

I. The Guarded Institutionalization of the ECHR

The drafting of the ECHR highlighted if anything the inherent problem of 'Europeanizing' human rights. If there was one superseding theme of these negotiations it was that human rights were at one and the same time both too integrated into national law and politics to be entirely entrusted to a new European court and too important to the idea of European integration to remain a question of national politics and law.[7] In practice this materialized in some rather delicate compromises. In respect of this analysis, the most important concerned the right to individual petition and the jurisdiction of the Court, which were both made optional in the 1950 Convention. This was done in a last ditch manoeuvre to evade a breakdown of the bargaining over the institutional mechanisms of European human rights. This, together with some other escape routes included in the last part of the negotiation, however implied that the political negotiation of European human rights was not put to rest with the signature in 1950 of the ECHR. And this prolonged negotiation concerned not only the drafting of additional Protocols to the Convention but also, and more importantly perhaps, of actually ensuring the institutional framework stipulated by the ECHR. What in practice occurred was that the Member States opted for a limited commitment to human rights which notably excluded the two trademarks of contemporary European human rights: the jurisdiction of the ECtHR and the right to individual petition before the Court.[8] First the Commission and then the nascent Court were thus in the unusual situation of having to prove their standards of human rights to the reticent Member States in order to convince them to accept the full package of European human rights. Effectively, the burden of proof had thereby been inverted.

It was well known at the time, particularly in light of the way that the Universal Declaration of Human Rights (UDHR) had fallen victim to Cold War bipolarities, that if human rights were to be ensured at the European level, it required both institutionalization and juridification. The latter seemed to have been achieved already in 1953 when ten Member States, including the UK but not France, had ratified the Convention and thereby made it effective.[9] But this achievement was

---

[7] For details on the drafting, see Chapter 2 above and Brian Simpson's seminal analysis, n 4 above.

[8] For a discussion of the continuous importance of these two features of the ECHR system, see Chapters 6, 10, and 11 below.

[9] Besides the UK, these were Denmark, Germany, Greece, Iceland, Ireland, Luxembourg, Norway, the Saar, and Sweden.

overshadowed by the fact that the actual institutionalization of the ECHR system at the end of the day required the Member States to accept the two central optional clauses on the right to individual petition and the jurisdiction of the Court. This in practice turned out to be a more prolonged process. Individual petition was eventually effective by 1955 when the required six acceptances had been received. The countries first taking this step were, in chronological order: Sweden (1952), Ireland (1953), Denmark (1953), Iceland (1955), the Federal Republic of Germany (1955), and Belgium (1955). Only in September 1958 were the necessary eight acceptances of the Court's jurisdiction confirmed. The countries in question were, in chronological order: Ireland (1953), Denmark (1953), the Netherlands (1954), Belgium (1955), the Federal Republic of Germany (1955), Luxembourg (1958), Austria (1958), and Iceland (1958). Only in 1959, nine years after the signature of the ECHR, was the Court finally operational.

The list of countries eventually accepting the two central powers of the ECHR system in the course of the 1950s has three striking absentees. Besides the Federal Republic of Germany, all other countries backing the ECHR were smaller European countries. Conversely, the two major European powers, France and the UK, as well as Italy, did not figure among the countries lending their support to the build-up of an effective European human rights system. This stood in sharp contrast to the fact that actors from precisely these three countries had undoubtedly been among the most influential in devising the institutional mechanisms of the system. As concerns France and the UK, their turnaround on European human rights has necessarily to be explained in light of their significant overseas problems during the 1950s and early 1960s where the cry for decolonization was gaining renewed momentum. While there was also a more general reluctance among many politicians and lawyers against entrusting an international court to monitor what they saw as their unique standards of human rights,[10] the greatest cause of concern was the escalating situation in a number of colonies, which made the craving for national sovereignty become even more pronounced than usual. Paradoxically, the self-proclaimed champions of human rights were not thereby exiled from the making of the European human rights system. The 1950 Convention provided that all Member States of the Council of Europe were entitled to a judge on the ECtHR. Ratification of the ECHR was, however, a condition for being (fully) represented in the Commission. This meant that both countries were to be represented on the ECtHR, but only the UK had a commissioner as France had only signed but not ratified the Convention.

These details on the initial process towards making the ECtHR operational underline if anything the largely unfinished conversion of European States into a common European legal framework. 'European integration through law' *versus* national sovereignty was hardly a settled issue. This implied that the nascent Court had to perform a delicate task of both getting the major powers aboard and at the same time developing a jurisprudence which took seriously the cases now being brought before the Strasbourg institutions concerning the Contracting States. In

---

[10] V. Evans, 'The European Court of Human Rights: A Time for Appraisal' in R. Blackburn and J. J. Busuttil (eds), *Human Right for the 21st Century* (London: Pinter, 1997).

this light, the nomination and appointment of commissioners and judges to the two institutions became an important exercise in striking a balance which could fulfil these potentially conflicting objectives. The formal requirements for holding office as a European judge were quite general: 'The candidates shall be of high moral character and must either possess the qualifications required for appointment to high judicial office or be jurisconsults of recognized competence' (Art 39(3) ECHR). Appointment was by majority vote in the Consultative Assembly of the Council of Europe based on a list of three nominees put forward by each Member State. The same voting procedure and nomination process applied to commissioners, yet the material requirements were only that they should act independently: they 'shall sit on the Commission in their individual capacity' (Art 23 ECHR).

A document containing the full list of all nominated candidates, recently made public by the ECtHR, sheds an interesting light on the first selection of judges for the highest office of European human rights.[11] From the perspective of the total list of nominees, the actual selection of candidates elucidates quite strikingly what were the de facto criteria for becoming a judge (and commissioner) at the Strasbourg institutions. What can be deduced is clearly that among European politicians of the day, the preferred candidates were all jurists with top academic degrees—typically doctorates—as well as an acquaintance with international politics and diplomacy. In other words, the nominees who were finally selected were not one-dimensional actors in terms of pure judges, academics, practising lawyers, etc but, rather, multi-dimensional in the sense of having knowledge of more fields of relevance.[12] Jurists who appeared formally independent—typically academics or jurists with an academic career background—and could exhibit somewhat of a track record in international politics and law were in practice to be selected over other candidates.[13]

This orientation towards intellectual resources in academic law combined with exposure to international affairs might seem unsurprising considering the general perception of international human rights law at the time as being an upshot of public international law. Hence, besides all being male and with an average age in their mid-60s, the 1959 bench entailed a highly experienced set of judges who for the most part had doctorates in law but also experience beyond academic law.[14] In that sense, the 1959 Court was, above all, a prolongation of the construction of international law, since the late nineteenth century, where the line of separation

[11] Council of Europe, Document IP/1249 PMGL/M-thn. 29.xii.58 (1958).

[12] It is a phenomenon vividly described in the work of Yves Dezalay and Bryant Garth on the entrepreneurs of the international legal field. See eg Y. Dezalay, 'Les courtiers de l'international: Héritiers cosmopolites, mercenaires de l'impérialisme et missionnaires de l'universel', 151–2 *Actes de la recherche en sciences sociales* (2004), 5.

[13] The commissioners were generally comparable although one finds a larger number of actors with experience in the practical offices of the legal system, including judges, lawyers, and prosecutors.

[14] Thereby they differed significantly from the judges of European Court of Justice. A. Cohen and M. R. Madsen, 'Cold War Law: Legal Entrepreneurs and the Emergence of a European Legal Field (1945–1965)' in V. Gessner and D. Nelken (eds), *European Ways of Law: Towards a European Sociology of Law* (Oxford: Hart Publishing, 2007).

between international law and politics had tacitly remained somewhat imprecise.[15]
Rather, as argued by Guillaume Sacriste and Antoine Vauchez, international law
served as a framework for stabilizing international politics, a civilized instrument of
ordering international politics and peace.[16] Moreover, in this process of civilizing
international politics by law, the very actors appointed to perform this task were
central to legitimizing the very same task and institutions. In other words, their
eminent individual and professional competences were the key to the legitimacy of
the nascent institutions, both in terms of legal practices and institutionalization.[17]
In the analytical scheme of Max Weber, the international clout of these eminent
lawyers was to give way to institutionalization following, abstractly speaking, the
process of the 'routinisation of charisma' famously described by Weber.[18]

II. Legal Diplomacy in Action

It is the underlying claim of this analysis that the collective and individual
characteristics of the judges and commissioners provide a means for understanding
the initial law-making of these institutions. Besides what has long been pointed
out by legal realists in terms of the influence of extra-legal factors on legal adjudication,[19] the actions of these actors had particular importance in respect of the
Strasbourg system as the institutional framework and the normative contents of
the ECHR that had yet to be fully developed. And this task was largely entrusted to
that very group of legal actors. That said, the importance of both their individual
and collective characteristics has to be correlated to the broader dynamics of
the emerging field of human rights of the time. Generally speaking, besides the
international legal dimension of the subject described above, in the 1950s the
field had been dominated by two issues which in human rights terms were closely
linked: the Cold War and decolonization.[20] Consequently, the question of human
rights in the 1950s was more a question of politics than law. Although the leading
NGOs at the time were for the most part legal organizations, they had more or less
explicit linkages to, respectively, Washington DC and Moscow, making them part
of a typical Cold War scheme of oppositions. The most striking example was
perhaps the practices of lawyers' organizations such as the International Commission

---

[15] See M. Koskenniemi, *The Gentle Civilizer of Nations: The Rise and Fall of International Law
1870–1960* (Cambridge: Cambridge University Press, 2001).

[16] G. Sacriste and A. Vauchez, 'Les bons offices du droit international: la constitution d'une autorité
politique dans le concert diplomatique des années 20', 26 *Critique Internationale* (2005), 101.

[17] Cf the analysis in Y. Dezalay and B. Garth, *The Internationalization of Palace Wars: Lawyers,
Economists, and the Contest to Transform Latin American States* (Chicago: University of Chicago Press,
2002).

[18] As described in M. Weber, *Wirtschaft und Gesellschaft. Grundriss der verstehenden Soziologie*
(Tübingen: Mohr, 1980), ch III, para 10.

[19] Such as Karl Llewellyn in the USA and Scandinavian realists such as Alf Ross.

[20] For a general analysis, see M. R. Madsen, *La genèse de l'Europe des droits de l'homme: Enjeux
juridiques et stratégies d'Etat (France, Grande-Bretagne et pays scandinaves, 1945–1970)* (Strasbourg:
Presses Universitaires de Strasbourg, 2010).

of Jurists (ICJ), pursuing a Western-oriented campaign for civil and political liberties, and their clash with the communist-dominated International Association for Democratic Jurists (IADJ) as part of the cultural Cold War.[21] While the ICJ sought to make human rights a question of Western liberty, the IADJ turned the rhetoric of liberty against the West in an attempt to denounce imperialism and advocate peoples' rights to self-determination.

It was at the height of these clashes that the ECtHR first opened its doors in 1959.[22] Needless to say, the countries most exposed to these clashes over human rights were the late-imperial societies of the UK and France.[23] Notwithstanding the hesitance exercised by precisely these States, they were in practice to dominate the Court during this tumultuous period. Concretely, the UK and France were to supply the first two presidents of the Court—respectively, Lord McNair (1959–64) and René Cassin (Vice-President 1959–64 and President 1965–7). Following Cassin, the Belgian lawyer-statesman Henri Rollin became President 1968–71 (after having been Vice-President 1965–7). He was then substituted by first Humphrey Waldock of the UK (President 1971–4 and Vice-President 1968–70) and then the Italian G. Balladore-Pallieri (President 1974–9 and Vice-President previously). Paradoxically, France, the UK, and Italy—the three countries institutionally and legally the least committed to the ECHR system, yet undoubtedly together with West Germany the most central to the broader project of European integration—took the lead on the bench.[24] One can, of course, only speculate on why—the Presidents and Vice-Presidents of both the Court and the Commission were elected by secret vote among the respectively appointed judges and commissioners—but it is plain to see that the late-imperial countries, regardless of their institutional commitments, were well placed.

The first case to arrive before the emerging European human rights system was in many ways to confirm both the worst fears of some of the drafters and the inevitability that colonial politics could not be kept outside the Strasbourg institutions. In 1956, Greece filed an interstate complaint concerning British practices on Cyprus, at the time a British Crown colony.[25] Greece alleged that the forceful British response to the insurrection triggered by, among others, the militant resistance movement EOKA (Ethnikí Orgánosis Kipriakoú Agónos), seeking self-determination and unification with Greece, was a violation of the ECHR. The case was explosive as it not only potentially opened up the possibility of a general showdown with the British Empire's human rights record in the colonies, but also concerned a long and complex conflict between Greece and Turkey over

[21] Cf H. Tolley, *The International Commission of Jurists: Global Advocates of Human Rights* (Philadelphia: University of Pennsylvania Press, 1994)

[22] The Commission had been operational since 1955. It was not until 1958, however, that the Commission found an individual application admissible.

[23] Belgium was also deeply exposed to these dynamics, as became clear during the 1960 Congo Crisis, which to a certain extent also was a Cold War proxy intertwined with the politics of decolonization.

[24] The role of the President was to direct the work and administration of the Court, as well as to preside over plenary sessions.

[25] *Greece v United Kingdom* Appl no 176/56 (1958).

Cyprus. But above all, it was an unwelcome development in London. Here the understanding had been that the important restrictions ensured by the optional clauses, conversely allowed the UK to use the ECHR as a tool of propaganda vis-à-vis the colonies. As a matter of fact, the UK had opted for extending the application of the ECHR to large parts of its empire in applying Art 63 ECHR ('the colonial clause'). Yet by Greece filing an interstate complaint before the Commission, the British strategy of evading the ECHR system by steering free of the Court and individual petition was thereby itself evaded. It was in any event an unpredicted development as it had been the general assumption during the negotiations that interstate complaints were highly improbable as the Convention was indeed a Convention among Western allies, most of them NATO allies.[26]

The only possible legal response at hand for the UK was to evoke Art 15 on 'public emergency threatening the life of the nation'. This did not, however, prevent the Council of Europe from authorizing a mission to investigate the claims of violations put forward by the Greeks. Aware of the seriousness of the situation and its potential effects on the whole of the remaining empire, the only real way out for the UK government was to bypass the Strasbourg system altogether by recourse to diplomacy. With the Zurich and London Agreements on Cyprus filed with the Commission, the latter had to resolve 'that no further action [was] called for'. It was obviously a heavy price to pay for imploding the case, but it was deemed necessary in the bigger picture. The unease the case was causing was not, however, limited to the defendants. In respect to the Strasbourg system more generally, the case was hardly an ideal occasion for striking the described balance between individual justice and recruiting the late-imperial States as full members of the system. This is apparent from the proceedings themselves. Emblematically, counsel for the prosecution in *Greece v United Kingdom*, the distinguished Belgian international lawyer and senator Henri Rollin, who two years later would be appointed to the ECtHR and subsequently serve as its President (1968–71), began his speech before the European Commission in the following fashion:

I am the first to admit the paradox—and personally I regret it—that by a chance of fate the first government to be brought to the bar by another government is the United Kingdom, which governs a country which surely, more than any other in Europe, has always shown concern for human rights.[27]

Perhaps inappropriate in a courtroom, but Rollin's point was hard to miss.

If, after all, the result of the *Cyprus case* was acceptable in light of the stakes, it was also a firm reminder of the fragility of the enterprise of institutionalizing and juridifying European human rights. And shortly after, another case, the *Lawless case*, was moving up through the system and becoming the first case before the ECtHR.[28] Lodged against Ireland, but not without relevance to a number of other countries, including notably the UK, it concerned the practice of detention without trial in Ireland in the context of a showdown with the IRA (Irish Republican

---

[26] A. W. B. Simpson, n 4 above, 4.   [27] Ibid, 322.
[28] *Lawless v Ireland* Appl no 332/57 (1961).

Army). In this case, first the European Commission and then the ECtHR found that these practices were in conflict with Art 5 ECHR, yet accepted derogation through Art 15 and did not, thus, find a violation of the ECHR. On this occasion, the European institutions themselves seem to have provided the necessary 'legal diplomacy' for striking a balance. The case also more generally suggests that the Strasbourg institutions were reluctant to turn loose the Convention and were certainly diplomatically perceptive when it came to questions of national sovereignty and insecurity. This seems to be more of a general phenomenon. In fact, a review of the number of applications admitted to the two bodies during the initial period of operation, sustains the argument that the Strasbourg institutions only very gradually embarked on devising European human rights jurisprudence.

Throughout the 1950s the Commission admitted five applications and some 54 during the subsequent decade. Importantly, only a very small number of these cases ended in actual decisions. The situation of the ECtHR was even more so striking: after ten years of operation, it had only delivered ten judgments, and of these only a handful found violations of the ECHR.[29] The Court was in fact out of business for a period of five years between 1960 and 1965 after it had been involved in the two cases in 1959 of *Lawless* and *De Becker*,[30] and finding violation in neither.[31] This has to be seen in the context of the fairly large number of applications lodged during the same period. What is certain, is that the Commission utilized fully its pre-screening competence to reduce the caseload thereby developing a very important jurisprudence on the notion of 'manifestly ill-founded' claims, that is, a jurisprudence on what are not human rights violations under the ECHR. Above all, what can be interpreted from these developments is that European human rights, after the turmoil of the *Cyprus case*, developed in a rather measured fashion. This necessarily has to be seen in light of the objective of ensuring the acceptance of the two key optional clauses by the major European States.

III. The Rise of the Integrationist Court

There is also little doubt that the institutional strategies devised in Strasbourg were well received in the Member States, observing sound judgement and necessary skills in 'legal diplomacy'. In the case of the UK, the observed reluctance and diplomatic flair of the Strasbourg institutions played a significant role when the decision for finally accepting the optional clauses on individual petition and the jurisdiction of Court was made in 1966.[32] Obviously, as pointed out by Anthony Lester, things were further complicated because accepting the clauses had to be considered not

---

[29] B. Dickson (ed), *Human Rights and the European Convention* (London: Sweet & Maxwell, 1997), 19.

[30] *De Becker v Belgium* Appl no 214/56 (1962).

[31] Another element influencing the institutionalization of the ECHR was the interface between the Court and Commission. I have left this issue out of the analysis.

[32] In 1967, individual petition was allowed for many individuals of the so-called dependent territories.

only in respect of the limited case law but also in respect of both decolonization and some unresolved issues deriving from the Second World War.[33] Yet, regardless of the various calculations carried out at the Foreign Office, the message was clear: Britain was aboard the European human rights train even if the acceptance was limited to a three-year period and then up for renewal.[34] In 1973, both Italy and Switzerland followed suit making France the only remaining hurdle.[35] Neverthe-less, in 1974, in the aftermath of President Pompidou's sudden death and with some distance from the traumas of the war in Algeria, France finally decided to ratify the Convention, as well as to accept the jurisdiction of the Court. It would, however, take the election of François Mitterrand in 1981 before the right to individual petition was accepted as part of a more general election pledge to human rights.[36] Nonetheless, the pattern was clear in terms of a European human rights system now finally legitimized and fully operational. This second incarnation of the Court was to take European human rights to a different level by turning the Convention into genuine European law and thereby make it a player in European integration.

Considering the rather limited activism exhibited during the previous period, the transformation in the late 1970s of the Court is indeed striking. In a series of landmark decisions the ECtHR laid out the fundamentals for the future under-standing of the Convention. If there was one common trend in these judgments, it was that they pushed the ECtHR beyond the mere intergovernmentalism of the previous period. Within the limited field of European human rights, the only viable way out of the hegemony of national sovereignty marking the initial period was by granting individuals—and individual rights—more importance in the balancing act between European human rights and national sovereignty. Retrospectively, the decisive importance of the institutionalization of individual petition in the 1970s was in fact precisely that it provided for adjusting the basic human rights equation more in favour of individuals and, thereby, the Convention. The degree of change is best illustrated by first briefly reviewing the jurisprudence up to the mid-1970s before examining the progressive jurisprudence during the second half of the 1970s.

Generally, up to the mid-1970s, the jurisprudence was marked by the measured development described above. Two cases decided by, respectively, the Commission and the Court, in the late 1960s—after the Court's five years of dormancy—each

---

[33] A. Lester, 'UK Acceptance of the Strasbourg Jurisdiction: What Really Went On In 1965', 46 *Public Law* (1988), 237.

[34] The latter was not as suspicious as it might look at first glance as indeed seven out of the eight first declarations of acceptance of the jurisdiction of the Court were limited to a fixed time period and, thus, up for renewal. Austria, Denmark, the Federal Republic of Germany, Iceland, and Luxembourg had specified this period to be three years—Belgium and the Netherlands initially accepted the jurisdiction for five years. See A. H. Robertson, 'The European Court of Human Rights', 9 *American Journal of Comparative Law* (1960), 18.

[35] Greece also re-ratified in 1974 after having left the Council of Europe in 1969. See further below.

[36] See eg É. Agrikoliansky, 'La gauche, le libéralisme politique et les droits de l'homme' in J.-J. Becker and G. Candar (eds), *Histoire des gauches en France* (Paris: La Découverte, 2003).

stand out in their own way.[37] The *Greek case* served for many as an important occasion for confirming the anti-totalitarian ethos held dear by many of the drafters of the Convention, who had mainly seen the Convention as a collective guarantee against the return of totalitarianism of any type in Western Europe.[38] Regardless of these high stakes, it was an intergovernmental case which, like the *Cyprus case*, was eventually to culminate in an extra-legal solution.[39] After the Commission in 1969 had concluded that the Greek colonels had violated the Convention, the junta simply decided to leave the Council of Europe, firing a farewell tirade at the Commission dubbing it 'a conspiracy of homosexuals and communists against Hellenic values'.[40] However, the junta's level of rhetoric was not to be the low point of the case. It was in itself highly problematic that a founding Member State (and NATO member) left the organization but, even worse, in the short term violent suppression only increased after the Greek exodus from the Council of Europe.[41] Human rights had been defended, but more abstractly than concretely.[42]

Another case, which might qualify more directly as a harbinger of the jurisprudence of the late 1970s, was the *Case Relating to Certain Aspects of the Laws on the Use of Languages in Education in Belgium*, better known as the *Belgian Linguistics case* of 1968.[43] In this strongly contested case, the Court found by a majority of 8 to 7 that a Belgian Act on access to education did not comply with Art 14 ECHR as it had no objective and reasonable justification, did not pursue a legitimate aim, and was not proportionate to the aim pursued. Although hardly speaking unanimously, this was a first warning to the Member States that although there was a certain margin of appreciation with regard to the fulfilment of their obligation, not every measure—or lack of measure—could be referred under the banner of subsidiarity. In other words, the interpretation of the ECHR was to take place according to the *effet utile* of the norms of the Convention.

While both cases indicate a change in the direction of a more effective application of the ECHR, they hardly transformed the system. It was only with the post-1975 jurisprudence of such remarkable cases as *Ireland v United Kingdom* (1978), *Tyrer v United Kingdom* (1978), *Marckx v Belgium* (1979), *Airey v Ireland* (1979), as well as a number of others,[44] that the course of European human rights took a new direction. Key notions such as 'living instrument' and 'practical and effective' developed in a flow of successive cases where the Court was not shy of finding violation. In *Golder v United Kingdom* (1975), the first UK case to arrive before the

---

[37] Two other cases of the same period—*Wemhoff v Germany* Series A no 7 (1968) and *Neumeister v Austria* Series A no 8 (1968)—are also noteworthy.

[38] *Greece v United Kingdom* Appl no 176/56 (1958).

[39] The interstate complaint had been submitted in 1967 by the Scandinavian governments and the Netherlands.

[40] A. W. B. Simpson, n 4 above, 144.

[41] In a similar way, the *Cyprus case* had been a disaster as its situation after the London and Zurich Agreements only worsened in terms of human rights.

[42] In the long run, it can be argued that the case served as a framework for activists opposing the Greek colonels.

[43] *Belgian Linguistics (No 2)* Series A no 6 (1968).

[44] For a list of the relevant judgments and case references, see n 1 above.

ECtHR after the acceptance of individual petition and the jurisdiction of the Court, the ECtHR found—with a very lengthy separate opinion by the English Judge Sir Gerald Fitzmaurize—that an inmate who had been deprived access to a lawyer to make a libel claim against a prison officer had been denied his right to a fair trial under Art 6 ECHR. The case basically explicated that without access to a court, the rule of law would be an illusion. A few years later, in *Airey v Ireland* (1979), the Court expanded further and found that the actual costs of separation in Ireland implied that the applicant, Mrs Airey, had been deprived of an effective right of access to the courts. Regardless of the absence of any formal barrier, the fact that the applicant could not pay for a lawyer and no legal aid was available infringed her right to access to a court and fair trial. Paragraph 24 of the judgment legendarily notes: 'The Convention is intended to guarantee not rights that are theoretical or illusory but rights that are practical and effective'.

The doctrine of 'practical and effective' was in itself of considerable importance to the interpretation of the Convention as it spelled out that the protection of the rights of the ECHR was not an abstract but a concrete obligation of the Member States and failure so to provide might constitute a violation of the Convention. In the cases *Tyrer v United Kingdom* (1978) and *Marckx v Belgium* (1979) the implications of the new approach were taken even further. In *Tyrer v United Kingdom* the Court faced the question of whether a British juvenile, Anthony M. Tyrer, had been subject to 'degrading punishment' contrary to Art 3 ECHR when sentenced to 'three strokes of the birch' for his assault of a senior pupil at school. Whether his right to dignity and physical integrity had been violated required establishing the general standards of society in this respect. In para 31, the ECtHR famously stated that the ECHR is 'is a living instrument . . . [and] must be interpreted in the light of present-day conditions . . . commonly accepted standards in the . . . members states'. Shortly after, in *Marckx v Belgium* (1979), the ECtHR confirmed that it was to conduct a dynamic interpretation of the ECHR in order to ensure up-to-date protection of human rights in Europe. A last crucial jurisprudential development is also linked to the interpretation of Art 3, namely the pronouncement in *Ireland v United Kingdom* (1978) that neither a national margin of appreciation nor derogation under Art 15 could justify the practice of inhuman and degrading treatment. Article 3 ECHR was a fundamental tenet of European human rights not to be derogated from, even in cases of national unrest and self-proclaimed emergency. With this judgment the *Lawless case* seemed suddenly to belong to a distant past.

IV. The ECtHR in the Transformation of Europe

What is apparent from this brief examination of the jurisprudence of the late 1970s is that the ECtHR, in the course of a few years, left behind the diplomacy of human rights and forged a doctrine which laid out at least three crucial issues in respect of the ECHR: a notion of fundamental rights (*Ireland*), a dynamic approach to the understanding of the ECHR (*Tyrer* and *Marckx*) and, finally, an obligation on the

Member States to protect the rights of the Convention effectively and practically (*Airey* and *Golder*). These decisions were certainly not all unanimous or without tensions between the Court and the Member States, but they successively pushed the Convention in the same direction of European human rights as a genuine form of law and as a force to be reckoned with and respected by all Member States. This dynamic framework for understanding and enforcing effective and practical legal rights was, in effect, to become the variant *strasbourgeoise* of the notion of the supremacy of European law and its uniform application being forged at the European Court of Justice (ECJ). While these developments might be seen as simply a metamorphosis of the ECHR, that is, an organic development driven by functional purposes already prescribed in the Convention, such a self-referential explanation does not, however, account for the obvious importance of extra-legal forces on legal evolution. Considering that the jurisprudence of the late 1970s practically qualifies as a small-scale revolution of European human rights, it begs the question of what facilitated this new jurisprudential direction.

The most simple and most often pronounced explanation for this change takes its lead from legal realism, suggesting that the substitution of the actors—the judges and commissioners—essentially accounts for the change of jurisprudence. Generally speaking, it appears plausible to allocate the transformation in jurisprudence to a radical change in the composition of the Strasbourg bench and, thereby, a change of institutional *habitus*.[45] However, in the specific case of the ECtHR, it turns out that the argument is problematic when the empirics are scrutinized more closely. In fact, what is striking is not difference but similarity when one compares the judges of 1959 and 1979 in terms of primary socio-professional profiles. Above all, the 1979 bench, like the 1959 bench, was dominated by actors who had had long spells in academia and exposure to the international field in various legal, diplomatic, and political functions.[46] If 80 per cent of the 1959 bench had a doctorate, in 1979 the figure was 70 per cent, underlining the significant continuity of academic lawyers in that sphere. Moreover, in 1979, the average age was still over 60 and male domination maintained; only one woman, the Dane Helga Petersen, had entered the Court. What one can observe is that the two generations of judges were essentially members of the same type of international legal academic elite. In fact, one of the most prolific actors of the 1979 bench turned out to be Pierre-Henri Teitgen, who besides having all the necessary academic credentials also happened to be the most influential drafter of the Convention some 25 years earlier. That the bench remained relatively unchanged only adds to the puzzle of how the legal output was so markedly different.

One is essentially left with a more structural explanation, unless of course the catalyst of change is allocated not to the socio-professional properties as above but

---

[45] This is also precisely the rationale behind making the nomination of judges a political question such as in the case of the ECtHR or, more strikingly, the US Supreme Court. Cf Chapters 4 and 6 below.

[46] As argued below in Chapter 4, such professional profiles generally speaking might suggest little judicial activism.

to the psychological features of the new bench or perhaps the political preferences of its individual members.[47] Contemporary sociology of law does indeed argue for the need for a structural framework for explaining legal evolution. The two main currents of contemporary sociology of law—Lumannian systems theory and Bourdieusian reflexive sociology of law—both suggest in different ways that law is structurally coupled to its surroundings.[48] It is precisely this interface that allows for a practice which is, in the famous words of Niklas Luhmann, at one and the same time normatively closed and cognitively open. In plain language, the genius of law is its ability both to respond to external circumstances—in lawyer's terms the *facts* but here not restricted to these—and to integrate these organically in a structure of norms. Thereby, the visible importance of extra-legal factors is obviously greatly diminished or even in some cases completely concealed. Their importance is, however, by no means thereby reduced. Thus, notwithstanding the claims of autonomy or semi-autonomy, law remains socially embedded and contingent on social change. And this is both true in terms of normative doctrinal evolution and institutional legitimacy.[49] Thus, following contemporary sociology of law, an international legal institution such as the ECtHR integrates its surroundings both legally and in terms of institutional strategies.

As demonstrated above, geopolitical issues, particularly Cold War politics, generally played a major role first in the drafting of the ECHR, and then in the initial jurisprudence where the question of decolonization directly and indirectly placed constraints on the practices of the Court. For the same reasons, it seems plausible that the shift in jurisprudence, beginning in the mid-1970s, can in a similar way be explained in respect of the broader structural transformation of the fields of human rights and European law in the period influencing the behaviour of the bench. In the 1970s, one can generally observe a renewed interest in international human rights both in terms of international politics and law. With the easing of relations in the Cold War as illustrated by the *détente* politics of the early 1970s, as well as the closure of the most violent of the colonial wars of independence, the question of human rights was gradually reinserted in international politics and law. Most importantly in respect of this analysis, human rights criticism was also increasingly directed at a set of new perpetrators to be found outside Western Europe: in Latin America, South Africa, Eastern Europe, as well as—at least in the

---

[47] As for the latter, this tends to be a prevalent variable when explaining judicial activism in other contexts such as the US Supreme Court. In respect of the European Courts, such explanations have also been used, eg by M. Rasmussen, 'The Origins of a Legal Revolution: The Early History of the European Court of Justice', 14 *Journal of European Integration History* (2008), 77. As for the ECtHR, it seems somehow far-fetched to argue along these lines, particularly in view of the actual protracted processes of institutionalization described here which undoubtedly related to the structural environment of the institution. For a somewhat similar approach to the ECJ, see A. Cohen, 'Dix personnages majestueux en longue robe amarante: La formation de la cour de justice des communautés européennes', 60 *Revue française de science politique* (2010), 227.

[48] N. Luhmann, *Das Recht der Gesellschaft* (Frankfurt: Suhrkamp Verlag, 1993) and P. Bourdieu, 'La force du droit: Éléments pour une sociologie du champ juridique', 64 *Actes de la recherche en sciences sociales* (1986), 3.

[49] Cf J. Habermas, *Faktizität und Geltung: Beiträge zur Diskurstheorie des Rechts und des demokratischen Rechtsstaats* (Frankfurt: Suhrkamp Verlag, 1992).

beginning of the 1970s—the USA and its conduct in Vietnam. Helped by this geographical transfer of the human rights struggle and the decline of Cold War human rights politics, Western Europe—like the USA under President Carter— came gradually to see itself, once again, as the cradle of human rights with somewhat of a mission abroad. The case of the former imperial societies of France and the UK is perhaps the most remarkable in this respect as they thereby transformed themselves from being subjects of human rights criticism to gradually reaffirming themselves as advocates of international human rights.

As in the case of the ECtHR, it was particularly in the second part of the 1970s that international human rights starting taking off in terms of becoming a substantive issue of international law and politics. The most well-known examples are perhaps the foreign politics devised by President Carter towards Latin-American military dictatorships and the negotiations of the Helsinki Final Act of 1975 which triggered and legitimized a series of 'watch' groups, including Human Rights Watch and Charter 77.[50] This further corresponds to the developments in the UN where the two Covenants finally came into force by the mid-1970s, providing a legalistic framework for international human rights. On the level of NGOs, a similar evolution can be observed. If, as described above, the initial NGO practices had been strongly marked by Cold War oppositional politics, the new leaders of the human rights movement, such as Amnesty International, sought explicitly to 'legalize' their human rights advocacy.[51] The new approach was recognized by an international society desperate for progress on the level of international human rights. In the late 1970s, in the course of only three years, Amnesty International received the Erasmus Prize (1976), the Nobel Peace Prize (1977), and the UN Human Rights Award (1978). After its more or less forced absence during the initial Cold War, the question of human rights was unquestionably making a comeback at the high table of international law and politics.

These intertwined developments, related to the launch of the post-war project of devising human rights as a matter of international law and politics, are also observable within Western Europe during the same period. In Western Europe in the early 1970s, most human rights activism was directed at non-democratic regimes outside the jurisdiction of European human rights: the Greek colonels, Spain under Franco and Portugal under Salazar. Yet, by the mid-1970s, the tide was turning and Greece, Spain, and Portugal were now integrating themselves into the ECHR framework.[52] Undoubtedly, this gave the institution a new and important legitimacy, but most significantly, it redefined the playing field making cases such as *Cyprus* and *Greece*, which had marked the initial period of operation, no longer likely to be brought before the Court. The *Irish case* was in fact to be the last of this series of highly delicate interstate complaints. And in this case the Court

---

[50] Cf D. C. Thomas, *The Helsinki Effect: International Norms, Human Rights, and the Demise of Communism* (Princeton: Princeton University Press, 2001).

[51] On the genesis of Amnesty International, see T. Buchanan, '"The Truth Will Set You Free": The Making of Amnesty International', 37 *Journal of Contemporary History* (2002), 575.

[52] Portugal and Spain signed the ECHR in 1976 and 1977, respectively.

stepped out of the smokescreen of post-war politics and underlined its primary commitment to European human rights by pointing out that Art 3 ECHR was a fundamental right from which there could be no derogation. This was not only an indication that the period of late-imperial special treatment had come to a close, but also that the ECtHR was not going to accept the kind of human rights games which characterized Latin America in the 1970s, where recourse to national emergency had become the preferred tool of Latin-American dictatorships to evade UN human rights.[53] With this decision, the ECtHR set itself apart as a leading institution in the international development of human rights law.

Although of crucial importance, these new geopolitics of human rights do not completely account for the changes in the course of the ECtHR. First, the developments at the ECtHR were also part of a distinct process of Europeanization both in terms of integrating European society and building European law. By the mid-1970s it is striking that all Member States of the European Economic Community (EEC) were now also full members of the ECHR system.[54] In fact, the change in commitment to the ECtHR analysed above happened to take place at the same time as the EEC undertook its first enlargement, and included Denmark, Ireland, and the UK.[55] This was to change the course of the EEC forever and create the process towards the development of the EU as we know it today. However, in the early 1970s the most important EEC-related development in this respect was taking place under the auspices of the ECJ. After an initial reluctance during the 1960s, the ECJ was now forging a jurisprudence on fundamental rights in terms of a set of unwritten general principles of Community law in such landmark cases as *Internationale Handelsgesellschaft* (1970), *Nold* (1974), *Rutili* (1975), and *Hauer* (1979).[56] Besides adding to the more general human rights momentum, the new ECJ jurisprudence also highlighted that human rights was not by definition a question of geopolitics and gross violations, but also concerned new social policy and citizens' rights in an increasingly united Europe.

Comparatively, the ECtHR cases of *Tyrer* and *Airey*, dealing respectively with corporal punishment and access to divorce, in a somewhat similar way raised the question of human rights in the evolving social fabric of West European society. As implied by the doctrine of dynamic interpretation, European human rights were the human rights of today's European society as a sum of societal development. As the Warren Court in *Trop v Dulles* (1958) had famously justified its progressive course by reference to societal progress in terms of 'evolving standards of decency in a maturing society', both European Courts deployed a notion of progressive

---

[53] It was the subject of a number of UN investigations, resulting finally in the so-called Questiaux Report of 1982.

[54] Of course with the exception of France's outstanding issue on individual petition.

[55] Norway did not join the EEC on this occasion following a 'no vote' at a referendum. Greece joined in 1981, and Spain and Portugal in 1986.

[56] Case 11/70 *Internationale Handelsgesellschaft mbH v Einfuhr- und Vorratsstelle für Getreide und Futtermittel* [1970] ECR 1161; Case 4/73 *J Nold, Kohlen- und Baustoffgroßhandlung v Commission of the European Communities* [1974] ECR 491; Case 36/75 *Roland Rutili v Minister for the Interior* [1975] ECR 1219; and Case 44/79 *Hauer v Land Rheinland-Pfalz* [1979] ECR 3727.

Europeanization—'ever closer Union' and 'present-day conditions [. . .] commonly accepted standards in the [. . .] members states'—in order to legitimize progressive European law.[57] Clearly, this only marginally links to the geopolitics of human rights addressed above. Nevertheless, it expresses a societal and legal evolution specific to Europe in which the idea of 'European integration through law' was a driving force. Moreover, the more general turn to rights in social policy to which both the ECtHR and the ECJ were to contribute significantly over the subsequent decades had a bearing on the jurisprudence of the ECtHR of the late 1970s. If European human rights had originally been envisaged and legitimized in terms of a collective guarantee against any forms of totalitarianism, in the 1970s human rights were also legitimized as a tool for social emancipation in a more permissive society.[58]

V. Conclusion

The multiple correspondence between the new jurisprudence of the ECtHR of the late 1970s and the social, legal, and political environments in which it was developed are striking. Indeed, it seems highly plausible to attribute the transformation of the ECtHR to the combined effects of the relative displacement of the human rights struggle to territories outside ECtHR jurisdiction and the new politics of 'juridicizing' human rights both in terms of international law and national politics. What is certain is that these more structural changes made the ECtHR a central institution for the realization of a set of objectives which all made the question of human rights—international, European, and national—more pertinent. Basically, structural constraints influenced the course of the combined set of actors involved in institutionalizing and juridifying human rights in Europe. What had kept the Court at bay for the first 15 years was to a large extent the strategies of the larger Member States who themselves were constrained in their engagement with human rights due to the structural transformation of the international field during the same period. In the 1970s, when finally 'liberated' from the heavy burden of decolonization, the same States helped legitimize the cause of human rights both in Europe and internationally, as well as on the level of national politics.[59] And together with the other developments in favour of human rights addressed above, this also greatly contributed to the eventual 'liberation' of the ECtHR.

---

[57] *Trop v Dulles* 356 US 86 (1958).

[58] The rights culture developed in the late 1960s and early 1970s is in itself an important variable in explaining the transformation of the ECtHR. A classic analysis of the rise of the politics of rights is found in S. Scheingold, *The Politics of Rights: Lawyers, Public Policy, and Political Change*, (2nd edn, Ann Arbor: University of Michigan Press, 2004).

[59] In fact, during the French election campaigns of 1974, Mitterrand had promised to make the drafting of a 'Charte des Libertés' a top political priority if he were elected. It was these electoral promises which were turned into reality by Giscard d'Estaing, when the newly elected President in July 1974 set up a commission of high court judges to draft a 'Code des Libertés Fondamentales de l'Invidu'. As a countermove, Mitterrand, assisted by the eminent lawyer, Robert Badinter, proclaimed the setting up of a commission to draft a 'Charte des libertés et droits fondementaux' in May 1975. This was only two days before the Communist Party was to publish its contribution to the battle: 'La Déclaration des Libertés'. Cf É. Agrikoliansky, n 36 above.

The human rights momentum of the late 1970s alone cannot, however, explain why the ECtHR went as far as it did in turning structural opportunity into legal practice. It would be mistaken simply to assume that the ECtHR joined the bandwagon of human rights euphoria of the 1970s (and 1980s). In fact, one reason that the ECtHR could develop as rapidly and progressively as it did was the processes of legitimization of the previous period; that is, legal diplomacy to an extent paved the way for the progressive integrationist jurisprudence of the late 1970s. In respect of this conversion, the ECtHR judges (and commissioners) played a crucial role. Helped by their tailored formation in academic law and exposure to international affairs, the judges managed to strike a balance in favour of the Member States when needed in the 1960s. In the late 1970s, a new set of judges—who greatly resembled the first bench—in a somewhat similar manner managed to strike a balance in favour of European law when it was most needed—and most viable. In fact, the most enduring contributions of the Strasbourg bench of the second period were not only the landslide decisions but also the continued reflexivity when dealing with human rights. The capacity was neither given by the Convention nor by the structures in which it operated but, rather, were the product of the collective skills of the small legal elite charged with institutionalizing and juridifying European human rights.

4

Politics, Judicial Behaviour, and Institutional Design

Erik Voeten

Into that strange compound which is brewed daily in the caldron of the courts, all these ingredients enter in varying proportions. I am not concerned to inquire whether judges ought to be allowed to brew such a compound at all. I take judge-made law as one of the existing realities of life.

Benjamin Cardozo (1921)

I. Politics and Rights Review: Inevitable but Uneasy Companions

When politicians delegate to judges the authority to interpret such abstract rights as freedom of expression and respect for private and family life, they allow judges to create compounds brewed from a motley crew of ingredients including legal text, statutes, precedent, judges' policy preferences, judges' perceptions of what society values, and collegial norms. The proportion in which the resulting brew features these ingredients varies across judges, courts, and cases. Yet, rights review inevitably introduces elements of subjectivity and judicial discretion. This is why the topic is viewed with such unease by strict legal positivists.

The subjectivity inherent to rights review invites politics into the equation. It offers politicians incentives to select judges who they think will interpret rights in accordance with their perceived interests and to reappoint judges who have proven loyal in that regard. It also presents politicians with opportunities to challenge the legitimacy of decisions they do not like. In all modern societies, judges who resolve disputes need to justify their decisions by telling the losing parties that 'You did not lose because we the judges chose that you should lose. You lost because the law required that you should lose.'[1] Politicians faced with sensitive defeats in the courtroom sometimes do not shy away from questioning the sincerity of such justifications. For example, Russian President Vladimir Putin called the

[1] M. Shapiro, *Courts: A Comparative and Political Analysis* (Chicago: University of Chicago Press, 1981).

European Court of Human Rights' (ECtHR) *Ilaşcu* decision 'a purely political decision, an undermining of trust in the judicial international system'.[2]

These types of allegations are not unique to the ECtHR. Charges that decisions are politically motivated also occur in mature constitutional democracies, including the USA. One cannot shield judges from these charges; one can only shield them from their consequences. Indeed, most reformers desire to improve the degree to which judges are insulated from political pressures, for example by creating non-renewable longer terms and by eliminating the role that governments play in the (re-)appointment process.[3] Yet, such reforms also carry potential costs. The ECtHR could lose legitimacy if its decisions appear motivated by political considerations but it may also lose legitimacy if it is seen as a wayward institution that is not accountable or responsive to democratically elected officials. Moreover, legitimacy may be tied to performance and efficiency. The greatest challenge currently facing the Court is the enormous backlog of cases. Institutional innovations that may make the Court more efficient may also increase worries about political influence; such as the idea that single judges can declare applications inadmissible as opposed to panels of three judges.

Legitimacy is crucial to any institution that operates in a compliance environment as insecure and complex as that of the ECtHR. Yet, as the above discussion clarifies, designing the institution to optimize legitimacy requires a set of complex trade-offs. Complicating matters further is that the actual effects of institutional design depend on how people (judges, leaders) respond to the incentives these institutions offer. Empirical studies of how judges behave can inform debates about how these institutional design trade-offs should be approached. If there is considerable evidence that politics affects decisions in normatively undesirable ways, then the case for institutional innovations that further insulate judges becomes stronger. If, on the other hand, the way politics interferes with justice appears modest, then this would strengthen the case for reforms that stress other goals (for example efficiency) where these conflict with reforms aimed at improving insulation.

In this chapter, I highlight in a non-technical manner the main findings from previously published quantitative empirical analyses.[4] I then discuss institutional and normative implications from these findings and highlight some areas where further empirical research could greatly enhance reform discussions. I argue that the evidence suggests that ECtHR judges are politically motivated actors in the sense that they have preferences on how best to apply abstract human rights in concrete

---

[2] Press conference, 11 January 2007, as quoted in B. Bowring, 'Russia's Relations with the Council of Europe under Increasing Strain', U-Russia Centre, available at: <http://www.eu-russiacentre.org/assets/files/15%20Feb%20Bowring%20article%20EU-RC.pdf>.

[3] See eg INTERIGHTS, *Judicial Independence: Law and Practice of Appointments to the European Court of Human Rights* (London: International Centre for the Legal Protection of Human Rights, 2003).

[4] E. Voeten, 'The Impartiality of International Judges: Evidence from the European Court of Human Rights', 102(4) *American Political Science Review* (2008), 417; and 'The Politics of International Judicial Appointments: Evidence from the European Court of Human Rights', 61(4) *International Organization* (2007).

cases, and not in the sense that they are using their judicial power to settle geopolitical scores. Politics matters in that governments more favourably disposed towards supranational integration tend to appoint more activist judges while those less favourably disposed generally select more restrained candidates. Politics also matters in that new governments sometimes choose not to re-elect sitting judges for partisan reasons. But there is no evidence that judges generally behave like diplomats in that they pursue the broader national interests of their States on the court. Nor are divisions among judges dominated by cultural differences. National bias is important but rarely influences the outcome of cases.

Normatively, these findings are generally favourable for the possibility of international review of rights issues. In some way, shape, or form politics will interfere with any attempt at judicial review of government respect for abstractly defined individual rights. The 'umpire' ideal that judges 'simply apply the law' is unattainable. Yet, political interference can come in many forms and some are more problematic than others. It is especially important that the Court has by and large not become an arena in which geopolitical or cultural battles are fought. Moreover, in any normative discussion, it is important to weigh how demands for accountability may interfere with demands for impartiality and independence. From a perspective of accountability, the notion that governments seek to influence the overall ideological direction of an international court may well be desirable. I conclude that it would be unwise to eliminate the role of governments in the appointment of judges but that the creation of a nine-year non-renewable term is a good idea that should reduce national bias. Given findings of national bias and given that little is known about the empirics of the admissibility process, I question the desirability of moving to one-judge admissibility panels, while acknowledging the efficiency advantages of such a move.

The chapter proceeds with an analysis of the role politics plays in the selection of judges. It then investigates national, cultural, and geopolitical biases. The final section offers normative and institutional implications.

II. Politics, Ideology, and the Selection of Judges

Politicians may care about the judges they select because these judges make decisions that affect the national interests of their governments and/or because politicians have preferences about how human rights should be interpreted. For the latter to be plausible, ideological divisions that matter in politics have to be relevant in the judicial arena as well. For example, in the USA the link between the political and judicial arenas is established by the relative ease by which both judges and politicians can be classified on a liberal–conservative continuum[5]. Consequentially, there is a long literature in US judicial politics that establishes

---

[5] M. A. Bailey and F. Maltzman, 'Does Legal Doctrine Matter? Unpacking Law and Policy Preferences on the US Supreme Court', 102(3) *American Political Science Review* (2008), 369.

that more liberal (conservative) politicians tend to appoint more liberal (conservative) judges.

Such links are plausible in the ECtHR context as well. The ECtHR takes decisions over some issues that divide politicians along traditional left–right lines; such as the degree to which property rights should be protected from government interference. More often, ECtHR judgments divide politicians along what some have called a 'new politics' dimension, which includes issues such as the extent to which gays are deserving of equal rights, politicians have the right to ban head-scarves, and other social issues.[6] Moreover, an ECtHR that finds that national practices or laws constitute violations of international law may be greeted with less enthusiasm by politicians who are generally sceptical towards increased European integration. Consequentially, it may be that governments which are more Euro-sceptic seek to select judges that advance a more restrained interpretation of the Convention.

A first indication that governments exercise their discretion in who they advance[7] for ECtHR judgeships is the variation in the backgrounds of international judges. For example, about one-third of ECtHR judges had experience as judges on high national courts.[8] Around one-quarter of judges were recruited from the *corps diplomatique* or domestic bureaucracies of States. The remainder of judges were academics, politicians (including former ministers of justice and parliamentarians), and private lawyers with experience in human rights litigation.

Does this variation matter? And, are certain types of governments more likely to appoint certain types of judges? In order to answer these questions it is first necessary to investigate what variation among ECtHR judges is about. Elsewhere,[9] I applied a quantitative methodology for estimating the location of judges along a single ideological dimension based on how individual ECtHR judges voted on cases (until 2006) that did not involve their home country. The methodology is identical to that used by scholars who estimate the degree to which US Supreme Court judges are liberal or conservative. Figure 4.1 plots the estimated ideal points and the 95 per cent posterior credible intervals of the 97 judges who voted at least ten times. The larger the posterior credible interval (the line in the figure) the more uncertainty there is about the precise location of a judge's ideal point. Large uncertainty reflects that the ideal points of some judges can be estimated more precisely than those of others, mostly due to varied numbers of votes.

The interpretation of these quantitative divisions among judges fits the qualitative literature that has interpreted divisions within the ECtHR as concerning the

---

[6] L. Hooghe, G. Marks, and C. Wilson, 'Does Left/Right Structure Party Positions on European Integration?', 35(8) *Comparative Political Studies* (2002), 965.

[7] In the post-Protocol No 11 system, governments no longer have absolute control over judicial appointments. Each government submits three candidates, who they may rank order. The Council of Europe's Parliamentary Assembly then votes on the list. The Assembly has occasionally selected a candidate other than the government's favourite and has refused to accept a few candidate lists for want of gender-balance or proper qualifications. Generally, however, the government's preferred candidate is elected.

[8] For more details on data collection see Voeten (2007), n 4 above.

[9] Ibid.

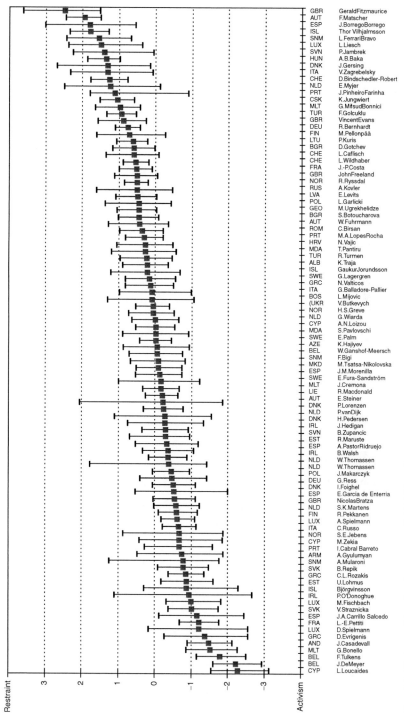

Fig. 4.1 Estimated levels of activism of ECtHR judges

size of the margin of appreciation that should be left to respondent States.[10] This division is generally labelled as being between those who favour 'judicial activism' and those who prefer 'judicial restraint'. I stick to these terms while noting their specific operationalization in the context of the ECtHR: given the legal facts of a case, an activist judge is more likely to rule in favour of the applicant than a judge on the self-restraint side of the spectrum. Thus, it is ultimately about the *degree of deference* a judge prefers to grant governments.

To the extent that the positions of judges are known through qualitative sources, the quantitative estimates have face validity. ECtHR judges whose previous careers were primarily as diplomats or bureaucrats are significantly less activist than are judges with other previous career tracks.[11] The British judge Sir Gerald Fitzmaurice is the most 'extreme' judge on the restraint side. Fitzmaurice was a legal adviser in the UK foreign office who became a well-known academic and a judge on the International Court of Justice (ICJ) (1960–73) before coming to the ECtHR in 1973. He is often cited as the prototype of the 'tough conservative' judge,[12] who sometimes angered his colleagues with long and opinionated dissents.[13] Another judge with a precisely estimated ideal point on the restraint side, the Austrian judge Franz Matscher, spent 17 years in the Austrian diplomatic service before joining the Court in 1977 and has openly expressed his concern about the ECtHR's activist tendencies by writing that the ECtHR has 'entered territory which is no longer that of treaty interpretation but is actually legal policy-making'.[14] Luzius Wildhaber proclaimed himself to be 'slightly more to the self-restraint side' in comparison to his colleagues,[15] which is confirmed by his ideal point estimate.

Similar observations can be made about many of the judges on the activist side of the spectrum. The Belgian judge Françoise Tulkens asserted in an interview that: 'One can speak of judges who are concerned about problems of the raison d'état and others who sympathize with the applicants. The raison d'état is more present here than I would have thought possible.'[16] The Italian judge Josep Casadevall (serving for Andorra) declared that 'Personally I am a judicial activist as to Article 6 with a bent to enlarge its scope.'[17] The French judge Louis-Edmond Pettiti,

---

[10] See eg F. J. Bruinsma, 'Judicial Identities in the European Court of Human Rights' in A. van Hoek, A. M. Hol, O. Jansen, P. Rijpkema, and R. Widdershoven (eds), *Multilevel Governance in Enforcement and Adjudication* (Antwerp: Intersentia, 2006); F. J. Bruinsma and S. Parmentier, 'Interview with Mr Luzius Wildhaber, President of the ECHR', 21(2) *Netherlands Quarterly of Human Rights* (2003), 185; D. W. Jackson, *The United Kingdom Confronts the European Convention on Human Rights* (Gainesville: University Press of Florida, 2007); C. C. Morrisson, *The Dynamics of Development in the European Human Rights Convention System* (The Hague: Kluwer, 1981).

[11] Mean activism score for diplomats and bureaucrats was 0.35 (number of judges: 24), for others —0.11 (number of judges: 73). P-value is 0.029.

[12] J. G. Merills, *The Development of International Law by the European Court of Human Rights* (Manchester: Manchester University Press, 1988).

[13] Bruinsma and Parmentier, n 10 above .

[14] R. McDonald, F. Matscher, and H. Petzold (eds), *Methods of Interpretation of the Convention in: The European System for the Protection of Human Rights* (Dordrecht: Martinus Nijhoff, 1993), 70.

[15] Ibid.

[16] Bruinsma, n 10 above , 211.

[17] Ibid, 225.

who has a background as an attorney (avocat) and human rights activist, had been singled out as the prototypical 'activist' in an earlier study.[18]

Political implications

The above demonstrates that there is structure underlying the disagreements among ECtHR judges.[19] How does this relate back to politics? My previous research suggests two links.[20] First, some political parties are more favourably disposed towards European integration and supranational institutions than are others. We may expect, then, that governments more at ease with supranationalism in general also have a tendency to appoint activist judges. Figure 4.2 shows evidence for this. The more favourable governments are towards EU integration (as measured by their party manifestos), the more likely they are to appoint an activist judge.[21] It should be noted that party positions towards EU integration are closely related to their positions on the substantive 'new politics' issues that many ECtHR judgments speak to.[22] That party politics matters in the selection of judges was also the conclusion of the INTERIGHTS report on the issue.[23] Moreover, there is anecdotal evidence that judges have not been reappointed for partisan reasons. For instance, the Austrian judge Willi Führman, a former Social-Democratic parliamentarian, was replaced after his party lost domestic elections. Likewise, the Moldovan judge Tudor Pantiru was ousted by the newly elected Communist government.[24]

Second, countries that were candidates for EU admission were more likely to appoint activist judges (see also Figure 4.2 below). The EU is a community of liberal States who view expansion as an attempt to broaden that community.[25] The so-called 'Copenhagen criteria' defined requirements for new members in an abstract manner: 'Membership requires that the candidate country has achieved stability of institutions guaranteeing democracy, the rule of law, human rights and respect for and protection of minorities.'[26] But how could aspiring members make credible commitments to protecting human rights? As Austrian Chancellor Franz Vranitzky put it in 1993:

---

[18] Jackson, n 9 above, 25.

[19] For a different conclusion (not based on a statistical analysis, see R. C. A. White and I. Boussiakou, 'Separate Opinions in the European Court of Human Rights', 9 *Human Rights Law Review* (2009), 37.

[20] Voeten (2007), n 4 above.

[21] For more information on the data, see ibid. The focus on EU integration rather than supranational integration more generally is driven by data availability.

[22] Hooghe, n 6 above.

[23] See n 3 above.

[24] 'Communists Announce Possible Recall of ECRH Judge Tudor Pantiru', *Moldova Azi*, 6 April 2001, available at <http://www.azi.md/news?ID=1415>.

[25] F. Schimmelfennig, 'The Community Trap: Liberal Norms, Rhetorical Action, and the Eastern Enlargement of the European Union', 55(1) *International Organization* (2001), 47.

[26] European Council in Copenhagen, 21–22 June 1993, 'Conclusions of the Presidency', SN 180/1/93 REV 1, 13.

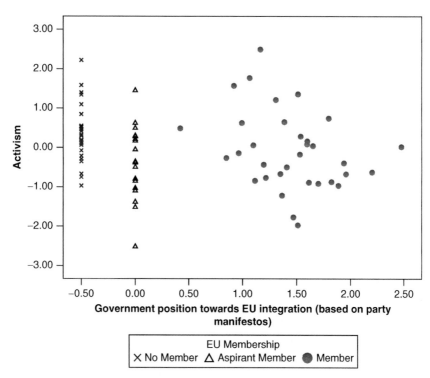

Fig. 4.2 Activism and government preferences

The economic and political realities of the present time, particularly in the former communist countries, are such that the Council of Europe is in fact the only organization capable of admitting these states to full membership without undue delay and so making them part of the European dynamic.[27]

Shortly after the agreement on the Copenhagen criteria during the June 1993 European Council meeting, the Council of Europe's heads of state agreed in principle to the Protocol No 11 reforms, in the Vienna Declaration of 9 October 1993. These reforms created the full-time independent ECtHR with compulsory jurisdiction, something that various States, most notably the UK, had opposed prior to the issue of enlargement.[28] Thus enlargement was a catalyst behind efforts to create a stronger ECtHR. One of the ways in which aspiring members could signal that they were serious about their commitment to human rights and international institutions was to send judges who were willing actively to apply international standards, perhaps even against their governments. Figure 4.2 presents some quantitative evidence for this. There is also qualitative evidence for this. For example, both Czech judge Karel Jungwiert and Slovak judge Bohumil Repik

[27] *Irish Times*, 11 October 1993, 8.
[28] For a concise view of British opposition, see 'Where Europe Rules', *The Guardian*, 11 October 1993, 19.

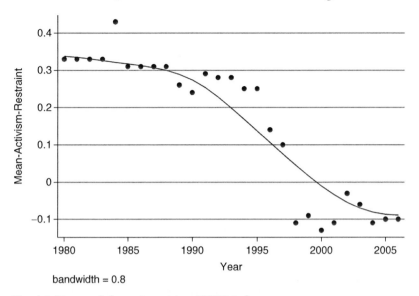

Fig. 4.3 Temporal change in activism ECHR judges

added paragraphs of text to their CVs to stress that they lost their formal positions in 1970 related to their activities in protesting the 1968 occupation of Czechoslovakia. Arold quotes several Western ECtHR judges and clerks who express their surprise at how independent from their home countries East European judges are relative to other judges.[29] Indeed, it turns out that East European judges are more likely to vote against their own government than are other judges (controlling for other factors).[30]

There is a visible trend towards a greater average degree of activism among ECtHR judges (see Figure 4.3 above). The overall trend towards increased activism concurs with observations from legal scholars[31] and is consistent with finding that the ECHR increasingly rules for the applicant (and thus against the government).[32] The trend in Figure 4.3 is a function of the replacement of restraint judges with more activist ones, not the effect of individual judges becoming more activist.[33] In this regard, especially the first election for the post-Protocol No 11 Court (1998) was important as it introduced a large number of new judges that were more activist than the judges they replaced.

[29] N. L. Arold, *The Legal Culture of the European Court of Human Right* (Leiden: Martinus Nijhoff, 2007), 311.

[30] Voeten (2008), n 4 above.

[31] See eg A. Mowbray, 'The Creativity of the European Court of Human Rights', 5(1) *Human Rights Law Review* (2005), 57.

[32] R. A. Cichowski, 'Courts, Rights and Democratic Participation', 39 *Comparative Political Studies* (2006), 50.

[33] The data are not sufficiently informative to allow for the estimation of a model in which the ideal points of individual judges vary over time.

These points serve as a useful reminder that political influences are not just there to restrain the activism of the ECtHR. Sometimes, politicians have incentives to put independently minded judges on the bench, even if those judges could take decisions that impose short-term costs on those very same politicians. Of course, this also implies that political winds could start blowing in the opposite direction, potentially resulting in a more restrained court. Some observers have argued that this is exactly what happened with the European Court of Justice (ECJ), when four ECJ judges were replaced following the controversial 1994 *Codorníu* judgment.[34] Karen Alter has also found evidence that Germany and France have appointed ECJ judges with an eye towards limiting judicial activism.[35] Allowing politics to play a role in the appointment of judges could thus help the Court become activist or restrained, suggesting that there is some responsiveness to changing electoral fortunes of political parties. Normatively, such responsiveness may well be desirable and enhance the legitimacy of the Court. In the next section, I evaluate potential sources of bias that are more problematic from a normative perspective.

III. National, Cultural, and Geopolitical Biases

The promise of legalizing international affairs derives its tenets from the notion that adjudication in legal institutions yields results that are different from those that come about through geopolitical (non-legal) means. Moreover, international courts aspire to transcend national cultural blinders and should not be biased against minority legal cultures. This section evaluates whether such promises are met by examining the role of national, cultural, and geopolitical biases in the decisions of ECtHR judges.

National bias

Figure 4.4 presents evidence on national bias on all (1,024) importance level 1 judgments issued between 1960 and 2006.[36] Nationality clearly mattered, although

---

[34] O. Costa, 'The European Court of Justice and Democratic Control in the European Union', 10(5) *Journal of European Public Policy* (2003), 744.

[35] Alter interviewed legal scholars and government officials in France, Germany, and the UK, as well as the Italian, Greek, Dutch, Belgian, French, German, British, and Irish judges at the ECJ (K. Alter, 'Who are the Masters of the Treaty?: European Governments and the European Court of Justice', 52(1) *International Organization* (1998), 125–52 at 139).

[36] As determined by the Court. The vast majority of judgments (5,042 or 69 per cent) are classified as having little legal significance. Judgments of importance level 2 (1,114) are not straightforward applications of case law but are also not considered to make new contributions to case law. Judgments of importance level 1 are deemed to make a significant contribution to the development of case law. Judges focus their separate opinions on the latter judgments. Whereas only 6 per cent of judgments of importance level 3 invite a concurring or dissenting separate opinion, 26 per cent of judgments of importance level 2 and 53 per cent of judgments of level 1 had at least one minority opinion. Many of the dissents on judgments of lower importance were repetitive and can thus not be treated as independent observations. For instance, Judge Ferrari-Bravo issued 133 identical dissenting opinions on alleged Italian art 6–1 violations, all in one day (28 February 2002).

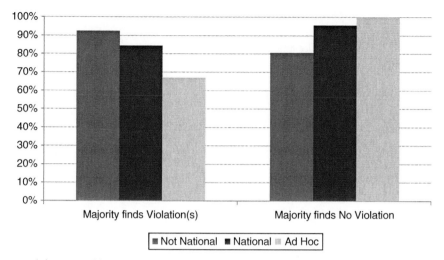

Fig. 4.4 National bias

not in a deterministic way. When the majority found no violation, 100 per cent of ad hoc judges and 95 per cent of regular national judges voted with the majority. This compares to 81 per cent of other judges. When the majority did find a violation, 33 per cent of ad hoc judges and 16 per cent of regular national judges dissented compared to only 8 per cent of other judges. These differences are statistically significant in a chi-squared test at p = 0.001. In all, ad hoc judges voted in favour of their home governments on 57 per cent of all important judgments, regular national judges on 50 per cent, and regular non-nationals on 35 per cent. Thus, while there are clear differences between the behaviours of nationals and non-nationals, national judges do not always vote in favour of their home government.

The existence of national bias has been demonstrated before.[37] The larger sample of cases examined in this study allows us to address the question that matters most for the functioning of the Court as a whole: how often do individuals lose cases because national judges are biased towards their home countries? After all, national judges are at best one of seven judges in a Chamber. In order to answer this question, we need to focus on the cases where the national judge was in a position to cast the pivotal vote to prevent a finding of a violation. There were 32 such instances in the data. Given that non-national judges were equally split, we would expect that if national judges had voted like the non-national judges, violations would be found in 16 judgments. In reality, the national judge voted in favour of the government on 24 of these cases. Thus, our best estimate is that there were

[37] F. J. Bruinsma and M. de Blois, 'Rules of Law from Westport to Wladiwostok: Separate Opinions in the European Court of Human Rights', 15(2) *The Netherlands Quarterly of Human Rights* (1997), 175; Jackson, n 9 above ; M. Kuijer, 'Voting Behaviour and National Bias in the European Court of Human Rights', 10(1) *Leiden Journal of International Law* (1997), 49.

eight cases of importance level 1 in which the government escaped a finding of a violation due to national bias. When viewed against the entire body of work by the ECtHR, this seems like an acceptable number, given the legal and political advantages of having national judges on the panels. One should keep in mind, however, that national judges also play a pivotal role in the admissibility process. It may well be that this conclusion would be much less favourable if we were better able to assess the role that national bias plays in deciding on the admissibility of cases. As such, making a national judge the sole judge responsible for admissibility decisions is problematic. Granting another single judge this responsibility has important efficiency disadvantages due to language difficulties and problems interpreting domestic legal systems.

Cultural bias

One of the most widely recognized challenges for international courts is to meld the main legal traditions of the world. The idea that internalized legal culture can influence judicial behaviour has firm roots in the study of comparative judicial behaviour,[38] although the empirical evidence for such effects on international courts is mostly negative.[39] Moreover, the possibility receives institutional recognition in the ECtHR and many other international courts. For example, the composition of the ECtHR's sections explicitly 'takes account of the different legal systems of the Contracting States'.[40]

Cultural bias in judicial behaviour reflects that judges may systematically assign different meanings to the same legal rules because they have internalized modes of legal reasoning specific to their domestic legal culture. Such effects may appear innocuous, yet they have some potentially troubling normative implications. If such cultural bias were prevalent, this would threaten the aspiration of international courts that they transcend national blinders and may lead to charges of bias from minority legal cultures. For example, it may be so that judges are more sympathetic towards arguments advanced by respondent States with similar legal systems. What may appear to a judge socialized in civil law as an entirely appropriate State action may seem inappropriate to a judge socialized and educated into a common law system, or vice versa.

In accordance with the literature, quantitative analyses of ECtHR decisions offer no evidence of strong cultural biases. There is no consistent evidence that shared legal culture makes a judge more lenient. Judges from French civil law countries

---

[38] eg G. A. Schubert and D. J. Danelski (eds), *Comparative Judicial Behavior: Cross-Cultural Studies of Political Decision-Making in the East and West* (New York: Oxford University Press, 1969); G. A. Schubert, 'Political Culture and Judicial Ideology: Some Cross-Cultural and Subcultural Comparisons', 9 *Comparative Political Studies* (1977), 363; M. Shapiro, n 1 above.

[39] Arold, n 29 above ; A. D. Renteln, 'Cultural Bias in International Law', 92 *American Society of International Law. Proceedings* (1998), 232; L. V. Prott, *The Latent Power of Culture and the International Judge* (Abingdon: Professional Books, 1979).

[40] Rules of the Court, available at: <http://www.echr.coe.int/NR/rdonlyres/D1EB31A8-4194-436E-987E-65AC8864BE4F/0/RulesOfCourtJuly2006.pdf>.

tend to evaluate other French civil law countries more favourably than non-French civil law countries, but the difference is not consistently statistically significant. The only consistent effect of legal culture is the opposite of cultural bias: judges from former socialist countries were harsher on other socialist countries than they were on countries without socialist heritage. This difference is consistently significant and substantively strong: a judge from a former socialist country was about 8 per cent more likely to find in favour of a violation when the respondent government was also a former socialist State than against any other respondent government. Since the analyses control for how other judges voted on an issue, this effect cannot be attributed to potentially more severe human rights violations by former socialist countries. I tested this further by evaluating whether judges from other legal traditions were also more likely to find a violation when a former socialist government was the respondent State but I found no evidence for such an effect.

The most likely interpretation of this finding is that these judges are especially sensitive to the way the remnants of socialist rule affect human rights. For example, one Western ECtHR judge notes that judges from socialist countries specifically reject State-governed economic regulation and suggested that 'behind this behaviour is their urge to change and develop away from the communist past'.[41] Thus, this observation is consistent with the notion that judges have policy preferences that shape the way they interpret alleged human rights violations. Such preferences may very well come from cultural experience but they do not equate to the type of cultural blinders that we should be normatively worried about. There are surely cases where civil or common law background shapes the perspective of judges but this has not led to a court that is dominated by cultural divisions or that is significantly biased for or against a legal tradition.

Geopolitical bias

The most serious threat to judicial impartiality is the possibility that judges may behave *as if* they were governments. Theoretically, judges could treat cases against important military, economic, and political allies of their national governments more favourably than cases against their governments' adversaries. If this were so, then the ECtHR would resemble a political institution more than a legal one. Posner and de Figuerido (2005) find evidence for such geopolitical biases among ICJ judges. The ICJ is a more likely context for such findings given that it primarily resolves interstate disputes over fairly high-stakes issues. On such disputes, geopolitics is more likely to enter the equation than on disputes between an individual and a government. Nevertheless, judges may feel pressure to take geopolitics into account. For example, a major Albanian opposition party was 'embarrassed' by the vote of the Albanian judge Ledi Bianku on the preliminary ruling in the *Hamza* case (which stayed the extradition of radical Muslim cleric Abu Hamza to the USA) stressing that 'Albanian representatives . . . should contribute to the efforts to build

---

[41] Quoted in Arold, n 29 above, 311. The judge was not identified as interviews were on the basis of anonymity.

the image of Albania, ... and to strengthen the friendship with countries, such as the United States, that have supported Albania for centuries.'[42] Such statements related to a preliminary ruling could pressure a judge to take geopolitics into account on a final ruling.

I tested whether ECtHR judges were more likely to vote in favour of the respondent government if that government represented an important trade partner or political or military ally of the judge's national government.[43] The measures used in this study were similar to those used by Posner and de Figuerido[44] in their study of the ICJ. I found no evidence for such geopolitical biases in the ECtHR, even when I limited the analyses to important votes or votes on Article 2 and 3 cases, on which security concerns presumably loom larger. This does not mean that judges do not occasionally consider geopolitical factors when they make decisions but that such considerations do not systematically affect the output of the Court. This may well be expected given the different nature of ECtHR rulings compared to ICJ rulings. Yet, it is important to establish nonetheless.

IV. Normative and Institutional Implications

The empirical evidence paints a mixed picture of the extent to which ECtHR judges at times considered factors other than the law when evaluating cases. Most clearly, judges evaluated their own countries differently from other countries. Moreover, there is ample evidence that the selection of judges is motivated by partisan politics and that judges are politically motivated actors in the sense that they have policy preferences on how best to apply abstract human rights in concrete cases. Yet, there is also good news. Cultural biases do not seem to have a systematic effect on how judges decide cases. From a normative perspective, perhaps the most important result is that there is no evidence that ECtHR judges are systematically motivated by geopolitical objectives of their home governments.

The results thus reject the 'umpire' ideal of judges, which has a long history in judicial ethics.[45] Yet, they also imply that the ECtHR is not just another international political institution in which judgments reflect geopolitical power struggles. How serious, then, are these deviations from the umpire ideal?

Let us first consider national bias. As noted earlier, national bias has only a small aggregate effect on ECtHR judgments. I estimated that States have escaped eight violations due to a strategic vote by a national judge. (This estimate goes up to 12 if one also considers issues other than importance level 1 judgments.) This estimate understates the true effect of national bias as it does not consider the admissibility

---

[42] 'Albanian party criticizes judge's vote against Hamza's extradition to USA', BBC Monitoring Europe—Political, supplied by BBC Worldwide Monitoring, 13 August 2008.

[43] See Voeten (2008), n 4 above.

[44] E. A. Posner and M. de Figueiredo, 'Is the International Court of Justice Biased?', 34 *Journal of Legal Affairs* (2005), 599.

[45] See M. E. Frankel, 'The Search for Truth: An Umpireal View', 103(1) *University of Pennsylvania Law Review* (1975), 123.

process, in which national judges could affect the fate of cases that are potentially damaging to their home governments. It would certainly be wise to investigate this possibility more closely as the reforms suggested under Protocol No 14 have the potential to increase the power of a single judge to block an application. Given language and expertise issues, that judge is probably either going to be, or be influenced by, the national judge.

Another feature of Protocol No 14 provides hope for improvement. The empirical analyses suggest that judges who are about to retire are less likely to exhibit national bias.[46] This suggests that making the terms of judges non-renewable has the potential to limit national bias. It should be noted, however, that the careers of judges are still potentially influenced by governments who hold the power to nominate these judges for other prestigious international or national positions.

That partisan politics plays a role in the selection of ECtHR judges is not a new finding. Indeed earlier studies by Flauss and INTERIGHTS concluded the same thing.[47] What is added here is that partisan selection indeed matters for how judges behave while on the court, not unlike how in the USA judges appointed by Democrats and Republicans tend to behave differently while on the court. The INTERIGHTS study, especially, is strongly negative regarding the role of partisanship in the selection of judges, presumably because it undermines the quality or impartiality of ECtHR judges. Yet, there is a redeeming quality to the role of partisanship in judicial appointments: it has the potential to increase responsiveness to democratically elected politicians. Since 1998, the political factors underlying the appointment of judges have mostly increased the activism and independence of ECtHR judges.[48] The logic of the argument suggests that this could be reversed if governments become disenchanted with supranational integration in general and the ECtHR's rulings in particular. That is, governments could increasingly start to appoint judges more towards the self-restraint side of the spectrum. This would be a legitimate exercise of democratic accountability that could help to counter criticisms that international courts remain unchecked and engage in 'wayward activism'. There are many less desirable ways in which governments could express their discontent. Most notably, influencing the ideological direction of the Court does not interfere with the normal judicial process in that it does not imply influencing individual cases. Moreover, it explicitly recognizes that the interpretation of what human rights mean involves a degree of political judgement. For this reason, it would seem unwise to advocate a move away from allowing governments a central role in the appointment of judges, as INTERIGHTS proposed. There are benefits to having a review court that is somewhat responsive to changes in broad ideological conceptions of how human rights should be interpreted but that keeps politics out of the courtroom discussions of individual cases.

---

[46] Voeten (2008), n 4 above.
[47] J. F. Flauss, 'Radioscopie de l'élection de la nouvelle Cour européenne des droits de l'homme', 9 *Revue Trimestrielle des droits de l'homme* (1998), 465; INTERIGHTS, n 3 above.
[48] Voeten (2007), n 4 above.

Together, this evidence suggests that with the exception of national bias, ECtHR judges essentially behave like normal judges on a review court. ECtHR judges are politically motivated actors in the sense that they have personal preferences on how best to apply abstract human rights in concrete cases, not in the sense that they are using their judicial power to settle geopolitical scores. Since interpreting human rights is a task that requires some political judgement, and since the judges are selected primarily by democratically elected governments, I do not find this conclusion normatively problematic. It may, however, be that this conclusion is wildly optimistic about the true degree to which politics interferes with ECtHR judgments. As noted before, there is virtually no empirical evidence about the admissibility process. Moreover, it may be that even if judges are not systematically swayed by political considerations, they may well be influenced on highly sensitive cases, something that is difficult to detect in quantitative studies. Judges depend on governments for the implementation of court decisions and for other forms of support, including budgetary support. The budget is obviously important given the severe backlog of cases. Lack of implementation also leads to more cases. More generally, judges may desire that their decisions have effects. Theoretically, anticipated government responses to decisions could influence the way judges decide cases. Other than some assertions about individual judgments,[49] there is no systematic empirical evidence that suggests to what extent this presents a problem for the impartiality of ECtHR judgments.

---

[49] M. Milanovic and T. Papic, 'As Bad As it Gets: The European Court of Human Rights' Behrami and Saramati Decision and General International Law', 58(2) *International Law and Comparative Law Quarterly* (2008), 267.

5

Civil Society and the European Court of Human Rights

Rachel A. Cichowski

In the last 50 years, the European Court of Human Rights (ECtHR) incrementally transformed human rights in Europe. The effects and role of Member States in this transformation is oft debated, problematizing the degree to which national sovereignty is unwillingly diminished or conversely the willingness of States to allow this evolution and expansion. We do know that over the last 50 years the European Convention on Human Rights and Fundamental Freedoms ('the Convention') system expanded in scope and jurisdiction, a transformation at times led by the ECtHR's jurisprudence and at other times initiated by State-led reforms. Yet from what we know generally about legal processes, the individuals who bring the claims, and the societal groups that support them, are critical to this dynamic. Despite their importance as initiators and users of the system, much less is known about the historical and present role of social activists and NGOs in ECtHR litigation. I argue that the evolution of the Convention system was and continues to be critically linked to a dynamic interaction between civil society and the ECtHR. The legitimacy of this process remains a fine balance between societal inclusion and domestic government support.[1]

Similar to the other chapters in this book, this analysis is concerned with the evolution of the Convention system and the ECtHR's jurisprudence. In particular, this chapter focuses on the historical interaction between civil society and the ECtHR asking if, how, and why social activists have mobilized Convention rights over the last 50 years. The study is also concerned with the effects of this mobilization–litigation dynamic for the Court's jurisprudence. Over 50 years ago

---

[1] The current debate around reforms to the European Convention system and in particular Russian opposition highlights that for the ECtHR an expanding case law protecting rights may enhance its legitimacy in the eyes of citizens, but at the same time cause a legitimacy crisis in the eyes of national executives. For further discussion of reforms see A. Mowbray, 'Faltering Step on the Path to Reform of the Strasbourg Enforcement System', 7(3) *Human Rights Law Review* (2007), 609; L. Caflisch, 'The Reform of the European Court of Human Rights: Protocol No 14 and Beyond', 6 *Human Rights Law Review* (2006), 403; S. Greer, *The European Convention on Human Rights: Achievements, Problems and Prospects* (Cambridge: Cambridge University Press, 2006).

13 national governments in Europe came together to construct an unprecedented supranational human rights regime. Legal entrepreneurs and activists were a critical motivating force behind the original negotiations and construction of this human rights regime.[2] Yet, ultimately, the resulting legal structure was crafted to preserve national sovereignty and privilege the role of national governments.[3] Civil society, NGOs, and even individual claimants were greatly restricted, if even allowed, under the founding Convention system.[4] However, the tides have changed. The ECtHR is now heralded around the world as a powerful international court able and willing to invalidate domestic legislation, constitutional provisions, and State action to fulfil its mandate of ensuring State compliance with the Convention—sometimes in the face of considerable national government opposition. Likewise, civil society, in the form of NGOs and individual legal activists, has become a central participant in the enforcement and development of human rights law in Europe—all with the effect of demanding and achieving more accessible legal institutions. The analysis examines this remarkable transformation.

This chapter provides a new perspective on ECtHR litigation by analysing how the evolution of the Convention system emerged through the processes of civil society mobilization and supranational litigation. I argue that much like domestic politics, social activism and litigation at the supranational level provide avenues for bringing about change in the institutions that govern human rights in Europe. By this, I mean that these processes can lead to reforms in the rules and procedures that govern human rights in Europe (that is, change in protection, access, and even opportunities to bring claims). Supranational litigation can enable individuals and groups, who are often disadvantaged in their own legal systems, to enforce these rights at the national and European level. ECtHR decisions can be particularly powerful in the extent to which they expand the scope or alter the meaning of

---

[2] M. R. Madsen, 'From Cold War Instrument to Supreme European Court: The European Court of Human Rights at the Crossroads of International and National Law and Politics', 32(1) *Law & Social Inquiry* (2007), 609 and 'Legal Diplomacy: Law, Politics and the Genesis of Postwar European Human Rights' in S.–L. Hoffmann (ed), *Human Rights in the Twentieth Century: A Critical History* (Cambridge: Cambridge University Press, 2011).

[3] Prior to the significant legal reforms that came with the implementation of Protocol No 11 (1998) the Convention provided two optional clauses that significantly preserved Member State power in this human rights system. Original Art 25 granted individuals the right to bring direct claims and original Art 46 granted the Court jurisdiction as final arbiter. After 1998, these measures became compulsory.

[4] As mentioned above, prior to 1998, the optional nature of original Art 25 actually created a situation in which individuals who were the victims of alleged Convention right violations, depending on whether a Member State had opted out of this provision, were not given access to this human rights claimant system directly, but could only 'assist' the European Commission of Human Rights in raising the complaint. Likewise, it was not until the Court itself interpreted (*Winterwerp v Netherlands* Series A no 33 (1979)) the Rules of Court, Rule 38(1) to allow third party intervention (in this case another State), that the door was opened for greater participation, civil society included, in this legal system. Today, this access, by individuals and NGOs, is enshrined and defined clearly in the Convention (Arts 34 and 36) and the Rules of Court (Rule 44) creating a much more accessible human rights mechanism than the one granted by the founding institutions in the 1950s.

European Convention provisions—rules that are otherwise relatively immune to alteration. This is not unique to the European Convention system, as courts and processes of legalization are increasingly shaping supranational and international governance at sites around the globe.[5] Further, individuals who may be excluded from domestic legal recourse can gain power and voice through the mobilization of public interest groups. This action can shape policy development as well as expand the boundaries of human rights by giving civil society a voice and place in international human rights regimes. A similar dynamic is evolving at the global level as civil society and transnational activists are increasingly present and participating in international politics.[6]

The chapter is organized as follows. First, I develop a framework elaborating how we can understand this dynamic interaction between civil society mobilization, ECtHR litigation, and its subsequent effects on the Court's jurisprudence. This conceptual framework suggests a set of general expectations that guide the empirical analysis. Second, the study turns to an analysis of the interaction between civil society and the ECtHR over a 50-year period to examine the important linkages between social activist mobilization and the judicial rule-making of the Court. The analysis has two sections. First, I provide a historical overview examining the role of NGOs and social activists' engagement in the Convention system. Next, I turn to an in-depth case study of Turkey and the UK in the area of minority rights to provide a more detailed analysis of this general mobilization–litigation dynamic over a 15-year period. The chapter concludes by suggesting a set of broader lessons that will help us to understand the role of NGOs in the European Convention system reforms in the future, and more generally in the development of international legal regimes.

I. Conceptualizing the Mobilization–Litigation Dynamic

Theoretically, we would expect to find complex linkages between mobilization and litigation.[7] As European rights and the ECtHR present social activists with the opportunity to bring legal claims, we would expect activists to mobilize and exploit

[5] K. Alter, 'Private Litigants and the New International Courts', 39 *Comparative Political Studies* (2006), 22; A.-M. Slaughter, 'A Global Community of Courts', 44 *Harvard International Law Journal* (2003), 191; and *A New World Order* (Princeton: Princeton University Press, 2004); R. A. Cichowski, 'Integrating the Environment: The European Court and the Construction of Supranational Policy', 5(3) *Journal of European Public Policy* (1998), 387 and 'Women's Rights, the European Court and Supranational Constitutionalism', 38 *Law & Society Review* (2004) and *The European Court and Civil Society* (Cambridge: Cambridge University Press, 2007); A. Stone Sweet, *On Law, Politics and Judicialization* (Oxford: Oxford University Press, 2004).

[6] M. Keck and K. Sikkink, *Activists Beyond Borders: Advocacy Networks in International Politics* (Ithaca: Cornell University Press, 1998); S. Tarrow, *The New Transnational Activism* (New York: Cambridge University Press, 2005).

[7] R. A. Cichowski and T. Börzel, 'Law, Politics and Society in Europe' in T. Börzel and R. A. Cichowski (eds), *Law, Politics and Society: State of the European Union* (Oxford: Oxford University Press, 2003); R. A. Cichowski, 'Courts, Rights and Democratic Participation', 39 *Comparative Political Studies* (2006), 50 and Cichowski (2007), n 5 above.

these opportunities. This litigation, in turn, can empower the ECtHR by providing the opportunity to clarify, enforce, and give meaning to Convention rights. In response to these supranational rules, individuals adjust their behaviour in a way that makes these institutions increasingly difficult to change. Furthermore, once these individuals and groups gain some access to this arena, they will push for greater inclusion. As the rights adjudication and enforcement process becomes more dependent on this increasingly present civil society, for legitimacy and efficiency reasons, we can expect the rules to change in a way that may offer more access to these actors. Through these processes supranational legal regimes can emerge and evolve. In this chapter, I examine how the Convention system may have been shaped by this dynamic process.

In any system of governance, mobilization and litigation can present avenues for institutional change and, thus, are particularly fruitful for exposing the many processes through which the Convention system—or a human rights regime— may evolve over time. Mobilization processes involve the strategic action of individuals and groups to promote or resist change in a given policy arena.[8] This study examines civil society legal activism. By movement activism I mean *sustained challenges, by individuals or groups with common purposes, to alter existing arrangements of power and distribution.* I adopt this general definition to examine the importance of both individual and group legal activism before the ECtHR.[9] Litigation enables actors to question existing rules and procedures. And the Court's judicial rule-making can lead to the creation of rules and procedures that sometimes serve as opportunities for action.[10] By judicial rulemaking I mean *a court's authoritative interpretation of existing rules and procedures, which results in the clarification of the law or practice in question.*

The choice to mobilize Convention rights by a group or individual begins as a result of action by individuals (or a group acting on behalf of individuals) that are either disadvantaged or advantaged by an available set of rules. This process is characterized by both action and at least some necessary rule or procedure (for example, in this case a Convention provision) that is invoked in the legal claim. In general, social activists and movements have experienced relative success at utilizing litigation as an avenue to pressure for social change and have done so by utilizing an explicit or implied set of rights.[11] Litigation before the ECtHR reveals a similar

---

[8] S. Tarrow, *Power in Movement: Social Movements and Contentious Politics* (Cambridge: Cambridge University Press, 1998); G. Marks and D. McAdam, 'Social Movements and the Changing Structure of Political Opportunity in the European Union' in G. Marks, F. Scharpf, P. Schmitter, and W. Streek (eds), *Governance in the European Union* (London: Sage Publications, 1996).

[9] Alongside collective action taken by movement organizations, scholars highlight the importance of activities carried out by individual activists who are often bound together in informal networks, but whose challenging action can be equally as effective as collective action by movement organizations (M. Katzenstein, *Faithful and Fearless: Moving Feminist Protest inside the Church and Military* (Princeton: Princeton University Press, 1998)).

[10] M. Shapiro, *Courts: A Comparative and Political Analysis* (Chicago: University of Chicago Press, 1981); A. Stone Sweet, *On Law, Politics and Judicialization* (Oxford: Oxford University Press, 2000).

[11] M. W. McCann, *Rights at Work: Pay Equity Reform and the Politics of Legal Mobilization* (Chicago: University of Chicago Press, 1994); Cichowski (2007), n 5 above; C. Harlow and R. Rawlings, *Pressure Through Law* (London: Routledge, 1992); C. Hoskyns, *Integrating Gender:*

dynamic with examples covering a host of legal domains from housing rights to racial discrimination. These NGOs may have both a direct impact on this litigation by representing the claimant, providing support for the litigation, or by submitting amicus curiae and also a more indirect effect by providing information on Convention rights and ECtHR case law to both the press and public more generally.[12] Stated generally, the mobilization–litigation dynamic begins with the following two factors: at least some necessary rule or procedure, embodying an explicit or implied right and the action on behalf of an individual or NGO to invoke this rule and bring a claim to Strasbourg. Without these two factors, we might expect this process to fail, or rather that there would be less involvement by civil society or social activists in ECtHR litigation.

This mobilization of Convention rights by individuals and civil society can activate and engage the ECtHR in the protection and expansion of rights. I argue that this mobilization can not only have a direct effect on the Court's jurisprudence but that this, in turn, can lead to an expansion of the Convention system, both the rights provided but also access to institutions. I start with the general assumption that through litigation a court's resolution of societal questions or disputes can lead to the clarification, expansion, and creation of rules and procedures that are structures of governance.[13] Thus, in any system of governance with an independent judiciary possessing judicial review powers, the judicial decision provides a potential avenue for institutional change. That is, a court's rule-making capacity operates within the institutional framework of an existing body of rules and procedures (in this case the Convention), yet a court's jurisprudence can subsequently alter these institutions. This approach is not unfamiliar to scholars of judicial politics.[14]

It is well documented elsewhere that these interpretations can significantly alter the original measure in a way that changes what is lawful and unlawful behaviour for individuals and public and private bodies operating under European law and its domestic implementation. The ECtHR's recent *Tebieti Mühafize Cemiyyeti* decision[15] is an example. The applicants in the case were an environmental NGO and

---

Women, Law and Politics in the European Union (London: Verso, 1996); L. Krämer, 'Public Interest Litigation in Environmental Matters Before European Courts', 8 *Journal of Environmental Law* (1996), 1; R. D Kelemen, 'Suing for Europe: Adversarial Legalism and European Governance', 39 *Comparative Political Studies* (2006), 76.

[12] The work of the UK-based AIRE Centre and the European Roma Rights Centre based in Hungary are both NGOs that have served these diverse roles in the enforcement and evolution of Convention rights. The JURISTRAS Project includes some documentation of group involvement in claims pertaining to minorities (funded by the European Commission under the 6th Framework Program (contract no 028398), 2006–9). See D. Anagnostou, 'Does European Human Rights Law Matter? Implementation and Domestic Impact of Strasbourg Court Judgments on Minority-Related Policies', 14(5) *International Journal of Human Rights* (2010), 721; D. Anagnostou and E. Psychogiopoulou (eds), *The Rights of Marginalised Individuals and Minorities in National Context* (Leiden: Martinus Nijhoff, 2010).

[13] Shapiro, n 10 above.

[14] Ibid; Stone Sweet, n 10 above ; C. N. Tate and T. Vallinder, 'The Global Expansion of Judicial Power: The Judicialization of Politics' in C. N. Tate and T. Vallinder (eds), *The Global Expansion of Judicial Power* (New York: New York University Press, 1995).

[15] *Tebieti Mühafize Cemiyyeti and Israfilov v Azerbaijan* Appl no 37083/03 (2009).

its former chairman and they brought a claim against the Azerbaijan government for wrongful dissolution of the association—claiming that the action infringed their right to freedom of association granted under Art 11. The ECtHR concurred finding the dissolution in violation of Art 11. The decision not only upheld the importance and need for NGO associations in domestic politics as enshrined in Art 11, but also modified the State powers embodied in the domestic NGO legislation that was at the heart of the dispute. In particular, the Court concurred that the domestic legislation was too general, giving the government a magnitude of interpretation that had wrongfully led to interference in civil society associations. The ECtHR's decision lays out what is and is not lawful action by governments regulating NGO action—a statement that could be seen as reaffirming an earlier action taken by the Committee of Ministers to strengthen the legal framework governing NGOs in Europe.[16]

Generally, this process can shape the ECtHR's jurisprudence with the effect of not only leading to expanded protection but also enhanced participation and access for NGOs. This process also highlights the potential legitimizing effects of ECtHR judicial rule-making by holding governments accountable to their society for the practical effects and meaning that is embodied in Convention rights provisions, an effect that can also enhance the transparency of both the rights and also the system by which they are protected.

Data and methods

To examine this process I created a series of datasets involving litigation before the ECtHR from 1955–2005. The decisions dataset is compiled from primary documents from the ECtHR including the *Yearbook of the European Convention on Human Rights, the European Commission and European Court of Human Rights* and *Reports of Judgments and Decisions/European Court of Human Rights*. The data is coded by respondent State, decision year, decision outcome, and Convention rights invoked. For the period up to 1998 I also include data on NGO third party interventions. I utilize this dataset mainly to extract cases during this longer period that involved NGO participation. A second dataset includes ECtHR decisions involving the UK and Turkey in the area of minority rights claims from 1991–2007. This includes cases invoking the following Convention provisions: Arts 3 (torture), 5 (liberty/security), 6 (fair trial), 8 (privacy), 9 (religion), 10 (expression), 11 (association), 14 (discrimination), and Art 1, Protocol No 1 (property rights). This dataset is created using data collected by the JURISTRAS Project.[17] The data is coded by respondent State, decision year, Convention rights invoked, and NGO

---

[16] See the Recommendation of Member States on the Legal Status of Non-governmental Organisations in Europe adopted by the Committee of Ministers in 2007, CM/REC(2007)14.

[17] JURISTRAS Project, n 12 above. See also D. Kurban, 'Protecting Marginalised Individuals and Minorities in the ECtHR: Litigation and Jurisprudence in Turkey' and S. Millns, C. Rootes, C. Saunders, and G. Swain, 'The European Court of Human Rights in the UK: Litigation, Rights Protection and Minorities' in Anagnostou and Psychogiopoulou, n 12 above, an elaboration of the data pertaining to the UK and Turkey.

and activist lawyer involvement. I chose to focus on litigation involving Turkey and the UK as both cases possess active involvement of social activist and NGOs over time. Further, the claims brought against these two countries even within the same policy area (minority rights) are quite different and so we are able to study the ways in which the mobilization may or may not vary depending on the legal domain of the claim.

As we begin this historical analysis of legal mobilization, it is important to highlight the Court's evolving role, as it is critically linked to why the ECtHR became a site for this type of social activism. The ECtHR's main function is to ensure State compliance with and the uniform interpretation of the Convention. Technically, the Court's jurisdiction involves international—not constitutional—law, such that the ECtHR does not have constitutional review powers. Yet interestingly, while Member States remain sovereign States in the Council of Europe system, the Convention rights as protected and interpreted by the ECtHR have served as a body of higher order norms and led to considerable constraint on what national legislators can do. As scholars such as Martin Shapiro observe of the ECtHR, 'the Court has rendered enough judgments that have caused enough changes in state practices so that it can be counted to a rather high degree as a constitutional judicial review court in the light of realities as opposed to the technicalities'.[18] Thus, the ECtHR becomes an interesting test of how NGOs and social activists can be engaged in individual rights adjudication even without constitutional review and also how the practical effects of administrative review can at times change both rights and access to these legal institutions.[19]

Further, a quick comparative overview illustrates the unique opportunity that the European Convention and the ECtHR served over the last 50 years in enabling rights claims above and beyond the domestic legal system. Figure 5.1 displays the standardized annual number of judgments from six of the oldest and consistently active international courts/dispute bodies: the International Court of Justice (ICJ), the ECtHR, the European Court of Justice (ECJ), GATT/WTO dispute settlement body/appellate panel, Inter-American Court of Human Rights (IACHR), and the Court of Justice of the Andean Community (ACJ). The data are standardized to account for the varying dates of first judgment and include a generally comparative category of judgments: final resolution of a concrete dispute before the court (for example, does not include advisory opinions etc). While this is just a snapshot of the work of international courts,[20] this comparison nonetheless illustrates the value of our historical analysis of ECtHR litigation. Why is there such considerable variation in caseload across these international courts, despite the similarities in some cases in age, institutional designs, and even private party access? Part of the answer is related to the critical and historical importance of social

---

[18] M. Shapiro, 'The Success of Judicial Review and Democracy' in M. Shapiro and A. Stone Sweet, *On Law, Politics and Judicialization* (Oxford: Oxford University Press, 2002), 155.

[19] Similarly Sterett has examined how administrative judicial review has served as quasi-constitutional review in a system with technically no constitutional law—the UK; see S. Sterett, *Creating Constitutionalism* (Ann Arbor: University of Michigan Press, 1997).

[20] See Alter, n 5 above, for a more comprehensive list.

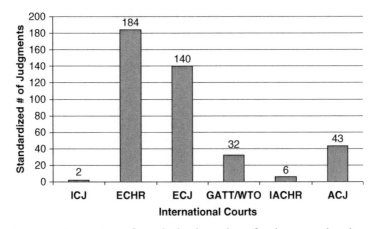

Fig. 5.1 Comparison of standardized number of judgments taken by international courts, 1949–2007

Source: Data compiled by the author from the websites of each of the courts, 2008.

activists and NGOs in supporting ECtHR litigation. The following analysis examines this dynamic.

II. Analysis: Social Activists and the ECtHR

We have seen that a set of general institutional factors can systematically affect the role that social activists can play in bringing litigation before the ECtHR. First, I examine the broad historical patterns in this mobilization and litigation dynamic highlighting the importance of NGOs, States, and the Court itself in expanding access to social activists. I then turn to a comparative country case study that provides a more nuanced examination of these general trends by providing an in-depth analysis of the social activists and NGOs involved in minority rights cases involving Turkey and the UK over a 15-year period.

Historical overview: expanding access and effects

We would expect this general dynamic to begin with at least some necessary rule or procedure that would enable social activists to invoke the European Convention provisions and bring a claim before the ECtHR. Not surprisingly, institutional access for NGOs was not a priority when States came together to negotiate the Convention in the late 1950s. Access for individual complaints was itself quite limited. Yet over time both individuals and social activists have increasingly gained access to the Court and, thus, have expanded the roles they play in ECtHR decision-making. These roles include direct victim (applicant), representing an applicant, intervening as a third party and acting as a larger support structure (such as serving as educator to both the public, other groups, and lawyers, providing legal information, and sponsoring litigation strategy workshops).

Under the original Convention system, individual petitioners did not have direct access to the Court. The original Art 25 recognized the right of individuals to file an application, yet it was an optional not compulsory mechanism. However, even when a State accepted Art 25, the European Commission of Human Rights served as the intermediary between the individual and the Court. Prior to 1994, only States and the Commission had standing to bring cases before the Court. In 1994, Protocol No 9 was adopted and individual access was reformed improving standing for individuals and groups. The Protocol amended original Arts 44 and 48 extending standing to individuals, NGOs, and groups of individuals. Individual access to the ECtHR underwent further reform in 1998. Protocol No 11, which governed the major reforms to the Convention institutions, also amended Art 25 and made individual access compulsory. Following these reforms, individuals were given both formal and practical access to the Court. These reforms also brought greater accessibility to NGOs. Today, the European Convention clearly provides the necessary rule or procedure for NGOs to file an application before the Court. Article 34 of the Convention provides:

The Court may receive applications from any person, non-governmental organisation or group of individuals claiming to be the victim of a violation by one of the High Contracting Parties of the rights set forth in the Convention or the protocols thereto. The High Contracting parties undertake not to hinder in any way the effective exercise of this right.

While the Convention provides the opportunity for NGOs to file an application, this must be understood clearly within the constraint of proving that the organization has itself directly experienced a violation of Convention rights. This is laid out in the ECtHR's case law.[21] Nonetheless, the Court's jurisprudence also reveals the diversity of organizations and entities that have successfully brought claims, including church associations,[22] media groups,[23] trade unions,[24] human rights groups,[25]

---

[21] See eg *Éskomoravsk v Czech Republic* Appl no 33091/96 (1999); *ARSEC and Others v Spain* Appl no 42916/98 (1999); *Association of Polish Teachers v Poland* Appl no 42049/98 (2003); *VgT v Switzerland* Appl no 24699/94 (2000); and in two other cases the ECtHR dismissed the claims of the NGO in the case on grounds of not being able to claim direct harm, *Éonka v Belgium* Appl no 51564/99 (2001) and *Asselbourg and Others* Appl no 29121/95 (1999).

[22] See eg *Johannische Kirche and Peters v Germany* Appl no 41754/98 (2001); *Christian Federation of Jehovah's Witness v France* Appl no 53430/99 (2001).

[23] See eg *Verdens Gang and Aase v Norway* Appl no 45710/99 (2001); *Pasalaris and Fondation de Presse v Greece* Appl no 60916/00 (2002); *Independent News and Media plc v Ireland* Appl no 55120/00 (2003).

[24] See eg *Unison v United Kingdom* Appl no 53574/99 (2002); *Federation of Offshore Workers' Trade Unions v Norway* Appl no 38190/97 (2002).

[25] A recent decision is one example, *Women on Waves & Others v Portugal* Appl no 31276/05 (2009) involving three NGOs, one Dutch and two Portuguese, who successfully won their claim that the Portuguese government had violated their Art 10 (freedom of expression) rights when it prevented the organizations from disseminating information about reproductive rights and abortion. See country case studies below for further examples.

and many companies.[26] Interestingly, the Court has also incrementally developed an 'indirect victim' approach that enables persons to bring a claim who were not directly affected, but who are close relatives and have a valid personal interest in having the violation confirmed.[27] This type of indirect representation is differentiated from a third party representing a direct victim or the continuation of proceedings by a relative, yet there have been notable exceptions. One example is *Karner v Austria* where the claimant's legal representative (non-relative) was allowed to continue the proceedings after the applicant's death.[28] While this evolving case law on 'indirect victims' has not previously provided a clear standing for NGOs as an applicant representing a victim, one ECtHR judge suggests it may be an 'indication of a possible evolution of the ECtHR's practice with regard to the role of representatives before the ECtHR'.[29] Thus, in the future, there may be an expanded opening for greater NGO participation in filing an application, beyond its role as a direct victim.

Over time NGOs have also come to play an important role through third party interventions. Again, if we look back, the ECtHR itself has largely been responsible for this expansion in access. The original Convention made no mention of third party intervention, but instead it has evolved by way of the Court's case law and today is codified in the Convention. Yet, the story is not only one of top-down reform; instead it has evolved as a result of the interaction between social activists and the ECtHR. The first request by a third party came in 1978 when the National Council for Civil Liberties requested to submit a brief in a pending case for an individual they had represented earlier in the legal process.[30] The Court denied the request. The following year, the UK government asked to intervene in the *Winterwerp* case against the Netherlands on the grounds it had a series of similar pending cases.[31] The UK government admitted it had no right to submit a brief but inquired whether Rule 38(1) of the Rules of Court might provide the basis: 'the Chamber may, at the request of a Party or of Delegates of the Commission or proprio motu, decide to hear . . . in any other capacity any person whose evidence or statements seem likely to assist it in the carrying out of its task.' The Chamber granted the UK leave to submit the brief but required that the information be submitted to the Court by delegates of the Commission rather than directly by the UK government. NGOs took notice and quickly followed suit with new requests. In 1981, the Court allowed the same indirect third party participation via the

---

[26] See eg *Comingersoll v Portugal* Appl no 35382/97 (2000); *Eielectric Srl v Italy* Appl no 36811/97 (2000).

[27] See eg the *Aksoy v Turkey* case (Appl no 21987/93 (1996)) was brought by the victim's father along with assistance from a Kurdish human rights group, the KHRP. This case is discussed in more detail in the country case study below.

[28] *Karner v Austria* Appl no 40016/98 (2000).

[29] N. Vajic, 'Some Concluding Remarks on NGOs and the European Court of Human Rights' in T. Treves et al (eds), *Civil Society, International Courts and Compliance Bodies* (The Hague: TMC Asser Press, 2005), 95.

[30] *Tyrer v United Kingdom* Appl no 5856/72 (1978).

[31] *Winterwerp v Netherlands* Appl no 6301/73 (1979).

Commission, but this time to a trade union, the Trades Union Congress (TUC).[32] Interestingly, the Court further expanded participation by also granting a TUC representative leave to participate in oral proceedings alongside the written documents submitted by the Commission on behalf of the TUC. What is the effect of this NGO participation? These TUC documents would later be cited directly in the Court's final decision finding a violation of Art 11.[33]

Following this trend developed in the case law, the ECtHR subsequently amended the then Rule 37(2) of the Rules of Court in 1983 specifically to allow third party participation both by States or any other person. Between 1984 and 1998 the Court has authorized 41 requests for third party intervention.[34] Today, following the adoption of Protocol No 11 in 1998, we see third party access and participation clearly specified in the Convention and the Rules of Court. Article 36 (2) of the Convention provides the President of the Court with the discretionary power to allow third party intervention:

The President of the Court may, in the interest of the proper administration of justice, invite any High Contracting Party which is not a party to the proceedings or any person concerned who is not the applicant to submit written comments or take part in hearings.

Likewise, Rule 44(2) of the Rules of Court govern similar provisions on third party participation.

Together, these are the necessary rules that have been both the cause and effect of social activist participation in ECtHR litigation. Clearly, these provisions do not create an open floodgate for NGO participation, but instead illustrate the persistence of NGOs to challenge constraints on accessibility to the Court and the power of the Court to allow increased participation over time—a decision which often takes place long before States clarified criteria for participation. In sum, while public interest organizations are rarely a litigant before the ECtHR, given the constraints of the Art 34 requirement of claiming to be a direct victim of an alleged violation of the Convention, they are able to participate in various ways and their involvement has directly impacted the development, reform, and implementation of Convention rights. We can see this most clearly when we look at the ways in which public interest organizations have at times shaped the decisions made by the ECtHR and even the policy positions held by national governments. The following are examples.

In the *Soering* case[35] concerning the UK's involvement in extraditing to the USA an individual accused of a capital offence, Amnesty International was granted leave to submit an amicus brief which was ultimately quoted by the Court in its judgment.[36] The group Article 19 (which focuses on the defence of freedom of

---

[32] *Young, James & Webster v United Kingdom* Appl nos 7601/76, 7806/77 (1981).
[33] Paras 31 and 64.
[34] See ECtHR, *Survey: Forty Years of Activity* (1998), 134–7.
[35] *Soering v United Kingdom* Appl no 14038/88 (1989).
[36] The ECtHR stated in para 102:

This 'virtual consensus in Western European legal systems that the death penalty is, under current circumstances, no longer consistent with regional standards of justice,' to use the

expression rights) filed amicus briefs in two cases[37] and played a key role in the Court's decision and dissenting opinions, and was ultimately used to support the Court's finding of a violation.[38]

The *Nachova*[39] decision was also particularly important not only for expanding Convention rights to find that Art 14 (prohibition of discrimination) also has a procedural element (obligation of the authorities to investigate possible racist motives), but also that the amicus briefs of three NGOs played prominently in the judgment. The three NGOs, the European Roma Rights Centre (ERRC), the International Centre for the Legal Protection of Human Rights (INTERIGHTS), and the Justice Initiative were all granted leave by the Court to file briefs. Together these groups have been directly involved (either as third party intervention or directly representing a claimant) in over 80 cases before the ECtHR. In sum, the number of cases involving NGOs is admittedly small compared to the total number of ECtHR cases. But the quality of the cases is high, meaning most of these groups are very strategic about choosing to participate in cases which they believe will lead to significant changes in European law. They thus see it as an opportunity to participate in the development of international human rights law, which would not only be used by the ECtHR in the future, but domestic courts and international courts throughout the world.

III. UK and Turkey Case Study

The above historical overview highlights the mobilization–litigation dynamic and the effects it can have for the expansion of rights and accessibility of the Convention system. In particular, we find NGOs mobilizing Convention rights and, subsequently, ECtHR decisions over time expanding rights that at times led to greater access, standing, and judicial obligation to protect. To elaborate how this litigation dynamic develops and in particular, give greater detail to the NGOs and activists involved and the effect on ECtHR jurisprudence, I provide a comparative country case study. In the remaining part of the analysis, I examine the interaction between social activists and the ECtHR in the context of minority rights cases against Turkey and the UK over a 15-year period, 1991–2006. Complementing the historical overview above, this more in-depth assessment enables us to examine the variation in NGO participation in these important cases. I will begin by examining the Turkish case and then turn to the UK.

---

words of Amnesty International, is reflected in Protocol No 6 to the Convention, which provides for the abolition of the death penalty in time of peace.

[37] *Observer & Guardian v United Kingdom* Appl no 13585/88 (1991); *Sunday Times v United Kingdom* Appl no 13166/87 (1991).

[38] The Court stated in para 60:

For the avoidance of doubt, and having in mind the written comments that were submitted in this case by Article 19 ... the Court would only add to the foregoing that Article 10 of the Convention does not in terms prohibit the imposition of prior restraints on publication, as such.

[39] *Nachova & Others v Bulgaria* Appl nos 43577/98, 43579/98 (2005).

We set out by looking at the patterns of participation across time and cross-nationally in Turkey. Table 5.1 displays the patterns of social activist involvement in ECtHR minority rights claims brought against Turkey by Convention rights invoked between 1991–2006. The vast majority of claims (90 out of 113 or 80 per cent) were brought by individual activists, rather than an NGO, on behalf of a Kurdish individual alleging a Convention rights violation. Interestingly, there were almost an equal number of activist British lawyers bringing these claims as there were Kurdish lawyers: 46 claims were represented by activist Kurdish lawyers and 44 were brought by UK-based lawyers. While certainly a smaller number than those brought by individuals, NGOs also played an important role in these minority rights claims from Turkey. Not surprisingly given the historical tensions between the State and the Kurdish community in Turkey, the main NGO that was successful at representing claimants came from outside Turkey. The UK-based Kurdish Human Rights Project (KHRP) acted as direct representative to the applicant in 23 of these claims.

Which Convention provisions were invoked in these minority rights claims and what variation exists across type of activist involvement in these claims? Article 3 (protection from torture) was raised in almost one-third of these claims reflecting ongoing questions of wrongful treatment by State police against Kurdish individuals. Further, successful minority rights claims from Turkey pertained mainly to severe ill treatment of the Kurdish community (killings, torture, and disappearances) by State police and thus violations of Convention provisions relating to bodily harm rather than general discrimination or civil rights. The KHRP invested its time and financial resources in claims that mainly involved Arts 3 (torture), 5 (liberty/security), and 8 (privacy). Interestingly, Art 6 (right to fair trial) was invoked most often by claims brought by Kurdish lawyers; a claim that seems familiar in almost all Council of Europe countries pertaining mainly to length of proceedings. It is not surprising that UK social activists might be less involved in cases that are not exhibiting a gross human rights violation, but pertain more to procedural inefficiencies.

As elaborated below in Table 5.1, the great majority of cases brought against Turkey involved Arts 3, 5, and 8. Interestingly, these are also the cases in which we see the greatest involvement of activists, including organized Kurdish lawyers, UK-based human rights lawyers, and also the KHRP. The KHRP was clearly a key actor in this litigation. This NGO was founded in 1992 and is based in London. It has a global mission in that it is not tied to a single country but instead is 'committed to the promotion and protection of the human rights of all persons living within Kurdish regions' with the aims 'to promote awareness of the situation of the Kurds in Iran, Iraq, Syria, Turkey and elsewhere, to bring an end to the violation of the Kurds in these countries, and to promote the protection of human rights of Kurdish people everywhere.'[40] The group utilizes international human rights mechanisms as a key instrument to protect Kurdish rights and the European

---

[40] Kurdish Human Rights Project 2008, p 1 (hereinafter 'KHRP').

Table 5.1 ECtHR decisions involving Turkey in the area of minority rights by Convention provision invoked in the case and litigant type, 1991–2006

Convention provision	Represented by activist Kurdish lawyer	Represented by activist UK lawyer	Represented by an NGO	Total
Art 3	11	16	7	34
Art 5	5	11	5	21
Art 6	15	2	0	17
Art 8	3	7	5	15
Art 9	0	0	0	0
Art 10	7	0	4	11
Art 11	2	0	0	2
Art 13	0	0	0	0
Art 14	0	1	2	3
Art 1, Protocol No 1	3	7	0	10
Total	46	44	23	113

Source: Data compiled by the author from the JURISTRAS Project reports funded by the European Commission under the 6th Framework Program (contract no 028398), 2006–2009.

Convention system has been its most successful avenue. Between 1992 and 2007 it represented over 500 applicants, and recognizes the importance of this individual procedure in attaining 'collective justice'.[41] We can see that the KHRP's involvement in this litigation has led to both an expansion in protection and also reform in European Convention procedures.

The *Aydin v Turkey* decision[42] was integral to expanding the scope and meaning of Art 3 and its prohibition of torture. In particular, this KHRP-assisted case, led to the ground-breaking decision that established rape as a form of torture. Prior to this ruling, rape was often categorized by many legal systems as a criminal act, underappreciating its potential systematic use by authorities in times of war. Thus, this ECtHR case law not only expanded Convention rights, but it also contributed to other legal developments in how rape would be prosecuted under international law.[43] Another important Art 3 decision with KHRP involvement was *Aksoy v Turkey*.[44] The case pertained to Zeki Aksoy who was shot in 1994 after receiving death threats for filing a complaint with the European Commission regarding mistreatment and torture he suffered while detained by the Turkish security forces. The case was brought by his father with the assistance of the KHRP. The ECtHR's

---

[41] KHRP, 25.
[42] *Aydin v Turkey* Appl no 23178/94 (1997).
[43] S. Eaton, 'Sierra Leone: The Proving Ground for Prosecuting Rape as a War Crime', 35(4) *Georgetown Journal of International Law* (2004), 874.
[44] *Aksoy v Turkey* Appl no 21897/93 (1996).

decision was important for publicizing the Turkish government's use of torture and also making clear that the Convention system took seriously such claims brought by individuals against their governments. Groups such as the KHRP understand the importance of utilizing the Convention system as a way of enhancing the accountability of domestic governments.

It is important to note that social activists may bring this litigation, sometimes formally through their work with NGOs such as the KHRP, but also working outside these organizations. In the case of Turkey, there are two legal activists that are particularly noteworthy for their involvement in bringing claims before the ECtHR. Kevin Boyle and Francoise Hampson are professors of law and fellows in the Human Rights Centre at Essex University in the UK. Both have distinguished careers of involvement in human rights litigation, in particular before the ECtHR. Boyle spent over a decade working specifically on bringing claims involving human rights violations in South East Turkey.[45] An examination of the case law from Turkey further details this involvement with their participation as legal representative to the applicant in 15 cases. This pair of lawyers has an excellent track record, with the ECtHR in almost all cases finding a violation of Convention rights, most involving Arts 3 and 8. For example, in the *Elci and Others v Turkey* case,[46] Hampson and Boyle assisted 16 Turkish nationals in bringing two complaints (that were later combined into one application) under Arts 3, 5, 8, and 25 and Art 1, Protocol No 1. The case involved a group of lawyers who were detained under the pretext that they were involved in criminal activities but in reality it was for their work representing individuals before the State Security Court and their wider human rights work. The ECtHR held that there was a violation of Arts 3, 5, and 8 in one or more of the 16 cases. The effect of this decision not only held the Turkish government accountable in all 16 cases, but also sent a clear message that the ECtHR will confront governments that limit access to legal institutions thus expanding the protection and access provided for those bringing rights complaints against their governments.

The UK provides us with an interesting comparison. Are social activists utilizing different strategies and invoking different Convention provisions in minority rights claims brought against the UK government? Table 5.2 displays the patterns of social activist involvement in ECtHR minority rights claims brought against the UK by Convention rights invoked between 1991–2006. The variation is remarkable, with the majority of these minority claims involving NGOs directly as the primary representative for the applicant (75 per cent), unlike the case of Turkey where NGOs played a lesser direct role in the litigation. NGOs served as the primary representative in 57 of these claims and were themselves applicants seven times. Activist lawyers were much more likely to operate through an NGO. Again, the UK is home to a very large number of international human rights organizations

---

[45] Their personal profiles are available at: Kevin Boyle <http://www.essex.ac.uk/law/people/academic/boyle.shtm> and Francoise Hampson <http://www.essex.ac.uk/law/people/academic/hampson.shtm>.

[46] *Elci and Others v Turkey* Appl nos 23145/93, 25091/94 (2003).

Table 5.2 ECtHR decisions involving the UK in the area of minority rights by Convention provision invoked in the case and litigant type, 1991–2006

Convention provision	Represented by activist UK lawyer	Represented by an NGO	Represented by a government commission	Applicant is an NGO	Total
Art 3	0	3	0	1	4
Art 5	0	1	0	0	1
Art 6	1	5	2	1	9
Art 8	2	10	2	0	14
Art 9	0	1	0	0	1
Art 10	0	2	0	0	2
Art 11	0	0	0	2	2
Art 13	1	8	0	1	10
Art 14	1	18	2	2	23
Art 1, Protocol No 1	1	9	0	0	10
Total	6	57	6	7	76

Source: Data compiled by the author from the JURISTRAS Project reports funded by the European Commission under the 6th Framework Program (contract no 028398), 2006–2009.

therefore these data are not surprising when compared to Turkey's lack of a similarly established local human rights civil society and organizations. Further, governmental commissions were involved with six claims illustrating a similar historical trend to that found in discrimination litigation before the ECJ in which a governmental body—the Equality Opportunities Commission—played a similarly important role bringing claims against the State.[47]

When we turn to look at the Convention provisions raised by either NGOs or individual activist lawyers there is a distinct pattern that is different from the claims invoked against the Turkish government. Nearly one-third of the claims involved Art 14 (discrimination); a fact that stands in stark contrast to the provision with a similar volume in Turkey—Art 3. NGOs invoked Art 14 in one-third of the cases where they served as primary representative to the applicant. Similar to Turkey, though, Arts 6 and 8 were also invoked in greater frequency in minority rights cases, with these claims making up another third of total claims. Yet unlike Turkey, Art 1, Protocol No 1 and Art 13 (effective remedy) made up almost one-third of the remaining claims. Examining the claims which involved NGOs as primary representative it is interesting to note that Art 14 received the great majority of their efforts (31 per cent) with Art 8 following close behind (17 per cent). Which

---

[47] Cichowski (2007), n 7 above.

Convention rights seemed most hospitable to associations or NGOs bringing direct victim claims? While the numbers are few as discussed above, Arts 3, 6, 11, 13, and 14 were all invoked by NGOs or associations claiming a direct violation of their Convention rights in these diverse areas of law—one example involved two trade unions which successfully argued that a UK law that enabled employers to de-recognize unions was a violation of Art 11 (freedom to associate) and the ECtHR concurred.[48]

We now turn to look more closely at NGO and social activist involvement in these cases. The most notable variation from the Turkish cases is the number and diversity of NGOs involved. Drawing from the larger dataset, we find that the UK is home to the largest number of NGOs that are systematically involved with applications before the ECtHR. Further, many of the key litigators and justice advocates before the ECtHR over the last 30 years are from the UK. Professors Boyle and Hampson are examples, as mentioned above, and Lord Lester of Herne Hill QC would be another.[49] As we saw from the Turkish case, these British social activists (the KHRP, for example) are not only involved in cases in their home country but are part of an increasingly important network of transnational public interest lawyers. The NGOs assisting in these cases included AIRE Centre, Justice, Children's Legal Centre, National Council of Civil Liberties, Stonewall, National Romani Rights Association, and Liberty. Due to space limitation, I will highlight a few of these NGOs and their activities in this case litigation.

The AIRE Centre is based in the UK and was set up in 1993 to assist individuals in obtaining rights provided through international agreements. Between 1993 and 2003 they were involved in more than 77 cases. The majority of their participation was in the form of directly assisting claimants with legal information (37 cases) or serving as a claimant's primary legal representative (37 cases) and a handful in which they were granted third party intervention (3 cases).[50] Further, the group is called upon by the Council of Europe and other international organizations to provide training on litigating Convention rights.[51] These cases have resulted in decisions finding violations in a host of legal domains, from failure in police protection (under Art 6) to family law (under Arts 6, 8, and 13). Nuala Mole from the AIRE Centre served on the legal team for the applicant in *D v United Kingdom*,[52] a case involving the deportation of an immigrant with AIDS to his home country, the remote island of St Kitts. The ECtHR found the UK in

---

[48] *Wilson, National Union of Journalists and Others v United Kingdom* Appl nos 30668/96, 30671/96, 30678/96 (2002).

[49] Lord Lester has a distinguished career as a human rights advocate and lawyer both before British courts but importantly before the ECtHR. In one recent example, he represented the applicants in *DH and Others v Czech Republic* Appl no 57325/00 (2007) which was a landmark decision on the meaning and effect of racial discrimination as protected under the Convention. His 40 years of work as a lawyer exemplifies the social justice activist who has utilized the courts to bring real legislative and legal reform.

[50] The Aire Centre, *Ten Year Review* (2003). The Report is available at: <http://www.airecentre.org/fileman/tenyearreview.pdf>.

[51] C. Harby, 'The Experience of the AIRE Centre in Litigating before the European Court of Human Rights' in T. Treves et al, n 29 above.

[52] *D v United Kingdom* Appl no 30240/96 (1997).

violation of Art 3 as deportation of a man in his condition to a place where he would have neither medical nor family support constituted 'inhumane and degrading treatment'. The ruling expanded the protection offered to non-nationals in the UK, especially those suffering from terminal illness.

Stonewall is also involved with equality and justice advocacy for the lesbian, gay, and bisexual communities. This is a professional lobbying organization that was set up in the UK in 1989 in opposition to anti-gay legislation.[53] Today that group has offices throughout the UK and has successfully mainstreamed their equality claim by garnering support from all the main political parties. While research, community and educational outreach, and parliamentary lobbying are their main activities, representatives from Stonewall are also involved in cases lodged before the ECtHR. In *Sutherland v United Kingdom*,[54] the applicant was represented by Stephen Grosz and also Angela Mason from Stonewall who lodged the complaint with the European Commission of Human Rights in 1994. The applicant in the case was questioning the lawfulness of a UK statute fixing the age of consent for lawful homosexual activities between men at 18 rather than that set for women at 16. He claimed that the statute was a violation of his right to privacy under Art 8 and was discriminatory and thus a breach of Art 14. This case is notable in that it led to direct legislative amendments by the UK government which lowered the age of consent to 16, despite repeated opposition from some parliamentarians. The government was held accountable to remove discriminatory practices, and the litigation in effect upgraded the law to meet current societal pressures. Stonewall is also a classic example of an NGO utilizing a wide array of venues to bring policy and social reform—through the courts (both at domestic and supranational levels), legislature, and larger public education campaigns.[55]

Liberty is another UK-based NGO that has played a critical role in the development of the ECtHR's case law. It was established in 1934 under the name the National Council for Civil Liberties. Their organizational goals are to 'promote the values of individual human dignity, equal treatment and fairness as the foundations of a democratic society' and it does so 'through a combination of public campaigning, test case litigation, parliamentary lobbying, policy analysis and the provision of free advice and information'.[56] Liberty has utilized the ECtHR as a venue for its test case litigation in the area of minority rights. The *Grant v United Kingdom* test case[57] is an example. The applicant in this case was a male–to-female transsexual and Liberty brought into question the fact that the applicant was disallowed a pension at the age of 60 despite the fact that she had a Gender Recognition Certificate as established through legislation adopted in 2004 following the ECtHR's *Goodwin* decision[58] which raised similar issues pertaining to new gender

---

[53] For more information on Stonewall see: <http://www.stonewall.org.uk/>.
[54] *Sutherland v United Kingdom* Appl no 25186/94 (2001).
[55] Cichowski (2006), n 7 above.
[56] Liberty, 'About' (2009), available at: <http://www.liberty-human-rights.org.uk/about/index.shtml>.
[57] *Grant v United Kingdom* Appl no 32570/03 (2006).
[58] *Goodwin v United Kingdom* Appl no 28957/95 (2002).

recognition for transsexuals. The ECtHR granted the applicant a pecuniary award finding a violation under Art 8. In the last ten years, Liberty has been directly involved in at least 26 cases before the ECtHR serving mainly in the role of primary legal representation (13), amicus briefs (12), and as mentioned above, one as actual claimant. Liberty's strategic litigation has led not only to an expansion in rights protections for minorities living in the UK but has also forced reforms in government mechanisms of societal control and monitoring which strengthened their importance governmentally.[59]

We have seen that NGOs, associations, and activist lawyers directly impact the number of cases coming before the ECtHR. They are important for the realization of Convention rights, especially when individual applicants lack the resources or expertise to bring these claims on their own. Likewise, as argued earlier, these ECtHR decisions can have a direct impact on democratic governance in the extent to which they expand the precision and scope of Convention provisions and provide greater protection. We know that the incorporation of Convention provisions into domestic law can expand the type of rights available to individuals and societal groups and the relative power they may gain in bringing claims against government action and acts. Yet ECtHR decisions can also be another source for rights development. Scholars have long recognized the power of courts as rule-makers, the extent to which their decisions change the precision, scope, and meaning of legal norms in the process of dispute resolution.[60]

IV. Conclusions

The relationship between NGOs and the ECtHR is truly exemplary. While clearly there is room for reform and improvements, there is much to applaud. Comparatively speaking, no other international court possesses such a rich history of engagement with and reliance on civil society and public interest representatives.[61] When we look back over the last 50 years, the number of cases involving NGOs is admittedly small compared to the total number of ECtHR cases. But the quality of the cases is high, meaning that most of these groups were very strategic about

---

[59] *Liberty & Others v United Kingdom* (Appl no 58243/00 (2008)) is an example of a case where Liberty was the applicant and the resulting decision pushed for greater government oversight. Liberty along with two civil liberties NGOs from Ireland brought a case before the ECtHR against the UK under Art 8 alleging wrongful interception of telecommunications traffic by the UK Ministry of Defence during which time the claimants were in regular phone contact with each other and also clients in order to discuss confidential legal matters. The Court's finding of a violation laid out clearly that while interception of telecommunications for national security purposes is lawful, the UK policy governing such action was 'not adequately accessible and formulated with sufficient precision as to be foreseeable'.

[60] See Shapiro, n 10 above.

[61] See Harby, n 51 above; A. Mohamed, 'Individual and NGO Participation in Human Rights Litigation before the African Court of Human and People's Rights: Lessons from the European and Inter-American Courts of Human Rights', 8 *Michigan State University Journal of International Law* (1999), 201; D. Shelton, 'The Participation of Nongovernmental Organizations in International Judicial Proceedings', 88 *American Journal of International Law* (1994), 626.

choosing to participate in cases which they believed would lead to significant changes in European law. They thus saw it as an opportunity to participate in the development of international human rights law, which would not only be used by the ECtHR in the future, but by domestic and international courts around the world.

Over time, this interaction between social activists and the ECtHR has expanded both rights protection and the accessibility of Convention institutions. This continues to be a dynamic and incremental process. First, the analysis reveals that social activist and NGO participation relied on a necessary set of rules granting access. Today, both the Convention and the Rules of Court explicitly grant access to NGOs either as a direct victim or in the form of third party intervention. If we look back over the last 50 years, we see that these rules evolved not at the initiation of States, but instead through the Court's jurisprudence and the strategic action of NGOs. Second, while these rules facilitated formal access for NGOs, the historical analysis also reveals NGOs playing myriad roles in the litigation process. Beyond this, their role as applicant or third party social activists was crucial in the role of representing applicants, and providing a general support structure to the Convention system. This includes educating the public on rights, assisting potential applicants seeking legal advice, and importantly transnational collaboration with other NGOs and legal advocates which ultimately led to an application.

Finally, the analysis highlights that this mobilization–litigation dynamic has real effects on the ECtHR's jurisprudence. The effects are twofold. NGOs play a critical direct role in the decision through their written documentation submitted through third party intervention. The analysis revealed that over time the ECtHR has systematically utilized this information and expertise to support its findings of a violation. These amicus briefs are often directly quoted by the Court in the final decision. The Court has linked this role to the spirit behind the requirements for third party intervention, namely the importance of involving organizations which may provide factual and expert information on the legal issues at hand.[62] NGOs also have a more indirect effect on ECtHR decisions. In particular, the findings reveal that social activists can shape the Court's decisions by the extent to which they are responsible for assisting in or representing significant cases before the ECtHR. NGOs are thus a crucial adjunct to the Convention proceedings by highlighting systematic human rights violations and giving the ECtHR the opportunity to hold States accountable. Thus, over time, NGOs were critical to the evolving jurisprudence of the Court and the precision, scope, and enforceability of human rights in Europe.

This analysis focused primarily on the historical interaction that has evolved between the Court and social activists. Yet, the findings also suggest a set of lessons that may help us to understand developments in the future. Scholars and practitioners alike acknowledge the challenges facing the Court and the detrimental effect that the Court's growing caseload is having on the effective and efficient protection

---

[62] Vajic, n 29 above, 97.

of Convention rights.[63] In particular, reforms in the proposed Protocol No 14, such as the creation of single-judge formations and an expansion of Committee powers, hope to increase the Court's efficiency. Yet as President Costa recently recognized, the proposed gains in efficiency are at the 20–25 per cent rate, and while useful, only scratch the surface of the Court's workload.[64] Thus, the findings illustrate the ways in which NGOs may increasingly be called upon to rectify these institutional deficiencies. NGOs and social activists stand to play a crucial role in potentially reducing the Court's caseload through their work in giving Convention rights meaning in the domestic legal system. By pressuring the executive, legislatures, and especially national courts to domesticate Convention rights, victims may find their complaints increasingly remedied in their home legal system. Further, legal advocacy groups also play a critical role in filtering out potential applicants whose cases would be inadmissible, through their work in providing legal advice, assistance, and education regarding Convention rights. Both these roles stand to diminish the overall number of complaints reaching Strasbourg.

A final lesson that the analysis suggests is the importance of international courts in expanding civil society access and participation in political and legal processes. Rather than State-initiated reforms, the ECtHR paved the way for greater access for NGOs both as direct victims and also participants as a third party in litigation before the Court. Yet supranational courts can also have an effect on NGOs within the domestic political and legal system, protecting their status as laid down in law and promoting their role as a counterweight to State activity.[65] Once these rules were created, NGOs have utilized the opportunity to demand and receive greater access, accountability, and transparency from their governments. It is this process of mobilization and litigation that has not only characterized the protection of human rights in Europe over the last 50 years, but has become the hallmark of good governance around the globe.

---

[63] Mowbray, n 1 above; A. Mowbray, 'Crisis Measures of Institutional Reform for the European Court of Human Rights', 9(4) *Human Rights Law Review* (2009), 647; and Caflisch, n 1 above, 403.

[64] Council of Europe Committee of Ministers, 'Explanatory Report to Protocol 14 to the ECHR', 12 May 2009, CM (2009), 58, para 3.

[65] One ECtHR decision elaborated the importance of associations in democratic societies and the Court did not hesitate to find an Art 11 violation when disproportionate State action led to the dissolution of the association in question. See *Tebieti Muhafize Cemiyyeti and Israfilov v Azerbaijan* Appl no 37083/03 (2009).

6

The European Court of Human Rights after 50 Years

*Anthony Lester**

It is a privilege to contribute to this distinguished book, marking the fiftieth anniversary of the European Court of Human Rights. There is much to celebrate about the Court's work. As its Deputy Registrar, Michael O'Boyle, observes:[1]

There seems to be unanimous agreement in Europe today that the European Convention on Human Rights...is one of the major developments in European legal history and the crowning achievement of the Council of Europe. The emergence of the authority of the European Court of Human Rights has been described as one of the most remarkable phenomena in the history of international law, perhaps in the history of all law.

However, it is important to think imaginatively and boldly about practical ways of alleviating the profound crisis which threatens the Court's achievements during its next half century, ways which go beyond useful but insufficient procedural changes, or increasing funding without tackling fundamental institutional problems. These are hard times across Europe as we face a deep economic crisis, but hard times might help to concentrate the minds of our European political and judicial leaders to tackle the worsening crisis of the Convention system. As O'Boyle has noted,[2] there is no or little public or media discussion about the Court's problems, and the arduous process of securing ratification of Protocol No 14, for example, took place 'under the radar' and was 'confined to the corridors in Strasbourg'.

In his speech on the occasion of the opening of the judicial year, on 30 January 2009, Mr Jean-Paul Costa, President of the Court, proposed a major conference in the first half of 2010, to articulate a new commitment, a reaffirmed legitimacy, and a clarified mandate for the Court. Coming only weeks after the Russian ratification of Protocol No 14, the Interlaken Conference held on 18 and 19 February 2010 was the first important step in the strategic response to the ongoing issues facing the

---

* The author is grateful to the staff at the Odysseus Trust for their help in preparing this chapter. His views have been informed by practical experience and discussion with many within the system to whom he is also grateful.

[1] M. O'Boyle, 'On Reforming the Operation of the European Court of Human Rights', 1 *European Human Rights Law Review* (2008), 1.

[2] Ibid at 11.

Court to be taken during the Swiss presidency. In reaffirming the commitment of States Parties to the role played by the Court in the protection of human rights in Europe, the Interlaken Declaration proposed a number of key reforms to the operation of the Court in the form of an 'Action Plan'. The swift implementation of these new reforms is essential to ensure the ongoing operational success of the Court. There is no doubt about the urgency of what is at stake—nothing less than the survival of a viable Convention system in which those it was designed to protect have confidence. And it is essential that the issues are openly discussed by the media and the public across Europe.

I. The Court's Past Life

> When to the sessions of sweet silent thought
> I summon up remembrance of things past,
> I sigh the lack of many a thing I sought,
> And with old woes new wail my dear time's waste.[3]

That was Shakespeare's melancholic recollection. But for me, remembrance of things past in using the Convention system as a human rights advocate brings happy memories and not 'old woes'. More recent and new woes are a different matter!

The master builders of the European Convention on Human Rights were determined, in the aftermath of a second terrible war in half a century, never again to permit State sovereignty to shield from international liability the perpetrators of crimes against humanity; never again to allow governments to shelter behind the argument that what a State does to its own citizens or to the stateless is within its exclusive jurisdiction, and beyond the reach of the international community. So they resolved to create a binding international code of human rights, with safeguards against abuses of power and effective remedies for victims of violations by Contracting States.

The birth pangs of the Convention were not easy. The European Movement approved a 'Declaration of Principles of the European Union'. It stated that:

No State should be admitted to the European Union which does not accept the fundamental principles of a Charter of Human Rights and which does not declare itself willing and bound to ensure their application.

The Consultative Assembly carried that proposal forward, seeking enforcement via an independent European Commission and Court. The proposal for a Commission, in addition to a Court, was made to protect the Court from being inundated with frivolous litigation and being exploited for political ends. The Commission was envisaged as a filter of admissible applications, as the fact-finding body, and as the body whose authorization was necessary for an individual to initiate proceedings before the Court.

---

[3] William Shakespeare, Sonnet 30.

The Committee of Ministers of the Council of Europe attempted to block the proposal for a Court, but, after a political struggle, the Consultative Assembly overcame opposition from governments, and the Convention and its institutions were born. What is now striking is the speed with which the Convention was drafted and adopted. It was prepared within the Assembly and not by diplomats meeting in secret. And, above all, there was a political will to create a new international human rights instrument and a supranational court without precedent.

It is more than 40 years since I argued my first case in Strasbourg. It was in the European Commission of Human Rights. It was also the very first case brought against the UK, soon after the British government had accepted the right of individual petition in January 1966.[4] At that time, when the Court was ten years old, it had dealt with only one case, *Lawless v Ireland*,[5] and acceptance of the right of petition was precarious. Several governments, including my own, used to accept the right only for limited periods of a few years at a time, playing a game of cat and mouse with the Commission, with the implied threat of non-renewal.

The Commission drew on the considerable diplomatic skills of Anthony McNulty and Hans-Christian Krüger, within the Secretariat, to win the confidence of governments, whose commitment to the system was precarious because of their concern to preserve national sovereignty and State power. The Commission was brilliantly led by its Presidents, each a fine jurist—including Max Sørensen and Carl Aage Nørgaard from Denmark, and Sir James Fawcett from the UK.

The right of individual petition was especially important to those in the UK because, 40 years ago, there was no developed British system of public law and judicial review. We had no framework of positive rights to match the Convention rights and freedoms; and, without a written constitution or human rights legislation, our common law system was in many respects ethically aimless. There was no recognition of fundamental human rights. Habeas corpus was easily overridden by positive law. The courts did not even recognize that racial discrimination was contrary to legal public policy.[6]

So British advocates like me began to use the Convention system to challenge administrative action, judicial decisions, and the laws made by our sovereign Parliament. We were used to developing legal principles in our common law system, and, in my case, I had the advantage of having studied American constitutional law before being called to the English Bar. It was a great advantage that the government's advocates—including Lord Slynn and Judge Sir Nicolas Bratza, as they later became as judges of the two European Courts—shared a common determination to make the system work fairly and effectively.

The idea of fundamental human rights was anathema to Jeremy Bentham and his Utilitarian ideology, as it was to the philosophy of the Scandinavian legal realism of Alf Ross and Axel Hägerström. British ministers and civil servants did not

---

[4] *Alam and Khan v United Kingdom* Appl no 2991/66 (1967) 24 CD 116.
[5] *Lawless v Ireland (No 3)* Series A no 3 (1961).
[6] A. Lester and G. Bindman, *Race and Law* (Harmondsworth: Penguin, 1972), ch 1.

welcome the prospect of European judges looking over their shoulders. As Sir James Fawcett, President of the Commission, once told me, the British pathology of human rights violations sprang from a tradition of uncontrolled administrative discretion. The benevolent paternalism of administrators was seen as preferable to judicial review. To put it only slightly unfairly, for many ministers and civil servants power was delightful, and absolute power was absolutely delightful.

I have told elsewhere[7] the story of the British experience in gradually coming to terms with the Convention system. I shall not repeat that story now. Just as it took the Nordic countries many years to make the Convention rights part of their legal systems, so it took some 30 years after acceptance of the right of petition for the UK to give domestic effect to the Convention rights in the Human Rights Act 1998.[8]

During the 1960s and 70s, the main business of the developing Convention system was carried out by the Commission, in fact-finding and giving opinions. Their work was of a very high standard, and the fact-finding, for example, in the interstate case between Ireland and the UK[9] was impressive by any standard.

The Court gave a handful of important judgments, for example, in *Wemhoff*,[10] *Neumeister*,[11] and the *Belgian Linguistics case*,[12] but at that stage the Commission referred cases to the Court infrequently. There was a feeling within the Commission that the Court was too remote and that the Commission was better able to interpret and apply Convention standards. That was gradually replaced by a reluctant recognition that the Court needed to develop the jurisprudence authoritatively. As more cases began to reach the Court, it won public confidence through a series of landmark cases—*Golder*,[13] *Kjeldsen, Busk Madsen and Pedersen*,[14] *Tyrer*,[15] *König*,[16] *Klass*,[17] *Marckx*,[18] *Sunday Times*,[19] *Winterwerp*,[20] *Dudgeon*,[21] *Sporrong and Lönroth*,[22] and *Lingens*,[23] to name just a few of the vintage judgments.

---

[7] See A. Lester, D. Pannick, and J. Herberg, *Human Rights Law and Practice* (3rd edn, London: LexisNexis Butterworth, 2009), ch 1. See also A. W. B. Simpson, *Human Rights and the End of Empire: Britain and the Genesis of the European Convention* (Oxford: Oxford University Press, 2001).

[8] The Coalition Government has announced plans to set up a Commission to examine the Human Rights Act 1998 and whether or not it should be replaced by a British Bill of Rights. HM Government, 'The Coalition: Our Programme for Government', May 2010. Available at: <http://www.cabinetoffice.gov.uk/media/409088/pfg_coalition.pdf>.

[9] *Ireland v United Kingdom*, 15 *Yearbook of the European Convention* (1972), 76.

[10] *Wemhoff v Germany* Series A no 7 (1968).

[11] *Neumeister v Austria* Series A no 8 (1968).

[12] *Belgian Linguistics case (No 2)* Series A no 6 (1968).

[13] *Golder v United Kingdom* Series A no 18 (1975).

[14] *Kjeldsen, Busk Madsen and Pedersen v Denmark* Series A no 23 (1976).

[15] *Tyrer v United Kingdom* Series A no 26 (1978).

[16] *König v Germany* Series A no 27 (1978).

[17] *Klass v Germany* Series A no 28 (1978).

[18] *Marckx v Belgium* Series A no 31 (1979).

[19] *Sunday Times v United Kingdom (No 1)* Series A no 3 (1979).

[20] *Winterwerp v Netherlands* Series A no 33 (1979).

[21] *Dudgeon v United Kingdom* Series A no 45 (1981).

[22] *Sporrong and Lönroth v Sweden* Series A no 52 (1982).

[23] *Lingens v Austria* Series A no 103 (1986).

The Court's case law makes[24] 'a continuing contribution to the evolving public law of Europe as the norms it contains are received into the national law and practice of 47 states', and has developed constitutional principles, including the judicial review of legislation, the principle of proportionality, the importance of freedom of political speech, and the full recognition of the dignity of the human person as a constitutional imperative.

For the first 30 years of the Court's life, Central and Eastern Europe were divided from the West by Winston Churchill's 'Iron Curtain'. The number of States Parties to the Convention was relatively small and most of them were well-established democracies which adhered to the rule of law. The Strasbourg machine coped well enough, with the Commission controlling the admissibility of applications and doing the fact-finding, and the Court deciding important issues of legal principle when cases were referred by the Commission or the respondent government for final adjudication.

The system was more user-friendly than was the English judicial system at that time. Today I feel nostalgic when I walk along the Allée de la Robertsau, past the unpretentious user-friendly building which housed the Commission and the Court, on my way to the modernist and functionalist palace of justice which now houses the Court and its staff.

In the early life of the Convention system, when the caseload was small, cases were argued for hours, occasionally even for days, in a friendly atmosphere. During coffee breaks we chatted with the Commissioners and judges and their staff. Admissibility decisions in important cases were fully reasoned and were usually reasonable too. The Commission acquired great expertise both in fact-finding[25] and in achieving friendly settlements compatible with human rights. The Commission was far better than the present Court in identifying urgent and important cases, a skill acquired over many years which appears to have been lost in the transition to the present system.

But, for all that, the old regime was imperfect. The judges and Commissioners were part-timers and included former agents of the governments which secured their appointment. The Secretariat and Registry staff had to do their best to uphold the integrity of the system. I remember a senior judge and former government legal adviser telling me that he saw it as his duty to uphold national interests! Of necessity the dedicated Commission staff came to assume a dominant role, seeing themselves as Platonic guardians of the Court's integrity and the European rule of law.

The procedures were cumbersome, repetitive, and inefficient. The right to effective national remedies under Art 13 was narrowly interpreted,[26] and not much attention was paid in individual cases to the need for systemic remedies for systemic violations.[27] The Committee of Ministers did not perform a useful role in independently

---

[24] O'Boyle, n 1 above, at 2.

[25] See eg in *Ireland v United Kingdom* Series A no 25 (1978).

[26] See Lester, Pannick, and Herberg, n 7 above, para 4.13.2.

[27] See Lord Lester of Herne Hill QC, 'The European Convention in the New Architecture of Europe', 5 *Public Law* (1996), 6.

supervising the execution of the Court's judgments or giving effect to the Commission's opinions. There was no equality of arms in access to the Court because, unlike governments, the applicants had no right of access and depended on the Commission to make a referral. That flaw was addressed in 1990 when Protocol No 9 enabled individual applicants to bring their cases to the Court after lodging their complaints with the Commission.

II. The Loss of Balance in the Reform of the System

In March 1985, the Swiss delegation to a European Ministerial Conference on Human Rights in Vienna proposed that the Commission and the Court should be merged into a single Court. The proposal was controversial, but I supported the creation of a single Court in the hope that it would promote speedy justice and enhance the Court's authority. A minority of governments, led by the UK, initially argued for a Court of First Instance to replace the Commission but their view did not prevail.

With hindsight it was a mistake to abolish the Commission. There will be considerable reluctance now, as Professor Caflisch observes,[28] to revert, in any form, to the two-tier system of the Commission and Court. Caflisch suggests[29] that 'in the long run, such a return may prove unavoidable'. But as the great economic reformer, John Maynard Keynes, reminds us from his grave[30] 'long run is a misleading guide to current affairs. In the long run we are all dead.' That is especially true when the patient is at risk of terminal decline and all that is available is palliative care. The need for a new streamlined two-tier system must be recognized as a high priority if we are to preserve both the right of individual petition and a Court able to command public confidence.

It took 13 years for the single Court system to be created by Protocol No 11, which came into force on 1 November 1998.[31] Europe had changed dramatically during those years, but unfortunately it was too late to argue that it would be better to retain the Commission to screen out inadmissible applications and do the fact-finding, working together with the Court to cope with the far-reaching effects of the enlargement of the Council of Europe.

Protocol No 11 dissolved the Commission, made the Court permanent and full time, and gave it compulsory jurisdiction for all individual applications. But it failed to provide a sufficient length of tenure to guarantee judicial independence, and it created further problems of overload from which the Court cannot recover without urgent and radical reforms.

---

[28] L. Caflisch, 'The Reform of the European Court of Human Rights: Protocol No 14 and Beyond', 6(2) *Human Rights Law Review* (2006), 414.

[29] Ibid.

[30] *A Tract on Monetary Reform* (1923), ch 3.

[31] See *Protocol No 11 to the Convention for the Protection of Human Rights and Fundamental Freedoms, restructuring the control machinery, established thereby* ETS No 155, *Explanatory Report*.

David Maxwell Fyfe, rapporteur of the drafting committee and one of its main architects, described the Convention in a speech made to the Parliamentary Assembly in 1950 as 'a beacon to the peoples behind the Iron Curtain and a passport for their return to the midst of the free countries'.[32] But when the proposal to create a single Court was first put forward, no one foresaw that the Soviet system was soon to collapse, resulting in a vast enlargement of the Council of Europe to its present membership of 47 States.

Everyone knows of the massive burdens the Court carries in attempting to deal with the backlog of applications and new complaints which have increased exponentially during the decade since Protocol No 11 came into force. Like Sisyphus, the Court is cursed to roll a huge boulder up a hill, only to watch it roll down again, and, in the absence of further reform, to repeat this throughout eternity! In 2008 alone, there were 50,000 new applications, 20 per cent more than in 2007. Fifty seven per cent of applications were lodged against just four States—the Russian Federation, Turkey, Romania, and Ukraine. They and Poland are the countries giving rise to the greatest number of judgments. In 2009, 57,200 applications were allocated to a judicial formation, while the backlog of cases reached 119,300 applicants.[33]

The Russian Federation is the worst offender.[34] Since it was admitted to the Council of Europe 13 years ago, it has failed to comply with its obligations under the Convention, including providing effective domestic remedies and abiding by the Court's judgments. Some 3,300 cases with similar factual background were lodged with the Court between August 2008 and January 2009 against Georgia concerning hostilities in South Ossetia.[35] It is reasonable to suppose that this has been done with encouragement from the Russian authorities.[36] Under the present Russian regime, there is seemingly little commitment to the European rule of law

---

[32] *Political Adventure: The Memoirs of the Earl of Kilmuir* (London: Weidenfeld & Nicolson, 1964), 183, quoting from his speech made in August 1950. The Earl of Kilmuir, formerly David Maxwell Fyfe, was a British Conservative MP who became Solicitor General, Attorney General, Home Secretary, and Lord Chancellor. He was Britain's chief prosecutor in the Nuremberg trials and conducted a brilliant and effective cross-examination of Hermann Göring.

[33] ECtHR Factsheet, 'Protocol 14: The Reform of the European Court of Human Rights'. See: <http://www.echr.coe.int/NR/rdonlyres/57211BCC-C88A-43C6-B540-AF0642E81D2C/0/CPProtocole14EN.pdf>.

[34] At the end of September 2010 there were 38,850 cases pending cases against the Russian Federation, constituting 27.8 per cent of all pending applications. See European Court of Human Rights Statistics, 2010 Pending cases pie chart at: <http://www.echr.coe.int/NR/rdonlyres/99F89D38-902E-4725-9D3D-4A8BB74A7401/0/Pending_applications_chart.pdf>.

[35] Press release issued by the Registrar, 14 January 2009.

[36] One may speculate that it was the interstate application brought by Georgia against the Russian Federation in respect of the events in South Ossetia in the summer of 2008 which caused the Russian Federation to retaliate by supporting the bringing of large numbers of individual applications against Georgia. Indeed, the Russian Prosecutor's Office has assisted South Ossetia residents in preparing complaints against Georgia to international and regional courts. On 12 August 2008, the prosecutor general of the Russian Federation, Yury Chaika, announced that he had created 'a special brigade of prosecutors that would provide legal assistance in preparing appeals and complaints to the European Court of Human Rights and the Hague International Criminal Court'. See Human Rights Watch, 'Up in Flames: Humanitarian Law Violations and Civilian Victims in the *Conflict over South Ossetia*', 23 January 2009, available at: <http://www.hrw.org/en/node/79681/section/31>.

and no sense of solidarity or collective responsibility with the other States Parties. And across Europe, *realpolitik* abounds. The Parliamentary Assembly and the Committee of Ministers have no appetite to apply dissuasive sanctions, for example by suspending voting rights in the Council of Europe, as was done for nine months in 2000 for alleged gross violations of human rights in Chechnya. And it is improbable that interstate proceedings will be taken against the Russian Federation (or other States) whose systemic and persistent violations place heavy and unacceptable burdens upon the Court and the Convention system. And I doubt whether the peoples of that long-suffering nation would benefit if the Russian Federation were expelled from the Council of Europe.

Alone among the 47 Member States, Russia's long-standing resistance thwarted the implementation of Protocol No 14, which had been devised as a means of improving the efficiency of the Convention system and reducing the Court's backlog.[37] Adopted by the Committee of Ministers in May 2004, Russia's long-awaited ratification in January 2010 paved the way for its adoption in June 2010. This may indicate a new willingness on the part of Russia to engage in a commitment to the Convention regime, but it remains to be seen to what extent the ratification amounts to a change of heart. Protocol No 14 contains a number of key institutional reforms. It:

(a) permits single judges to declare cases inadmissible where they are clearly without merit;

(b) permits committees of three judges (instead of Chambers of seven judges) to give judgments in repetitive cases where the Court's case law is already well established (for example, the many cases on length of proceedings);

(c) introduces a new admissibility requirement concerning cases where the applicant has not suffered a significant disadvantage, provided that the case has already been considered by the domestic courts, and provided that there are no general human rights reasons why the application should be examined on its merits;

(d) provides for a single term of office of nine years for the judges of the Court;

(e) gives the Committee of Ministers new powers to bring proceedings before the Court against a party that refused to abide by one of the Court's judgments, and to request the Court to give an interpretation of a judgment;

(f) allows the Commissioner for Human Rights to submit written observations and take part in proceedings before the Court; and

(g) provides that the European Union may accede to the Convention.

Under current circumstances, the Court's caseload is likely to increase at an annual rate of about 14 per cent. Regardless of the accession to Protocol No 14 the load will probably only increase, as it will as more States ratify Protocol No 12, enabling cases to be brought under a free-standing guarantee of equal treatment without

---

[37] Protocol No 14 was adopted by the Committee of Ministers on 13 May 2004.

discrimination.[38] However, while Protocol No 14 is not a panacea, its provisions need to be translated into short-term practical measures while longer term solutions are discussed and developed.

The Court's expenditure is borne by the Council of Europe.[39] Its expenditure accounts for a quarter of the Council's total budget, but it needs more money to function properly. It does not have its own ring-fenced budget.[40] Its budget is part of the general budget of the Council of Europe. The contributions of Member States to the Council of Europe are fixed according to scales taking into account population and gross national product. The Court's budget for 2010 amounted to €58,588,600. Since 2000, the Council of Europe's budget has been prepared on the basis of zero real growth (that is, the same amount as the previous year to take into account inflation, salary adjustments, etc). Since 2006, the principle of zero growth has been extended to Member States' contributions. In 2009, the Court received an extra €1,542,300 for its enhancement programme (for the creation of seven additional posts in the Department of Execution of Judgments and 47 additional posts in the Court). A group of leading human rights NGOs have rightly observed that[41] the Court 'has been hampered by a lack of sufficient human and financial resources'. The Ministers' Deputies have made it clear to the Secretary General of the Council of Europe[42] that 'they would not accept proposals departing from the principle of zero real growth in member states' contributions'. Within the confines of the total Council of Europe budget, it has been treated generously, but the underlying problem is that the Court should not have to compete for resources within the overall budget. It needs its own budget calculated according to its needs in delivering what the Convention requires, without being constrained by the requirement of zero growth for the rest of Council of Europe expenditure.

The resources at the Court's disposal are meagre compared with those of the European Court of Justice (ECJ). To give one example, the ECJ's library budget for acquisitions is about €800,000 per year, while that of the Strasbourg Court is €70,000 and reducing. Of course the European Courts have different functions, but it is difficult to understand why the European Union should fund the Luxembourg

---

[38] Matching Art 26 of the UN International Covenant on Civil and Political Rights.

[39] Art 50 of the Convention.

[40] Unlike the Inter-American Court of Human Rights which, in accordance with Art 72 of the Inter-American Convention on Human Rights, draws up its own budget and submits it for approval to the General Assembly through the General Secretariat which may not introduce any changes to it. In accordance with Art 26 of its Statute, the Court administers its own budget.

[41] Amnesty International, the European Human Rights Advocacy Centre, INTERIGHTS, JUS-TICE, Liberty, the International Commission of Jurists, and the AIRE Centre, 'Comments on Reflection Group Discussions on enhancing the long-term effectiveness of the Convention system', DH-S-GDR (2009) 008, March 2009, para 50. They refer to the Report of the Group of Wise Persons, 15 November 2006, para 37, which noted that 'no other international court is confronted with a workload of such magnitude while having at the same time such a demanding responsibility for setting the standard of conduct required to comply with the Convention.'

[42] 'Budgets of the Council of Europe for the financial year 2009', Report on Economic Affairs and Development (Rapporteur, Mr Paul Wille), Doc 11599, 25 April 2008, Explanatory memorandum, para 14.

Courts so generously while the Council of Europe deprives the Strasbourg Court of the financial and human resources needed to perform its Herculean labours.[43]

It is also essential, as the Group of Wise Persons recommended[44] that, in the interests of enhancing the Court's independence and effectiveness, the Court should be granted 'the greatest possible operational autonomy, as regards in particular the presentation and management of its budget and the appointment, deployment and promotion of its staff'. It is important too, as the Group of Wise Persons also recommended,[45] for the judicial system of the Convention to be made more flexible and for there to be a Statute of the Court.

Since the accession to Protocol No 14 in January 2010, the Court's rules have changed significantly, allowing for greater flexibility and the faster processing and dismissal of cases. Prior to the introduction of Protocol No 14, the Court was forced to spend most of its time striking out inadmissible cases. The new 'Protocol No 14' introduces changes in three areas. It bolsters the Court's ability to strike out clearly inadmissible applications by allowing single judges to do so. The Protocol introduces a new power to refuse to hear cases in which the applicant has not suffered a significant disadvantage, so that the Court can focus on cases which raise important human rights issues. And, it provides the Court with measures for dealing more efficiently with repetitive cases, so that the Court will have significant new powers to punish States that repeatedly fail to comply with its judgments. It can now initiate proceedings of non-compliance in the Grand Chamber of the Court, and these sanctions can potentially include suspension or expulsion from the Council of Europe.[46]

Even though the giving of reasons is an important safeguard encouraging a rational and fair process of decision-making, there is no duty for the Court to give reasons for rejecting an application without communicating it to the government. The applicant is informed of the decision by a peremptory letter reminiscent of the reply to the young narrator in Ring Lardner's novel *The Young Immigrants* who asked her father tenderly whether he was lost on the journey to their new home. '"Shut up," he explained.'

This peremptory procedure is adopted even in cases raising novel issues of interpretation and application of the Convention which are of general importance, and where lawyers have taken great care on behalf of applicants in cases which deserve to be communicated to the respondent governments. The rejection letters inform them that:

The decision is final and not subject to any appeal . . . You will therefore appreciate that the Registry will be unable to provide any further details about the Committee's deliberations or to conduct further correspondence relating to its decision in this case.

---

[43] The 2010 budget for the ECJ is €329,300,000, about 5.5 times the budget of the European Court of Human Rights.

[44] Report of the Group of Wise Persons to the Committee of Ministers, CM(2006)203, 15 November 2006, para 124.

[45] Ibid, paras 127–8.

[46] ECtHR Factsheet, n 33 above.

I recognize that the absence of proper reasons does not mean that behind the scenes there has been an absence of detailed reasons to inform the Committee in reaching inadmissibility decisions, but it would enhance public confidence if they or a summary of them could be provided to applicants. There is widespread dissatisfaction among applicants and their advocates about the current practice.

The Court's refusal to provide short but clear reasons for decisions on inadmissibility is unacceptable, given that every proposal to the Committee is accompanied by a report containing the grounds for the proposed rejection of an application. It would not be a significant burden for this analysis to provide the basis for a short, clear set of reasons, and it is wrong to suppose that only the Committee needs to see that analysis. The Court should surely set a good example to national courts and administrators in the way in which it communicates its decisions to applicants.

Several of the senior Registry staff are old personal friends. We grew up together as the system grew and changed. They do a fine job as Platonic guardians of the *acquis*, but I hope they will forgive my observing that they are somewhat inbred. The Section Registrars and Deputy Section Registrars are grown from within the Registry, and their experience is not enriched by adding those from outside with experience of running and reforming overburdened national courts. This old friend may be forgiven for saying that younger advocates representing applicants often complain (privately) that they find access to Registry staff difficult and believe that government agents have much easier access.

III. The Independence of the ECtHR

Seven years ago, INTERIGHTS (the International Centre for the Legal Protection of Human Rights) published a report by a group of eminent jurists[47] describing the current system of appointments to the Court, in light of the principles of judicial independence. It contained a number of recommendations. In particular, the report proposed that the Council of Europe should devise and distribute minimum standards for national nomination procedures, and should set up an independent group of experts in international human rights law to make recommendations to the Parliamentary Assembly after having interviewed the candidates. In the words of INTERIGHTS' report, internal processes are 'often inadequate, politicised and so opaque that they are barely understood.... There is no meaningful review of these procedures at the international level, and no effective safeguards against arbitrariness.'

---

[47] *Judicial Independence: Law and Practice of Appointments to the European Court of Human Rights,* May 2003. The authors were: Professor Dr Jutta Limbach, former President of the Federal Constitutional Court of Germany (Chair); Professor Dr Pedro Cruz Villalón, former President of the Constitutional Court of Spain; Mr Roger Errera, former member of the Conseil d'Etat and of the Conseil supérieure de la magistrature in France; Professor Dr Tamara Morshchakova, former Vice President of the Constitutional High Court of the Russian Federation; the Rt Hon Lord Justice Stephen Sedley, of the English Court of Appeal; Professor Dr Andrzej Zoll, former President of the Constitutional High Court of Poland; and myself, as Hon President of INTERIGHTS.

The Parliamentary Assembly has recently called for improvements in national and European procedures, building upon the INTERIGHTS report.[48] They recommend new requirements to make the selection process fair and transparent, and to make it possible for judges to retain judicial office in their own countries while serving as members of the Court, thereby strengthening judicial independence. Fortunately, the rigid and inflexible requirements imposed by the Assembly to secure gender balance have been interpreted by the Court in an advisory opinion so as to secure appointment on the basis of personal merit rather than gender.[49]

Strasbourg judges do not manage the cases in any real sense; that key responsibility is left to the Registry staff. It is the staff who manage the cases and make the vital selection as to which cases have priority and which cases are sent to the judges in batches for summary disposal. Lord Woolf noted in his Review[50] that within the 20 divisions in the Registry, arranged primarily according to language and country, 'there is constant pressure to meet targets and increase productivity'. And again, according to Lord Woolf,[51] the lawyers in the Registry 'work to fulfil numerical targets; they have to complete a certain number of cases each year ... it is often the more important Chamber cases that get left at the bottom of the pile'. It is a factory system, dominated by the Registry, attempting to achieve high productivity in delivering mass production of mainly negative decisions.

Even cases which have been given priority treatment by the Court—urgent cases involving arbitrary arrest and detention, solitary confinement, inhuman and degrading treatment threatening an applicant's health and life, the coerced sterilization of Romani women, and other gross abuses—may be left in abeyance for years. As I know from personal experience, when the lawyers in these cases write to the Registry, they are simply told to wait. The judges remain in ignorance of the way in which priorities are being determined or operated by the Registry. There is a lack of transparency about the relationship between the judges and the Registry, and a lack of a proper system of judicial oversight to ensure that urgent cases are given proper priority. I understand that the Court has been examining this problem and look forward to the publication of the new system for ensuring that urgent cases are dealt with expeditiously. It is really important that the criteria are clear and transparent and widely available.

The Convention envisages[52] that the Court is to be assisted by legal secretaries. It is presumably for the judges, in partnership with the Registry, to decide how that assistance should be provided. Unlike the judges of the ECJ and the International

---

[48] Report of the Committee on Legal Affairs and Human Rights, 'Nomination of candidates and election of Judges to the European Court of Human Rights' Parliamentary Assembly Doc 11767, 1 December 2008. See also Parliamentary Assembly Resolution 1646 (2009).

[49] The Court held that 'in not allowing any exceptions to the rule that the under-represented sex must be represented, the current practice of the Parliamentary Assembly is not compatible with the Convention'. Advisory opinion on certain legal questions concerning the lists of candidates submitted with a view to the election of judges to the European Court of Human Rights, Strasbourg, 12 February 2008.

[50] *Review of the Working Methods of the European Court of Human Rights*, the Rt Hon Lord Woolf et al, December 2005, at 53.

[51] Ibid, 55.   [52] Art 25.

Court of Justice, Strasbourg judges are not assisted by their own *référendaires* in analysing the facts, the law, and the case law, and in seeking to improve the reasoning in the decisions and judgments. They depend on lawyers within the Registry who may be assigned to them in particular cases. If judges wish to do independent research they often have to do it themselves.

It is unlikely that extra funds would be made available to pay for additional support for the judges, but it is important to ensure that their working conditions are such as to attract able candidates to become and remain members of the Court, and that the judges are able themselves to decide cases with adequate time for analysis and reflection. It is also essential to involve the judges themselves in case management. This has been done in the UK with great success, after judges have received the necessary training in case management.

It is also essential in the interests of judicial independence for salaries to be sufficient, and for serving judges to have both security of tenure and security when they return to their home countries after their term of office. Protocol No 14 gives them nine years' tenure, but does not provide for judicial retirement benefits. In 1997, the Committee of Ministers adopted a resolution on the status and conditions of service of judges of the Court to be set up under Protocol No 11.[53] It provided that the conditions of service would be governed by provisional regulations which would be reviewed by the Committee of Ministers within 12 months following the entry into force of Protocol No 11. That review did not take place.

The 'provisional' regulations which remain in force require the judges to provide, at their own expense, for their retirement or pension benefits corresponding with the period of their terms of office, as well as arranging, at their own expense, for insurance for temporary or permanent incapacity to work due to illness or accident, costs of health care, and death. Judges of the Court are well paid while they are in office, but it is very important that they should have proper social cover and security for their retirement. Otherwise, they will fear the consequences if they displease the government of their country and are not renewed in office, leaving them with no prospects of earning a living in a worthwhile occupation on their return home or receiving a pension. This has already happened in at least two cases of judges who were not re-elected, and constitutes a serious threat to judicial independence. There is no justification for treating them less favourably than the judges of the International Court of Justice,[54] or the ECJ.[55]

---

[53] Resolution (97) 9 adopted on 10 September 1997.

[54] The UN General Assembly fixes the conditions for retirement pensions for those judges of the International Court of Justice who have served a full nine-year term at one half the annual salary. There are differing amounts for those serving for shorter or longer periods: Art 32 of the Statute of the Court.

[55] The terms and conditions for judges and advocates-general of the ECJ are set out in European Communities staff regulations. Members of the ECJ belong to the contributory final salary pension scheme paid for from the general EU budget. A contribution of 10.25 per cent is deducted from their monthly basic salary. After ceasing to hold office, members of the ECJ are entitled to a pension for life payable from the age of 65. The amount of pension is calculated on the basis of 4.275 per cent of their final basic salary per year in office. The maximum pension is 70 per cent of the basic salary last received.

Members of the ECJ are entitled to sickness, occupational disease, industrial accident, and birth and death benefits under a social security scheme funded by the Communities, to which they contribute

IV. Serving Justice

Professor Caflisch has asked[56] whether the increase in the Court's output has been at the expense of quality. As a serving judge, he cannot answer that important question. I agree with the group of leading human rights NGOs that:[57]

> The Court has ensured that applicants have obtained redress for violations of human rights when states have failed to provide an appropriate remedy. In doing so it has played a crucial role in holding states accountable for these violations.... The judgments of the Court have provided essential guidance... on the steps necessary to respect and secure fundamental human rights.

Despite the intolerable conditions in which it has to work, the Court has continued to produce landmark judgments of high quality.[58] However, in important areas there is a lack of consistency and coherent principles in Chambers judgments which await clarification by the Grand Chamber.

For example, although the Court's case law includes landmark judgments explaining and applying the fundamental right to free expression, it has often been closely divided, and its reasoning has always suffered from a use of ad hoc balancing under the margin of appreciation doctrine which lacks legal certainty and adherence to clear principles.[59] In recent cases, the Court's case law on free expression has become less consistent and coherent and faithful to legal principle. In the core area of political expression where a speaker seeks to criticize governmental actions, the Court has rightly emphasized that restrictions on speech will be permitted only in the most exceptional circumstances.[60] Because of the role played by politicians in a democratic society, the limits of acceptable criticism of such persons are wider than with respect to private persons.[61]

---

2 per cent of their basic salary. This scheme reimburses 80 per cent of medical costs. See House of Lords Hansard, cols WA165–6, 18 June 2008.

[56] See n 28 above, 405.

[57] Amnesty International et al, n 41 above, para 2.

[58] Recent important Grand Chamber judgments include *Ilascu v Moldova and Russia* Appl no 48787/99 (2004); *Bosphorus Hava Yollari Turizm Ve Ticaret Anonim Sirketi v Ireland* Appl no 45036 (2005); *DH and others v Czech Republic* Appl no 57325/00 (2007); *Saadi v Italy* Appl no 37201/06 (2008); *Nachova v Bulgaria* Appl no 43577/98 (2005); *Hirst v United Kingdom (No 2)* Appl no 74025/01 (2005); *Sørensen & Rasmussen v Denmark* Appl no 52562/99 (2006); *Jalloh v Germany* Appl no 54810 (2006); *Dickson v United Kingdom* Appl no 44362 (2007); *S and Marper v United Kingdom* Appl no 30562/04 (2008); *A and Others v United Kingdom* Appl no 3455/05 (2009); *Rantsev v Cyprus and Russia* Appl no 25965/04 (2010), 22; *Orsus and Others v Croatia* Appl no 15766/03 (2010), 337; *Konstantin Markin v Russia* Appl no 300078/06 (2010), 1435.

[59] A. Lester, 'Universality Versus Subsidiarity: A Reply', 1 *European Human Rights Law Review* (1998), 73.

[60] See eg *Castells v Spain* Series A no 236, 14 *European Human Rights Review* (1992), 445, para 46. However, in the recent case of *Karako v Hungary* (Appl no 39311/05 (2009)) the Court accepted in principle that defamatory comments made in the course of an election campaign by a political opponent could constitute a breach of the claimant's Art 8 rights, although in that case they were insufficiently serious to do so.

[61] *Lingens v Austria* Series A no 103 (1986); *Worm v Austria* Appl no 22714/93 (1997), para 50; *Colombani v France* Appl no 51279/99 (2002).

Unfortunately, in some of its recent decisions concerning situations of conflict between freedom of expression and the right to protection of one's reputation, the Court has not fairly weighed the various interests against each other in order to ascertain whether a fair balance has been struck between the competing rights and interests. Rather, the decisions display a disproportionate weight being given to reputational rights. The most striking example of this is the case *Lindon, Otchakovsky-Laurens and July v France*,[62] as well as the decisions which show the emergence of a dangerous doctrine pursuant to which court-imposed standards or claimed duties of responsible journalism are being invoked to police the way in which the press reports on matters of clear public interest. It is hoped that the Court will curtail the development of this doctrine and return to applying the established jurisprudence which rightly accorded substantial importance to the role and duties of the press in a democratic society, particularly when commenting on the actions of political actors or other public figures.

The problem with the Court's loose invocation of the margin of appreciation is that it removes the need for the Court to discern and explain the criteria appropriate to particular problems. What is needed is a careful, skilful, and consistent application of the principle of proportionality. That is lacking in some of the Court's recent case law.

On 28 January 2010,[63] the President of the Court, President Costa, cited the entering into force of the Lisbon Treaty, Russia's ratification of Protocol No 14, and the Interlaken Conference as three reasons for optimism regarding the Court's reform. However, he also noted that the ever-increasing caseload of the Court meant that urgent reform is ever more necessary. At a press conference in 2009, President Costa outlined a road map for reform. He said that the main lines of the reform were clear, and that they would involve:

comprehensive implementation of the Convention standards at domestic level; effective execution of the Court's judgments by member states to ensure that the Court was not overloaded with large numbers of similar cases and a re-structured protection mechanism allowing the Court's efforts to be concentrated as a matter of priority on the important well-founded cases.[64]

---

[62] *Lindon, Otchakovsky-Laurens and July v France* Appl nos 21279/02, 36447/02 (2007), in which Judge Loucaides said 'The right to reputation should always have been considered as safeguarded by Article 8 of the Convention, as part and parcel of the right to respect for one's private life . . .'. There is some indication of a recent change of direction: in *A v Norway* Appl no 28070/06 (2009) the Court drew attention to the fact that Art 8 does not expressly provide for a right to protection against attacks on personal reputation, unlike Art 12 of the Universal Declaration of Human Rights and Art 17 of the International Covenant on Civil and Political Rights. Further, in *Karako v Hungary* ECHR Appl no 39311/05 (2009) the Court said 'In the Court's case-law, reputation has only been deemed to be an independent right sporadically . . . and mostly when the factual allegations were of such a seriously offensive nature that their publication had an inevitable direct effect on the applicant's private life.'

[63] ECtHR, Press release issued by the Registrar, 'President Costa expresses optimism about prospects for reform', 28 January 2010. See: <http://cmiskp.echr.coe.int/tkp197/view.asp?action=html&documentId=861681&portal=hbkm&source=externalbydocnumber&table=F69A27FD8FB86142BF01C1166DEA398649>.

[64] ECtHR, Press release issued by the Registrar, 'Press conference with the President of the European Court of Human Rights', 29 January 2009. See: <http://cmiskp.echr.coe.int/tkp197/

These praiseworthy aspirations are not likely to be achieved in the current political climate. Comprehensive implementation of the Convention standards at domestic level could happen only if there were the necessary collective will within the Council of Europe and among the governing national authorities to achieve this. That will is at present lacking. And the judicial systems in many European States are not yet genuinely independent and impartial in dealing with human rights cases and other politically sensitive cases. In Professor Caflisch's words, 'A reason for the high number of applications from Eastern Europe is the distrust of individuals vis-à-vis their national judicial systems.'[65]

Effective execution requires speedy and full compliance by the States with their obligation to abide by the Court's judgments and effective monitoring of the obligation of States Parties to abide by the Court's judgments. Many governments are not complying with that obligation, and are not called to account by their Parliaments for failing to do so.[66] At the end of 2009, about 8,600[67] cases were pending before the Committee of Ministers of the Council of Europe in its supervisory capacity. Despite the best efforts of the dedicated staff of the Director-ate of Human Rights, the Committee finds it difficult to muster sufficient collective energy to secure speedy and proper execution by recalcitrant governments.

President Costa did not amplify his reference to a 'restructured protection mechanism'. This could mean a judicial filtering system as recommended by the Group of Wise Persons, or a new two-tier system of Commission or Court of First Instance and a Final Court, or further limiting or even abolishing the right of individual petition. I would suppose that President Costa agrees with the Group of

---

view.asp?action=html&documentId=846335&portal=hbkm&source=externalbydocnumber&table=F69A27FD8FB86142BF01C1166DEA398649>.

[65] See n 28 above, 405. That is why the proposal by Professor Laurence R. Helfer to embed the Convention regime as a 'deep structural principle' in national legal systems lacks practical reality: 'Redesigning the ECHR: Embeddedness as a Deep Structural Principle of the European Human Rights Regime', 19 *European Journal of International Law* (2008), 125. Every Contracting State has already purported to do this, but Helfer's proposals depend on the existence of independent and impartial courts willing to act in partnership with the European Court of Human Rights, eg by asking the Strasbourg Court to review the Convention-compatibility of existing or proposed legislation. Apart from the matter of the capacity of national courts to carry out this task in many Contracting States, this proposal would further burden the Court with the need to give advisory opinions on proposed or actual legislation. It would interrupt and delay the law-making processes of national legislatures, and would tend to violate the separation of the judicial from the other branches of government.

[66] Committee of Ministers, 'Supervision of the execution of judgments of the European Court of Human Rights', 1st annual report, 2007, Council of Europe, March 2008; Recommendation CM/Rec (2008) 2 of the Committee of Ministers to member states on efficient domestic capacity for rapid execution of judgments of the European Court of Human Rights; Parliamentary Assembly Resolution 1516 (2006) on Implementation of judgments of the European Court of Human Rights; Committee on Legal Affairs and Human Rights, AS/Jur (2008) 24, 26 May 2008. In the UK, the Joint Parliamentary Committee on Human Rights monitors the government's response to the judgments of the European Court of Human Rights as well as of the judgments of domestic courts: 'Monitoring the Government's Response to Human Rights Judgments: Annual Report 2008', HL Paper 2173; HC 1078, 7 October 2008.

[67] Enhancing Parliament's role in relation to human rights judgments, Fifteenth Report of the Joint Committee on Human Rights, Session 2009–10, HL 85/HC 455 (para 3).

Wise Persons[68] that to give the Court a discretionary power (analogous to the *certiorari* procedure of the US Supreme Court) to decide whether or not to take up cases would be:

alien to the philosophy of the European human rights protection system. The right of individual application is a key component of the control mechanism of the Convention and the introduction of a mechanism based on the *certiorari* procedure would call it into question and thus undermine the philosophy underlying the Convention. Furthermore, a greater margin of appreciation would entail a risk of politicising the system as the Court would have to select cases for examination. The choices might lead to inconsistencies and might even be considered arbitrary.

In my view, the problems of the present system should not result in yet further procedural obstacles to the right of individual application. As Michael O'Boyle rightly observes[69] the success of the Convention system is 'undoubtedly linked to the immeasurable value over the years of the right of individual petition' and that right should not be 'trammelled or curtailed in any way'. Instead, there is a pressing need to create a new streamlined two-tier system which would enable the Grand Chamber of the Court to concentrate its efforts, as a matter of priority, on cases involving serious questions of public importance about the interpretation and application of the Convention. At the same time, there needs to be a body— whether a judicial filtering system within the Court, or a Commission or a Court of First Instance—to deal fairly and speedily with admissibility in all cases. In my view, it would be important for the body to be able to establish the facts, as was done by the European Commission of Human Rights.

V. A View to the Future

A new Protocol No 15 will be needed to make these changes, but there are reforms which could now be made without waiting for further amendments to the Convention. The Court is rightly requiring State authorities to provide effective remedies and to eliminate systemic practices which violate Convention rights. The pilot judgment procedure is important in enabling the Court to deal with repetitive complaints that highlight such practices. But the Court needs to develop a fair procedure for dealing with pilot cases so that other parties with a common interest are able to be represented. And the Committee of Ministers must be more vigorous in ensuring that States introduce effective general measures to eliminate systemic and structural problems and provide effective remedies to victims.

In addition, the Court should enable its judges to decide, in cooperation with the Registry, which cases should be given priority, and what procedure should be adopted for those cases. The criteria should be developed and made public.

---

[68] Report of the Group of Wise Persons to the Committee of Ministers, CM(2006)203, 15 November 2006, para 42.
[69] See n 1 above, 3–4.

The power conferred on the Secretary General of the Council of Europe to obtain explanations from Contracting States on the manner in which their internal laws ensure the effective implementation of the Convention has fallen into disuse. It should be activated. And the Committee of Ministers should be more rigorous in requiring States to abide by judgments of the Court by which they are directly bound, as well as seeking to ensure that judgments of general importance are given effect across Europe—the so-called *erga omnes* principle.

President Costa has rightly called for a Special Conference to consider the future of the Court and Convention system. It should consider what kind of Court we need, and with what level of political and financial support. There is an urgent need to take stock and strengthen the foundations of what has been built up over the past 50 years. One risk in holding such a conference is that it could be used to dismantle, to wreck, and to weaken. The moment of reform of any type is always a dangerous one. There are certainly States whose governments would dearly love to have the opportunity to hobble the Court. But the risks should be faced and overcome.

To adapt the poet's description of the Mosaic Code,[70] the ethical and legal code protected by the Convention system is 'a moon for mutable lampless men'. It is often described as a beacon of hope for the 800 million peoples of Europe. But the lamplighters who lit the beacon more than half a century ago are no more, and the light will fail unless our generation rekindles the flame. Let us hope that those who govern us will take heed.

---

[70] Isaac Rosenberg, 'The Jew'.

PART II
LAW AND LEGITIMIZATION

7

The Reform of the Convention System: Institutional Restructuring and the (Geo-) Politics of Human Rights

Robert Harmsen

A language of imperative reform, suggesting that measures are urgently required to save a system at breaking point, has perhaps in its own way become something of a reassuring constant for those concerned with the institutional system established by the European Convention on Human Rights (ECHR). For some three decades now, discussions of the reforms needed to deal with a rapidly (indeed exponentially) growing caseload have figured prominently in any analysis of the future prospects of the Convention system. Already in 1983, the then European Commission on Human Rights expressed its concern at the 'serious backlog' of cases which risked developing, and stressed that it was 'high time to provide the organs of the Convention with the means to cope with this situation, while maintaining the quality of their work and the confidence which they enjoy'.[1] At the time, the Strasbourg institutions were dealing with an average of some 400 new petitions per year. It need hardly be added that this sense of urgency has not diminished in the present period, where the European Court of Human Rights (ECtHR) is confronted with over 50,000 new petitions per year, and an accumulated backlog over the 100,000 mark.

There have, of course, been major reform efforts in the intervening years. One need hardly be reminded that the entire institutional architecture of the Strasbourg system was overhauled in the 1990s, with the entry into force in 1998, after long negotiations, of Protocol No 11. It rapidly became apparent, however, that the new structures (centred on a single, full-time court), if undoubtedly permitting certain advances, were nonetheless in themselves not entirely adequate to face the growing pressures on the Strasbourg system. Only two short years after the establishment of the new court, a further reform process, 'the reform of the reform', was initiated. The November 2000 Rome Ministerial Conference on Human Rights called on

---

[1] Memorandum of 17 November 1983, cited in 'Functioning of the Organs of the European Convention on Human Rights: Assessment, Improvement and Reinforcement of the International Control Machinery set up by the Convention', Report submitted by the Swiss Delegation to the European Ministerial Conference on Human Rights, Vienna, 19–20 March 1985, reprinted in 5 *Human Rights Law Journal* (1985), 99.

the Committee of Ministers to identify the measures necessary for the Court to maintain its effectiveness relative to the 'new situation' in which it found itself.[2] This process of reflection subsequently led to the drafting of Protocol No 14, containing a further package of reform measures intended to secure the efficient functioning of the Convention system, opened for signature in May 2004. Long stalled by Russian non-ratification,[3] Protocol No 14 finally entered into force on 1 June 2010. Yet, long before this date, this new reform package also appeared to have been overtaken by events—widely coming to be seen as a necessary, but by no means sufficient, remedy for the system's persisting ills. To this end, two major reports, the 2005 report of Lord Woolf on the working methods of the Court[4] and the more wide-ranging 2007 report of the Group of Wise Persons,[5] sought to set the stage for a further round of reform discussions—'the reform of the reform of the reform', to use a tellingly awkward phrase. A new round of reform discussions was subsequently launched by the February 2010 'Interlaken Declaration',[6] setting out both a 'road map' and an 'Action Plan' for the ongoing adaptation of the Convention system over the course of the next decade.

What to make of this constant refrain of reform? The more comforting response, and that which shapes much of the official discourse surrounding the reform process, is that the Court is essentially the 'victim of its success'. A uniquely effective instrument of human rights protection, having established a wide-ranging and ambitious human rights jurisprudence, the Court, it is argued, has a natural 'attractiveness' for a growing range of litigants. The burgeoning numbers of applications with which the Court must deal are thus simply the price of its success, albeit a price which it can perhaps ill-afford given its current resources.

There is obviously much to be said for the 'success story' explanation of the ongoing reform preoccupations of the Strasbourg system. Clearly, the attractiveness of the Convention system to growing numbers of applicants in a growing range of countries is, in some sense, an undoubted testimony to the system's independence

---

[2] European Ministerial Conference on Human Rights, Rome, 3–4 November 2000, Declaration: 'The European Convention on Human Rights at 50: What Future for the Protection of Human Rights in Europe?', H-conf(2000)001.

[3] Faced with the repeated refusal of the Russian Duma to ratify Protocol No 14, moves were made in May 2009 to secure a partial, provisional implementation of the Protocol's key institutional provisions. A Protocol No 14 bis and attendant 'Agreement of Madrid' were adopted, both of which allowed States to opt in to the application of the Protocol's reformed judicial procedures as regards cases lodged against them, pending the entry into force of the text in its entirety.

[4] Lord Woolf, *Review of the Working Methods of the European Court of Human Rights*, December 2005, available at: <http://www.echr.coe.int/NR/rdonlyres/40C335A9-F951-401F-9FC2-241CDB8A9D9A/0/LORDWOOLFREVIEWONWORKINGMETHODS.pdf>.

[5] *Report of the Group of Wise Persons to the Committee of Ministers*, 15 November 2006, CM(2006) 203. See also *Future Developments of the European Court of Human Rights in the light of the Wise Persons' Report: Colloquy organised by the San Marino Chairmanship of the Committee of Ministers of the Council of Europe* (Strasbourg: Council of Europe, 2007).

[6] High Level Conference on the Future of the European Court of Human Rights, Interlaken Declaration, 19 February 2010, available at: <http://www.eda.admin.ch/etc/medialib/downloads/edazen/topics/europa/euroc.Par.0133.File.tmp/final_en.pdf>. See further the collected *Preparatory Contributions*, published by the Directorate General of Human Rights and Legal Affairs, Council of Europe, H/INF (2010).

and effectiveness. Yet, at the same time, it would clearly be inadequate to examine contemporary reform debates only in terms of the need to 'manage success'. The Court's 'success' is not only that of its own 'attractiveness', but also that, necessarily, of wider dysfunctions or shortcomings in the protection of fundamental rights at the national level. In particular, the Court has seen its role shift in the past two decades from a position in which it functioned essentially as an arbiter of the 'good faith' limits of State power, to one in which it must increasingly deal with serious systematic or systemic violations of fundamental rights. This shift, largely (though not exclusively) tied to the process of enlargement which has seen the Council of Europe expand to a 47-member pan-European organization, has itself called forth further proposals for reform. Here, however, the focus is not so much on the internal mechanics of the Court itself, but rather on the quality of its own systemic relationships with both the Committee of Ministers in its supervisory role and national authorities.

It is thus against this background that the present chapter will survey the major reform processes in the period from the early 1980s through to 2010. The analysis encompasses the formal amendment of the Convention by both Protocols No 11 and No 14, as well as wider changes of practice, but cannot treat in any detail the—at the time of writing—newly launched Interlaken process. The intention through-out is not to provide a detailed analysis of the various reforms concerned, which would be both beyond the scope of this chapter and largely superfluous given the ample literature already available. Rather, these reform processes will be interro-gated as a means to understand the wider evolution of the role of the Convention institutions including, notably, such points of significant consensus or dissensus as have emerged. It will be argued that the core narrative which emerges from such an examination is one which highlights a shift from an almost exclusive concern with questions of institutional mechanics and efficiency to one which has displayed an increasing (if still limited) concern with questions of the constitutional architecture and overriding objectives of the Convention system. If a welcome broadening of concern, it is nonetheless finally argued that reform discussions have thus far continued largely to neglect the wider (geo-)political realities within which the system operates—and that it is precisely such a heightened awareness of the system's political environments which must shape future debate if the Strasbourg institutions are to retain their relevance and effectiveness across a highly diverse set of national human rights situations.

I. Protocol No 11

In retrospect, perhaps the most striking feature of the discussions surrounding Protocol No 11 is their comparatively limited scope. Clearly, the Protocol itself was of substantial import, effecting an overhaul of the institutional machinery of the Convention system which replaced the part-time, two-tiered structure of the Commission and the Court with a full-time, single-tiered (with qualification) Court structure. Yet, though producing a major change, and doing so against the background of a dramatic, co-temporal expansion of the membership of the Convention community, the discussions and negotiations surrounding the Protocol generally assumed a remarkably restricted form—restricted largely to questions of institutional mechanics, and correspondingly eschewing wider considerations of the role or purpose of the Convention system. Discussions, simply put, remained substantially focused at the level of *how* to secure the better functioning of the institutions, in a context where there did not as yet appear to be a need to pose deeper questions as to *what* purposes those institutions were intended to serve.

The main line of division which emerged in the negotiations over Protocol No 11 was unquestionably that concerning the merger of the Commission and the Court. The early running in the reform debates was made almost entirely by proponents of a merger of the two existing Strasbourg institutions into a single, full-time court. The 1985 Swiss proposal to the European Ministerial Conference on Human Rights, which may be seen to have launched formal deliberations over major institutional reform, squarely backed the option of a single, full-time Court as 'the most rational way of effectively ensuring international control of the undertakings accepted by the European States under the Convention'.[7] The single court proposal further won broad expert and governmental backing the following year at the Neuchâtel Colloquy on institutional reform organized under Swiss auspices.[8] As Francis Jacobs noted in his concluding remarks to the conference, only the 'somewhat intriguing combination' of the Court Registrar and the UK government representative appeared to dissent from the prevailing consensus.[9]

A waning of the initial momentum generated by the Swiss proposal, however, progressively saw significant doubts surface as to the wisdom of the proposed merger. This was notably embodied in separate Dutch and Swedish counterproposals, both tabled in 1990, which effectively sought to maintain the existing two-tiered control structure, but in a reformed guise with the Commission upgraded to a fully judicial institution in its own right.[10] Debate about *the* reform thus transformed itself into—occasionally quite ill-tempered—discussions about the relative merits of competing 'single court' and 'two-tiered' reform proposals, with advocates of the two positions actively canvassing support amongst national governments over the period 1990–3. Although the balance of opinion in the Council of Europe's pivotally placed Steering Committee on Human Rights[11]

---

[7] See n 1 above, 114.

[8] The full proceedings were published in 8 *Human Rights Law Journal* (1987), 1.

[9] 'General Report', 8 *Human Rights Law Journal* (1987), 195–6.

[10] 'Modification of the Judicial Control Mechanism of the European Convention on Human Rights: An Overview of the Proposals made by the Dutch and Swedish Authorities', report prepared by the Committee of Experts for the Improvement of Procedures for the Protection of Human Rights (DH-PR), reprinted in *Human Rights Law Review* (1993), 41. The Dutch government acted on the basis of an experts' report drawn up by a group under the chairmanship of ECtHR Judge Pieter van Dijk. The group came to back the two-tiered option despite having started its work from 'the virtually unquestioned starting-point that merger was the obvious solution'. See K. de Vey Mestagh, 'Reform of the European Convention on Human Rights in a Changing Europe' in R. Lawson and M. de Bois (eds), III *The Dynamics of the Protection of Human Rights in Europe: Essays in Honour of Henry G. Schermers* (Dordrecht: Martinus Nijhoff, 1994), 346.

[11] Usually identified by its French acronym CDDH (*Comité directeur des droits de l'homme*).

initially appeared to be tilted towards some form of two-tiered solution, this was gradually reversed so that by the end of 1992 a clear majority of States backed the single court solution.[12] The endgame of the negotiations consequently focused on crafting a proposal which would combine the adoption of a single court model with sufficient concessions to win over the remaining proponents of the two-tiered option. This was achieved by the so-called 'Stockholm Compromise' of May 1993, which saw agreement reached on the principle of allowing for the exceptional rehearing of cases within a single court structure.[13] Undoubtedly an artful political compromise, the resultant provision was also one of the most heavily, and not unreasonably, criticized aspects of the new institutional order.[14]

That which concerns us here is not, however, the coherence of the compromise reached (which has, in practice, proved quite workable), but rather the terms of the debate—or, more specifically, the very limited terms of the debate surrounding the two institutional alternatives. In essence, it is striking that the discussions, though heated at times, remained restricted to the presentation of two alternative modes of operation of the Convention system, neither of which were articulated as representing wider, competing visions of the nature, place, or limits of that system. The single court was presented as the more efficient solution, and one which was perfectly adequate given the 'subsidiary' nature of the European level of supervision.[15] The maintenance of the two-tiered structure, by way of contrast, was largely justified in terms of minimizing disruption to the functioning of the existing institutional system, while also maintaining a clear appellant possibility within the Convention system.[16] Beyond these arguments, however, the division between the two camps did not appear to correspond to any deeper set of discernible political preferences. Although some allegations appeared in French-language literature suggesting the existence of a 'Germanic lobby' which had coordinated its efforts to push for the single court solution as a means of limiting the Convention's reach into national politico-legal systems,[17] these claims were strongly rebutted by well-placed participants in the process.[18] Moreover, such claims would appear to carry little a priori weight insofar as it is difficult to sustain the case that a full-time, single-tier institution is, in some undefined manner, *intrinsically* less well placed to maintain basic standards of human rights protection than the other alternatives

---

[12] A. Drzemczewski, 'A Major Overhaul of the European Human Rights Convention Control Mechanism: Protocol No 11', VI(2) *Collected Course of the European Academy of Law* (1995), 122.

[13] Ibid, 160–1.

[14] For an overview of initial criticisms of Protocol No 11, see H. G. Schermers, 'Adaptation of the 11th Protocol to the European Convention on Human Rights', 20 *European Law Review* (1995), 559.

[15] See eg A. Drzemczewski, 'The Need for a Radical Overhaul', *New Law Journal* (1993), and 'Putting the European House in Order', *New Law Journal* (1994).

[16] See eg H. G. Schermers, 'The Eleventh Protocol to the European Convention on Human Rights', 19 *European Law Review* (1994), 367.

[17] The criticisms are (uncritically) summarized in J. F. Flauss, 'Le Protocole no 11: Côté Cour', 2 *Bulletin des droits de l'homme* (1994), 3.

[18] See notably O. Jacot-Guillarmod, 'Comments on Some Recent Criticisms of Protocol No 11 to the European Convention on Human Rights' in *Eighth International Colloquy on the European Convention on Human Rights* (Strasbourg: Council of Europe, 1996).

under discussion.[19] Rather, the claims themselves appear to fit into a wider pattern in which divisions had appeared within the European human rights community largely in function of differing weights of personal or institutional loyalties, or differing expert assessments of the practical needs of the system, rather than on the basis of more far-reaching, principled oppositions reflecting fundamentally different views of the purposes of the Convention system itself.

The negotiations surrounding Protocol No 11 do, in this respect, point to the emergence of a human rights policy domain significantly defined by the existence of an 'epistemic community' as defined by Peter Haas: 'a network of professionals with recognized expertise and competence in a particular domain and authoritative claim to policy-relevant knowledge in the area'.[20] Sociologically, this 'human rights epistemic community' was made up of legal professionals working both in and around the Strasbourg institutions, including the wider communities of human rights lawyers, legal academics, and governmental officials concerned with the development of the Convention system.[21] This group broadly shared a set of professional norms rooted in the practice and development of human rights law, as well as an attendant commitment to maintain and develop the distinctive European *acquis* in the area. This sense of community was, moreover, reinforced by the participation of many of these actors in ongoing discussions surrounding the Convention system. These debates found their principal expressions in a limited number of specialist journals, together with the regular publication of *Festschriften* or *Mélanges* bringing together many of the community's more prominent figures to honour one of their own. Much of this discussion, moreover, tended to bridge practitioner and academic concerns—in part, during this period, reflecting the 'part-time' character of the Strasbourg institutions, in which members of both the Commission and the Court continued to pursue their parallel national (often academic) careers.

Politically, the central role played by this 'epistemic community' bears further emphasis. In essence, the claim being put forward here is that, by the 1980s, the West European system of human rights protection had achieved a degree of political legitimacy such that questions of its institutional development were largely considered to be 'technical matters', best—and safely—left to the determination of the relevant legal experts. The definition of the parameters for the reform of the human rights system, as detailed above, was thus largely left to those experts, whose discussions centred on issues of practice and process. Wider political concerns, notably as regards issues of national sovereignty and the limits of the European

---

[19] It might be noted, in this respect, that both the Court's long-serving President Rolv Ryssdal and the Council of Europe's Director of Human Rights, Peter Leuprecht, were among the more prominent proponents of the single court solution.

[20] P. M. Haas, 'Introduction: Epistemic Communities and International Policy Co-ordination', 46 *International Organization* (1992), 3.

[21] The role of the national representatives in the CDDH and its subcommittees (including the Committee of Experts for the Improvement of Procedures for the Protection of Human Rights or DH-PR), variously called upon to act as both governmental representatives and independent experts, merits further investigation both in the present reform process and in the longer term development of the Convention system.

regime, were correspondingly little present. Moreover, further following Haas's model,[22] external political intervention appeared to be forthcoming only where the experts themselves were divided. A degree of political pressure appears to have been applied to the expert committees in order to achieve a compromise solution between the two reform proposals prior to the Council of Europe's (first ever) summit in October 1993 in Vienna—but even here, that pressure appears to have been applied principally so as to force the experts to achieve an agreement amongst themselves, rather than with a view to privileging a particular outcome.[23]

The very high degree of political consensus which had come to surround the West European system was further borne out by the relative ease of acceptance of the second major aspect of Protocol No 11, that which might be termed the 'full judicialization' of the Convention protection system. From the early stages of the reform process, proposals had been put forward, taking stock of the evolution of the Convention system, to render obligatory the optional right of individual complaint (ex Art 25) and to remove the judicial role of the Committee of Ministers (ex Art 32). To this could be added the recognition of the compulsory jurisdiction of the Court (ex Art 46) and the right of individual petitioners to bring cases before the Court (optionally instituted by Protocol No 9), insofar as these developments would not otherwise take place in light of the more general reform of the institutional structures. Interestingly, the predominant, and largely unchallenged, presentation of these reforms was that of removing anomalies from the operation of the system; key aspects of the interstate bargain struck in 1950, viewed at the time as necessary safeguards of national sovereignty, had come to be widely perceived as anomalous relative to the evolution of a system which had successfully established its judicial credentials on the basis of a growing body of individual litigation.[24] Indeed, throughout the reform process, no major or systematic opposition appears to have been mounted to this '*achèvement*' or 'full realization' of the institutional system—though a number of more limited rearguard actions were attempted. Most notably, at a relatively late stage in the proceedings (March 1994), a UK government in the throes of a more general post-Maastricht Euroscepticism sought to revert to a system in which the right of individual petition would be recognized by five-year renewable national declarations.[25] The Major government, finding itself

---

[22] '[I]n cases in which scientific evidence is ambiguous and the experts themselves are split into contending factions, issues have tended to be resolved less on their technical merits than on their political ones': Haas, n 20 above, 11.

[23] The generic pressure to have 'something' for the Summit communiqué, but without significant substantive intervention, was confirmed by a number of interviewees during research undertaken by the present author on the genesis of Protocol No 11 in the spring of 1998.

[24] See eg Ronny Abraham who, after identifying the vestigial non-judicial aspects of the Convention system as one of the well-springs of reform, went on to criticize the pre-Protocol No 11 decisional role of the Committee of Ministers in the following terms: 'One is allowed to think that such an anomaly, no doubt inevitable in the context of the initial drafting of the Convention, is hardly acceptable today...': R. Abraham, 'La Réforme du mécanisme de contrôle de la Convention européenne des droits de l'homme: Le Protocole no 11 à la Convention', 40 *Annuaire français de droit international* (1994), 620–1. Abraham was the French representative on the CDDH and the DH-PR in the period leading to the agreement of Protocol No 11.

[25] Drzemczewski, n 12 above, 174–6.

isolated apart from some Turkish interest, did not, however, persist in pursuing this option.[26]

If reflective of a broad political consensus in some of its aspects, Protocol No 11 was nonetheless not, as already suggested, informed by a wider politico-institutional vision of the role of the new Court. Little attention was focused on wider systemic issues, with neither the Court's relationship with its national counterparts nor its position within the wider Council of Europe system being the subject of sustained reflection. Perhaps more strikingly, the question of enlargement also did not figure with any prominence in the later (post-1989) stages of the drafting process. Although the then ongoing enlargement of the Council of Europe was cited by proponents of reform as likely still further to aggravate problems of the Convention institutions' *quantitative* caseload, there appears to have been little consideration of how this enlargement might *qualitatively* reshape the types of cases which could make their way to Strasbourg. The picture which emerges is thus that of a somewhat surprisingly insulated process, reflective of the considerable achievements of the West European human rights system, and the political and expert consensus which had formed around it, but structurally little attuned to the new challenges which the institutions were about to face.

II. Protocol No 14

Relative to Protocol No 11, Protocol No 14 is a markedly modest document, making 'no radical changes to the control system established by the Convention'.[27] Rather, it essentially consists of a package of relatively limited reforms intended to allow for the more efficient functioning of the Convention system, in light of the early experiences of the new Court and the continuing growth in the number of cases coming to Strasbourg. Yet tellingly, the drafting of Protocol No 14 took place against the background of far more wide-ranging debates than those which had been associated with the much more ambitious Protocol No 11. Increased, post-enlargement pressures on the Court have, predictably, led to more sharply defined discussions concerning the institution's core purpose(s), and its limits. Most particularly, debates have taken shape, both in relation to aspects of the Protocol and more widely, pitting distinctively articulated 'constitutionalist' and 'individual justice' visions of the role of the Court.

As with Protocol No 11, core features of Protocol No 14 do, again, largely concern the internal institutional mechanics of the control system, seeking to increase its 'processing capacity'. It is in this vein that a new single-judge formation is introduced and empowered to declare applications as inadmissible 'where such a

---

[26] The issue was also, according to media reports, the subject of a conflict within the British cabinet. The Foreign Secretary, Douglas Hurd, supported accepting the European consensus, while the Home Secretary, Michael Howard, battled to maintain the status quo. See 'Howard Defeat on European Court Rights', *The Times*, 9 May 1994.

[27] Protocol No 14, Explanatory Report, CETS No 194, at para 35.

decision may be taken without further examination'.[28] In a similar vein, the remit of three-judge committees is expanded so as to be able to render judgments in meritorious cases which fall within the well-established boundaries of the Court's existing case law.[29] Yet, beyond this concern with the Court's internal functioning, Protocol No 14 also marks a modest departure relative to the more 'insulated' Protocol No 11, further incorporating limited provisions which concern the articulation of the Court's relationship with the wider Council of Europe system. Specifically, Protocol No 14 sees the first recognition in a Convention text of the Council of Europe's Commissioner of Human Rights, given a general right of third party intervention before the Chambers of the Court.[30] It also creates two new institutionalized channels of communication between the Court and the Committee of Ministers. The Committee, by a two-thirds majority, is empowered to bring infringement proceedings before the Court where it deems that a Member State has failed to comply with a decision, as well as to request an interpretive ruling from the Court where questions have arisen in the enforcement of a decision.[31] These provisions are not without problems, creating difficulties of their own, particularly in the case of the envisaged infringement procedure. Here, the Court had publicly expressed its 'unease' at the introduction of this procedure, noting amongst other considerations that it risked creating confusion in relation to the 'existing clear distinction between the political/executive branch of the Council of Europe and its judicial branch'.[32] Nonetheless, these modest provisions do signal a clear awareness on the part of the Protocol's drafters of the importance of the links between the Court and the Convention's wider institutional machinery in ensuring its proper overall functioning. These specific provisions of the Protocol must, moreover, be placed against the background of the text having been first adopted together with a further package of measures by the Committee of Ministers (one resolution and three recommendations) dealing with the linkage between Strasbourg and the national level.[33]

If further reforming the institutional mechanics of the control system and marking a small 'systemic turn', the aspect of Protocol No 14 which has garnered

---

[28] Protocol No 14, Art 6, inserting a new Art 27 ECHR.

[29] Ibid, Art 8, amending Art 28 ECHR.

[30] Ibid, Art 13, creating a new Art 13(3) ECHR. The Commissioner, with the backing of the Parliamentary Assembly, had campaigned for a more far-reaching provision, creating a form of '*actio populatis*' whereby he would have been empowered to bring cases directly before the Court. Many members of the CDDH, however, felt that the assumption of such a 'prosecutorial' role would sit poorly with the office's core functions as regards the promotion of human rights in the Member States (as well as its potential role in aiding States in the execution of Court decisions). For a wider discussion of the question, see M. I. van Dooren, 'Betere naleving van het EVRM door vergorting van de rol van de Human Rights Commissioner', 28 *NJCM-Bulletin* (2003), 530–3.

[31] Protocol No 14, Art 16, amending Art 46 ECHR.

[32] Response of the European Court of Human Rights to the CDDH Interim Activity Report prepared following the 26th Plenary Administrative Session, 2 February 2004, at para 29. If ultimately unable to block the adoption of the provision, the Court was, nonetheless, successful in its opposition to the introduction of a system of '*astreintes*' (financial penalties), which had been strongly advocated in the Parliamentary Assembly.

[33] See nn 55–8 below.

by far and away the most critical attention is nonetheless that of its introduction of a new admissibility criterion. In addition to the existing criteria, the Protocol allows the Court to rule a petition as inadmissible where 'the applicant had not suffered a significant disadvantage', unless the case otherwise raised what the Court deems to be important questions and provided that it had been duly heard by a national tribunal.[34] The precise scope of this new admissibility criterion is open to doubt. The measure's proponents clearly view it as something of a readily usable 'catch-all' clause, giving the Court a more expeditious means of removing large numbers of otherwise inadmissible cases from its overloaded docket. In this vein, the *Explanatory Report* to the Protocol lauds the measure as potentially facilitating 'the more rapid disposal of unmeritorious cases', going on to specify that 'Once the Court's Chambers have developed clear-cut jurisprudential criteria of an objective character capable of straightforward application, the new criterion will be easier for the Court to apply than some other admissibility criteria'.[35] Yet, critics have argued that decisions made under this new provision risk being far from 'clear-cut' or 'straightforward'. In effect, as finally agreed,[36] the provision will require the Court to make three separate determinations concerned respectively with the putative importance of the alleged violation for the applicant, the putative importance of any questions raised for the wider respect and development of human rights, and the existence of an effective domestic remedy.[37] It thus becomes difficult to see, a priori, how this mechanism might operate any more expeditiously than the existing admissibility criteria. Indeed, it might prove, in practice, to be little more than a form of *de minimis* clause, an additional criterion by which a small percentage of currently admissible cases would be removed from the Court's docket. Nevertheless, whatever its likely practical effects, the new criterion does clearly raise major—and sharply contested—questions of principle. The underlying logic of the criterion, suggesting that the Court was not bound to treat *all* violations of human rights, but only those of a 'more serious' character (however defined), was taken by critics as marking the beginning of an unacceptable redefinition of the institution's role—in this, both paralleling and further fuelling a more general debate about the nature and limits of the Strasbourg Court's remit.

This more general debate, in terms now well set out in the literature, opposes what have been labelled as 'constitutional' and 'individual justice' visions of the role

---

[34] Protocol No 14, Art 12, amending Art 35(3) ECHR.

[35] Explanatory Report to Protocol No 14, para 79.

[36] A majority of the Court had, notably, expressed its support for the introduction of a more sweeping criterion, which would have allowed for a declaration of inadmissibility whenever 'respect for human rights as defined in the Convention and the Protocols thereto does not require examination of the application': Response, n 32 above, para 21. The envisaged provision, which would have given the Court a very flexible (not to say open-ended) instrument of docket control, was rejected by the CDDH.

[37] See M. A. Beernaert, 'Protocol 14 and New Strasbourg Procedures: Towards Greater Efficiency? And at What Price?', 9 *European Human Rights Law Review* (2004), 544; R. A. A. Böcker, 'Protocol nr 14 bij het EVRM: hervorming van de hervorming', 79 *Nederlands Juristenblad* (2004), 1842.

of the Court.[38] 'Constitutionalists'[39] essentially argue that the core function of the Court is that of a pan-European standard-setter, with individual cases in effect serving as the vehicle by which problems are signalled and principles established. Following from this logic, it is not the primary role of the Court, even if this were practically possible, to provide a remedy for every individual-level violation of human rights. Rather, it is the function of the Court to ensure that national legislation and practice remains consistent with Convention standards, and that adequate remedies are provided at the domestic level where this may be in doubt. By way of contrast, the individual justice model holds that it is precisely the provision of remedies for individual-level violations of human rights which is the institution's *raison d'être*, as well as the distinctive marker of its 'success' relative to other regional or international human rights instruments. Proponents of the individual justice model further argue that any attempt by the Court to restrict its caseload—either by way of the 'significant disadvantage' criterion or through the adoption of a more robust US-style *certiorari* mechanism—would seriously risk compromising its legitimacy. Here, they argue that the diversity of the Convention community would not allow for the easy or readily accepted operation of a *certiorari* procedure,[40] while also pointing to the attendant problems of real or perceived 'fairness' likely to arise in a scenario where the Court would be seen as 'picking and choosing' those matters which it thought worthy to pursue.[41]

The lines of division surrounding the two positions are interesting. The Court itself was divided on the question. Its President, Luzius Wildhaber, was a prominent advocate of the constitutionalist position—having played a key role in launching the debate by way of a widely cited 2002 article in the *Human Rights Law Journal*.[42] In the article, President Wildhaber pointedly posed the dilemma facing the Court, and called for a corresponding redefinition of its role:

---

[38] For fuller discussions, see S. Greer, *The European Convention on Human Rights: Achievements, Problems and Prospects* (Cambridge: Cambridge University Press, 2006); R. Harmsen, 'The European Court of Human Rights as a "Constitutional Court": Definitional Debates and the Dynamics of Reform' in J. Morison, K. McEvoy, and G. Anthony (eds), *Judges, Transition, and Human Rights: Essays in Memory of Stephen Livingstone* (Oxford: Oxford University Press, 2007).

[39] The term is presently used in a comparatively broad, political sense, suggestive of the foundational or constitutive importance of the issues on which the Court is called to adjudicate. This is significantly distinct from the more technical question of the extent to which the ECtHR performs functions analogous to those of a constitutional court (typically on the Kelsenian model) in a domestic politico-legal system. On this latter question, see J. F. Flauss, 'La Cour européenne est-elle une Cour constitutionnelle?' in J. F. Flauss and M. de Salvia (eds), *La Convention européenne des droits de l'homme: Développements récents et nouveaux défis* (Brussels: Bruylant, 1997) (also reprinted in 36 *Revue française de droit constitutionnel* (1999)).

[40] Cf F. Benoît-Rohmer, 'Il faut sauver le recours individuel...', 38 *Recueil Dalloz* (2003), 2584 and 'Les perspectives de réforme à long terme de la Cour EDH: "*certiorari*" versus renvoi préjudiciel', 14 *Revue universelle des droits de l'homme* (2002), 313.

[41] Cf W. Thomassen, 'Het individuele klachtrecht moet behouden blijven: Over het Europees Hof voor de Rechten van de Mens en zijn toekomst', 28 *NJCM-Bulletin* (2003), 11.

[42] L. Wildhaber, 'A Constitutional Future for the European Court of Human Rights?', 23 *Human Rights Law Journal* (2002), 161 (also published in the *HRLJ*'s French and German language sister publications).

Will we really be able to claim that with say 30,000 cases a year, full, effective access can be guaranteed? Is it not better to take a more realistic approach to the problem and preserve the essence of the system, in conformity with its fundamental objective, with the individual application being seen as a means to an end itself, as the magnifying glass which reveals the imperfections in national legal systems, as the thermometer which tests the democratic temperature of States? Is it not better for there to be far fewer judgments, but promptly delivered and extensively reasoned ones which establish the jurisprudential principles with a compelling clarity that will render them de facto binding *erga omnes*, while at the same time revealing the structural problems which undermine democracy and the rule of law in parts of Europe?[43]

The Court's Registrar, Paul Mahoney, was similarly amongst the more vocal proponents of the constitutionalist thesis—stressing, in provocative language, that the Strasbourg institution risked becoming a pan-European 'small claims court' if it were not more clearly refocused on its broader public policy function.[44] At the same time, however, strong voices made themselves heard amongst the judges in defence of maintaining a system in which the Court continued to see its principal role as that of providing remedies to all individual victims of human rights violations who petition it. Most notably, the three Benelux judges together with their Andorran counterpart[45] published a joint note in which they strongly argued that an admissibility criterion of the type ultimately incorporated in Protocol No 14 would do little to improve the Court's efficiency, while seriously compromising its hard-won credibility and authority.[46] In their view, the reform risked further placing the European system on the wrong side of welcome international trends, by restricting access to the Court at the very moment when the 'judicialization' of international human rights protection appeared to be gaining ground.

These issues also resonated in the academic community of human rights specialists. Here, the constitutionalist position garnered some support. Professor Rick Lawson, for example, argued in memorable terms that the Court could only act to guarantee that 'the ship of state is seaworthy', but could not 'rescue every drowning person'.[47] Majority academic opinion, however, came down squarely on the side of the individual justice thesis. Proponents of this position argued, inter alia, that the Court essentially derived its legitimacy from its role as a guardian of individual rights, and that its function as a 'standard-setter' could not be divorced from this provision of individual justice.[48]

---

[43] Ibid, 164.

[44] P. Mahoney, 'An Insider's View of the Reform Debate (How to Maintain the Effectiveness of the European Court of Human Rights)', 29 *NJCM-Bulletin* (2004), 175.

[45] Judges Josep Casadavell (Andorra), Marc Fischbach (Luxembourg), Wilhelmina Thommassen (the Netherlands), and Françoise Tulkens (Belgium).

[46] 'Pour le droit de recours individuel', reprinted as Annex 3 in G. Cohen-Jonathan and C. Pettiti (eds), *La réforme de la Cour européenne des droits de l'homme* (Brussels: Bruylant, 2003).

[47] R. Lawson, 'De mythe van het moeten: Het Europees Hof voor de Rechten van de Mens en 800 miljoen klagers', 28 *NJCM-Bulletin* (2003), 130.

[48] T. Barkhuysen and M. L. van Emmerick, 'De Toekomst van het EHRM: Meer middelen voor effectievere rechtsbescherming', 28 *NJCM-Bulletin* (2003), 298.

Finally, in contrast to the debates surrounding Protocol No 11, the very active role assumed by human rights NGOs in the discussions surrounding Protocol No 14 and wider attendant issues should be underlined.[49] Leading human rights NGOs intervened, in particular, to express their opposition to the introduction of the new admissibility hurdle, strongly making the case that the Court must remain a refuge for all those who have suffered a violation of their rights for which they cannot find adequate remedy within their domestic legal system. The joint response document addressing the proposed reform of the Convention, signed by 114 NGOs, thus pointedly observed in relation to the 'significant disadvantage' criterion: 'We consider that *all* violations of human rights are "significant" and that the individual victim, members of the community, and the integrity of the authorities suffer "disadvantage" when violations of human rights go without redress'.[50]

If somewhat robustly expressed, the practical consequences of these divisions must not, however, be overstated. At base, the Court, by its nature, will continue to perform both functions—that of 'constitutional standard-setting' and that of providing individual remedies—with the question being rather more one of how these two functions are to be balanced. In this regard, it is perhaps worth underlining that the constitutionalist/individual justice division does not appear to translate as a more general line of division within the Court; well-defined 'schools' of Convention interpretation, grounded in differing views of the underlying purposes of the system, do not appear to have emerged.[51] Indeed, it might be argued that the most important aspect of this debate concerned not the substantive definition of the two positions, but rather the fact that it was taking place at all. In many respects, a dialogue of this type, involving both members of the Court and wider concerned publics, was groundbreaking; never before had the broad terms of the institution's mandate and future development been discussed in such a sustained fashion. In this, moreover, the debates about and around Protocol No 14 are reflective of a more general trend. As discussed in the following section, reform discussions have increasingly sought to move beyond a vision of the Court as an 'isolated institution', rethinking the wider pattern of institutional relationships which make up the Convention system.

---

[49] The increased presence of NGOs in the reform process merits further investigation. Speculatively, three factors might variably account for this enhanced role: (a) a more general increase in the level of engagement by human rights NGOs with the Convention system, particularly in the post-enlargement period (cf Cichowski, Chapter 5 above); (b) a desire for greater openness or transparency on the part of Council of Europe authorities; and (c) the increased ease of communication and ready availability of the relevant documentation via the internet (in contrast to all but the final stages of the discussions surrounding Protocol No 11).

[50] (Updated) Joint Response to Proposals to Ensure the Future Effectiveness of the European Court of Human Rights, April 2004, para 28, available at: <http://www.amnesty.org/en/library/info/IOR61/008/2003>. See also J. Wadham and T. Said, 'What Price the Right of Individual Petition?: Report of the Evaluation Group to the Committee of Ministers on the European Court of Human Rights', 7 *European Human Rights Law Review* (2002), 169.

[51] It might, however, be noted that the four judges who were signatories to the joint brief 'Pour le recours individuel', cited at n 46 above, are all placed towards the 'activist' end of the spectrum developed by Voeten in Chapter 4 above.

III. The Wider Canvas of Reform

The wider pattern of reform discussions surrounding the Convention, as suggested in the previous sections, is one which has seen a 'unique' focus on the Court itself (as with Protocol No 11) progressively give way to a wider systemic view. This systemic perspective is, as the name suggests, one which views the Convention as being rooted in a *system* of human rights protection, which concerns not only the Court, but also national-level authorities and the political organs of the Council of Europe. This systemic turn has, in part, been borne of immediate practical necessity, as the Strasbourg institutions seek to lighten their own excessive load by 'repatriating' problem areas back to a national level a priori better able to provide individual remedies in a large number of repetitive cases. Yet, beyond the inevitable pressures of 'the numbers', this systemic turn also reflects a wider rethinking of institutional roles triggered by the now fully apparent effects of enlargement on the Strasbourg system. Most notably, issues of implementation, long confined to the relative margins of discussions about the Convention system,[52] have come to assume an increasing prominence in a context where the traditional presumption of a 'good faith' response by Member States to Court decisions no longer uniformly holds store.

A full understanding of the reform of the European human rights system consequently entails that one move beyond an exclusive concern with the 'heavy machinery' of amending protocols to the Convention, further examining the more modest, but significant practical adaptations which have been made by the Strasbourg institutions in response to their radically changed circumstances. The present section does this, looking at the practical rearticulation of the relationships between the three main actors in the implementation of the Convention—the Committee of Ministers, the Court, and national authorities.[53] Specifically, the first section, focused on the Committee of Ministers, surveys the development of a more detailed normative framework by the Committee for national implementation, as well as the reform of its own working practices in its supervisory role. This is in turn followed by a discussion of the principal jurisprudential innovations by which the Court has concomitantly sought to rearticulate its relationship with the wider Convention system, re-emphasizing the primary responsibility of national authorities,

---

[52] C. Tomuschat, 'Quo Vadis, Argentoratum?: The Success Story of the European Convention on Human Rights—And a Few Dark Stains', 13 *Human Rights Law Journal* (1992), 401.

[53] Beyond the Convention system *stricto sensu*, the Parliamentary Assembly, through its Legal Affairs and Human Rights Committee, has also taken an increasing interest in the effective enforcement of Court decisions (notably through the work of successive rapporteurs, Erik Jurgens and Christos Pourgourides). The committee monitors and publicly reports on the execution of Court judgments, treating both specific cases and more general problems. It has also passed a number of recommendations and resolutions seeking to define good practice and encourage reform in the area. See, inter alia, Resolution 1226(2000) on the execution of judgments of the European Court of Human Rights, adopted 28 September 2000, as well as Resolution 1516(2006) and Recommendation 1764(2006) on the implementation of judgments of the European Court of Human Rights, adopted 2 October 2006.

while also by extension placing greater onus on the supervisory role of the Committee of Ministers. A generally heightened awareness of the need for the Convention system to function *as a system* will thus be shown to have clearly emerged over the course of the past decade. Such welcome developments must, however, be further placed against the sombre background of a situation in which the limits of the essentially 'consensus-based' Convention system, when faced with structural violations of human rights, have also become increasingly apparent.

The Committee of Ministers

A revitalized concern with questions of national-level implementation already found expression at the very beginning of the 2000s with a January 2000 Committee of Ministers recommendation calling on Member States to make provision for the reopening of judicial proceedings in light of ECtHR judgments.[54] The recommendation essentially sought to resolve an anomaly whereby individual plaintiffs who had won a favourable decision in Strasbourg might subsequently be unable to obtain a remedy before domestic courts insofar as, by definition, they had already exhausted all domestic remedies.

Four years later, as already noted, the agreement of Protocol No 14 was accompanied by the simultaneous adoption of a package of measures intended to improve the domestic application of the Convention. This package included three recommendations concerned respectively with: ensuring that an appropriate place is given to the Convention in relevant university and professional training courses;[55] providing for the vetting of the Convention compatibility of domestic legislation and administrative practice;[56] and securing improved domestic remedies for the redress of violations of Convention rights.[57] This was further complemented by a resolution calling on the Court clearly to identify the existence of a 'systemic problem' in its judgments, so that such underlying or structural deficiencies might be prioritized by the Committee of Ministers in its supervisory role.[58] This latter recommendation gave practical effect to the Court's request for the introduction of a 'pilot judgment' procedure whereby an individual case might be used as an exemplar for the treatment of a wider problem generating a substantial body of applications.[59]

---

[54] Recommendation Rec(2000)2 on the re-examination or re-opening of certain cases at domestic level following judgments of the European Court of Human Rights. Adopted by the Committee of Ministers, 19 January 2000.

[55] Recommendation Rec(2004)4 on the European Convention on Human Rights in university education and professional training. Adopted by the Committee of Ministers, 12 May 2004.

[56] Recommendation Rec(2004)5 on the verification of the compatibility of draft laws, existing laws and administrative practice with the standards laid down in the European Convention on Human Rights. Adopted by the Committee of Ministers, 12 May 2004.

[57] Recommendation Rec(2004)6 on the improvement of domestic remedies. Adopted by the Committee of Ministers, 12 May 2004. This should be seen in conjunction with the Court's *Kudla* line of jurisprudence. See n 72 below.

[58] Resolution Res(2004)3 on judgments revealing an underlying systemic problem. Adopted by the Committee of Ministers, 12 May 2004.

[59] Position Paper of the European Court of Human Rights on Proposals for the Reform of the European Court of Human Rights and Other Measures set out in the Report of the Steering

More recently, the Committee of Ministers agreed upon a further recommendation in 2008 concerned with the 'rapid execution' of ECtHR judgments at the domestic level.[60] Amongst other measures, this recommendation called on Member States to designate a coordinating body or individual to assume overall responsibility for the national execution of judgments. This most recent recommendation thus joins a growing body of prescriptive norms whereby the Member State governments of the Council of Europe have, collectively, set out increasingly detailed road maps for the correct domestic implementation of the Convention, covering both the direct remedy of adjudicated violations and the wider anchoring of Convention norms in practice and 'culture' at the national level.

This has been further accompanied by the significant reform of the working practices of the Committee of Ministers in its supervisory capacity. Following a Norwegian initiative, new working methods were adopted in 2004 which both systematized the follow-up of national implementation measures (including the introduction of the so-called 'status sheet'—a summary document on the follow-up of each judgment) and streamlined discussions in human rights meetings so as to focus more clearly on problem areas.[61] The supervisory process has also, to a limited extent, been opened up to external interveners. New rules adopted in May 2006 notably made explicit provision for the receipt of communications from NGOs and national human rights institutions,[62] apt to be of particular importance when the Committee is dealing with instances of generalized or systemic violations. The general accessibility of information concerning the supervisory process has also been markedly improved. A (well-designed) website allows for the easy tracking of the implementation of all judgments on a State-by-State basis. The Committee, following a recommendation made during the 2004 high-level Oslo seminar,[63] further adopted the practice from 2007 and onwards of issuing annual reports which provide an overview of the enforcement of judgments.[64] Overall, there have thus been important moves towards both formalizing the supervisory system and, more importantly, rendering it more

---

Committee for Human Rights of 4 April 2003 (CDDH(2003)006final), 23 September 2003, at paras 43–6. The Court's later insistence that the mechanism be adopted by way of Convention amendment failed, however, to sway the CDDH. For the Court's position, see Response, n 32 above, para 37c. The subsequent use of the pilot judgment procedure is discussed at nn 74 et seq below.

[60] Recommendation Rec(2008)2 on efficient domestic capacity for rapid execution of judgments of the ECtHR. Adopted by the Committee of Ministers, 6 February 2008.

[61] Human Rights working methods—Improved effectiveness of the Committee of Ministers' supervision of execution of judgments, Ministers' Deputies information document, 7 April 2004, CM/Inf(2004)8 Final. See further the 'Norwegian Non-Paper: Summary of New Working Methods adopted by the Committee of Ministers' Deputies in April 2004' in *Reform of the European Human Rights System: Proceedings of the High-level Seminar, Oslo, 18 October 2004* (Strasbourg: Directorate General of Human Rights/Council of Europe, 2004).

[62] Rules of the Committee of Ministers for the supervision of the execution of judgments and of the terms of friendly settlements, 10 May 2006, rule 9.2.

[63] 'Conclusions of the Seminar' in *Reform of the European Human Rights System*, n 61 above, at 7, 11 (para 23), available at: <http://sutyajnik.ru/rus/echr/etc/reformeurhrsystem.pdf>.

[64] Available at: <http://www.coe.int/t/DGHL/Monitoring/Execution/Documents/Publications_en.asp>.

publicly transparent. Criticisms concerning aspects of the system's accessibility may certainly still be made.[65] Equally, issues also arise as regards the comparatively limited resources possessed by the execution of judgments unit within the Council of Europe secretariat.[66] Nonetheless, one could reasonably argue that the procedures currently in place provide, at base, adequate means for the 'naming and shaming' of persistent violators.

The real question, indeed, for the supervisory organs of the Council of Europe system is now rather less that of their ability to track and publicize persisting violations, than that of the potentially limited impact of such public 'shaming'. While the keys to Convention compliance, as discussed further below, remain at the national level, the 'added-value' of the Convention's intergovernmental enforcement mechanism is that of a form of peer pressure. National authorities possessed of the sentiment that they are part of a community of 'like-minded States', whose collectively evolving standards are accepted as a legitimate benchmark, will generally see the rectification of identified shortcomings as an obligation.[67] Yet, if this sense of a shared consensus has not established itself, or at the least is not otherwise developing relative to wider dynamics of constraint and cooptation (such as those associated with a candidacy for EU membership), then problems of compliance are likely to ensue for which the system has little in the way of response beyond the necessarily double-edged sword of suspension or expulsion.[68] It is in this deeper sense, rather than because of any obvious procedural shortcomings, that enforcement clearly will remain the Convention system's 'Achilles heel'.[69]

The Court

The systemic turn seen in the development of new mechanisms and procedures at the level of the Committee of Ministers has also found expression in the

---

[65] Cf P. Leach, 'The Effectiveness of the Committee of Ministers in Supervising the Enforcement of Judgments of the European Court of Human Rights', 51 *Public Law* (2006), 443.

[66] This point was raised in a number of the *Preparatory Contributions* to the February 2010 Interlaken Conference, including the Opinion of the Steering Committee for Human Rights (at 23), the Joint NGO Appeal (at 34), and the Contribution of the Secretary General of the Council of Europe (at 48).

[67] On the more general logics of compliance as regards international human rights regimes, see A. Moravcsik, 'Explaining International Human Rights Regimes: Liberal Theory and Western Europe', 1 *European Journal of International Relations* (1995), 157; T. Risse, S. C. Ropp, and K. Sikkink (eds), *The Power of Human Rights: International Norms and Domestic Change* (Cambridge: Cambridge University Press, 1999).

[68] There might, however, be some scope for the development of more graduated sanctions, including exclusion from the holding of particular responsibilities within the organization (such as its chairmanship) or the suspension of voting rights (following the example of the Parliamentary Assembly, which suspended the voting rights of its Russian members in 2000–1 over human rights violations arising from the Chechen conflict). This subject was broached as part of the 2004 Oslo high-level meeting, but appears to have generated comparatively little subsequent discussion. See n 63 above, at 7, 12 (para 28).

[69] S. Greer, 'Protocol 14 and the Future of the European Court of Human Rights', 50 *Public Law* (2005), 92.

jurisprudence of the Court. Abandoning what critics from within the Strasbourg system had termed its unnecessary adherence to a strict 'case-by-case' approach, with a corresponding reticence to enunciate general principles,[70] the Court has in the post-enlargement period increasingly demonstrated a willingness to identify underlying or systemic problems in instances where large numbers of identical complaints (so-called 'clone cases') are finding their way onto its docket. Moreover, where it has identified such general failings, the Court has further engaged in what might be termed 'remedial dialogues' with the Member States concerned. Here, though formally reaffirming the principle of Member State discretion as regards the means of executing judgments, the Court has nonetheless effectively taken to prescribing the acceptable parameters of remedies (and proscribing unacceptable ones) in a manner and at a level of detail which would not have been conceivable in earlier periods.

These jurisprudential developments, in turn, point to a somewhat different conceptualization of the overall pattern of institutional relationships within the Convention system. A classic logic of 'subsidiarity', implying a national level which is conceived in terms separate from and prior to a secondary European supervisory system, has been significantly superseded by a logic akin to that which Christoffersen has termed 'primarity'.[71] In this optic, national institutions are themselves conceived as Convention institutions, entrusted with the primary responsibility, as part of the overall ECHR system, to ensure the substantive protection and development of the enumerated rights (and this irrespective of the formal terms of incorporation of the Convention into the national legal order).

The Court has, unsurprisingly, shown a particular disposition to engage in broad 'remedial dialogues' with Member States over the vexed question of Art 6(1) cases concerned with the undue length of proceedings. Seeking to dam the flood of such cases coming to Strasbourg, the Court has repeatedly insisted on the need for appropriate domestic remedies to be put in place and, where it deemed it necessary, given Member States detailed guidance as to the (in)adequacy of the solutions adopted. It is in this vein that one must read the Court's landmark *Kudla* jurisprudence,[72] which has seen the historically little used Art 13 ECHR guarantee of 'the right to an effective remedy' assume a new life as a separate ground for the finding of a violation. This remedial approach has also been much in evidence in the Court's handling of the 'Pinto Law' saga in Italy, where a series of Strasbourg decisions have both supported and sanctioned national authorities and, through doing so, have progressively defined the

---

[70] See R. Harmsen, 'The European Convention on Human Rights after Enlargement', 5 *International Journal of Human Rights* (2001), 32–3.

[71] J. Christoffersen, *Fair Balance: A Study of Proportionality, Subsidiarity and Primarity in the European Convention on Human Rights* (Dordrecht: Martinus Nijhoff, 2009).

[72] *Kudla v Poland* Appl no 30210/96 (2000). See further R. Harmsen, 'The European Court of Human Rights as a "Constitutional Court": Definitional Debates and the Dynamics of Reform' in Morison, McEvoy, and Anthony, n 38 above, 42–5.

parameters of a Convention-compatible remedy for delay of proceedings at the domestic level.[73]

The development of a more systemic dimension in the Court's jurisprudence has nonetheless found perhaps its most prominent expression in the development of the pilot judgment mechanism. As discussed in the previous section, the Committee of Ministers had adopted a resolution in May 2004 inviting the Court to identify cases in which its finding of a Convention violation pointed to an 'underlying systemic problem'. The desired invitation having been secured, the Court did not wait long to make use of it—handing down its first pilot judgment the following month in the case of *Broniowski v Poland*.[74] Here, having found a violation of Art 1 of Protocol No 1 ECHR in the individual case with respect to the compensation scheme adopted by the Polish government for those who had been historically dispossessed of properties east of the Bug River, the Court went on to note that this violation originated in a 'systemic problem' which the respondent State was more generally obliged to correct. In keeping with this verdict, the Court also then suspended proceedings in the 167 further cases dealing with the same question pending before it, while the Registry worked with the Polish government to find a satisfactory overall remedy for the shortcoming identified. This process drew to a successful close the following year with the agreement of a friendly settlement.[75] This settlement, beyond the individual case, crucially incorporated a declaration by the Polish government whereby it undertook to implement a series of specified general measures in accordance with the Court's decision to provide a comparable standard of relief to all other current and potential Bug River applicants.

This first use of the pilot judgment procedure was widely heralded as a success. Notably, both the Woolf Report[76] and the Wise Persons' Report[77] singled out the procedure for favourable comment and encouraged its further development. Yet, despite this initially very positive reception, little immediate use was made of the new tool. Speaking at the 2008 Stockholm Colloquy, the Court's Registrar, Erik Fribergh, noted that only one further 'full' use of the pilot judgment had been made in the four years after *Broniowski*[78]—a second Polish case, *Hutten-Czapska*, which dealt with the reform of Communist-era rent controls.[79] Inevitably, a certain sense of disappointment thus crept in relative to earlier expectations.

---

[73] See notably *Brusco v Italy* admissibility decision of 6 September 2001, Appl no 69789/01 and *Scordino v Italy (No 1)* judgment of 29 March 2006, Appl no 36813/97. See further S. Wolf, 'Trial Within a Reasonable Time: The Recent Reforms of the Italian Justice System in Response to the Conflict with Article 6(1) of the ECHR', 9 *European Public Law* (2003), 189.

[74] *Broniowski v Poland* (Merits and Just Satisfaction) judgment of 22 June 2004, Appl no 31443/96.

[75] *Broniowski v Poland* (Friendly Settlement) Appl no 31443/96 (2005).

[76] Woolf, n 4 above, 39–40.

[77] *Report of the Group of Wise Persons*, n 5 above, paras 100–5.

[78] E. Fribergh, 'Pilot Judgments from the Court's Perspective' in *Towards Stronger Implementation of the European Convention on Human Rights at National Level: Colloquy organised under the Swedish Chairmanship of the Committee of Ministers of the Council of Europe* (Strasbourg: Council of Europe, 2008), 90.

[79] *Hutten-Czapska v Poland* Appl no 35014/97 (2006) (Merits and Just Satisfaction) and *Hutten-Czapska v Poland* Appl no 35014/97 (2008) (Friendly Settlement); Fribergh, n 78 above, 90, does,

The limited use of the procedure appeared, moreover, to derive from certain intrinsic practical and political limitations. Practically, the pilot judgment mechanism would seem to be well-suited only to cases in which a 'class action' logic is operable—that is, circumstances in which a potentially large, but clearly delimited, group share a common grievance amenable to collective resolution.[80] Politically, and more contentiously, it also requires a situation in which the respondent State concerned is itself amenable to negotiation—that is, willing to engage constructively with the Court in finding a resolution to the problem identified, given that the logic of the pilot judgment procedure is essentially one, at the more general level, of a legally framed negotiation. This might thus, a priori, be thought to exclude many of precisely those Member States where the existence of serious systemic problems currently presents the Court with some of its greatest challenges.[81]

In 2009, the Court moved to address these concerns head-on, in a case which looks set to be a litmus test for the wider possible applicability of the pilot judgment procedure (if not, indeed, a test of the effective limits of the Strasbourg system itself). The *Burdov (No 2)* case was seized upon by the Court as a pilot judgment so as to deal with the more general structural problem of the non-enforcement of judgments in Russia.[82] To this end, the operative part of the judgment placed an obligation on the Russian authorities to adopt 'an effective domestic remedy or combination of such remedies which secures adequate and sufficient redress for non-enforcement or delayed enforcement of judgments' within six months of the definitive publication of the judgment. The Court also placed an obligation on the Russian authorities to provide adequate redress within one year in all comparable cases pending before the Court at the time of the publication of the judgment. Proceedings in the case of newly introduced complaints were, at the same time, adjourned for a one-year interval from the date of publication. The overall architecture of the decision thus sought to create a breathing space within which the

---

however, note that there had been a number of 'semi-pilots' during this period, in which the Court made use of aspects of the pilot judgment procedure in dealing with cases which raised more general structural or systemic problems. See eg *Lukenda v Slovenia* Appl no 23032/02 (2005). Here, the Court urged the Slovene authorities to take general measures to address the 'major problem' of backlogs in the domestic court system leading to repeated violations of Art 6(1)—but did not opt for a 'full pilot' procedure which would presumably have entailed the provisional adjournment of the some 500 'reasonable time' cases then pending before it from the country.

[80] See further A. Gattini, 'Mass Claims at the European Court of Human Rights' in S. Breitenmoser et al (eds), *Human Rights, Democracy and the Rule of Law: Liber Amicorum Luzius Wildhaber* (Baden-Baden: Nomos, 2007).

[81] Cf W. Sadurski, 'Partnering with Strasbourg: Constitutionalisation of the European Court of Human Rights, the Accession of Central and East European States to the Council of Europe, and the Idea of Pilot Judgments', 9 *Human Rights Law Review* (2009), 397. Sadurski suggests that pilot judgments may—not altogether unproblematically—concentrate on the post-transition States of Central and Eastern Europe, given what he regards as both their likely ineffectiveness in the case of more serious violators and a possible reticence to apply the procedure in the case of the more established West European democracies.

[82] *Burdov v Russia (No 2)* Appl no 33509/04 (2009).

underlying problem might be addressed, while also placing clear and time-limited obligations on the respondent State.

Relative to earlier cases, the use of the pilot judgment mechanism in *Burdov (No 2)* marks a bold new development. As regards the perceived practical limits of the procedure, the Court has clearly moved beyond a more traditional 'class action' logic. In contrast to both *Broniowski* and *Hutten-Czapska*, the present judgment seeks to tackle an extensive structural dysfunction where the broad range of potential victims do not necessarily form, as the Court itself noted, 'an identifiable class of citizens'.[83] Politically, the decision has also, even more clearly, been delivered against a particularly problematic Member State whose predisposition to negotiate and whose immediate capacity to implement a Court-mandated reform of domestic institutional structures might themselves reasonably be questioned. It is in these respects that the *Burdov (No 2)* case ambitiously pushes the boundaries of the pilot judgment procedure.

Yet, though ambitious, the Court also displayed an awareness of the potential limits of the mechanism. While imposing tight time limits as regards the introduction of domestic remedies consonant with the obligations imposed by Art 13 ECHR, the Court nonetheless explicitly recognized that the wider process of judicial reform is not one which may be jurisprudentially engineered from Strasbourg, but which rather requires an active political engagement at the national and the European levels. Addressing the issue of reforms intended to remedy the underlying violations of Art 6 and Art 1 of Protocol No 1 ECHR, the Court commented:

> this process raises a number of complex legal and practical issues which go, in principle, beyond the Court's judicial function. It will thus abstain in these circumstances from indicating any specific general measure to be taken. The Committee of Ministers is better placed and equipped to monitor the necessary reforms to be adopted by Russia in this respect. The Court therefore leaves it to the Committee of Ministers to ensure that the Russian Federation, in accordance with its obligations under the Convention, adopts the necessary measures consistent with the Court's conclusions in the present judgment.[84]

Relative to these concerns and expectations, the initial follow-up to *Burdov (No 2)* has perhaps inevitably been rather inconclusive. While the Russian authorities were unable to introduce a domestic remedy within the (arguably unrealistic) six-month period specified in the judgment, such a law did enter into force on 4 May 2010. Similarly, the Russian authorities proved unable to deal with the full backlog of related cases within the one-year time limit set by the Court, but did signal their willingness to continue to tackle the problem as expeditiously as possible—citing, amongst other explanations for the delay, the existence of more than double the number of some 700 related applications initially identified in the pilot judgment.[85] Globally, the Court's use of the pilot judgment mechanism has thus served as a useful impetus for (relatively) accelerating domestic reforms as regards the

[83] Ibid, para 129. [84] Ibid, para 137.
[85] Letter of 4 May 2010 from the Representative of the Russian Federation at the European Court of Human Rights to the First Section Registrar, subsequently communicated (with response) to the Committee of Ministers. Doc DH-DD(2010)257, 1086th DH meeting, 1–3 June 2010.

immediate question of compensatory relief. The deeper question of the extent to which such external leverage might contribute to resolving underlying dysfunctions remains, however, necessarily unanswered at this stage.[86]

Building on *Burdov (No 2)*, the Court itself has notably continued to push further in the same direction, deploying two subsequent pilot judgments in comparable Moldovan and Ukrainian cases later the same year.[87] As the Court continues down this path, the implications and logics of its wider systemic turn thus also become correspondingly more apparent. A jurisprudence predicated on the implementation of general remedies for structural deficiencies inevitably requires that the Court develop a different—and denser—pattern of relationships with the other actors in the wider Convention system than that which had sufficed in an earlier era characterized by the 'case-by-case' resolution of more discrete or limited violations.[88]

IV. Conclusion

While it is clear that a constant refrain of reform focused on an ever-expanding caseload has marked discussions surrounding the Convention system for three decades now, it should be equally clear that the underlying realities which those reforms seek to address have dramatically changed. The major institutional overhaul effected in 1998 by Protocol No 11 appears, perhaps somewhat paradoxically, as the last act of the post-war West European human rights system—relatively little direct attention having been paid during the Protocol's long genesis to the new challenges which were to be posed to the Strasbourg system by its transformation into a pan-European jurisdiction. The new century has, however, seen the Strasbourg institutions become fully apprised of their dramatically altered circumstances. The modest changes proposed by Protocol No 14 were thus, in contrast to their far more wide-ranging predecessor, accompanied by a much deeper discussion of the nature and limits of the Convention system itself—opposing well-articulated 'constitutional' and 'individual justice' visions of the European Court's role. More generally, the 2000s also saw the emergence of a heightened 'systemic' awareness, highlighting the need for the human rights system, across its political and its judicial dimensions, to function as a whole. This greater systemic awareness has given rise to a significant clarification and improvement of the working methods of the Committee of Ministers in its supervisory role. It has

---

[86] See further P. Leach, H. Hardman, and S. Stephenson, 'Can the European Court's Pilot Judgment Procedure Help Resolve Systemic Human Rights Violations?: *Burdov* and the Failure to Implement Domestic Court Decisions in Russia', 10 *Human Rights Law Review* (2010), 346.

[87] *Olaru and Others v Moldova* judgment of 28 July 2009, Appl nos 476/07, 22539/05, 17911/08, and 1313607 and *Yuriy Nikolayevich Ivanov v Ukraine* judgment of 15 October 2009, Appl no 40450/04.

[88] The further development of the pilot judgment procedure in particular will also see the Court face growing pressures to formalize the criteria for its use and application, beyond the perhaps inevitably somewhat piecemeal approach which has characterized its initial phase. See notably point 7b) of the 'Action Plan' adopted as part of the Interlaken Declaration, n 6 above.

equally seen the Court jurisprudentially reposition itself within the wider Convention system, more directly engaging the responsibility of national (and by extension European) authorities for the provision of general remedies to identified Convention violations.

Yet, this systemic turn has thus far been little accompanied by considered reflections on the wider (geo-)politics of the Convention system, despite the obvious centrality of the problematic of enlargement for understanding the system's current dilemmas. On the one hand, the quasi-official character of much of the discussion, taking place in Council of Europe or intergovernmental fora, tends by its nature to militate against an explicit consideration of the highly variable levels of democratic practice found in the post-enlargement Convention community. On the other hand, the relative failure of political scientists to engage with the Convention system has also perhaps led (with honourable exceptions) to a relative dearth of more critical examinations of the variable patterns of Convention compliance which are emerging and, even more, of the implications of such variations for longer term system legitimacy.[89] Nonetheless, it is such questions surrounding the politics—and political science—of the Convention system which are likely to be crucial in understanding its future development. Much will ride on the system's (continued) ability to encompass and respond effectively to the highly variegated set of human rights challenges found across the full range of Convention Member States.

The Convention community may now be seen to encompass three broad types of national human rights situations: those of established democracies, (post-)transition States, and States in which the basic norms of democratic governance and the rule of law have significantly failed to take hold.[90] There are, as such, obvious differences in the role which Strasbourg may be expected to play relative to each of these differing situations. While one should not be complacent as regards either the possible existence of systemic problems (as readily demonstrated by the surfeit of Italian delay of proceedings cases) or the challenges potentially posed by the post-9/11 'security state', the principal 'value added' of the Convention system for (most of) its West European Member States is likely to continue being that of an 'evolutive' standard-setter, pushing the boundaries of human rights practice in accord with evolving societal demands. In the case of (post-)transition States, by way of contrast, the system is most likely to have its strongest impacts in supporting—if not accelerating—the latter stages of politico-legal reform processes, while also acting as an adjudicator of the vestigial issues associated with the transition

---

[89] A notable recent exception is H. Keller and A. Stone Sweet (eds), *A Europe of Rights: The Impact of the ECHR on National Legal Systems* (Oxford: Oxford University Press, 2008).

[90] This argument is further developed in R Harmsen, 'The Transformation of the ECHR Legal Order and the Post-Enlargement Challenges facing the European Court of Human Rights' in G. Martinico and O. Pollicino (eds), *The National Judicial Treatment of the ECHR and EU Laws: A Comparative Constitutional Approach* (Groningen: Europa Law Publishing, 2010), 27–53. See also Greer, n 38 above, 60–135; P. A. Jordan, 'Does Membership have its Privileges?: Entrance into the Council of Europe and Compliance with Human Rights Norms', 25 *Human Rights Quarterly* (2003), 660.

itself (such as measures concerned with property restitution or civic disenfranchise-
ments imposed because of individuals' positions under the previous regime).[91]
Finally, the system must also increasingly confront situations in which either
political order has simply broken down or in which forms of significantly non-
democratic rule have maintained or even consolidated themselves since Convention
accession. Here, at the very least, the boundaries of the system are being taken to—
if not past—the breaking point of that which might be accomplished by a logic of
judicial enforcement.

The Convention institutions are consequently faced with the not inconsiderable
challenge of maintaining the cohesion and ultimately the legitimacy of the system
across this highly divergent range of situations. Exceptional demands are placed on
the Court, which must craft a jurisprudence which maintains both an overall
coherence and a more specific relevance across a range of cases which include
established democratic, newly democratic, and significantly undemocratic regimes.
The wider Convention system must also, moreover, be shaped so as to accommodate substantially different configurations of key actors in different circumstances.
Most obviously, the status and role of national judiciaries varies considerably across
the Convention community, in ways which must inevitably have an impact on the
intensity and quality of their dialogues with Strasbourg. Equally, the role of NGOs,
and particularly that of international or 'foreign' NGOs, is also likely to differ
markedly in different national contexts—highlighting questions concerned with
the relationship of the Court's judicial function to wider functions of human rights
advocacy. The Convention's core institutional trialogue—encompassing the Court,
the Committee of Ministers, and national authorities—must thus correspondingly
allow for different balances and dynamics so as to optimize effective implementation and enforcement.

It is relative to this reality that the next phase of reform discussions surrounding
the Convention system should move from the simply 'systemic' to the more
broadly 'environmental'—recognizing that the functioning of the system as a
whole must be conceived and adapted in line with the political environments in
which it operates.[92] This is not to deny the importance of dealing with the problem
of the Court's caseload and the attendant need for ongoing procedural reforms.
Rather, it is to set these institutional reforms in their wider contexts, arguing that
institutional reform must ultimately be conceived in relation to political purpose.
The question, if not the answer, thus becomes a relatively straightforward one: what
(variable) roles can Strasbourg best and most effectively play in the protection and
development of human rights across the diverse members of a pan-European
community, and how might the institutions best be reformed so as to achieve

[91] See M. Varju, 'Transition as a Concept of European Human Rights Law', 14 *European Human Rights Law Review* (2009), 170.

[92] The present emphasis on the wider political environments of Convention implementation parallels Helfer's stress on national 'embeddedness' as a cornerstone of reform. See L. R. Helfer, 'Redesigning the European Court of Human Rights: Embeddedness as a Deep Structural Principle of the European Human Rights Regime', 19 *European Journal of International Law* (2008), 125.

this result? As discussions surrounding the 'reform of the reform of the reform' take place over the coming years, it is imperative that they move to incorporate such a more explicitly grounded understanding of the potential and the limits of the Convention system in relation to the complicated geopolitical realities of which it forms a part.[93]

---

[93] The initial signs as regards the Interlaken process are not, in this regard, particularly promising. While both the declaration finally adopted and the preparatory contributions for the conference moved still more resolutely in the direction of recognizing the need to address reforms at a 'systemic' level, the wider political environments in which the Convention must operate again failed to generate significant attention. Only the submission of the Secretary General of the Council of Europe offered a brief nod towards such wider dimensions, suggesting that 'the Convention's procedures might become more flexible' so as to create 'an upward dynamic' in which States which have 'got their house in order' would interact differently with the Court than those presenting serious and persisting problems. See n 6 above, 45.

8

Constitutional v International? When Unified Reformatory Rationales Mismatch the Plural Paths of Legitimacy of ECHR Law

Stéphanie Hennette-Vauchez

The European system of human rights protection seems to be in constant reformatory turmoil. Protocol No 11 that merged the European Commission (ECommHR) and Court (ECtHR) of human rights is famous for being one of its most drastic alterations but also quickly appeared to both actors and observers to be notoriously unable to help the whole system deal with an increasing caseload emanating from the expanding geographical reach of the Convention. Consequently, negotiations over the next big reform (Protocol No 14, signed in 2004 but whose entry into force was delayed until Russia finally agreed upon ratification in January 2010) started shortly after[1] and were soon paralleled by yet other reformatory initiatives such as the Group of Wise Persons set up after the 2005 Warsaw meeting of the Heads of State and Government of the Council of Europe Member States with the objective to 'consider the long-term effectiveness of the ECHR control mechanism, including the initial effects of Protocol No 14'[2] (the 'reform of the reform of the reform', according to Judge L. Caflisch[3]).

This uninterrupted and at times chaotic reform process has however favoured the stabilization of reformatory rationales. In particular, one alternative has become the basic framework against which reformatory options and individual

---

[1] It was less than two years after the entry into force of Protocol No 11 that the reform process was launched again during the Inter-ministerial Conference held in Rome on the occasion of the 50th anniversary of the Convention's signature. A declaration adopted during the conference led to the creation of an ad hoc committee of the Council of Europe's Committee of Ministers. Later, the Committee of Ministers also created an 'Evaluation Group' on 7 February 2001 (EG Cour (2001) 1 of 27 September 2001) with the objective of coming up with reform proposals. Still later on 4 April 2003, the Steering Committee for Human Rights published an important report on the basis of which negotiations over what was to become Protocol No 14 really began, and a final report in April 2004 which was to become the text of the Protocol as adopted by the Ministers on 12 May 2004.

[2] The group's final report was published on 15 November 2006 and is available at: <https://wcd .coe.int/ViewDoc.jsp?Ref=CM%282006%29203&Sector=secCM&Language=lanEnglish&Ver= original&BackColorInternet=9999CC&BackColorIntranet=FFBB55&BackColorLogged=FFAC75>.

[3] L. Caflisch, 'The Reform of the European Court of Human Rights: Protocol 14 and Beyond', 6 *Human Rights Law Review* (2006), 415.

positions alike now tend to position themselves: allegedly, the European system of human rights has to choose between its 'constitutional' and its 'international' identity. Although they have not initiated it, nor can they be held responsible for the many variations on the same theme that have subsequently thrived, the duo, formed at the beginning of the 2000s by then President and Registrar of the ECtHR Luzius Wildhaber and Paul Mahoney, excelled in framing the debate in such terms. They often expressed the view that 'the Convention and its complaint based enforcement mechanism should not be viewed as aiming at providing individual relief for as many European citizens as possible'[4] but rather at focusing on 'decisions of "principle," decisions which create jurisprudence'.[5] They presented the necessary reform of the Convention system to be constrained by a choice between two competing perspectives—and favoured the constitutional one over the international:

One perspective, that of 'individual justice,' views as the soul of the Convention the entitlement of each and every complainant to examination of his or her complaint and, if it is upheld, to individualized relief. The other, that of 'constitutional justice' regards the Convention as a constitutional instrument of European public order in the field of human rights, and thus the mechanism of individual applications as the means by which defects in national protection of human rights are detected with a view to correcting them; thereby raising the general standard of protection of human rights, both in the country concerned and in the Convention community of States as a whole.

The purpose of this chapter is to challenge the relevance of this alternative (or at least, of some of its usages) to the extent that it is ill-adapted to the empirical reality that needs to be reformed—a reality we argue is much more national than *trans*national. The idea that will be developed is that the 'constitutionalist talk' based on this false alternative[6] between individual and constitutional justice readily speaks a 'transnational' language that is hardly audible in the national settings—yet those are the settings in which the Convention primarily operates.[7] This demonstration is based on the idea that the ECHR's identity and effects are conceptualized and experienced in a variety of different universes and that the hermeneutics of ECHR law are quite different depending on whether they are articulated on the transnational or the national plane. In other words, the claim here is that there is no

---

[4] P. Mahoney, 'New Challenges for the European Court of Human Rights Resulting from Expanding Case Load and Membership', 21 *Penn State International Law Review* (2002), 105.

[5] L. Wildhaber, 'The Role of the European Court of Human Rights: An Evaluation', 8 *Mediterranean Journal of Human Rights* (2004), 28.

[6] One can indeed coin it a 'false alternative', for all the people who refer to it actually side with the constitutionalist reading of the Convention and its future, thus transforming its other branch (the internationalist one) into a non-existent option.

[7] By all accounts, the ECHR created a subsidiary human rights protection system and the primary judicial enactor of the Convention is the national judge. The ECtHR is to intervene only after all national remedies have been exhausted. In addition, the ECHR does not prescribe the modes by which it is to be introduced within national legal orders; in fact, it does not even make incorporation compulsory. As a result, the status of the Convention varies greatly from one country to another, and depends on the constitutional framework that defines the relationships between national and international law.

such thing as one 'ECHR law'. Rather, there exists the Strasbourg case law, on the one hand, and no less than 47 national versions of its appropriation, on the other hand. Additionally, each of these bodies of ECHR law leads to a plurality of theorizations. On these premises, while it is acknowledged that there is indeed a genuinely transnational hermeneutic universe within which specific conceptualizations of the ECHR are put forth,[8] it is also insisted that the pragmatic effects of the ECHR only deploy at the national levels and therefore that the very nature and status of the ECHR are not a matter of ECHR (transnational) law but of national law.

It will thus be argued here that the discourse on the ECHR that emanates from this transnational hermeneutic universe and favours a 'constitutional' reading of the Convention over an 'international' one runs the risk of reducing the plurality of national constructions of ECHR law[9] under the univocal and irrelevant banner of 'transnational constitutionalism'.[10] The pitfalls of such a reductionist approach are not only theoretical misunderstandings. The tragic fate of the 2004 Treaty establishing a Constitution for Europe serves as a good illustration of the pragmatic and political effects of the 'transnational' imposition of constitutional semantics over ill-prepared polities and under-estimated conceptual resistances. Legal categories do not exist in themselves; they are always embedded in particular legal and political cultures, and the risk of the transnationalization of traditionally national legal categories is that of uprooting them—thus preventing them from performing what they generally do. As Anne Lise Kjaer puts it: 'Law is not a matter of text. Legal rules expressed in legal texts are surface law and only the tip of an iceberg. What actually matters is how people act and think in real life'.[11] This is why in 1958 when Sir Humphrey Waldock, a British international law professor who had chaired the International Law Commission and was to serve as president of both the ECommHR and the ECtHR, called the ECHR a possible 'constitutional code of human rights'[12] for the free Europe, or when the Court ruled in 1995 that the

---

[8] M. R. Madsen, *L'émergence d'un champ des droits de l'homme dans les pays européens. Enjeux professionnels et stratégies d'Etat au carrefour du droit et de la politique*, PhD Thesis, Ecole des hautes études en sciences sociales, Paris (2005).

[9] See, already 25 years previously, A. Drzemczewski, *European Human Rights Convention in Domestic Law: A Comparative Study* (Oxford: Clarendon Press, 1983).

[10] This chapter will thus only address the issue of the extent to which the 'constitutionalist paradigm' fails to serve as an accurate descriptive tool of what ECHR law is made of—that is, in large parts, of national law. It will not address other more theoretical questions faced by this constitutionalist paradigm; but research on this issue has been undertaken within a collective research project, see S. Hennette-Vauchez (ed), *La Convention européenne des droits de l'homme vue d'ailleurs. Acteurs du dehors et du dedans dans la promotion d'une norme de référence*, Rapport pour la mission de recherche Droit & Justice, January 2010.

[11] A. Kjaer, 'Language as Barrier and Carrier of European Legal Integration' in H. Petersen, A. L. Kjaer, H. Krunke, and M. R. Madsen (eds), *Paradoxes of European Legal Integration* (Aldershot: Ashgate, 2008), 151.

[12] Cited by E. Bates, Chapter 2 above. Such claims were not isolated; see eg the words of P. Modinos in 1962 (Modinos has been the head of the Council of Europe's Human Rights Directorate, the Commission's Secretariat, then the Court's Registrar, and was eventually appointed as the Deputy Secretary General of the Council of Europe): 'It is no exaggeration to say that the Convention is a genuine European Code of Human Rights..... The authors of the Convention have

Convention had become 'a constitutional instrument of European public order', *different things were being heard (understood) in different places* and this is what the present chapter will aim at establishing.

This chapter's methodology rests on the following grounds. The basic hypothesis is that, absent any ontological concept of human rights[13] it is not law itself (or, for that matter, legal categories, rulings, . . .) that have caused the oft-mentioned evolution of ECHR law from international to domestic law,[14] but people equipped with particular legal tools. Subsequently, the constitutional semantics that are increasingly applied to the ECHR will first be replaced in a genealogical perspective, in order for their true and often forgotten story to (re)appear clearly: they are in large part a product of insiders to the ECHR system (Section I). However, this transnational discourse cannot live in itself; and its audiences are national, hence the need to study its local receptions. This will be done throughout two case studies: France and Italy. The legal debates that have accompanied the ECHR over the years in these two High Contracting Parties will be analysed in order to show the diversity of the 'receptions' and adaptations of the constitutional semantics spoken from within what we have called the transnational ECHR hermeneutic universe (Section II).

I. The 'Transnational–Constitutional' Reading of the ECHR: Past, Present, Future

The ECHR really is an important convention, well beyond the solace it might have brought over its 60 years of being in force to many individuals who have seen their rights redressed. For, indeed, the ECHR is a cornerstone in the history of the creation of a transnational universe of human rights protection: it is both this nascent universe's most accomplished realization[15] and therefore the strong foundation upon which it has been able to develop and spread around the world.[16] More specifically, the ECHR has also played an instrumental role in the way we conceive and think of human rights, by means of affirming their *legal* nature and

---

succeeded in laying down the constitutional rules without which the Political community could not exist': P. Modinos, 'Effects and Repercussions of the European Convention on Human Rights', 11 *International and Comparative Law Quarterly* (1962), 1107.

[13] For an overview of theoretical questions on this issue, see M. Dembour, *Who Believes in Human Rights?: Reflections on the European Convention* (Cambridge: Cambridge University Press, 2006).

[14] This is a commonly held analysis of one of the main evolutions undertaken by ECHR law since 1950; see eg the speech delivered by P. Mahoney on his departure from the Court's Registry in 2005, thanking several groups of actors who had, in his view, helped to transform the ECHR from 'an esoteric specialty of international law into a major subject of national law': P. Mahoney, 'Réflexions d'un greffier de la Cour européenne des droits de l'homme à l'heure du départ', 17(4) *Revue universelle des droits de l'homme* (2005), 1.

[15] See Madsen n 8 above.

[16] There subsists an interesting and crucial research agenda linked to the relations between the space of the ECHR and those of other international human rights covenants such as that of the ILO or, better, the Inter-American Convention on Human Rights.

contributing to the autonomization of human rights law as a branch of law per se,[17] as distinct from both international law (many premises of which it departs from— such as its interstate nature or the centrality of the rule of reciprocity) and national law (over which it readily claims primacy[18]). Such impressive outcomes can be explained by the fact that the people who early on were appointed to Strasbourg and operated the system (Convention people[19]) were not merely a new group of judges ensuring that yet another international convention was enforced. Rather, it was a strongly cohesive[20] set of multi-skilled individuals who were tied together not only by feelings of institutional loyalty or socio-professional resemblances but also, and strikingly so, by a shared vision of law. It will be argued here that as far as human rights law went, this vision was, early on, very 'constitutionalist' and therefore that it has provided strategic support to more recent scholarly enterprises that aim at affirming the expansion of constitutionalization processes worldwide.

The politics of legal theory: from 'monism', '*ordre public*', and '*ius cogens*' to human rights as the 'constitutional' vector of European unification

The sheer desire of the lawyers-politicians who formed the first generation of Convention people in Strasbourg to establish the fact that what they were doing was law (thus: something 'scientific'), and not politics or diplomacy,[21] is noteworthy. Prominent members of these first generations of Convention people thus actively promoted the production and dissemination of human rights science and scholarship. Particularly conspicuous in this respect were the undertakings of individuals such as René Cassin, the first French judge on the Court and its second president, who in 1968, together with Karel Vasak of the ECommHR's secretariat and W. J. Ganshof van der Meersch (a prominent Belgian judge and politician, and professor at the Free University of Brussels, who was to be appointed as a judge in the Strasbourg Court in 1973 and later serve as its vice-president), launched both

---

[17] S. Hennette-Vauchez, 'L'Europe au service du droit des droits de l'homme. Réalité politique, entreprise savante et autonomisation d'une branche du droit', 80 *Politix* (2010/11), 57.

[18] D. Shelton, 'Hierarchy of Norms and Human Rights: of Trumps and Winners', 65 *Saskatchewan Law Review* (2002), 304.

[19] The expression 'Convention people' here serves to designate not only judges of the ECtHR and members of the ECommHR, but also a wider but instrumental group composed of those who worked in the former's Registry, the latter's Secretariat, and the Council of Europe's Human Rights Directorate. On the justification of this wide perspective, see S. Hennette-Vauchez, 'Divided in Diversity? National Legal Scholarship(s) and the ECHR', European University Institute, RSCAS Working Paper Series (2008).

[20] On this particular aspect of the first generations of 'Convention people', see Hennette-Vauchez, n 17 above.

[21] On the importance of the political-diplomatic credentials of these first generations of 'Convention people', and the extent to which diplomacy permeated the activity of the European human rights system for a lasting 10–15 years, see M. R. Madsen, 'From Cold War Instrument to Supreme European Court: The European Court of Human Rights at the Crossroads of International and National Law and Politics', 32(1) *Law & Social Inquiry* (2007), 137 and 'Legal Diplomacy: Law, Politics and the Genesis of Postwar European Human Rights' in S.-L. Hoffmann (ed), *Human Rights in the 20th Century: A Critical History* (Cambridge: Cambridge University Press, 2010).

the *Revue des droits de l'homme* and the Institut International des Droits de l'Homme. The *Revue des droits de l'homme* was conceived by this trio as an instrumental means of turning the protection of human rights into an actual legal enterprise; as Cassin himself put it in one issue of the journal: 'We want to prove that human rights are scientific' (*nous voulons apporter la preuve que les droits de l'homme sont une science*).[22] The endeavours of Vasak and Ganshof van der Meersch strongly echo this objective: while the first was in charge of an ambitious programme of listing all the existing courses of human rights law in European law schools and crafting syllabus and training sessions in order to train law professors in this new branch of law,[23] the second created and held the first chair of ECHR law at the University of Brussels.

This new legal science of human rights rested on several instrumental theoretical and conceptual pillars, some of which are worth detailing here. The first of these is constituted by a then revolutionary package of ideas in the field of international law such as a monist representation of the legal order which granted international law norms precedence over national ones, combined with the notion that the individual was a relevant subject of international law. This latter affirmation in particular was a necessary condition for the success of the whole enterprise of creating international (here, European) human rights law, which by definition presupposed the possibility for international legal norms to reach out to the individual. It was a real breakthrough in international law theory which entailed piercing a hole in the States' veil of sovereignty. Strikingly, numerous Convention people were active academic promoters of the recognition of the relevance of the individual within international law.[24] As to the monist view that founded the primacy of international over national law, ideas expressed at the second international colloquy on the Convention held in Vienna in 1965 by several Convention people are very illustrative. Among them, Alfred Verdross, a prominent Austrian international law professor who had been appointed to the Court in 1959, strongly expressed the views that: 'it is indispensible to substitute a monist theory to the dualist one and include international and domestic law into one legal system' (*il est indispensable de substituer à la théorie dualiste une théorie moniste qui englobe le droit international et le droit interne dans un système juridique*) and 'At any rate, the norms of the Convention must reach the rank of constitutional norms. . . . Convention norms will only be well-respected when all contracting parties' legal orders include provisions according to which these norms, having become an integral part of domestic orders, can only be amended by means of constitutional modifications' (*Il faut en*

---

[22] R. Cassin, III(4) *Revue des droits de l'homme* (1970), 555.

[23] This endeavour produced ever-lasting results as the Institut International des Droits de l'Homme still organizes an annual training session on human rights.

[24] See the publications by Eustathiades (member of the ECommHR), 'Les sujets du droit international et la responsabilité internationale : nouvelles tendances', 84 *RCADI* (1953), 397–633; Cassin (judge and president of the ECtHR), 'L'homme, sujet de droit international' in *La Technique et les principes de droit public. Etudes en l'honneur de Georges Scelle*, vol 1 (Paris: Pichon, 1950), 67–91; Mosler (judge at the ECtHR), 'The International Society as Legal Community', 140 *RCADI* (1974), 1–320; Norgaard (member and president of the ECommHR), *The Position of the Individual in International Law* (Copenhagen: Munksgaard, 1962); Sperduti (member of the ECommHR), "L'individu et le droit international", 90 *RCADI* (1956), 727–849.

tout état de cause que les normes de la Convention accèdent au rang de lois constitu-tionnelles.... Les normes de la Convention ne seront parfaitement respectées que si l'ordre juridique de tous les Etats contractants comporte une disposition selon laquelle ces normes, qui sont devenues partie intégrante du droit interne, ne peuvent être amendées qu'à la suite d'une modification de la Constitution).[25]

Interestingly, these ideas resulted in the notion that international human rights law (hence, the ECHR) embodied something like a 'public order' common to European countries. Authors such as Henri Rolin, a notorious Belgian lawyer, law professor, and Member of Parliament who was appointed to the ECtHR in 1959 and later served as its president, W. J. Ganshof van der Meersch or H. Mosler, another famous internationalist who also served as a Strasbourg judge, were all strong promoters of the concept of an international public order. Sir Humphrey Waldock, Gerald Fitzmaurice (judge at the ECtHR), Lord McNair (president of the ECtHR), but also Alfred Verdross were all strongly involved, in their multiple capacities (the first two not only as academics but also as members of the Interna-tional Law Commission), in the promotion and eventual elevation of the concept of *ius cogens*.[26] This concept in its undefined nature has proven very useful as a receptacle for human rights and this did not slip through the Convention people's hands; Giuseppe Sperduti for instance, a ECommHR member for a lengthy 33 years, insisted that human rights were the content of *ius cogens*.[27] Other Convention people have focused on the concept of *ius commune* which ECHR law was contributing to,[28] and others yet on the 'objective nature' of human rights law.[29]

All in all, what this subtle mix of theoretical options and idealist articles of faith has favoured is the early mobilization of constitutional semantics for describing the ECHR by many insiders to the system. Whereas some boldly affirmed the 'constitutional' nature of the Council of Europe's most prominent achievement[30] and others remained on the more cautious lines of equating ECHR law with 'objective' norms forming a 'European public order', all were

---

[25] A. Verdross, 'La place de la CEDH dans la hiérarchie des normes juridiques' in *Les droits de l'homme en droit interne et en droit international* (Brussels: Presses Universitaires de Bruxelles, 1968), 92.
[26] A. Gomez-Robledo, 'Le *jus cogens* international: sa genèse, sa nature, ses fonctions', 172 *Recueil des cours de l'Académie de droit international de l'Haye* (1981), 37, 41, 43, 70, 74.
[27] G. Sperduti, 'Richiamo ai diritti dell'uomo', 2 *Rivista internazionale dei diritti dell'uomo* (1991), 320.
[28] M. de Salvia, 'L'élaboration d'un *ius commune* des droits de l'homme dans la perspective de l'unité européenne: l'œuvre accomplie par la Commission et la Cour européennes des droits de l'homme' in *Protecting Human Rights: The European Dimension. Studies in Honor of G. Wiarda* (Cologne: Carl Heymanns Verlag, 1988), 555–66.
[29] K. Vasak, 'Vers un droit international spécifique des droits de l'homme' in K. Vasak (ed), *Les dimensions internationales des droits de l'homme. Manuel destiné à l'enseignement des droits de l'homme dans les universités* (Paris: UNESCO, 1978), 711.
[30] Robertson (head of the Council of Europe's Human Rights Directorate), *Constitutional Devel-opments in the Council of Europe* (Brussels: Institut d'Etudes Européennes, 1964); Modinos (head of the ECommHR's Secretariat, Registrar of the ECtHR, and then Secretary General of the Council of Europe), 'Effects and Repercussions of the European Convention on Human Rights', 11 *International and Comparative Law Quarterly* (1962), 1097–108.

simultaneously consecrating constitutional semantics which we know later fully germinated, for multiple key Convention people have sided with a constitutional reading of the ECHR. At the Academy of European Law, president of the Court Rolv Ryssdal and president of the Commission Jochen Frowein successively delivered courses entitled 'On the Road to a European Constitutional Court' and 'The ECHR as the Public Order of Europe',[31] Pierre-Henri Imbert, the former head of the Human Rights Directorate,[32] Hans-Christian Krüger as head of the Commission's secretariat,[33] Michele de Salvia, who worked at the ECommHR's secretariat from the 1960s until he became its head in the 1990s and then was appointed to be the Court's Registrar,[34] Evert Alkema, a member of the Commission[35] as well as, as mentioned above, Registrar Paul Mahoney[36] or President Wildhaber:[37] all endorsed these semantics over the years. Even the current president of the Court Jean-Paul Costa, although significantly more cautious in his recourse to constitutional semantics, does not clearly part from them.[38] In other words, even though the Convention world has almost exponentially grown in size and number over the years and is now less cohesive than before, such ideas remain commonly shared by its members. Some have argued that there is a 'common legal culture' among members of the Court;[39] regardless of the accuracy of such a qualification, it remains empirically ascertainable that many insiders to the Convention system have or still share this 'constitutionalist' perspective on the ECHR.

[31] R. Ryssdal, 'On the Road to a European Constitutional Court', *Recueil des cours de l'Académie de droit européen* (Dordrecht: Martinus Nijhoff, 1991); J. Frowein, 'The ECHR as the Public Order of Europe' in *Recueil des cours de l'Académie de droit européen* (Dordrecht: Martinus Nijhoff, 1992).

[32] P. Imbert, 'Pour un système européen de protection des droits de l'homme' in *Mélanges en hommage à Louis-Edmond Pettiti* (Brussels: Bruylant, 1998), 458.

[33] H. Krüger, 4 *Human Rights Information Bulletin* (special issue) (2000); Madsen (2007), above n 21.

[34] M. de Salvia, 'La Cedu a 50 anni dalla sua firma: speranza e perseveranza', 2 *Rivista internazionale dei diritti dell'uomo* (2000), 414.

[35] E. Alkema, 'The European Convention as a Constitution and its Court as a Constitutional Court' in P. Mahoney (ed), *Protecting Human Rights: the European Perspective. Studies in Honour of R. Ryssdal* (Cologne: Carl Heymanns Verlag, 2000).

[36] Mahoney, n 4 above and 'Thinking a Small Unthinkable: Repatriating Reparation from the European Court of Human Rights to the National Legal Order' in L. Calfisch, J. Callewaert, R. Liddel, P. Mahoney, and M. Villiger (eds), *Droits de l'homme, Regards de Strasbourg. Liber Amicorum Luzius Wildhaber* (Kehl: N. P. Engel, 2007).

[37] L. Wildhaber, 'A Constitutional Future for the European Court of Human Rights?', 23(5–7) *Human Rights Law Journal* (2002), 16 and 'The European Court of Human Rights: the Past, the Present, the Future', 22 *American University International Law Review* (2006), 521.

[38] J.-P. Costa, 'La Cour européenne des droits de l'homme est-elle une cour constitutionnelle?' in P. Gélard (ed), *Constitutions et Pouvoirs: Mélanges en l'honneur de Jean Gicquel* (Paris: Montchrestien, 2007).

[39] N. Arold, *The Legal Culture of the European Court of Human Rights* (Leiden: Martinus Nijhoff, 2007).

Constitutional semantics applied to the ECHR outside the Convention world

These early and authoritative constitutional readings of the ECHR have furthermore lent much support to more recent scholarly enterprises which seek to apply a constitutionalist lens to many legal orders—and even to unify them under the banner of transnational constitutionalism.[40] From the point of view of international law, it has been argued that the ECHR has turned into the core value system of the emerging international constitutional order.[41] From the point of view of comparative constitutional law, it has been argued that the ECtHR is now a constitutional court, mostly because of the authority it has acquired over national legal orders and the similarities in the types of cases brought before it and the methods it uses with those of national constitutional courts.[42] From the perspective of human rights law, it has also been argued that the constitutionalization route was the only viable option for a system the *raison d'être* of which, as well as geographic and demographic scope and caseload, have been altered in dramatic ways over the half-century of its operation.[43] While all these works blossom on the otherwise fertile theoretical grounds of post-State transnational constitutionalism,[44] one that readily associates rights with courts (and potentially, international courts), proportionality with a new and rights-oriented method of adjudication,[45] and 'constitutional human rights' with peremptory norms of *ius cogens*,[46] it is also noteworthy that they also rely heavily upon the legitimacy of the Convention people's constitutionalist vision. Statements by Wildhaber and Mahoney are recurring references in Stone Sweet and Greer's approaches, whereas the piece by de Wet draws most of its theoretical insights from the academic writings (which, as noted above, were and remain firmly situated in the field of international law) of authors who also happened to be insiders to the ECHR system such as Verdross, Henry G. Schermers (a member of the ECommHR), or Frowein.

---

[40] J. L. Dunoff and J. P. Trachtman (eds), *Ruling the World? Constitutionalism, International Law, and Global Governance* (Cambridge: Cambridge University Press, 2009); N. K. Tsagourias (ed), *Transnational Constitutionalism: International and European Models* (Cambridge: Cambridge University Press, 2007).

[41] E. de Wet, 'The Emergence of International and Regional Value Systems as a Manifestation of the Emerging International Constitutional Order', 19 *Leiden Journal of International Law* (2006), 611; see also C. Tomuschat, 'The European Court of Human Rights Overwhelmed by Applications: Problems and Possible Solutions' in R. Wolfrum and U. Deutsch (eds), *The European Court of Human Rights Overwhelmed by Applications: Problems and Possible Solutions* (Berlin: Springer, 2009).

[42] A. Stone Sweet, 'Sur la constitutionnalisation de la Convention européenne des droits de l'homme', 80 *Revue trimestrielle des droits de l'homme* (2009), 923.

[43] S. Greer, *The European Convention on Human Rights: Achievements, Problems, Prospects* (Cambridge: Cambridge University Press, 2006).

[44] J. Weiler and M. Wind, *European Constitutionalism Beyond the State* (Cambridge: Cambridge University Press, 2003).

[45] A. Stone Sweet and J. Mathews, 'Proportionality Balancing and Global Constitutionalism', 47 *Columbia Journal of Transnational Law* (2008), 73.

[46] M. Scheinin, 'Impact on the Law of Treaties' in M. Scheinin and T. Kammings (eds), *The Impact of Human Rights on General International Law* (Oxford: Oxford University Press, 2009).

There is much to comment upon in relation to both this 'constitutionalization' discourse and some of its theoretical underpinnings. It gives an arguably exaggerated central place to human rights in law for it turns them into unmistakable vectors of 'constitutionalization' regardless of the many remaining theoretical blind spots of human rights theory—and especially *legal* theory. In its internationalist version, not only does it take the very existence of norms of *ius cogens* for granted, thus ignoring (or at least not making up to) much of the theoretical dispute about peremptory norms,[47] but it also draws an equation between human rights and norms of *ius cogens*[48] in an arguably under-problematicized manner. In its comparative constitutionalist version, this discourse can be said to be overconfident in associating judicial (constitutional) review, proportionality, and higher standards of human rights protection—in a manner which places it at risk of imposing a US-type centrality of the judiciary in European settings where the notion of an all-judiciary protection of fundamental rights resonates as far less legitimate and satisfactory. These elements of critique will not be further developed here; rather, the focus in the remainder of the chapter will be placed on the tendency of both these versions of the constitutionalist discourse to either overlook or hide the lasting relevance of *national* normative orders.

II. No Longer International but Certainly Not Constitutional: Rehabilitating a *National* Perspective on the ECHR

In this section, legal discourses over the ECHR in France and Italy as case studies will be presented. It will be established that 'constitutional semantics'

---

[47] This equation is rather situated in time and space. For a useful recollection of theorizations of *ius cogens* from 17th-century political through to mid-20th century legal arenas, see A. Gomez-Robledo, 'Le *jus cogens* international: sa genèse, sa nature, ses fonctions', *Recueil des cours de l'Académie de droit international* (1981). He insists on the conceptual links between *ius cogens* and natural law:

> Chez les classiques du droit international, de Vitoria à Vattel, dans la majorité pour le moins, le droit naturel assume la fonction qui correspond dans l'actualité au ius cogens . . . Il existe en effet entre le ius cogens et le ius naturale une étroite parenté, celle que leur confère le fait d'être des normes supérieures, au plus haut de l'échelle hiérarchique, ainsi que le fait d'être tous deux non dérogeables par le biais de toute convention particulière qui leur serait contraire.

He thus explains that it should come as no surprise that the discussions about turning the notion into positive law within the International Law Commission after the Second World War received enthusiastic support from natural law theory supporters and the Holy See. In fact, the Holy See's representative at the Vienna Convention was none other than René-Jean Dupuy, a French international law professor who would later become the first French member of the ECommHR, who then expresses the Vatican's satisfaction and deep belief in the *ius cogens*/human rights equation:

> Le Saint Siège ne peut que se rallier à toute tentative de placer au-dessus du pouvoir certains principes fondamentaux. Dans sa doctrine, ce rôle est assuré par le droit naturel. . . . Le Saint Siège se demande s'il ne serait pas possible, même si l'on renonce à dresser une énumération des normes qui composent le ius cogens, de dégager un principe d'interprétation donnant à cette notion une valeur plus concrète. Pour le Saint Siège, ce dénominateur commun se trouve dans le principe de la primauté des droits de l'homme.

[48] Scheinin, n 46 above.

are hardly relevant in those national settings and that if they are at all, they have very different meanings in both examples: whereas they are mostly used in a 'preservation-of-the-national-legal-order' fashion in Italy, they (implicitly) support a technically much looser desire to affirm a 'symbolic-axiological' primacy of human rights in France.

The ECHR and the strong Italian internationalist legal tradition

There is a strong and vivid tradition of international law in Italy. Italian jurists take pride in the existence of a 'German–Italian' approach to international law, that led by Triepel and Anzilotti. Certainly, the Italian tradition of international law is rather at odds with all the idealistic faith that has enabled ECHR law to contribute to the juridical revolution that international human rights law stands for: it is dualist and refuses to consider that national law can be deemed invalid for the (sole) matter that it contradicts international law; it firmly holds on to an inter-sovereign State approach to international law that only painstakingly allows for the acceptance of some relevance of the individual. In fact, even the Italian jurists who have served in Strasbourg (presumably those most inclined to accepting the premises on which European human rights was to be built) retained significant parts of this Italian international law traditionalism that thus singled them out in otherwise strongly cohesive crowds: Giorgio Balladore Pallieri held strongly dualist views even after his appointment as a judge in Strasbourg[49] and Giuseppe Sperduti is the single member of the Commission who dissented from the recourse to the concept of *ordre public* in the 1961 *Austria v Italy* decision.[50] However, and regardless of the potential case to be made for sheer inadequacy between the ECHR and the Italian 'traditionalist internationalist' perspective, it is beyond doubt that internationalists remained for a long time the only legal scholars actually to pay attention to the ECHR in Italy. They are the ones who wrote the early articles on the Convention,[51] published the first monographs on the topic,[52] spoke about the ECHR in legal conferences,[53] and so on.[54]

The reason it is interesting to stress this centrality of international law specialists in Italy in the dissemination process of ECHR law from Strasbourg to Rome,

---

[49] G. Balladore Pallieri, *Diritto Internazionale Pubblico* (8th edn, Milan: Giuffrè, 1962).

[50] In a separate opinion, he insisted that the notion central to the Commission's decision that the ECHR represented a piece of a 'communitarian public order' rested on 'highly approximate' grounds.

[51] See the references in C. Mazzi, 'Bibliografia italiana sulla Cedu', *Rivista di diritto internazionale privato e processuale* (1986).

[52] See the volumes by G. Biscottini, *La Convenzione Europea dei Diritti dell'Uomo nell'applicazione giurisprudenziale in Italia* (Milan: Giuffrè, 1981); V. Grementieri, *L'Italia e la Cedu* (Milan: Giuffrè, 1989); S. Bartole, *Commentario Alla Convenzione Europea Per La Tutela Dei Diritti Dell'uomo E Delle Libertà Fondamentali* (Padua: CEDAM, 2001).

[53] F. Capotorti, 'Les interférences dans l'ordre juridique interne entre la Convention européenne des droits de l'homme et d'autres accords internationaux' in *Les droits de l'homme en droit interne et en droit international* (Brussels: Institut d'Etudes Européennes, 1968); C. Zanghi, 'The Effectiveness and Efficiency of the Guarantees of Human Rights enshrined in the ECHR' in Council of Europe (ed), *4ème Colloque international sur la CEDH* (Strasbourg: Conseil de l'Europe, 1970).

[54] For further references, see Hennette-Vauchez, n 19 above.

Palermo, and Milan, is that there is a case to be made for the idea that Italian internationalists were more likely to remain hermetic to the notion that the ECHR would be part of something like a 'European public order' (let alone a constitutional order) than domestic law specialists. As is well known, international law specialists are not necessarily at ease with highly disputed notions such as 'public order', '*ius cogens*', and the like. And thus it should come as no surprise that traditional Italian internationalists barely discussed the notion of 'objective' obligations that would derive from the Convention. In other words, what Italian international law scholars have been saying about the Convention is the following: the ECHR is an international law device that is to be introduced within the national legal order and the application of which (and thus, status, strength, etc) is a matter of domestic law.[55] No less, but no more.

Granted, a shift has occurred over time in scholarly perceptions of the ECHR in Italian legal academic circles; and many domestic lawyers now pay attention to and comment on ECHR law. As far as academic interest of domestic lawyers is concerned, specific mention must be made with regards to criminal law specialists. Indeed, for many years the ECHR all but began and ended with Arts 5 and 6 in the eyes of its Italian audience. For that reason, it cannot be overlooked that early on (and certainly after Italy was condemned for the first time in the *Artico* case in 1980[56]), specialists of procedure and penal law in general were at the forefront of explaining, commenting on, and writing about the ECHR.[57] This, however, can be explained as a mostly *mechanical* effect of the ECommHR and the ECtHR's case law—and most of these publications do not reveal a genuine interest in the ECHR in itself (its identity, its nature, its effects...) but only address the issue of systemic defaults within the Italian judicial and criminal system. In fact, other branches of Italian law that remained long immune from ECHR-based condemnations whole-heartedly ignored the Convention until recently. For instance, administrative lawyers seem not to have been particularly interested in ECHR law;[58] in fact the first monograph on Italian administrative law and the ECHR was not published until 2007.[59] The same seems to be true with respect to civil law: one if its great figures, Professor P. Rescigno, noted in 2001 that the influence of the ECHR on private law had 'only been scarce'.[60]

Constitutionalists, however, are now paying attention to the ECHR in growing numbers. Interestingly, however, there is a strong case for this belated constitutionalist

[55] B. Conforti, 'The New European Court of Human Rights Between International and Domestic Law', IX *Italian Yearbook of International Law* (1999), 3.

[56] *Artico v Italy* Series A no 37 (1980).

[57] The leading publication in this respect is M. Chiavario, *La CEDU nel sistema delle fonte normative in materia penale* (Milan: Giuffrè, 1969).

[58] G. Greco, 'La Cedu e il diritto amministrativo in Italia', *Rivista italiana di diritto pubblico comunitario* (2000), 26.

[59] S. Mirate, *Giustizia Amministrativa e Cedu: l'altro diritto europeo in Italia, Francia e Inghilterra* (Naples: Jovene, 2007).

[60] P. Rescigno, 'Cedu e diritto privato' in *Convegno in occasione del cinquantenario della Convenzione del Consiglio d'Europa per la protezione dei diritti umani e delle libertà fondamentali, in onore di Paolo Barile* (Rome: Academia Nazionale dei Lincei, 2000).

interest in the ECHR to be but a consequence of what has come to be perceived as shortcomings in the internationalist approach. Indeed, the Italian constitution of 1947 puts forth a strongly dualist approach to international law: all international norms such as treaties must be introduced into the national legal order by a national legal Act and, subsequently, the international norm is vested with the authority and normative rank of this introductory device. As far as the ECHR is concerned, it was introduced into the Italian legal order by a law of 1955 and the strict and mechanical application of constitutional provisions thus implies that it has legislative rank. However, both courts and scholars have regularly expressed unease with this situation, and the idea that the ECHR was too important by its nature to be potentially overruled by posterior national legislation made its way in the Italian landscape,[61] based on the notion that the ECHR's position within the Italian legal order is 'very different than the one it ought to be' (*ben diversa di quella che la Cedu dovrebbe avere*).[62] The Constitutional Court itself ruled in 1993 that the ECHR provisions had been introduced into Italian law by 'atypical competences of the State' and that they consequently could not be repealed or modified by national legislation.[63] The Supreme Judiciary Court echoed the Constitutional Court six years later by ruling that since they reflected 'general principles of the legal order', ECHR provisions had a 'specific force of resistance' to posterior legislation.[64] Scholarly commentary has also been prolific on the diverse ways in which it could be argued that the ECHR could be said to escape this tragic fate of international law within the Italian constitutional order.[65] For instance, it has been argued that the Italian constitution's reference to 'inviolable rights' (art 2) encompassed ECHR provisions and thus bestowed upon them constitutional value. It was also claimed that a detour through EC law, and the obligation it imposes on Member States to respect its direct application and primacy, made it possible to consider that ECHR provisions were superior in rank to legislative norms—especially after the ECJ had started referring to the ECHR as a standard of fundamental rights protection within the EC.[66] In other words, constitutional law has been used in a partially instrumental (and highly imaginative) manner by Italian jurists, in order to

---

[61] For a review: A. Cassese, 'L'efficacia delle norme italiane di adattamento alla Convenzione europea dei diritti dell'uomo', *Rivista di diritto internazionale privato e processuale* (1969), 918.

[62] G. Gerin, *La nuova Corte europea dei diritti dell'uomo* (Trieste: IIEDH, 2000), 72.

[63] CC, sent 10, 1987; see also Cass 8 July 1998, in *Rivista Internazionale dei Diritti dell'Uomo* (1998), 970.

[64] Cass 10 July 1993, *Medrano*.

[65] It is noteworthy that Italian Convention people have been forerunners in this enterprise—from B. Conforti's *principio di specialità sui generis* that enables him to claim that since by definition international treaties have been concluded as obligations, their bindingness should not be blocked or altered by norms of domestic legal orders (B. Conforti, *Lezioni di diritto internazionale* (Naples: Editoriale Scientifica, 1982)) to M. de Salvia's call for a ready constitutionalization of the ECHR (M. de Salvia, 'L'acculturazione incompiuta al diritto europeo dei diritti dell'uomo', 2 *Rivista internazionale dei diritti dell'uomo* (2000), 447).

[66] For overviews of these theories: F. Donati, 'La Cedu nell'ordinamento italiano', 3 *Il Diritto dell'Unione Europea* (2007), 691; P. Pustorino, 'Sull'applicabilità diretta e la prevalenza della Cedu nell'ordinamento italiano', 1 *Rivista internazionale dei diritti dell'uomo* (1995), 134.

argue that the ECHR could not (and should not) be subject to the *lex posterior derogat legi priori* rule.

But this 'constitutional' approach of the ECHR within Italian legal scholarly discourse does not at all speak the same language as the constitutional semantics that emanated from within the Convention world early on. In fact, it goes in the opposite direction, for the Italian constitutionalists' interest in the ECHR really is a matter of hierarchical rank of norms, and has only served to oppose the internationalist perspective that potentially subjected the Convention to modification by posterior legislation. It does not, however, amount (or only in marginal proportions) to sustaining the idea according to which the Convention should have (or has) constitutional value—and a fortiori, supra-constitutional value.

This very technical/normative understanding of the Italian constitutional reading of the ECHR is only confirmed by recent evolutions in positive law. At the end of 2007, the Constitutional Court issued two important decisions that tentatively clarified the status of the ECHR in Italian law. Without explicitly ruling that the ECHR was of constitutional value, the Court did decide that even posterior national legislation had to respect the Convention and that this was a potential matter of constitutional review. But the Court also affirmed its monopolistic competence in examining that particular issue, and all inferior and regular courts before which it is raised are obliged to defer the question to the Constitutional Court.[67] In other words, what is at stake here is a rather *traditional* form of constitutional argumentation: constitutional law is applied to the ECHR insofar as (and only insofar as) it provides answers to the question of the normative rank of the ECHR *within the Italian constitutional order* (no constitutionalism beyond the State at stake here). The positive law landscape as stabilized by the recent decisions by the Constitutional Court unquestionably maintains the ECHR within the borders and under the authority of national (constitutional) law. Therefore, although there has indeed been a shift from an originally solely internationalist eye on the Convention to one that is now increasingly constitutionalist within the Italian scholarly debate over the ECHR, 'constitutionalist' in this particular case does not convey the idea of fundamental importance and allegedly normative primacy that it is sometimes associated with (cf supra-constitutionalism); nor does it correspond to a transnational-beyond-State concept of constitution. Quite differently, it is only in a national legal order's integrity-preservation fashion that constitutional semantics are applied to the ECHR.

The ECHR 'au pays des droits de l'homme'

In France, the picture is both similar and different. It is similar in that academic interest in the ECHR was ignited in a rather slow fashion (and actually slower in the French case than in the Italian one), a fact that arguably has much to do with the great activism of Convention people who for a long time occupied in a somewhat monopolistic fashion the then narrow space that was provided for ECHR law in

---

[67] O. Pollicino, 'Case note 4(2)', *European Constitutional Law Review* (2008).

academic *loci*.[68] It is also similar in that the case of France also verifies the hypothesis that internationalist academic arenas and scholars were forerunners in opening up to the ECHR. Thus, until well into the 1980s scholarly pieces on the ECHR remained few in number and were almost systematically published in international law journals. The status of ECHR studies and commentaries in the prestigious *Revue Générale de Droit International Public* is emblematic in that respect: one article was published in 1964 on the United Nations and regional organizations of human rights[69] and only later were some cases such as the famous *Ireland v United Kingdom* case of 1978 commented upon (note that it is another clue of the strongly internationalist perspective on the ECHR that only an inter-state case should be commented upon). But it is not until well into the 1980s[70] that substantial pieces addressing ECHR law appeared.[71]

---

[68] Given our hypothesis on the crucial role of 'Convention people' in generating academic interest in the ECHR in the early years (especially during the 1950s–60s), it is probably hardly surprising that genuine French academic interest arose later than in the Italian case. For indeed, France's late ratification of the ECHR (1974) accounts for the absence (or at least greater rarity) of French representatives in Strasbourg. It must be recalled that even though a French senator had been appointed at the ECommHR in the very early years in the name of the importance of France, on the one hand, and the hopefully imminence of the French ratification, on the other hand, he stopped attending and was not replaced as it became clear that ratification did not rank sufficiently high on the French political agenda. As a consequence, there was no French member at the Commission until René-Jean Dupuy was appointed in 1974. Granted, the situation was different at the Court, since René Cassin was elected judge in 1959 (he even served as a vice-president immediately, and as a president as of 1965). He undoubtedly played a crucial role within the Court but it must, however, be kept in mind that the Court only delivered two judgments while he sat at the Court (*Lawless v Ireland (No 3)* Series A no 3 (1961); *De Becker v Belgium* Series A no 4 (1962) and . . . none during his presidency (he left the Court in 1968 in order to allow for regeneration, before the *Use of Languages in Belgium, Neumeister*, and *Wemhoff* judgments were delivered. And this only partial presence of France within the Strasbourg institutions until 1974 verifies more generally that it not only affected the Commission and the Court, but also all the institutions that accompany them: the Commission's Secretariat, the Court's Registry, etc. It is therefore clear that there were fewer French than Italians who could spread the ECHR word from Strasbourg (this obviously does not mean there were none; one only has to recall the importance of names such as Marc-André Eissen, who joined the Council of Europe in the mid-1950s, to prove to the contrary; they were, however, fewer and therefore their importance were bound to be less).

[69] G. Guyomar, 'Nations Unies et organisations régionales dans la protection des droits de l'homme', *Revue générale de droit international public* (1964), 687.

[70] This could be linked to the fact that, as of 1983, Professor P.-M. Dupuy joined the editorial board of the journal, together with Charles Vallée. An internationalist but also son of France's first member of the ECommHR (R. J. Dupuy), it can be hypothesized that Dupuy was more likely to be acquainted with and sensitive to human rights law. In any event, there is a case to be made for the reverse idea according to which the former sole editor-in-chief had reason not to pay much interest to the ECHR. Ch. Rousseau, to start with, had been on the very first list of candidates for judge at the ECtHR that France presented to the Council of Europe's Parliamentary Assembly in 1959. As is well known, R. Cassin was appointed. Interestingly, this could be linked to Rousseau's theoretical stance on the field of international law, for an element he has thoroughly insisted upon throughout his career is that immorality (eg contrariness to human rights) cannot per se invalidate an international agreement. This, obviously, is very much at odds with the conception of international law that has been most successful both in the foundations and the functioning of the ECHR, best embodied by A. Verdross's strong views to the contrary or H. Rolin's credo in such a concept as an 'international public order' (see H. Rolin, 'Vers un ordre public réellement international?' in *Hommage d'une génération de juristes au président Basdevant* (Paris: Pedone, 1960), 441.

[71] P.-H. Imbert, 'Les réserves à la CEDH devant la Commission de Strasbourg', 3 *Revue générale de droit international public* (1983), 580; F. Sudre, 'La première affaire française devant la Cour européenne des droits de l'homme: L'arrêt Bozano du 18 déc. 1986', 2 *Revue générale de droit international*

However, the French case also differs from the Italian one for a reason intrinsic to the very structure of legal curricula in French law schools, for indeed a new course was created in 1956 and became compulsory after 1962, that is essentially a human rights law course (*Libertés publiques*). As a result, a growing group of law professors who specialized in human rights started emerging quite early on in France, and logically some of them became interested in the ECHR and not (necessarily) from the point of view of international law. Hence, the French configuration became propitious to the ECHR being treated as a human rights law matter, and not simply as one of international law. The chronicle entrusted to Robert Pelloux by the *Annuaire Français de Droit International* from the early 1960s onwards is telling in this respect, for Pelloux was not an internationalist. Rather, he had a human rights/ civil liberties profile. Similar observations can be made apropos another important ECHR law chronicle published between the years 1978 and 1982 authored by Patrice Rolland, another non-internationalist *Libertés publiques* specialist. Therefore the specificity of the French case may be summarized as follows: whereas the ECHR was initially viewed mainly as an international law device to be commented upon in international arenas by international law specialists,[72] it also raised the interest of a nascent group of human rights law scholars who were not (necessarily) trained in international law and thus imported legal concepts and qualifications from their domestic law background and began to apply them to the ECHR .

This initial mapping (observable well into the 1980s) of French legal scholars' interest in ECHR law was confirmed and accentuated from the 1990s onwards in the sense that domestic law specialists chose to focus on European human rights law in ever-greater numbers. Domestic law journals started devoting more editorial space to ECHR law: upon her appointment as editor-in-chief of the *Revue de science criminelle et de droit penal comparé* in 1984, Mireille Delmas-Marty[73] launched a biannual chronicle devoted to ECHR law (interestingly though, it was not entrusted to an academic but to Louis-Edmond Pettiti who was then serving at the ECtHR); and shortly after, Frédéric Sudre[74] convinced the *Revue française de droit administratif*

---

public (1987), 533 and 'La notion de peines et traitements inhumains et dégradants dans la jurisprudence de la Commission et de la Cour européenne des droits de l'homme', *Revue générale de droit international public* (1984); G. Cohen-Jonathan, 'Les réserves à la CEDH', 2 *Revue générale de droit international public* (1989), 273.

[72] See ibid; G. Cohen-Jonathan, *La Convention européenne des droits de l'homme* (Aix-en-Provence: Presses universitaires d'Aix-Marseille, 1989); Imbert, n 71 above; F. Sudre, *Droit international et européen des droits de l'homme* (Paris: Presses universitaires de France, 1992); Sudre (1987) and (1984), n 71 above.

[73] A specialist of criminal law, M. Delmas-Marty began looking at ECHR law in the 1980s as a means of sustaining her broader *ius commune* fuzzy logic theoretical stance. There is a direct correlation between her appointment as editor-in-chief of the *Revue de science criminelle* and the launch of an ECHR law chronicle (held mostly over the years by Convention people: L.-E. Pettiti, P. H. Teitgen, F. Tulkens) which was the first of its kind. For more information and references, see Hennette-Vauchez, n 19 above, 26).

[74] Initially an internationalist, F. Sudre shifted to ECHR law soon after his doctoral dissertation. By the end of the 1980s, he developed an intense activity devoted to the ECHR. After publishing a monograph on international and European human rights law, he organized many conferences on the ECHR, wrote reports, and acted as a coordinator of many collective research projects, and also published extensively. Consequently, he generated something akin to an ECHR law school. To this

(1991),[75] the *Revue universelle des droits de l'homme* (1992), the *Semaine juridique* (1996), and the *Revue du droit public* (1999) also to launch ECHR law chronicles under his (sometimes lasting) authority. During the first half of the 1990s, a new generation of ECHR law specialists began to appear. It was formed of jurists who were no longer international but domestic law specialists—public law specialists but later also private law specialists.[76] Established scholars were turning to the ECHR[77] and, maybe even more significantly, young scholars were starting to sense that ECHR law was a subject of study susceptible to being valued as a worthwhile academic specialty—by the mid-1990s, a significant number of PhD dissertations (the key to an academic career) were successfully being defended on subjects related to ECHR law.[78] Hence, a specific community of human rights law/ECHR law specialists quite rapidly emerged within French academia—a profile that is generally not met so strongly elsewhere (and especially not in Italy).

This, again, is where academics' profiles and discourses are cohesive, for French legal scholarship is rather eager (and, in any event, much more so than its Italian counterpart) to view the ECHR as an element of a European public order. In fact, the concept of *ordre public* is central to Andriantsimbazovina's ECHR law chronicles in the *Cahiers de droit européen*[79] and he has recently defined the concept of

day, he has supervised close to ten PhD dissertations on ECHR law—some of which by students who have since become professors themselves. For more information and references see Hennette-Vauchez, n 19 above, 26.

[75] Interestingly, this first ECHR law chronicle by Sudre is also co-authored by a Strasbourg insider: Vincent Berger. However, it soon shifts to an all-academic undertaking, as well as the other chronicles Sudre is in charge of. Colleagues who join in the chronicles include Henri Labayle (an EU law specialist) and Joël Andriantsimbazovina and Laurent Sermet (administrative law specialists).

[76] J. Marguénaud, CEDH *et droit privé: l'influence de la jurisprudence de la Cour Européenne des Droits de l'homme sur le droit privé français* (Paris: La Documentation Francaise, 2001) and *La Cour européenne des droits de l'homme* (Paris: Dalloz, 1996).

[77] Cohen-Jonathan, n 71 above ; M. Delmas-Marty, *The European Convention for the Protection of Human Rights: International Protection versus National Restrictions* (Boston: Martinus Nijhoff, 1992); J.-F. Flauss, *La Satisfaction Equitable Dans Le Cadre De La Convention Europeenne Des Droits De L'homme: Perspectives D'actualité* (Saarbrücken: Europa-Institut der Universität des Saarlandes, 1995); J.-F. Flauss, Les droits de l'homme comme éléments d'une constitution et d'un ordre publics européens, 52 *Les Petites Affiches* (1993), .8; Sudre, nn 71 and 72 above ; P. Wachsmann, *Le Protocole N 11 a La Convention Européenne des droits de l'homme: Actes de la table-ronde Organisée le 22 septembro 1994 par l'Université Robert Schuman à Strasbourg* (Brussels: Bruylant, 1995).

[78] J. Andriantsimbazovina, *L'Autorité des décisions de justice constitutionnelles et européennes sur le juge administratif français: Conseil constitutionnel, Cour de justice des communautés européennes et Cour européenne des droits de l'homme* (Paris: LGDJ, 1998); A. Braconnier, *Jurisprudence de la CEDH et droit administratif français* (Brussels: Bruylant, 1997); H. Fourteau, *L'application de l'article 3 de la Convention européenne des droits de l'homme dans le droit interne des états membres: l'impact des garanties européennes contre la torture et les traitements inhumains ou dégradants* (Paris: LGDJ, 1996); B. Maurer, *Le Principe de respect de la dignité humaine et la convention européenne des droits de l'homme* (Paris: La Documentation française, 1999); C. Picheral, *L'ordre public européen. Droit communautaire et droit européen des droits de l'homme* (Paris: La Documentation Française, 2001); L. Sermet, *Convention européenne des droits de l'homme et contentieux administratif français* (Paris: Economica [pour] Centre d'Études et de Recherches Internationales et Communautaires, Université d'Aix-Marseille III, 1996); L. Potvin-Solis, *L'Effet des jurisprudences européennes sur la jurisprudence du conseil d'état français* (Paris: LGDJ, 1999).

[79] J. Andriantsimbazovina, 'L'élaboration progressive d'un ordre public européen des droits de l'homme', *Cahiers de droit européen* (1997), 'Splendeurs et misères de l'ordre public européen des droits

European public order as instrumental in the very definition of the ECHR's identity as well as in the autonomy of human rights law.[80] Sudre has written two pieces on the subject,[81] Cohen-Jonathan has been one of the first promoters of the concept[82] in France, and Flauss has also published many pieces on the subject.[83] This must be due to the 'domestic law' (and, in fact, predominantly administrative law) profile of many of these ECHR law specialists for, unlike internationalists, domestic lawyers are very familiar with the concept of public order; not to mention the fact that whereas its very relevance and existence are disputed in international law, that is certainly not the case with domestic—administrative—law. Further-more, as far as the identity of human rights law specialists is concerned, there is a strong case to be made for the fact that in large numbers, they have been or are 'believers'[84] in the notion of a *ius commune* that the Convention would somehow either favour or embody. There is, indeed, in France a strong trend within human rights law specialists that considers human rights (and thus ECHR law above all) as the expression of 'higher' norms and values.[85] In other words, although the constitutional paradigm does not explicitly play a prominent role in French jurisprudence, there is an underlying symbolic-axiological rationale to many a legal discourse on European human rights law that resembles some understandings of the word 'constitutional' (that is, 'of higher value'). Thus, if at all, constitutional semantics applied to the ECHR in France would refer to yet another understanding of the concept—one that looks neither to the political identity of the Convention nor to the modalities of its normative integration within national legal orders, but one that conveys the universal and humanistic promise of human rights.

III. Conclusion

This chapter has called for increased attention to the national level in legal discourse on European human rights law. Promoters of the constitutional/international

---

de l'homme', *Cahiers de droit européen* (2000), and 'La cour européenne des droits de l'homme à la croisée des chemins', *Cahiers de droit européen* (2002), 735.

[80] J. Andriantsimbazovina, 'L'ordre public européen des droits de l'homme: l'affirmation de l'autonomie du droit né de la CEDH?', *Annuaire de droit européen* (forthcoming).

[81] F. Sudre, 'Existe-t-il un ordre public européen?' in P. Tavernier (ed), *Quelle Europe pour les droits de l'homme?* (Brussels: Bruylant, 1996) and 'L'ordre public européen' in *L'ordre public: ordre public ou ordres publics? Ordre public et droits fondamentaux* (Brussels: Bruylant, 2001).

[82] G. Cohen-Jonathan (ed), 'Responsabilité pour atteinte aux droits de l'homme' in SFDI, *La respons-abilité dans le système international* (Paris: Pedone, 1991), 110.

[83] Flauss, n 77 above.

[84] M. Dembour, *Who Believes in Human Rights: Reflections on the European Convention* (Cambridge: Cambridge University Press, 2006).

[85] This has been observed in particular throughout French legal scholarship's recent infatuation with the human dignity principle: C. Girard and S. Hennette-Vauchez, *La dignité de la personne humaine. Recherche sur un processus de juridicisation* (Paris: Presses universitaires de France, 2005); S. Hennette-Vauchez, 'When Ambivalent Principles Prevail. Leads for explaining recent Western legal orders' infatuation for the human dignity principle', 10(2) *Legal Ethics* (2007), 193; E. Dreyer, 'La fonction des droits fondamentaux dans l'ordre juridique', 182/11 *Recueil Dalloz* (2006), 748.

alternative themselves cannot not deny the national level's importance; in fact, many of them rejoin in insisting on the importance of greater 'embeddedness'[86] of the ECHR within national legal orders. They tend, however, to overlook the importance the ECHR's strong dependence vis-à-vis national legal orders by maintaining the debate over the ECHR's future within a transnational framework that simply *does not make much sense on a national scale* because national legal actors (first of which are national constitutional courts) are hardly eager to accept the concept (let alone the authority) of a truly constitutional international level. Examples in this respect are numerous and can be found in many other instances than the Italian or the French cases on which this study has focused: from the notorious *Görgülü* ruling of the German Federal Constitutional Court[87] to other less conspicuous but highly significant trends of case law emanating from other European constitutional courts. One such example is the Spanish who have developed a 'flexible' jurisprudence regarding the authoritativeness of ECHR law in a pragmatic case law sustained 'less [by] the result of a principled linkage [between national constitutional law and ECHR law] than as a favourable exercise of discretion by the Tribunal Constitucional in the great number of cases where the stakes are not too high'.[88] Nico Krisch's analysis shows that even though there is certainly a post-national arena of judicial conversation, 'domestic courts insist on the ultimate supremacy of their own legal order over European human rights law'.[89] Therefore, it can be argued that because it fails to take into consideration the extraordinary variety of statuses that the ECHR is awarded in the 47 national legal orders to which it applies, the constitutional/ international alternative paradigmatic to the ECHR's reformatory discourse needs to be reconsidered as the product of a transnational perspective on the ECHR. Being thus based only on a partial picture, this alternative and the general 'constitutionalization' discourse it serves and readily applies to the ECHR may be said to run the risk of being purely theoretical and potentially entertaining no correspondence whatsoever with the national legal realities of ECHR law—realities that it is claimed should be the number one horizon of the reform agenda.[90]

---

[86] Following the words of L. Helfer, 'Redesigning the European Court of Human Rights: Embeddedness as a deep structural principle of the European Human Rights Regime', 19 *European Journal of International Law* (2008), 125.

[87] *Bundesverfassungsgericht*, 2 BvR 14841/01, 14 October 2004—a ruling by which the Court ruled that ordinary German courts are under the obligation to disregard judgments of the ECtHR if they are incompatible with central elements of the domestic legal order, legislative intent, or constitutional provisions.

[88] N. Krisch, 'The Open Architecture of European Human Rights Law', 71(2) *Modern Law Review* (2008), 191.

[89] Ibid, 215.

[90] Granted, such a pitfall not only exposes European human rights but international human rights law in general—as established by D. Shelton (n 18 above, 303):

> In general theory and practice diverge: there seems to be a pronounced gulf between the views of scholars and those of states and most international tribunals on the supremacy of human rights law . . . Despite the efforts of proponents, state practice and judicial decisions are sparse in recognizing and giving effect to either the doctrine of ius cogens or that of obligations erga omnes.

This analysis that insists on the risks of disconnection between a transnational constitutionalist paradigm applied to the ECHR and the reality it intends to analyse could actually be stretched further, in the sense that there are many other legal orders that are currently being analysed through a similar lens, such as the European Union, the United Nations, or the World Trade Organization—to name but a few. Not only are all these legal orders increasingly referred to in constitutional parlance, it is also often understood that their abiding by human rights norms and standards has done much to favour its purported relevance. Hence, it seems that human rights are viewed by many as a constitutionalizing device. This ought to raise many questions for further investigation,[91] among which: Are 'human rights' a stable and unequivocal concept in all these legal orders? Doesn't the assertion according to which 'human rights' are 'constitutional' (or lead to 'constitutionalization') necessarily rest on axiological conceptions of (here, international) law that have been seriously challenged?[92] In other words, isn't the 'constitutionalization-through-human-rights' paradigm (arguably a sibling of the 'integration-through-law' one[93]) putting itself at risk of pragmatic failure because of its voluntary ignorance of important critical strands of both international law and human rights law that should by now have caused legal actors to think (at least) twice before invoking any sort of correspondence between normative and axiological prevalence?

[91] For some leads, Hennette-Vauchez, n 17 above.

[92] See notably M. Koskenniemi, 'Les droits de l'homme, la politique et l'amour' in *La politique du droit international. Doctrines* (Paris: Pedone, 2007, 203) and *The Gentle Civilizer of Nations: The Rise and Fall of International Law, 1870–1960* (Cambridge: Cambridge University Press, 2002).

[93] A. Vauchez, 'Integration-through-law: contribution to a socio-history of European common-sense', European University Institute Working Papers Series, 2008/10; and A. Vauchez, *L'en-droit de l'Europe*, Habilitation thesis, Université Paris 1 Panthéon Sorbonne, January 2010.

9

Diplomatic Intrusions, Dialogues, and Fragile Equilibria: The European Court as a Constitutional Actor of the European Union

Laurent Scheeck

The role of the European Court of Human Rights (ECtHR) in the EU is a paradoxical case of asymmetrical inter-institutional power relations in Europe. In the society of European legal actors, it indeed happens that the most powerful institutions do not necessarily prevail over more fragile, yet sophisticated and highly institutionalized normative entrepreneurs. In this vein, the thesis of this chapter is that, contrary to the intuitive assumption that the EU's legal system is much more powerful than the Council of Europe's human rights regime, ECtHR norms have progressively been superimposed over EU norms within the EU itself—in the absence of any formal institutional linkage between the EU and the Council of Europe.

This evolution is seen as a direct result of the ECtHR's 'diplomatic intrusions' into the EU system and its high-profile dialogue with both EU judges and political actors. Over the last three decades, the linkage between the two European systems has had a progressively reinforcing relationship in many unexpected ways. It might even be the case that the European Convention on Human Rights (ECHR) norms have nowhere been as strong as in the EU system, where they became an important instrument for the Court of Justice of the European Union (CJEU, the former ECJ) in its quest to enforce the primacy of EU law.

The evolving linkage between the EU and the Court, which has led the Strasbourg judges to become very powerful actors inside the EU system is not an automatic process. It is rather the result of complex legal entrepreneurship, the mobilization of both public and private actors, the increasing presence of legal actors in political fora, the emerging dialogue and even solidarity between European judges, and the many unintended and unexpected consequences of jurisprudential entanglement between Courts, which reciprocally intruded into each other's legal realms before transforming their linkage into a form of strategic interdependence.

While it is possible to trace back these evolutions empirically from a historico-politico-sociological perspective, an investigation into the role of the Court in the

EU also shows, however, that the resulting complex equilibriums, as well as the judge-driven jurisprudential politics that have allowed for an era of peace in a sometimes turbulent EU–Council of Europe relationship, remain very delicate, and possibly ephemeral. The role of the Court still largely resides on jurisprudential principles and, even more so, on the discursive highlighting of mutually beneficial jurisprudential evolutions by an epistemic community of judges, academics, and lawyers fighting for the protection of human rights beyond the State and/or the constitutionalization of the EU. The fate of the judicial protection of human rights in Europe nowadays greatly depends on the cooperation of lawyers and judges, who might not have the same institutional and political incentives to increase their cooperation in the future as their predecessors had in the past.

How can a relatively isolated court like the ECtHR have a considerable normative and political impact on a much bigger European organization, especially since the EU has not yet acceded to the ECHR? How can the ECHR prevail in the future, given that the EU's Charter of Fundamental Rights has become legally binding with the ratification of the Lisbon Treaty? Will EU fundamental norms and the CJEU sideline the ECHR and the Strasbourg Court in the near future as the Charter has now come into force? Will the EU succeed to accede to the ECHR, as the new Lisbon Treaty foresees it, despite the growing Member State resistance to transnational human rights instruments? This chapter tries to answer these questions. Their very nature hints at the fact that the ECHR and its Court still face the risk of disconnection from the EU system (or worse, indifference), even though there is no doubt that over the last 20 years, the Strasbourg Court has had a regime-changing impact on the EU.

The 'diplomatic intrusion' of the ECtHR into European affairs and its diplomatic political and juridical dialogue, has not only transformed the way in which the CJEU sets its priorities, defines its autonomy, and interprets EU law, but it has also deeply influenced EU law and treaty-making. As a result of these interactions, this research aims to demonstrate that even within the EU, ECHR norms are now sometimes more important than the most fundamental principles of EU law, such as the four freedoms. It gives empirical evidence for these claims based on a socio-historical analysis of jurisprudence, political and judicial discourses and their evolution, and on an in-depth study of the dialogue of European judges. Nonetheless, many political and legal uncertainties have resurfaced since the EU's new treaty has come into force, and doubts can be raised whether the future role of the ECtHR in the EU will be comparable to its recent past.

I. A Diplomatic Intrusion

The ECtHR has penetrated into the EU's legal order on numerous occasions. The EU became an object of the Strasbourg Court's attention by the end of the 1970s as the human rights judges began receiving applications alleging violations of the ECHR by the European Community. In almost 30 years of very careful, often hesitating, jurisprudential politics, the human rights judges have put the EU under considerable pressure to make the EU accede to the ECHR. The ECtHR has indeed not shied away from controlling human rights at the EU level with time. Yet, Strasbourg's interference in the EU's constitutional space has been a slow and gradual process, hence we prefer to qualify this process as a 'diplomatic intrusion' rather than a form of inter-institutional 'aggression'.[1]

It was by the end of the 1970s that Strasbourg was confronted with an EC-related question for the first time. In 1978, the Court assessed the *CFDT v the European Communities and, in a subsidiary manner, the collective of their Member States and the Member States taken individually* case.[2] At the time, the European Commission of Human Rights determined it did not have jurisdiction because the EC was not a Contracting Party to the ECHR. Subsequently, the European Commission of Human Rights reiterated this jurisprudence in various cases related to the EC.[3] In the case of *M & Co v The Federal Republic of Germany*,[4] the Commission confirmed its jurisprudence by stating that the EC Member States remain responsible for the implementation of Community acts and cannot escape the guarantees foreseen by the ECHR, but also that it was unable to examine procedures and decisions of EC institutions. In this affair, the Commission brought in a new principle with regard to the hierarchical relationship between the two legal orders. It introduced a '*solange*' (that is, a principle of equivalent protection comparable to the German Constitutional Court's 1986 *Solange* decision) in which it declared that a transfer of competences to the EC is not excluded 'as long as' fundamental rights receive an equivalent protection at the EC level. But unlike the German court, the ECtHR excluded the possibility of monitoring EU acts on their respect for fundamental rights, giving the impression that it gave up every form of control over the EU.[5]

The ECtHR only started to rule on EU-related cases in the mid-1990s and in doing so considerably reinforced the interaction between Strasbourg and the EU. In the *Procola v Luxembourg* case[6] or *Cantoni v France* case,[7] the Court did not refrain, for instance, from controlling the compatibility of national laws implementing EU law with the ECHR.

By the end of the twentieth century, the Court's control became more direct. In 1999, Strasbourg made a decisive move with its *Matthews* judgment.[8] The case

---

[1] L. Scheeck, 'The relationship between the European Courts and integration through human rights', 65 *Zeitschrift für ausländisches öffentliches Recht und Völkerrecht* (2005), 837.
[2] *CFDT v the EC and, in a subsidiary manner, the collective of their Member States and the Member States taken individually* case Appl no 8030/77 (1978).
[3] See eg the cases *Dalfino* (1985) not reported, *Dufay v The European Communities* Series A (1989), *De la Fuente* (1991) not reported.
[4] *M & Co v The Federal Republic of Germany* Appl no 13258/87 (1990).
[5] A. Bultrini, 'La responsabilité des Etats membres de l'Union européenne pour les violations de la Convention européenne des droits de l'homme imputables au système communautaire', 49 *Revue trimestrielle des droits de l'homme* (2002), 16; R. Lawson, 'Confusion and Conflict? Diverging Interpretations of the European Convention on Human Rights in Strasbourg and Luxembourg' in R. Lawson and M. de Blois (eds), *Essays in Honour of Henry G. Schermers*, vol 3, *The Dynamics of the Protection of Human Rights in Europe* (Dordrecht: Martinus Nijhoff, 1994).
[6] *Procola v Luxembourg* Appl no 14570/89 (1995).
[7] *Cantoni v France* Appl no 17862/91 (1996).
[8] *Matthews v United Kingdom* Appl no 24833/94 (1999).

concerned deciding whether the UK could be held responsible for not having organized European elections in Gibraltar in 1994 and the Court concluded that the UK (as well as all the other EU Member States) was responsible for the consequences of the Maastricht Treaty, effectively sanctioning for the first time a Contracting Party for an EU-related issue.[9]

To this day, the ECtHR has not pronounced a sanction in cases directed against the EU Member States taken collectively on the basis that the latter are responsible for the acts of international institutions to which they have delegated political and legal authority, even though the number of requests directed against the Member States has been increasing.[10]

Yet, the Court usually undertakes a very detailed scrutiny of EU law in all EU-related cases, thus providing some form of external control despite the fact that its hands are mostly tied. Above and beyond the question of Strasbourg's jurisdiction, it appears that its judges have already been scanning the EU for human rights violations for a very long time, and that, meanwhile, they do so in most areas of EU politics. Besides institutional questions, the Court had to deal with, for instance, the EU's economic and social policies, with questions of democracy and asylum policy in the EU, the way it deals with terrorism, and how it applies international sanctions.

On 30 June 2005, the *Bosphorus Airways v Ireland*[11] decision made another step forward.[12] The final judgment appears to be a compromise between those judges who pleaded for an 'annexation' of the EU to the ECHR and those who did not want to intrude into the EU's legal order at a moment when the Member States were seriously considering making the EU accede to the ECHR. This compromise comes down to a 'presumption of equivalent protection' as elaborated in the *M & Co* case, but the Court also states, for instance, that it presumes that an EU Member State will not depart from the Convention when it implements EU acts and that 'any such presumption can be rebutted if, in the circumstances of a particular case, it is considered that the protection of Convention rights was manifestly deficient'.[13] Put differently, the ECtHR was at the same time willing to wait until the EU had formally adhered to the ECHR even though it had also declared that it could sanction Member States for EU-related acts if they violate the ECHR. The 'Bosphorus test' has subsequently been successfully applied in cases such as *Biret v the 15 EU Member States* of 9 December 2008.[14] Yet, this very same approach was also ignored in *Boivin v Belgium and France and 32 Council of Europe Member*

---

[9] O. de Schutter and O. L'Hoest, 'La Cour européenne des droits de l'homme juge du droit communautaire: Gibraltar, l'Union européenne, et la Convention européenne des droits de l'homme', 36 *Cahiers de droit européen* (2000), 1–2.

[10] See eg *Soc Guérin Automobiles v the 15 EU Member States* Appl no 51717/99 (2000); *Segi ea and Gestoras Pro Amnestia v the 15 EU Member States* Appl no 6422/02 (2002); and *Senator Lines v the 15 EU Member States* Appl no 56672/00 (2004).

[11] *Bosphorus Hava Yollari Turizm Ve Ticaret Anonim Şirketi v Ireland* Appl no 45036/98 (2005).

[12] S. Douglas-Scott, 'The Bosphorus Case: Human Rights in the EU and ECHR', 43 *Common Market Law Review* (2006), 243.

[13] See n 11 above, para 156.

[14] *Biret v 15 Member States of the European Union* Appl no 13762/04 (2008).

States.[15] In this case, which was closely comparable to the *Bosphorus* case, a request was directed against Eurocontrol. Even though that organization had no direct relation with the EC as such, the judges had to deal with a situation where the Member States did not directly intervene in the acts that led to the alleged violation of the ECHR, and the impossibility of creating a direct link between 'supranational acts' and the Contracting Parties had led the judges to declare the request inadmissible. Such hesitations still exemplify the self-restraint of the ECtHR with regard to other international organizations, as long as they have not acceded to the ECHR.

Finally, it appears, however, that the ECtHR has been forced to look at the human rights situation in the EU on a regular basis as more and more EU-related cases have been brought to Strasbourg, despite the absence of a formal EU accession to the ECHR and despite the legal uncertainties related to its competence to review EU acts. The ECtHR judges have, however, been patient enough to avoid the scenario of a 'forced accession', especially with regard to acts that *only* concern EU institutions and where the Member States were in no way involved. In such cases, only a formal EU accession to the ECHR would be likely to lead the Court to declare such cases judiciable. Whereas the judges of the European Court have proved that they feel able to act even without the EU joining the ECHR, ferocious incursions into the EU would probably have been counterproductive. Instead, the leaders of the Strasbourg Court have complemented their jurisprudential diplomacy with a regular informal dialogue with the judges of the EU's main Court, progressively fostering common interests.

II. The Discourse of Cooperation

Since the end of the 1990s, the judges and court officials of both European Courts have been meeting on a regular, but not formally institutionalized, basis. While such meetings have taken place since the 1970s, they started to be held on an annual basis only at the end of the twentieth century. These bilateral meetings—as well as the judges 'direct encounters during legal academic and practitioners' conferences or their contributions to the impressive body of literature on the relationship between the EU, the Council of Europe, and their Courts—have had a considerable impact on the evolution of the protection of human rights in Europe.[16] The presidents of both Courts have played the most important part in the

---

[15] *Bovin v 34 State Members of the Council of Europe* Appl no 73250/01 (2008).

[16] See eg L. Wildhaber and J. Callewaert, 'Espace constitutionnel européen et droits fondamentaux. Une vision globale pour une pluralité de droits et de juges' in N. Colneric, D. Edward, J. P. Puissochet, and D. R. Colomer (eds), *Une Communauté de droit. Festschrift für Gil Carlos Rodriguez Iglesias* (Berlin: BWV-Berliner, Wissenschafts-Verlag, 2003); F. Tulkens and J. Callewaert, 'La Cour de justice des Communautés européennes, la Cour européenne des droits de l'homme et la protection des droits fondamentaux' in M. Dony and E. Bribosia (eds), *L'avenir du système juridictionnel de l'Union européenne* (Brussels: Editions de l'Université de Bruxelles, 2002); J. P. Costa, 'La Convention européenne des droits de l'homme, la Charte des droits fondamentaux de l'Union européenne et la problématique de l'adhésion de l'Union européenne à la Convention', EUI Working Paper, 2004/5 (2004).

effective rapprochement between the two institutions. Luzius Wildhaber (ECtHR) and G. C. Rodriguez Iglesias (ECJ), who were presiding over the two Courts at that time, were the main consolidators of this special relationship, whereas Advocate General Francis Jacobs, an ECHR specialist, played a pre-eminent role with regard to the very emergence of this dialogue. In the absence of any formal ties between the EU and the Council of Europe, it has indeed been up to the European judges to regulate their sometimes conflicting[17] relationship in what appear to be high-profile diplomatic meetings in order to provide a means for coherence without uniformity.

With regard to their own relationship, the European judges' diplomatic interactions and jurisprudential gifts have had the double advantage of tempering each Court's potential for intrusions into the other Court's legal order. The meetings and encounters have also helped to highlight, and indeed sometimes even celebrate, the mutually supportive effects of both Courts' reciprocal actions.

The mutual benefits of the Courts' rapprochement have been discovered in this way and the dynamics of 'cross-fertilization'[18] between the two Courts have been highlighted. It has also been asserted that the impression of mutual defiance between the two Courts is 'in fact the opposite of what happens in reality',[19] just as the complementarity between the two systems has been stressed when it comes to protecting rights, especially with regard to the ECHR–Charter relationship where the Convention is described as an instrument of external control and the Charter as an internal 'constitutional' instrument. Similarly, the absence of an EU accession to the ECHR has been qualified as an outdated anomaly by one ECJ judge,[20] a very telling evolution given that in 1996 the ECJ made a direct EU accession to the ECHR impossible through its Opinion 2/94.[21]

Yet, if the EU's accession to the ECHR would not change existing judicial practices and would only acknowledge the preferences of the European Courts, it could have a major institutional impact with regard to the relationship between the two Courts. Only a formal accession could transform the fragile equilibrium between the two European Courts into a more stable linkage. Much uncertainty

---

[17] E. Bribosia, 'Le dilemme du juge national face à des obligations contradictoires en matière de protection des droits fondamentaux issus des deux orders juridiques européens' in Dony and Bribosia, ibid; L. Burgorgue-Larsen, 'Senator Lines c les 15 États de l'Union européenne, DR, du 10 mars 2004, *Chronique de la Cour européenne des droits de l'Homme*, 35 *Recueil Dalloz* (2004), 2533–4; Council of Europe, 'Cancellation of hearing in the case, Senator Lines GmbH v the 15 Member States of the European Union', press release issued by the Registrar, 16 October 2003; F. Krenc, 'La decision Senator Lines ou l'ajournement d'une question delicate', 61 *Revue trimestrielle des droits de l'homme* (2005), 121; O. de Schutter and Y. Lejeune, 'L'adhésion de la Communauté à la Convention européenne des droits de l'homme. A propos de l'avis 2/94 de la Cour de justice des Communautés', 32 *Cahiers de droit européen* (1996), 5–6; P. Wachsmann, 'L'avis 2/94 de la Cour de justice relatif à l'adhésion de la Communauté européenne à la Convention européenne de sauvegarde des droits de l'homme et des libertés fondamentales', 32 *Revue trimestrielle de droit européen* (1996), 467.

[18] F. G. Jacobs, 'Judicial Dialogue and the Cross-Fertilization of Legal Systems: The European Court of Justice', 38 *Texas International Law Journal* (2003), 547.

[19] J. P. Puissochet and J. P. Costa, 'Entretien croisé des juges français', 96 *Pouvoirs. Les cours européennes. Luxembourg et Strasbourg* (2001), 161 (ECJ Judge Puissochet).

[20] A. Rosas, 'Fundamental Rights in the Luxembourg and Strasbourg Courts' in C. Baudenbacher et al (eds), *The EFTA Court: Ten Years On* (Oxford: Hart Publishing, 2005).

[21] Wachsmann, n 8 above.

over the protection of human rights at the EU level and the two Courts' role would disappear upon accession. It would once and for all confirm the ECJ's 'internal' and the ECtHR's 'external' role with regard to the judicial control of human rights in the EU. Strasbourg would be reassured that the ECJ would stop referring to the ECHR with the possible constitutionalization of the Charter of Fundamental Rights, because for some actors the Charter was intended to replace the Convention. The Charter would then indeed be more comparable to an 'internal' constitutional fundamental rights document, rather than to a second 'external' supranational instrument for the protection of human rights comparable to the ECHR. For the moment, actors in both Courts will remain on their guard until the EU's accession to the ECHR confirms their Courts' respective roles with regard to the protection of human rights in Europe. As the Courts have entangled themselves and their organizations in a web of constraining relations, it now seems that a formal accession would have more advantages than disadvantages—even for those actors who had been opposing the EU's accession to the ECHR.

The discourse of cooperation appears at several levels. For example, some authors such as Francis Jacobs have highlighted the very punctual role of the ECtHR in helping to enforce EU obligations on the national level. For instance, in 1993, the European Commission of Human Rights strongly encouraged national courts to make preliminary references to the ECJ in the *Soc Divagsa v Spain*[22] and *Fritz and Nana S v France*[23] cases—requests which were all declared inadmissible—when it ruled that a refusal by a national court to seek advice from the ECJ could lead to a violation of the ECHR and could be contrary to the right to a fair trial. In this way Strasbourg indeed supported the system of preliminary references to the ECJ.[24] A sanction from Strasbourg would no doubt have had a discouraging effect on national judges to make preliminary references to the ECJ[25] and would not have been appreciated in Luxembourg. Furthermore, in 1997, the ECtHR condemned Greece[26] for not executing a Council of State ruling based on an ECJ preliminary decision,[27] thus strongly reminding the Greek administration of the supremacy of EU law. Similarly, in the *Dangeville*[28] and *Cabinet Diot et SA Gras*[29] cases against France, the ECtHR condemned France for failing to bring French law into line with EU law. So, whereas Strasbourg has partly annexed the EU, it also feels responsible for controlling the EU Member States' neglect to apply EU law—thus promoting the implementation and coherence of European law.

As interesting as these cases are, the very fact that those actors who try to bring closer the two European Courts emphasize very integral moments of jurisprudence

[22] *Divagsa Company v Spain* Appl no 20631/92 (1993).
[23] *F S and N S v France* Appl no 15669/89 (1993).
[24] L. Burgorgue-Larsen, 'Chronique de jurisprudence comparée', 4 *Revue de droit public* (2004), 1051.
[25] E. Bribosia, n 8 above.
[26] *Hornsby v Greece* Appl no 18357/91 (1997).
[27] D. Spielmann, 'Un autre regard: la Cour de Strasbourg et le droit de la Communauté européenne' in *Libertés, justice, tolérance. Mélanges en hommage au Doyen Gérard Cohen-Jonathan*, vol II (Brussels: Bruylant, 2004).
[28] *S A Dangeville v France* Appl no 36677/97 (2002).
[29] *S A Cabinet Diot and S A Gras Savoye v France* Appl nos 49217/99, 49218/99 (2003).

and try to convert them into history-making decisions is also very telling about the importance they attach to the convergence of the Courts. Selective a posteriori rationalizations of case law are a very powerful tool to construct jurisprudence and to inflect it into a direction that favours the positive dialogue of the European judges. The European Courts' relationship has not, however, evolved linearly from conflict to cross-fertilization and the case law of the two systems has led to some conflicts and it still contains potential for further conflict. It is undoubtedly due to the mobilization of a very proactive and powerful epistemic community of leading lawyers and judges that the discourse of rivalry has gradually been replaced by a discourse of cooperation and complementarity.[30] This community has not only been active in legal fora, but it has also extended its activism to political arenas in recent times.

III. The EU Politics of the ECtHR

The ever closer linkage between the ECtHR and the EU is not only the result of the socialization between judges and long-term jurisprudential interactions, but also of the mobilizations of the most important actors of the Court (and academia) in favour of a complementary relationship between the EU and the ECHR. With regard to issues like, for instance, the accession of the EU to the ECHR and the hierarchical relationship between the Charter of Fundamental Rights and the Convention, the judges and officials of the Strasbourg Court have been very present in the EU's political fora over the last decade.

Indeed, many Strasbourg actors—such as Luzius Wildhaber, when he was the president of the ECtHR; Jean-Paul Costa, the acting president; Johan Callewaert, a key official of the court; or judges like Marc Fischbach or Professor J. A Frowein, a former member of the Commission of Human Rights; and Hans Christian Krüger in his capacity of Deputy Secretary General of the Council of Europe— have become the ambassadors of their Court in the EU. This is evident, for example, during the drafting of the Charter of Fundamental Rights, or at the Convention for the Future of Europe which drafted the EU's constitutional treaty, which was later transformed into the Lisbon Treaty.

As Johan Liisberg and Pierre Drzemczewski have shown,[31] these actors have played a fundamental role in the Convention for the Charter of Fundamental Rights by insisting that references to the ECHR should be included in the Charter, and insisting on the complementarity of the Convention and the new

---

[30] L. Scheeck, 'La diplomatie commune des cours européennes' in A. Vauchez and P. Mbongo (eds), *Dans la fabrique du droit européen. Scènes, acteurs et publics de la Cour de justice des Communautés européennes* (Brussels: Bruylant, 2009).

[31] J. B. Liisberg, 'Does the EU Charter of Fundamental Rights Threaten the Supremacy of Community Law?', 38 *Common Market Law Review* (2001), 1171; P. Drzemczewski, 'The Council of Europe's Position with Respect to the EU Charter of Fundamental Rights', 22 *Human Rights Law Journal* (2001), 19.

EU instrument for the protection of human rights. These observers also insisted on the fact that the ECHR only provides a minimum standard and they welcomed a Charter that would deepen the protection of rights. For Fischbach and Krüger, the hardest fight with the other participants of the Convention was over the idea of mentioning the jurisprudence of the ECtHR and not only the Convention as such in the text. After having successfully managed to include a reference into a horizontal clause of the Charter, it was eventually taken out again after this idea met strong resistance. However, the representatives of the Council of Europe nevertheless managed to convince the participants to include a reference into the preamble of the Charter with the support of other members of the Convention.

Similarly, the protagonists of the ECtHR tried to seize the window of opportunity opened by the negotiations on the European constitution. For example, in January 2003, Luzius Wildhaber officially called for an EU accession to the ECHR at a press conference at the Court,[32] three months after the 'Giscard Convention' published its first draft proposal for a European Constitution. During this second Convention, the ECtHR judge Fischbach also made an intervention at the so-called 'Vitorino group' on the Charter and a possible EU ECHR accession, where he once again stressed the complementarity of the Charter and the Convention and insisted on the importance of an EU accession to the Convention,[33] while the Secretary General of the Council of Europe, Walter Schwimmer, published a very detailed report on the technical and legal modalities of an EU accession.[34] In the same vein, the Council of Europe co-organized a large conference on the 'Council of Europe's contribution to the EU' in Santiago de Compostela on 3–4 June 2002 where many EU politicians and ECJ judges and officials also attended. At this conference, as at many others, the main topic was again the question of an EU accession and complementary EU–Council of Europe cooperation.

These actions have no doubt helped to prepare the ground for a successful entry of the idea of an EU accession to the ECHR into the European treaties. The presence of actors from Strasbourg in other European political arenas has no doubt had a decisive impact on the perception of the importance of the ECHR and its institutions. In the coming years, when the question of a concrete EU accession will be debated, the role of these ambassadors of the ECHR will be equally important. Meanwhile, the importance of the ECHR and its jurisprudence has been strongly acknowledged by the ECJ, not only because of the pressure coming from Strasbourg, but also for 'internal' reasons.

---

[32] ECtHR, 'Call for European Union to accede to European Convention on Human Rights', press release, 28 January 2003.
[33] European Convention, 'Summary of the meeting held on 17.09.02 chaired by Commissioner António Vitorino', Working group 'Charter/ECHR', WG II 10, CONV 295/02, 26 September 2002.
[34] Council of Europe, 'Étude des questions juridiques et techniques d'une éventuelle adhésion des CE/de l'UE à la Convention européenne des droits de l'homme', *Report adopted by the Steering Committee for Human Rights (CDDH), 53th meeting*, 25–28 June 2002, DG-II(2002)006.

IV. Saving the Primacy of EC Law through the Supremacy of ECHR Law

Long before the regular dialogue and quest for harmony between the European Courts emerged, the ECHR had already found its place in the EU thanks to the ECJ's instrumentalization of the Convention. When it comes to explaining the role of the ECHR in the EU, it appears that the ECJ has played a fundamental role. It has massively imported the ECHR into the EU's legal order in the absence of having its own legal means at its disposal. In the 1950s, the drafters of the European treaties did not plan for any kind of protection of citizens with regard to the action of Community institutions. Yet, the question of human rights protection at the European level progressively appeared when private actors started to mobilize before the ECJ,[35] when some judges and law professors[36] started to write about this problem and when national constitutional courts bound the fate of the European Communities and of the primacy of EC law to the judges' ability to protect rights.

As of the end of the 1960s, the ECJ started to protect human rights.[37] During the 1970s, the pressure on the ECJ to do so increased, most of all because some national constitutional courts, especially the German Constitutional Court, did not accept the primacy of European law, arguing that rights were not sufficiently protected in the European Communities. By the end of the 1970s, the ECJ was increasingly confronted with human rights cases, and its judges started to rely on the ECHR in its *Nold*[38] decision, only a few days after France had signed the ECHR and two weeks before the German Bundesverfassungsgericht's first *Solange* decision.[39] Since Karlsruhe did not take into account this effort to guarantee the protection of rights, the ECJ judges probably had to push even further for their guarantees for the protection of human rights. The ECHR has been an important tool in this respect. Individual Articles of the ECHR were mentioned explicitly from 1975 onwards[40] and the ECJ has confirmed this evolution in hundreds of other cases subsequently, but it was only in the *P/S and Cornwall County Council* case[41] that the ECJ for the first time made reference to the ECtHR case law, showing increasing respect for the interpretation of the Convention by the Strasbourg Court. Similarly, in the *Baustahlgewebe GmbH* case,[42] the ECJ also directly

---

[35] Case C-1/58 *Friedrich Stork and Cie v High Authority of the European Coal and Steel Community* [1959] ECR 17.

[36] P. Pescatore, 'Die Menschenrechte und die Europäische Integration', 2 *Integration* (1969), 103–36; M. Waelbroeck, 'La Convention européenne des droits de l'homme lie-t-elle les Communautés européennes?', *Droit communautaire et droit national* (1965), 305–18.

[37] See Case C-29/69 *Erich Stauder v City of Ulm—Sozialamant* (1969).

[38] Case C-4/73 *J Nold, Kohlen- und Baustoffgroßhandlung v Commission of the European Communities* (1974).

[39] BVerfGE 37, 271, 29 May 1974.

[40] See Case C-36/75 *Roland Rutili v. Ministre de l'intérieur* (1975).

[41] Case C-13/94 *P v S and Cornwall County Council* (1996).

[42] Case C-185-95 *Baustahlgewebe GmbH v Commission of the European Communities* (1998).

referred to the Court's case law on the right to a fair trial enshrined in Art 6 ECHR.[43]

From a qualitative point of view, the ECHR law and jurisprudence also has a very special place in EU law thanks to the judges. Some years after the dialogue of the European judges intensified, the *Schmidberger, Internationale Transporte und Planzüge* case of 2003,[44] for instance, put the ECHR on top of the EU's normative hierarchy. Indeed, in this case, the Luxembourg Court favoured rights as protected by the ECHR—more specifically, freedom of expression—over economic rights— freedom of movement of goods—as granted by the EU treaties. In the *Omega Spielhallen- und Automatenaufstellungs-GmbH* case of 14 October 2004,[45] the ECJ also had to seek an equilibrium between fundamental liberties and human rights. If the judgments are very careful not to argue explicitly that ECHR norms are more important than the four freedoms, it very clearly appears that those actors who had invoked the ECHR won their cases, while those who had invoked the most fundamental EU principles lost. It is difficult to say if these cases will be the first in a long line of jurisprudence, but it seems clear that as long as both national constitutional courts and the ECtHR put pressure on the ECJ to protect rights well, one can expect the judges in Luxembourg to respect the ECHR and its jurisprudence 'à la lettre'. Setting up any of these jurisdictions might be highly counterproductive, while quoting the ECHR seems like a safe way to protect the EU's legal order from European or national jurisprudential attacks. In this context, the references to the ECHR by the ECJ come as no surprise since it is the best instrument to protect the primacy of EU law. The lawyers from Strasbourg like this form of self-regulation. The *Schmidberger* case[46] is indeed not only a good example of the ECJ judges protecting rights in an exemplary manner: according to Takis Tridimas, the Court also 'pre-empted Strasbourg'[47] in this case, when it put human rights before fundamental freedoms. With regard to national actors, the Convention is a means to show national constitutional courts that the ECJ is respecting Europe's most prominent human rights instrument, which all the Member States have ratified, including their own and it might thus help to tame their resistance.

Thus, it comes as no surprise that the ECHR has become the ECJ's most important instrument for the protection of human rights. From 1998 to 2005, the ECHR is referred to 7.5 times more frequently than *all* other human rights

---

[43] G. Cohen-Jonathan, *Aspects européens des droits fondamentaux* (Paris: Montchrestien, 2002), 184.

[44] Case C-112/00 *Eugen Schmidberger, Internationale Transporte und Planzüge contre Republik Österreich* (2003). See also A. Alemanno, 'À la recherche d'un juste équilibre entre libertés fondamentales et droits fondamentaux dans le cadre du marché intérieur. Quelques réflexions à propos des arrêts Schmidberger et Omega', 4 *Revue du droit de l'Union européenne* (2004), 1; J. Morijn, 'Balancing Fundamental Rights and Common Market Freedoms in Union Law: Schmidberger and Omega in the Light of the European Constitution', 12 *European Law Journal* (2006), 15.

[45] Case C-36/02 *Omega Spielhallen- und Automatenaufstellungs-GmbH v Oberbürgermeisterin der Bundesstadt Bonn* (2004).

[46] See n 44 above.

[47] T. Tridimas, The European Court of Justice and the Draft Constitution: A Supreme Court for the Union?, *Social Science Research Network*, Working Paper Series (2004). Available at: <http://papers.ssrn.com/sol3/papers.cfm?abstract_id=490603>, 37.

instruments the ECJ occasionally relies on—including the Charter of Fundamental Rights—despite the fact that the EU has not acceded to the ECHR and that there is no legal obligation for the ECJ to refer to the Convention (although the ECJ never goes so far as to feel bound by the ECHR).[48] Regarding the Charter, it is to be expected that since its ratification the ECJ will more often rely on its own instrument. The direct references to this normative source will very probably increase, probably also to the detriment of the ECHR.

Such an evolution will not necessarily mean that both European systems will separate from now on, especially because the Charter is not in contradiction with the Convention on any point and since the Convention allows for the possibility of going beyond the rights protected by the conventional system. The possibility of a separation exists, however, and in the absence of a swift EU accession to the ECHR, the evolution of the relationship between the CJEU and the ECtHR will largely depend on the dialogue of its judges.

V. The Uncertain Future of the European Court's Role in the EU

The legal orders of the ECtHR and the CJEU increasingly overlap and their relationship has become more complex. Each Court could harm the 'other' European Court, yet the European judges can also uphold each other's legal regime. Given that one cannot expect that all the decisions in both Courts will take into account the Courts' mutual interests in the future, it can be expected that conflict and cooperation, defiance and loyalty will continue to coexist in the future.

As both Courts face more political resistance from governments and more judicial resistance from national (constitutional) courts than ever before, the continuing dialogue appears to be in their interest. As long as the judges continue to meet and solemnly to celebrate their strategic interdependence, the mutually reinforcing dynamics are likely to continue to dominate the linkage between the European Courts, independently of how the respect of human rights evolves in the different parts of Europe. A complete separation of the EU and its Member States from the Council of Europe, as some authors have envisaged,[49] still does not appear to be a valid option. However, a stronger convergence also seems unlikely given the fact that not all EU and Council of Europe Member States might eventually agree on an EU accession to the ECHR. With regard to the jurisprudential politics of the European Courts, a gradual normative and judicial separation with fewer and fewer cross-references is also more plausible than ever before as the Charter of

---

[48] L. Scheeck, 'The Diplomacy of European Judicial Networks in Times of Constitutional Crisis' in F. Snyder and I. Maher (eds), *The Evolution of the European Courts: Institutional Change and Continuity* (Brussels: Bruylant, 2009).

[49] A. G. Toth, 'The European Union and Human Rights: The Way Forward', 34 *Common Market Law Review* (1997), 491; for an overview of all scenarios see J. Y. Carlier, 'La garantie des droits fondamentaux en Europe: pour le respect des compétences concurrentes de Luxembourg et de Strasbourg', 13 *Revue québécoise de droit international* (2000), 37. For another pluralist approach, see N. Krisch, 'The Open Architecture of European Human Rights Law', 71 *Modern Law Review* (2008), 183.

Fundamental Rights has come into force. It would indeed come as no surprise if the ECJ started to rely mainly on the Charter and less on the ECHR in the coming years. In more recent cases, such as *Masdar (UK) Ltd v Commission*,[50] it already appears that the Court prefers to rely *exclusively* on this new internal document and that it ignores the ECHR in a rather ostensive way.[51]

However, such an evolution cannot necessarily be interpreted as a separation of these two European human rights systems. On a jurisprudential level, the ECHR still remains very present in the ECJ's case law for the moment. Its prominence in history-making judgments, such as the famous *Kadi* case, where the Convention stands alongside the Charter, is very telling in this respect—especially because the references to the Convention are in this case much more numerous.[52] On a judicial level, the way both Courts embrace each other's jurisprudence (or not) will indeed be decisive for the future of the Courts' relationship and the protection of human rights in Europe. On a discursive level, the future status of the ECHR and the ECtHR will depend on the communication effort of the European judges and their continued willingness to maintain or even deepen their existing relationship. On all these levels there are no particular signs of a 'decoupling' between the European Courts, as things currently stand.

In the absence of an EU accession to the ECHR, the evolution of the ECtHR's role in the EU will greatly depend on how the judges manage their relationship with the Luxembourg Court. Unfortunately, the ECtHR's position is not enviable in this respect. While the political climate for an EU accession has been relatively favourable over the last years, as shown by the creation of a legal basis for such a possibility in the failed European constitution and in the Lisbon Treaty, it is not certain that the Member States will be able to agree on the principle and even less on the exact modalities of such a development. The opt-outs of some Member States with regard to the Charter of Fundamental Rights hint at the problem: since it is impossible to get all the EU Member States to ratify the EU's Charter, how likely is it that there will be agreement on a potentially even more controversial ECHR accession? Given this uncertainty, it is also unlikely that the ECtHR would go beyond its standing jurisprudence and proceed to a forced annexation of the EU. In this respect, the Court is condemned to an unsatisfactory status quo. If it goes beyond its actual case law, it risks fostering disagreement on an ECHR accession; but how long will Strasbourg have to be patient, since no one knows when the accession to the ECHR will appear on the EU's political agenda and, most importantly, how long it will take to negotiate the 'technical' details?

The Charter has been controversial mainly because of the EU's increasing power to control human rights with regard to national acts directly or indirectly related to EU law. An EU accession to the ECHR would incidentally reinforce the power of

---

[50] Case C-47/07 *Masdar (UK) Ltd v Commission* (2008).

[51] L. Burgorgue-Larsen, 'Chronique de jurisprudence comparée 2008', *Revue de droit public* (2009), 6.

[52] Joined Cases C-402/05 P and C-415/05 P *Kadi & Al Barakaat v Council of the European Union*, 3 *Common Market Law Reports* 41 (2008).

EU institutions as well as the debate about the scope of their power with regard to protecting human rights. The ECtHR would not only be strengthened in its capacity to protect rights with regard to EU acts, but also in its control of national measures implementing EU law. Since the ECHR would remain a mandatory standard of reference for the CJEU if the EU acceded to the Convention, the Strasbourg system would also be indirectly reinforced through the system of the Luxembourg Court's preliminary decisions. The implementation of these judgments is mandatory for national judges and the more they are filled with ECHR norms and references to Strasbourg's jurisprudence, the more forceful their impact will be at the national level. Even if, of course, the main objective of such an accession would be to protect individuals from the actions of EU institutions, political debates about the scope of European human rights protection are to be expected in many Member States for these reasons.

There is now a risk that the window of opportunity for an EU accession is gradually closing. Future EU presidencies might put this accession on the EU's agenda—as did Spain during the first semester of 2010—and there will no doubt be new mobilizations by the 'Convention people'[53] themselves. But given the still possible disagreement even on the very principle of such an accession and surely on its exact modalities, the European Court will probably remain confronted by the scenario of non-accession for quite some time, despite the provisions of the Lisbon Treaty and the Council of Europe's Protocol No 14. Since the CJEU is currently less dependent on Strasbourg than in the past, given that it now has its own human rights instrument, the ECtHR will have to be more careful than ever before not to upset the judges in Luxembourg. And given that the Court's role and the position of its jurisprudence in the EU is still highly dependent on the ECJ judges, it is also very likely that the European Court will avoid declaring receivable and sanctioning EU related acts in the future.

For instance, EU-related applications are quite often linked to previous CJEU decisions. The ECtHR has never sanctioned such a case until now, but if it did it would expose the Court of Justice as a transgressor of human rights (and incidentally put into danger the supremacy of EU law). For this reason, the ECtHR will probably not move beyond its standing *Bosphorus 'solange'* jurisprudence of equivalent protection, even though the latter has often been criticized for not going far enough by those observers and actors who would like Strasbourg to be more insistent and consequential when it is faced with potential violations of human rights by the EU.

If Strasbourg started to sanction EU acts before the EU's formal accession to the Convention, it would run the risk of retaliation from the ECJ judges. As the EU grows more powerful, the ECJ could easily sideline the ECHR and its Court. It could, for example, stop aligning its case law or exclusively rely on the Charter of Fundamental Rights. Since the Charter has come into force, the risk of being disavowed by the ECtHR is smaller for the CJEU than the danger of Strasbourg

---

[53] S. Hennette-Vauchez, 'Divided in Diversity: National Legal Scholarship(s) and the European Convention of Human Rights', EUI Working Paper, RSCAS 2008/39.

being sidelined (or 'forgotten') by the Court in Luxembourg. Any overzealous activism in the absence of an EU accession would be politically counterproductive. It would not necessarily convince the EU Member States to accelerate an accession to the Convention and it could also trigger a more defiant approach in Luxembourg with regard to the ECHR. The ECJ could also stop quoting the ECHR without the risk of lowering the standard of protection of human rights in the EU (since the Charter is seen as a more sophisticated text in this respect). It could even begin to interpret the Charter in a different way, leading to divergences of interpretation which would, in turn, lead to loyalty shifts of national judges who may be inclined to rely more often on the Luxembourg jurisprudence than on the Strasbourg case law when it comes to protecting rights. The less the ECtHR puts Luxembourg under pressure, the more it reduces the risk of being sidelined by the ECJ. Put differently, despite the historically reinforcing relationship and complementarity, despite the mutually beneficial dialogue, both Courts are now at a crossroads. The CJEU will probably take the lead in interpreting rights in a more contemporary manner since it has a more modern rights text at its disposal. Such an evolution could be extremely positive for the ECtHR as well, since it could rely on this jurisprudence to strengthen and complete its own jurisprudence. From this perspective, the multiplication of human rights instruments in Europe and even increasing competition between judicial actors could be to the benefit of human rights.

Indeed, the ECtHR does not shy away from quoting the ECJ and EU law. It had already taken over several advancements of ECJ case law, for example with regard to questions such as the right to have a name, self-incrimination, or the right to keep one's state of physical health secret.[54] The ECtHR has also referred to the Charter and the ECJ's case law on many occasions, even to operate reversals of case law.[55] It did so in December 1999 in the *Pellegrin v France* case[56] for instance[57] and another classic example is the *Goodwin v United Kingdom* case,[58] where the ECtHR strengthened its argument by referring to an ECJ decision and by quoting the Charter.[59]

However, there is now another serious risk of both European systems drifting apart, which is related to the non-EU accession to the ECHR after the Charter of Fundamental Rights came into force. If Strasbourg might find inspiration in the Charter to strengthen its own jurisprudence, it will have less power than ever before to protect individuals from an ever-more powerful EU. Indeed, the ECtHR has already taken a very careful approach not to upset the judges in Luxembourg and

---

[54] D. Simon, 'Les droits du citoyen de l'Union', 12(1–2) *Revue universelle des droits de l'homme* (2000), 44.

[55] L. Burgorgue-Larsen, 'L'art de changer de cap. Libres propos sur les nouveaux revirements de jurisprudence de la Cour européenne des droits de l'homme' in *Libertés, justice, tolérance. Mélanges en hommage au Doyen Gérard Cohen-Jonathan* (Brussels: Bruylant, 2004).

[56] *Pellegrin v France* Appl no 28541/95 (1999).

[57] L. Burgorgue-Larsen, *Libertés fondamentales* (Paris: Montchrestien, 2003), 168–9.

[58] *Goodwin v United Kingdom* Appl no 28957/95 (2002).

[59] D. Spielmann, n 15 above, 1463; L. Burgorgue-Larsen, n 30 above.

this situation is not likely to change. Hence, there will probably be no effective in-depth 'external' control of EU acts for a long time. And with the expansion of EU law at the national level, the ECHR might gradually lose ground in those Council of Europe Member States that have also acceded to the EU. By fighting each other, the European Courts run the risk of reciprocally unravelling their authority and the leaders of the two Courts are more than aware of this and, for that reason, there will be no war of European judges. However, the ECtHR's fight for protecting rights in the EU has once again become more difficult and, for the sake of human rights, the Strasbourg Court would benefit if it did not have to take into account very complex inter-institutional concerns when it came to decide on potential ECHR violations by an ever-more powerful EU.

VI. Conclusion

After decades of fruitful informal cooperation, the judicial self-management of the relationship between the two European courts remains relatively brittle. The protection of human rights remains a fundamental challenge in European societies as the political resistance to European human rights instruments grows. For now, the drifting apart of the EU and the Council of Europe remains in the hands of a new generation of judicial leaders in an enlarged Europe and in the absence of political decisions to make the EU accede to the ECHR. Despite the ambient optimism after the ratification of the Lisbon treaty, which foresees such an acces-sion, the final negotiations might prove to be far less consensual.

There are reasons for optimism however. The legal linkage between EU and ECHR norms inside the EU system has to be seen in terms of complex equili-briums, but the political weight and normative value of ECHR law sometimes appears to have an even higher status in EU law than EU law itself as a result of the reciprocal actions of the European Courts. Moreover, the emerging strategic interdependence between the Court of Justice of the European Union and the ECtHR is based on the (not very explicit) acceptance of the normative domination of the Strasbourg court. Despite the strong will of the Luxembourg judges to protect their court's autonomy, the ECHR has indeed become an invaluable tool to protect the primacy of EU law in the face of the multiplication of old and new forms of national judicial and political resistance to legal integration in Europe.

Today, the European human rights regime is best characterized by the multiple interdependences of judicial institutions at both European and national levels, which are simultaneously competing and cooperating in a highly complementary manner. It is no doubt because of its pro-activeness that the ECtHR has become a centrepiece of this regime in which it provides an external form of control on national and, increasingly, EU acts but in which each court also tends to maintain a high degree of autonomy, arguably, for the general benefit of human rights.

Tomorrow, changing political contexts, the recent failure of the EU's political constitutionalization, economic and social contingencies, changing judicial leaders and the possible shift of institutional interests towards centralisation and accumulation of institutional power, rather than decentralised cooperative sharing of rights protection, might however cause a backward surge, arguably, to the detriment of human rights.

While the leaders of the European courts took a long time to acknowledge their mutual interest to cooperate, their successors are now confronted with a situation where the institutional interests to cooperate are not necessarily given in the same way any more. In the absence of strong political support, the future of human rights in the EU will henceforth continue to depend on both the diplomacy of the European judges and the shrewdness of the judges of the European Court of Human Rights.

10

Individual and Constitutional Justice: Can the Power Balance of Adjudication be Reversed?

Jonas Christoffersen

I. The Need for a New Approach to ECHR Adjudication

The European Court of Human Rights (ECtHR) is overburdened and today provides a largely inaccessible human rights remedy. Most European citizens think twice about filing complaints with the Court and many of those who do have insufficient knowledge of the admissibility conditions. Moreover, some States have failed to rectify systematic defects in their legal systems. The result is well known: the vast majority of cases are either manifestly ill- or well-founded, and the Court is in practice inaccessible to many of those who really need its help.

History has shown us that the Strasbourg Court cannot fix its problems by itself, and that streamlining and reforming the Court's procedures does not rectify the Court's failings. It is now time to look beyond the horizon and reconsider the power balance between national and international authorities. The most striking feature of the life of the European Convention on Human Rights (ECHR) so far is perhaps the institutional balance having tilted in favour of the Court. The Court became the central focus despite the fact that it was intended to provide only a subsidiary measure of protection. The institutional focal points were intended to be the authorities of the Member States of the Council of Europe and the international institutions played, and were meant to play, an insignificant role.

My key argument is that we need to go back to the roots of the dynamic between the national and international authorities and work to make States the prime focus of attention. The Contracting States should perform their primary obligation under the ECHR to secure the rights and freedoms of the ECHR to everyone within their respective jurisdictions. This means first and foremost that the States must implement the ECHR in their domestic legal orders and follow the case law of the Court; but States must also do more than that. States may and must, depending on the circumstances, deviate from the case law of the Court and independently strike a fair balance between opposing forces and provide their own answers to pertinent human rights issues. States need to provide answers that have higher legitimacy than those given by the Court.

My argument is based on the observation that the Court is already in the process of revising its role, and that the entry into force of Protocol No 14 will accelerate the development towards an increasingly restricted international human rights remedy. The decreasing capacity and role of the Court as an institution granting relief to individual applicants necessitates a (re-)vitalization of the independent capacities and powers of national authorities that must act independently with a view to securing the rights and freedoms of the ECHR.

The institutional power balance between national and international authorities is not easily restored, but the last 25 years of constant reform should tell us that there is no other way out of the current impasse. If the power balance is not restored, the Court—and with it the Convention—will fall apart. In brief, we need to understand that there are clear limits on the Court's role as an institution granting individual relief, just as there are limits on the role of the Court as an institution granting constitutional relief. The limits on the Court's role are real and necessitate a new approach to human rights adjudication in Europe.

II. The Court's Limited Role in Providing Individual Justice

The Crown jewel of the Convention is the right of individual petition, but the jewel does not shine as brightly as it used to. The Court simply has neither the capacity nor the power to provide individual relief to the extent needed in the present day Council of Europe. The Court cannot get to the bottom of cases and provide sufficient answers to all disputes. This is not a critique of the Court and the way its members administer its powers. It is simply a fact that we cannot avoid addressing any longer.

The Court's role is already changing. The caseload facing the Court has also played a part in its development since the mid-1980s and everyone following the work of the Court will recognize the changes in the number of applications, organization of the Court, internal procedures, etc.

Constitutional justice has been the name of the game since the Court's changing role was addressed by the Court's then President, Luzius Wildhaber, in an article published in English, German, and French in 2002. Wildhaber envisaged that the Court would take on a 'constitutional' role adjudicating 'essentially public-policy issues'[1] and asked rhetorically:

Is it not better for there to be far fewer judgments, but promptly delivered and extensively reasoned ones which establish the jurisprudential principles with a compelling clarity that will render them de facto binding erga omnes, while at the same time revealing the structural problems which undermine democracy and the rule of law in parts of Europe?[2]

---

[1] L. Wildhaber, 'A Constitutional Future for the European Court of Human Rights', 23 *Human Rights Law Journal* (2002), 163.
[2] Ibid, 164.

Wildhaber hoped at the time that structural reforms would relieve the Court of the burden of a mass of unfounded complaints and help to 'preserve the coherence and quality of the leading judgments, the judgments of principle, the judgments that contribute to the Europe-wide human rights jurisprudence, that help to build up the European "public order".'[3] Since 2002, the caseload has, however, continued to increase and the minor reform of Protocol No 14 is not likely to solve the problem, just as the outcome of the further reform initiatives foreseen in the Interlaken Declaration are unlikely fundamentally to change the circumstances of human rights protection in Europe.

Moreover, the Court already plays a constitutional role in the sense described by Wildhaber. The Court has always faced the tension between the desire to safeguard the rights of individuals, to develop the standards, to elucidate the substantive content of the ECHR, and to retain room for manoeuvre in future cases. In *Ireland v United Kingdom*, the Court accordingly stated that it has the obligation 'to elucidate, safeguard and develop the rules instituted by the Convention'.[4]

It is no new thing to discuss the tension between the Court's role as an institution granting individual relief, on the one hand, while developing the standards of the ECHR, on the other hand. Yet, the shift from individual relief (individual justice) to general development (constitutional justice) is likely to increase in the future.

The constitutional role of the Court has been marketed with a view to solving the Court's caseload problems, but if we scratch the surface of Strasbourg adjudication we will soon realize that the Court's limited role as an institution granting individual relief makes necessary a new approach to human rights adjudication in Europe.

The new approach is, admittedly, based on old knowledge, namely that there is— and has always been—a gap between the standards *actually* enforced by the Court and the standards that *could and/or ought* to be enforced by the Court. The gap is an inevitable consequence of—as well as directly proportionate to—the limitations on individuals' access to full review by the Court. The gap emerges as a result of several factors that are best addressed by looking at different categories of limitations on the Court's review addressed below.

Subsidiarity vis-à-vis the Member States

The principle of subsidiarity (sometimes also referred to as the margin of appreciation/fourth instance principle) restricts the Court's powers of review and thus places corresponding wider obligations on Member States.

The Court for the first time described its standard of review in the *Belgian Linguistic case* observing that the disproportionality of differential treatment must be 'clearly established'.[5] Further, it recognized the discretion of States alongside the subsidiarity of its review observing that 'it cannot assume the role

---

[3] Ibid, 163.
[4] *Ireland v United Kingdom* Series A no 25 (1978), para 154.
[5] *Belgian Linguistic case* (Merits) Series A no 6 (1968), 34, para 10.

of the competent national authorities, for it would thereby lose sight of the subsidiary nature of the international machinery of collective enforcement established by the Convention'.[6] There is no reason to go deeper into the subsidiarity principle here and it suffices to recall that the principle is qualified in different ways.

(a) The evidential qualification: the Court exercises restraint if the assessment of evidence and facts gives reason to doubt.[7]

(b) The procedural qualification: the Court exercises restraint if the quality of the national decision-making procedures so warrants.[8]

(c) The legitimacy qualification: the Court exercises restraint if the legitimacy of the national decision-maker calls for it.[9]

(d) The normative qualification: the Court exercises restraint if the standards are not sufficiently clear.

These qualifications are well known as factors affecting the margin of appreciation and they are (of course) of general applicability throughout the ECHR.[10]

The impact of the principle of subsidiarity on the standard of protection of the ECHR raises complex issues of the interaction between national and international authorities. There is no doubt that the principle of subsidiarity affects the Court's review. The question is what should be made of the impact.

As regards the factual qualification, it is commonplace that the Court's inability to arrive at a proper appreciation of the factual context of a case affects the substantive weighing and balancing. The institutional setting places national authorities in a better position and thus enlightens them with better knowledge of the factual circumstances. The Court's restraint due to the inability to assess facts is inherent in the structure of the enforcement machinery (inherent-restraint) and raises the question whether domestic authorities should accept a factually flawed assessment or correct it and strike a different balance. In my view, a national institution with better access to a proper appreciation of the facts of the matter should take the better factual appreciation into account and strike a fair balance on that basis rather than leaving the balancing act to the Court.

A much less clear approach can be taken to the procedural and legitimacy qualifications, because the interaction between procedure, legitimacy, and substance is murky to say the least. We normally accept that the Court's review is limited due to its institutional reluctance (self-restraint) against overruling the domestic assessment if the domestic procedures followed and/or the legitimacy of the domestic decision-maker supports legitimacy of the domestic decision. But that does not mean that the

---

[6] Ibid, 34–5, para 10.
[7] Y. Shany, 'Toward a General Margin of Appreciation Doctrine in International Law', 16 *European Journal of International Law* (2006), 913.
[8] D. Feldman, 'Establishing the Legitimacy of Judicial Procedures for Protecting Human Rights', 13(1) *European Review of Public Law* (2001), 139.
[9] P. Mahoney, 'Judicial Activism and Judicial Self-Restraint in the European Court of Human Rights: Two Sides of the Same Coin', 11 *Human Rights Law Journal* (1990), 81.
[10] J. Christoffersen, *Fair Balance* (Leiden: Martinus Nijhoff, 2009), 227–318.

domestic authorities should take advantage of the room for manoeuvre and stretch the margin of appreciation to breaking point. The national authorities should strike a balance in light of their superior legitimacy and should not take advantage of the fact that the legitimacy of their decisions affects the Court's choice within the margin of interpretation.

The international–national divide has been an issue ever since the ECHR was drafted and it is in my view counter-intuitive to think that procedure and legitimacy do not play a role. The crucial questions are how much weight is attached to domestic procedure and legitimacy, and how domestic authorities should respond to the weight placed by the Court on the subsidiarity principle. Should domestic authorities clothe themselves in a procedural garment and thus enlarge their discretion, or should they rather be mindful of the substance of the ECHR and stay away from the outer boundaries of the Court's subsidiary review, although the Court will be likely to grant them an enlarged measure of discretion as a result of the subsidiarity of its review?

It should also be mentioned in brief that the Court has adopted a particular variant of the subsidiarity principle in the *Bosphorus case*. The Court invented a presumption of ECHR compliance in respect of State implementation of legal obligations flowing from the membership of an international organization 'as long as the relevant organisation is considered to protect fundamental rights, as regards both the substantive guarantees offered and the mechanisms controlling their observance, in a manner which can be considered at least equivalent to that for which the Convention provides'. The presumption is subject to rebuttal 'if, in the circumstances of a particular case, it is considered that the protection of Convention rights was manifestly deficient'.[11] The underlying philosophy is that the Court will not fully review each and every case concerning the implementation of States' 'strict international legal obligations'.[12] The access to ECHR review is restricted accordingly and the Luxembourg Court should not take advantage of the subsidiarity of the Strasbourg Court's review.

Access restricted by Protocol No 14

The Court's role as an institution granting individual relief is further restricted by the new admissibility criteria in Art 35(3)(b) which dictates that the Court shall declare inadmissible any individual application, provided:

the applicant has not suffered a significant disadvantage, unless respect for human rights as defined in the Convention and the Protocols thereto requires an examination of the application on the merits and provided that no case may be rejected on this ground which has not been duly considered by a domestic tribunal.[13]

---

[11] *Bosphorus Airways v Ireland* ECHR 2005-VI (2005), paras 155–6.
[12] See also ibid, para 157.
[13] Protocol No 14, Art 12.

The current admissibility criterion 'manifestly ill-founded' applies alongside the 'significant disadvantage' criteria and the Court shall thus dismiss applications that may be well-founded but have caused no 'significant disadvantage'. The new criterion may thus lead to cases being declared inadmissible despite a violation of the ECHR, although the early practice may not fall into this category.[14]

The scope of the new criterion is difficult to measure as the wording is open to interpretation and limited practice exists.[15] The construction of a low admissibility threshold is suggested when the explanatory report makes reference to cases of a 'trivial nature',[16] the 'more rapid disposal of unmeritorious cases',[17] and the risk of the ECHR system becoming 'totally paralysed'.[18] A higher threshold is indicated, on the other hand, when emphasis is placed on the Court's need to focus on 'important human rights issues'[19] as well as on the assessment of the need for examination 'from the broader perspective of the law of the Convention and the European public order to which it contributes'.[20]

The potential impact of the proposed threshold is hard to estimate and the interpretation of the provision was left to be worked out by the Court over time[21] as the Court was intentionally given a 'very broad margin of discretion'[22] to develop its case law gradually.[23] The Court is more likely to adopt an extensive interpretation of the criterion as the caseload has increased significantly, just as political calls are now made—by the Steering Committee and the Interlaken Declaration—for giving full effect to the criterion.[24]

Further restrictions in the future

If in the future, an amendment to the enforcement machinery is adopted to restrict the access to international review to examine gross and systematic violations, or if

---

[14] Council of Europe, *Explanatory Report to Protocol No 14 to the Convention for the Protection of Human Rights and Fundamental Freedoms, amending the control system of the Convention* (2004), para 79. See *Ionescu v Romania* Appl no 36659/04 (2010) and *Korolev (II) v Russia* Appl no 5447/03 (2010).

[15] Protocol No 14 has generated considerable debate in legal literature. Thorough analysis of the preparatory works are provided by eg M. Eaton and J. Schokkenbroek, 'Reforming the Human Rights System Established by the European Court of Human Rights', 26 *Human Rights Law Journal* (2005), 1; and P. Lemmens and W. Vandenhole (eds), *Protocol No 14 and the Reform of the European Court of Human Rights* (Antwerp, Oxford: Intersentia, 2005).

[16] Council of Europe, n 14 above, paras 82 and 83.

[17] Ibid, para 79.

[18] Ibid, para 78.

[19] Ibid, para 37.

[20] Ibid, para 77.

[21] Evaluation Group, *Report of the Evaluation Group to the Committee of Ministers on the European Court of Human Rights of 27 September 2001*, EG Court (2001) 1, para 94.

[22] Steering Committee for Human Rights (CDDH), *Interim Report of the CDDH to the Committee of Ministers 'Guaranteeing the long-term effectiveness of the European Court of Human Rights' of 18 October 2002*, CM(2002)146, para 41.

[23] Council of Europe, n 14 above, paras 80 and 84.

[24] Steering Committee for Human Rights (CCDH), *Opinion on the issues to be covered by the Interlaken Conference*, CCDH(2009)019 Addendum I of 1 December 2009, 6, para 28 (ii), and Interlaken Declaration of the High Level Conference on the Future of the European Court of Human Rights of 19th February 2010, 5, para 9(c).

the Court is granted power to choose cases for review (writ of certiorari), it is clear that the Court's role as an institution granting individual relief will be further restricted.

Such development is not impossible although it was firmly rejected when Protocol No 14 was negotiated. It has been revived by the Steering Committee which mentions:

In the longer terms, there lies the possibility that the Court may one day develop to have some degree of power to choose from among the applications it receives those that would receive judicial determination. The time is not yet ripe, however, to make specific proposals to this end.[25]

The suggestion was not included in the Interlaken Declaration, but a more political role of the Court may be established in the future.

Conclusion

The Court's role in providing individual justice is already today limited by the subsidiarity principle and the inherent limits on the Court's review. The limits are bound to be felt even more strongly in the future and the question emerges whether the Court can provide another kind of justice—now and in the future?

III. The Court's Limited Role in Providing Constitutional Justice

The Court's restricted ability to grant individual justice makes it tempting to develop the other limb of the Court's activity, namely the provision of constitutional justice. However, just as there are clear limits on the Court's ability to grant individual justice, so are there significant limits to the Court's power to provide constitutional justice.

We need to understand the fundamental nature of these limits before we subscribe to what may be left of the notion of a constitutional role of the Court in the sense described by Wildhaber.[26] And we need to accept that the solution is not to be found in Strasbourg.

The individual and the enforcement machinery

The most important factor defining the Court's role is the role of individual applicants in the development of the enforcement machinery. While the Court early on took steps to include the applicants in its proceedings,[27] and while Protocol No 9 from 1990 recognized the *locus standi* of individual applicants,

---

[25] Steering Committee for Human Rights, ibid, 4, para 15.
[26] See n 1 above.
[27] *Lawless v Ireland* (Preliminary objection) Series A no 1 (1960); *Lawless v Ireland* Series A no 3 (1961), 61, para 44; *De Wilde, Ooms and Versyp ('Vagrancy Case') v Belgium* (Question of procedure) Series A no 12 (1970).

individuals were only granted *locus standi* at the entry into force of Protocol No 11 in 1998.

Nonetheless, the role of individuals formed the Court's review when it decided that it should not engage in an abstract review of the case after the applicant had withdrawn his complaint in light of new legislation passed in Belgium.[28] Although the Court may review in the abstract the compatibility of domestic law with the requirements of the ECHR, the Court generally maintains that 'it is not the role of the Convention institutions to examine *in abstracto* the compatibility of national legislative or constitutional provisions with the requirements of the Convention'.[29] An exception may be provided where the Court decides to continue the review of a case of general interest despite the absence of an individual interest in the case such as in *Karner v Austria* concerning the possible discontinuation, after the applicant's death, of a case concerning discrimination of homosexuals.[30]

The Court may thus continue the examination of a case in the absence of individual interests, but no provision allows for the dismissal of applications or the discontinuation of proceedings due to the lack of general interest in a case.

The restricted advisory jurisdiction

The Court's role as an institution granting individual relief, rather than generally developing the ECHR, is so fundamental that it has been codified in the delimitation of the Court's advisory jurisdiction pursuant to Art 47. Article 47 provides that the Court may render advisory opinions 'on legal questions concerning the interpretation of the Convention and the Protocols thereto' (Art 47(1)), while at the same time excluding opinions dealing

with any question relating to the content or scope of the rights or freedoms defined in Section I of the Convention and the Protocols thereto, or with any other question which the Court or the Committee of Ministers might have to consider in consequence of any such proceedings as could be instituted in accordance with the Convention.

The extremely narrow delimitation of the advisory jurisdiction was considered necessary to 'ensure that the Court shall never be placed in the difficult position of being required ... to make a direct or indirect pronouncement on a legal point with which it might subsequently have to deal as a main consideration in some case brought before it'.[31] The Court is, in other words, empowered not to make general statements of principles, but rather to deal with specific issues when they emerge.

---

[28] *De Becker v Belgium* Series A no 4 (1962), 26, para 14.

[29] *McCann and Others v United Kingdom* Series A no 324 (1995), para 153 and standing case law. See eg H. Golsong, 'The European Court of Human Rights and the National Law-Maker: Some General Reflections' in F. Matscher and H. Petzold (eds), *Protecting Human Rights: The European Dimension—Studies in Honour of Gérard J. Wiarda* (Cologne: Carl Heymanns Verlag, 1988).

[30] *Karner v Austria* ECHR 2003-IX (2003), para 26. A friendly settlement was likewise rejected in *Ukrainian Media Group v Ukraine* Appl no 72713/01 (2005), due to the serious nature of the complaint.

[31] *Decision on the Competence of the Court to give an Advisory Opinion* ECHR 2004-IV (2004), para 33 and *Advisory Opinion on Certain Legal Questions concerning the Lists of Candidates Submitted with a*

The non-political role of courts

Another concern is the political role of the Court. As Professor Wildhaber suggests in Chapter 11 below, the Court may be well advised to be more careful in its promotion of new human rights standards. The development and elucidation of general standards sits ill with the Court's general reluctance to intervene in domestic matters, just as there are limits to how far the Court's legitimacy can carry it into the field of dynamic interpretation.

The traditional desire gradually and cautiously to develop case law inclines the Court to focus on the circumstances of specific cases rather than pronouncing sweeping statements of principle. The tendency is in line with general experience, which shows that judges and law-makers alike are commonly unable to foresee the nature and detail of future disputes. Law-makers thus make general law for the courts to interpret and apply to specific cases. Judges, conversely, prefer not to make general statements and commonly stick to the review of specific cases. Notions relating to the role of courts in the development of fundamental rights will continue to provide limits, albeit unclear limits, to the Court's constitutional role.

The nature of the ECHR

Finally, it is a well-known fact that the substantive content of the ECHR is worked out in a process of weighing and balancing. While the process of weighing and balancing may result in more or less specific ad hoc rules (precedents) that are immediately applicable to other cases and other States, experience derived from 50 years of ECHR adjudication suggests that it is not possible to describe with sufficient precision the international obligations of general applicability.

A general elucidation of the ECHR's standards cannot very often be made in the abstract. This does not mean that the Court may not take steps to increase the general applicability of its judgments, for example by resorting to obiter dicta[32] or by giving broader statements of principle.[33] Likewise, the Court may deliver pilot judgments of general applicability even if the situation of the individual applicant has been resolved.[34]

Yet a significant measure of concretization is necessary to bring the norms of the ECHR into action, simply because the weight accorded to relevant considerations cannot be determined in the abstract. This is well known and we see it every time

---

View to the Election of Judges to the European Court of Human Rights (2008), para 37 with reference to the preparatory works. Unsuccessful attempts were made during the negotiation of Protocol No 11 to widen the scope of the Court's advisory jurisdiction, see A. Drzemczewski, 'Advisory Jurisdiction of the European Court of Human Rights: A Procedure Worth Retaining?' in P. Nikken (ed), *Modern World of Human Rights—Essays in Honour of Thomas Buergenthal* (San José: Inter-American Institute of Human Rights, 1996), 510–11.

[32] See eg *Nikitin v Russia* ECHR 2004-VIII (2004), paras 44 and 60.
[33] See eg *Al-Nashif v Bulgaria* Appl no 50963/99 (2002), para 137.
[34] See eg *Hutten-Czapska v Poland* ECHR 2006-VIII (2006), para. 217.

we read a judgment in which the Court elaborates its general principles and then proceeds to apply those principles to the facts of specific cases. This step in the adjudicatory process is often the most important—and who should take care of this if not the Court itself?

Conclusion

The Court has always faced the choice between generally developing the standards of the ECHR and granting individual relief in specific cases. The traditional focus on individual relief is codified in the delimitation of the Court's advisory jurisdiction pursuant to Art 47 and deeply embedded in the culture of the Court and the environment surrounding it. The principal character of the majority of norms of the ECHR makes a process of weighing and balancing inevitable, just as the development and elucidation of general standards sits ill with the Court's general reluctance to intervene in domestic matters and to approach matters from a broader perspective of human rights policy.

Accordingly, the nature of the system provides a fundamental challenge to the development of the Court's role as an institution granting what may be called constitutional justice. It should not easily be assumed that adjudication in specific cases can be avoided. Since the Court cannot do the job on its own, our attention must turn elsewhere, namely towards national authorities.

IV. The Member States' Increasing Role under the ECHR

The presently ongoing shift in the institutional power balance away from the Court and towards national authorities is perhaps less of a revolution than international human rights lawyers and activists would like to think. As Stéphanie Hennette-Vauchez argues in Chapter 8 above, ECHR law is already subject to a significant measure of pluralism due to its varying implementation in the laws of the 47 Member States of the Council of Europe.

The changing role of the Court away from individual towards constitutional justice entails a return to a less centralistic understanding of the system. For 50 years, our minds have been set to think of the Court as the core institution of the ECHR. But the centre can no longer be the Court. The centres are and should be the Member States.

The institutions set up to supervise States' performance in the field of human rights and fundamental freedoms were never supposed to walk in solitude the path to improved human rights protection. The Commission and Court were designed to perform a supplementary—or subsidiary—supervisory function. The States were supposed to take the lead. National authorities have the advantage of being directly and democratically legitimated by their constitutional set-up, and national authorities are in direct and continuous contact with the vital forces of their countries. Further, national authorities have a better understanding of the circumstances of their respective societies and are best placed to adjudicate human rights disputes in good faith and in accordance with international standards. This is why we have the principle of subsidiarity. The principle justifies the Court's increasing focus over the last six to seven years on different ways of making the ECHR more effective in the national legal orders, in particular by introducing a range of procedural obligations designed to secure a better implementation of the rights and freedoms of the ECHR.[35]

Now, one of the key questions emerging as a result of the ongoing change in the role of the Court is this: how should the Court's changing role affect the role of national authorities? Domestic authorities have, admittedly to varying degrees, become accustomed to looking closely at the Court's practice to identify the proper interpretation of the ECHR. Yet the shifting power balance is likely to entail a deregulation of the ECHR's standards, unless the Contracting Parties decrease their dependence on the Court and increase their interpretative independence. As a matter of practice and principle, the decreased access to international review should be made up by an increased national review.

In the following I argue that the Contracting Parties' role in the implementation of the ECHR cannot be restricted to one of closely following the Court's case law. Rather than being highly dependent on the Court in the interpretation of the ECHR, the pluralism of the ECHR should be recognized and domestic authorities should be willing and able to depart from the Court's case law and provide the answers to human rights responses that they are best placed to provide. The argument is based on several elements that I will describe below.

National authorities and Protocol No 14

The negotiations leading to Protocol No 14 shed light on the perceived role of national authorities. The proposed new role of the Court raised concern among members of the Steering Committee[36] and the Parliamentary Assembly[37] who feared that the right of individual petition would be limited without improving the Court's effectiveness. Members of several delegations considered that the new provision could be viewed as sending 'a negative message to national authorities that the latter could disregard certain minor violations of the Convention'.[38] The concern was particularly valid in respect of 'those States Parties where the national judiciary as yet did not take the Convention and its case law sufficiently into account'.[39]

---

[35] Christoffersen, n 10 above.

[36] Steering Committee for Human Rights, n 22 above, para 39 and Reflection Group, *Activity Report of the Reflection Group under the Steering Committee of Human Rights on the Reinforcement of the Human Rights Protection Mechanism (15 June 2001)*, CDDH-GDR(2001)010, Section II.

[37] Committee on Legal Affairs and Human Rights, *Report of 23 April 2004 on the Draft Protocol No 14*, Doc 10147 (2004), para 44.

[38] Steering Committee for Human Rights (CDDH), *Interim Activity Report of the CDDH, Guaranteeing the long-term effectiveness of the European Court of Human Rights—Implementation of the Declaration adopted by the Committee of Ministers at its 122th Session (14–15 May 2003)*, CDDH (2003)026, para 34.

[39] Ibid, para 34.

The Austrian delegation accordingly proposed an important amendment reaffirming the primary role of national authorities[40] with a view to creating 'a further incentive for States Parties to assume fully their responsibility under the convention'.[41] The crux of the Austrian amendment was that insignificant applications could be dismissed only if 'the object of the application has been duly examined by a domestic tribunal according to the Convention and the Protocols thereto and in the light of the case law of the Court'.[42] The Austrian amendment reflected a precondition expressed by the Evaluation Group, namely that effective domestic remedies are available to the applicant.[43]

The final Protocol adopted the rule that a case may not be rejected on the grounds of lack of significant disadvantage if it 'has not been duly considered by a domestic tribunal', which condition is intended to ensure that every application receives judicial review on the national or international level.[44] Although this does not expressly require review in light of the case law of the Court, the underlying view reflects the integrated review of procedure and substance. If the case has been adequately handled at the domestic level, the domestic discretion (margin of appreciation) will be enlarged with the effect that minor violations of the ECHR shall be dismissed.

Protocol No 14 is further based on the premise that the new admissibility criterion should not lead to a deregulation of international human rights law.[45] On the contrary, it was recognized in the explanatory report to Protocol No 14 that the Court's 'evolving and extensive interpretation' of the ECHR was a factor affecting the increased case law.[46] Instead of availing themselves of the opportunity to deregulate the ECHR, the Contracting Parties took active steps to avoid such development by including the caveat that every case must receive judicial examination on the national or international plane. The increase in the admissibility threshold was thus delicately balanced by emphasizing the obligation to secure full respect of the ECHR's standards. It can thus safely be concluded that the domestic authorities are obligated to interpret and apply the ECHR in good faith and in light of international standards despite the restricted access to the Court's international review.

National dependence of the Court

The interaction between national and international law depends on national law, and varies from State to State. Yet, no one can avoid the question: how clear must an interpretation of the ECHR be before domestic authorities—according to national law—are allowed and/or obligated to take the ECHR into account?

---

[40] Ibid, para 34.   [41] Ibid, para 37.   [42] Ibid, para 36.

[43] Evaluation Group, n 21 above, para 94.

[44] Council of Europe, n 14 above, para 82.

[45] As regards the Evaluation Group, see A. Mowbray, 'Proposals for Reform of the European Court of Human Rights', *252 Public Law* (2002), 262.

[46] Council of Europe, n 14 above , para 13.

Domestic authorities will commonly consider the ECHR inapplicable if the provisions, including as interpreted by the Court, are not sufficiently specific and determinate to allow either self-execution or implementation.[47] Domestic authorities do not have complete freedom in the interpretation of the ECHR, and they will normally be assumed to approximate their interpretation of the ECHR to the Court's interpretation of the ECHR.

The substance of the ECHR varies from fairly specific and concrete rules to very vague and indeterminate principles. The vague character of many norms places the doctrine of clarity at a prominent place in the implementation of the ECHR. If domestic authorities make the existence of very clear and specific rules a requirement of the implementation of the ECHR, the implementation runs the risk of becoming illusory. Due to the vague and indeterminate nature of most of its norms, the ECHR is likely to be viewed as comprising programmatic and/or injudiciable rights and freedoms. If the ECHR shall be brought to life, a weighing and balancing of counterweighing principles is required in order to arrive at sufficiently specific and determinate norms. One of the Court's most important functions is exactly to specify the content of the ECHR by weighing and balancing the counterweighing considerations.

If the Court's practice, in pursuit of constitutional justice, becomes more abstract or general, the necessary balancing act must increasingly be conducted by domestic authorities; an increased decentralization must go hand in hand with increased decentralized independence. The domestic independence ought thus to be inversely proportionate to the access to individual relief. The less international review, the more national review.

The Court interprets the ECHR only insofar as cases are brought before it,[48] and the independent role of domestic authorities is particularly relevant in the absence of case law illustrating how the Court might interpret and apply the ECHR. The absence of case law cannot necessarily be taken to imply the absence of ECHR rights,[49] although the presence of case law will of course help to provide the required clarity.[50] Some measure of independent interpretation by domestic authorities is required in respect of those areas of the ECHR that are not yet the subject of case law or are the subject of old or otherwise disputable case law. Moreover, any precedent is subject to interpretation. The Court has not expressed its view on the domestic requirement of clarity, but it seems to assume that

---

[47] See eg *Sardinas Albo v Italy* ECHR 2004-I (2005), para 48 and *Vermeire v Belgium* Series A no 214-C (1991), para 24.

[48] *Handyside v United Kingdom* Series A no 24 (1976), para 48.

[49] T. Ojanen, 'The Times they are a-Changing—The Reaction of European Courts and National Courts' in J. Petman and J. Klabbers (eds), *Nordic Cosmopolitanism—Essays in International Law for Martti Koskenniemi* (Leiden, Boston: Martinus Nijhoff, 2003), 203–4.

[50] *Vermeire v Belgium*, n 47 above, paras 23–4 in which the Belgian government defended the Belgian judiciary's non-application of Arts 8 and 14 arguing that they were not 'sufficiently precise and comprehensive' and 'thus not suitable for direct application by the domestic courts', but the Court found 'nothing imprecise or incomplete about the rule which prohibited discrimination' between children borne in or out of wedlock based on *Marckx v Belgium* Series A no 31 (1979).

the interpretation adopted by the Court should be followed at the domestic level as well.[51]

A consequence of the clarity doctrine is that domestic authorities await the Court's development of the ECHR. The Norwegian Supreme Court has stated, for example, that Norwegian courts must use the Court's methods of interpretation, except that it falls in the first place to the Court to develop the ECHR.[52] The Court, on the other hand, expects the Contracting Parties to develop the standards of the ECHR. The inherent stalemate caused by domestic dependence on the Court was resolved in favour of the Court's evolutive interpretation in *Steel and Others v United Kingdom*:

It is of crucial importance that the Convention is interpreted and applied in a manner which renders its rights practical and effective, not theoretical and illusory. A failure by the Court to maintain a dynamic and evolutive approach would risk rendering it a bar to reform or improvement.[53]

The primary development by the Court of the standards of the ECHR is less than optimal seen both from the perspective of the power balance between the Court and the Contracting States, as well as from the perspective of individual applicants who turn to the Court to bring about a development in the standards of the ECHR.

The appropriate rigidity of domestic clarity requirements should be regarded in the light of the absence of effective access to international review. Human rights complaints, which for institutional reasons cannot be entertained internationally, may call for individual relief at the domestic level. There would, of course, be little need for domestic authorities to exercise any measurable amount of independence, if the Court had no backlog of cases and provided access to speedy review, and if only truly trivial cases were dismissed by the Court.

If, however, the Court takes the job of saving the enforcement machinery from the ever-increasing caseload seriously, a wide interpretation of the 'significant disadvantage' criteria should be adopted. A wide interpretation would entail that, subject to the other criteria, only individuals who have been subjected to (not in) significant human rights violations can expect to gain access to the international enforcement machinery. Similarly, the ongoing proceduralization and indeed the principle of subsidiarity in general may entail the adoption of standards of protection that cannot always be taken to reflect the proper standard of the ECHR, simply because the precedential value of the Court's practice may be institutionally flawed.

---

[51] *Pla and Puncernau v Andorra* ECHR 2004-VIII (2004), para 62; *Van Kück v Germany* ECHR 2003-VII (2003), paras 77–84; and *Storck v Germany* ECHR 2005-V (2005), para 93 (Art 5) and, similarly, paras 147–8 (Art 8).

[52] NRt 2000.996, NRt 2002.557, and NRt 2003.359.

[53] *Stafford v United Kingdom* ECHR 2002-IV (2002), para 68; *Christine Goodwin v United Kingdom* ECHR 2002-VI (2002), para 74; and *Mamatkulov and Abdurasulovic v Turkey* Appl nos 46827/99, 46951/99 (2003), para 105.

National independence of the Court

A Catch 22 is inherent in the interaction between the roles of the Court and the Contracting Parties. On the one hand, the Court may seek to generalize its judgments in order to increase the precedential value, whereas the national authorities may require specific judgments in order to accept the binding force of the ECHR in domestic law. The more the development goes in the direction of general judgments, the harder domestic implementation will become—and the greater will be the pressure on the Court. Domestic dependence on the Court's practice thus poses challenges to the future development of the interaction between national and international authorities.

European human rights law has become surprisingly centralized, at least in theory. In practice, however, we may expect to find a pluralistic legal order in which human rights standards vary from State to State, and from institution to institution. Legal pluralism is often viewed as a challenge to law, which is assumed to provide clear and uniform answers to disputes.

However, we need to base a renewed understanding of the interaction between national and international law and authorities on normative grounds justifying the legitimacy of different minimum standards of protection depending on the institutional setting of the adjudicator or other decision-maker. Many human rights defenders would regard with great scepticism the practice of a national court which decided not to follow (blindly) the practice of the European Court. Yet, the time has come not only to recognize *as fact* that the balance might not be struck the same way in different institutional settings—that is, nationally and internationally. The time has come also to accept *as legitimate* the striking of a different balance nationally.

Legal pluralism as an actual fact

The ECHR is prima facie pluralistic in the sense that the enforcement system is highly decentralized. The ECHR may and must be interpreted and applied not only by the Court (Art 19), but in particular by domestic authorities (Art 13). The Preamble identifies the maintenance and further realization of human rights as one of the methods available to achieve 'greater unity' between the members of the Council of Europe, but the ECHR does not advance legal integration by harmonization of national human rights standards.

The diversity is expressly authorized by Art 56(3), which allows a Contracting Party to extend the ECHR to territories for which it is responsible. The ECHR 'shall be applied in such territories with due regard, however, to local requirements'. Far from being an exception to a general rule of uniformity, the provision enacts the general principle of diversity[54] inherent in international human rights law as well as

---

[54] Compare *Tyrer v United Kingdom* Series A no 26 (1978), para 38 and *Piermont v France* Series A no 314 (1995), para 59 with eg *Dudgeon v United Kingdom* Series A no 45 (1981), para 56. See also

in other areas of international law.[55] The diversity of human rights standards under the ECHR is commonly addressed in terms of the margin of appreciation. Legal practice and doctrine on the ECHR has a long-standing tradition of accepting pluralism and diversity under the ECHR[56] and it has long been recognized that the standards may vary according to the circumstances prevailing in different States.[57]

Yet, the question remains whether the diversity allowed within the boundaries of the ECHR may, under the circumstances, extend as far as to obligate the Contracting Parties to strike a different balance by neutralizing the impact of the principle of subsidiarity on the Court's review. The crux of the matter is whether different interpretations can be of equal legitimacy.

From a positivistic and monocentric point of view, it may be considered impossible to accept that institutional factors influence the legitimacy of human rights standards. How can a human rights violation be denied in one institutional setting and recognized in a different setting? Would not one of the institutions have to be wrong?

An example is provided by the then UK House of Lords. Subsequent to the terrorist attacks in the USA in 2001, the UK government derogated from Art 5 for the purpose of allowing prolonged detention of terrorist suspects who could not be expelled within the time limit set by Art 5(1)(f). In December 2004, the House of Lords reviewed the compatibility with Art 15 of the derogation. I shall refrain from commenting on the substance of the House of Lords' conclusion and stick to one aspect of the case. Lord Hope of Craighead reiterated the view of the Council of Europe's Human Rights Commissioner on the rationale behind the margin of appreciation, 'it is . . . precisely because the Convention presupposes domestic controls in the form of preventive parliamentary scrutiny and posterior judicial review that national authorities enjoy a large margin of appreciation in respect of derogations'.[58] Lord Rodger of Earlsferry likewise observed, 'indeed the considerable deference which the European Court of Human Rights shows to the views of the national authorities in such matters really presupposes that the national courts

---

Py v France ECHR 2005-I (2005), which considered a violation of the right to vote justified under Art 56, para. 3.

[55] C. D. Stone, 'Common but Differentiated Responsibilities in International Law', 98 *American Journal of International Law* (2004), 276.

[56] See eg E. Kastanas, *Unité et diversité: Notions autonomes et marge d'appréciation des états dans la jurisprudence de la Cour européenne des droits de l'homme*, vol 35 (Brussels: Bruylant, 1996); A. W. Heringa, 'The "Consensus Principle"—The Role of Common Law in the ECHR Case-Law', 3 *Maastricht Journal of European and Comparative Law* (1996), 108; and E. Benvenisti, 'Margin of Appreciation, Consensus, and Universal Standards', 31 *Journal of International Law and Politics* (1999), 842.

[57] See eg *Mathieu-Mohin and Clerfayt v Belgium* Series A no 113 (1987), para 56; *Vogt v Germany* Series A no 323 (1995), para 59; *Rekvényi v Hungary* ECHR 1999-III (1999), para 47; *Murphy v Ireland* ECHR 2003-IX (2003), para 38; *Kyprianou v Cyprus* Appl no 73797/01 (2004), para 84; *Ilascu and Others v Moldova and Russia* ECHR 2004-VII (2004), para 411; *Refah Partisi (The Welfare Party) and Others v Turkey* ECHR 2003-II (2003), para 95; *Leyla Sahin v Turkey* ECHR 2005-XI (2005), para 115; *Jahn and Others v Germany* ECHR 2005-VI (2004), para 89; *Melnychenko v Ukraine* ECHR 2004-X (2004), para 55; *Py v France*, n 54 above, para 46.

[58] *Opinion 1/2002 of 28 August 2002 on certain aspects of the United Kingdom's derogation from Article 5(1)*, paras 7 and 8.

will police those limits'.[59] However, the fact that the observance of the limits drawn by the ECHR is reviewed at the domestic level does not necessarily mean that a different line must be drawn; domestic authorities must not necessarily subject domestic measures to stricter scrutiny than the Court.

Yet, Lord Hope expressed the view that national authorities have an obligation not only to form an opinion on the conformity of the derogation with the requirements of the ECHR, but further that the domestic courts' review is wider than that of the European Court:

> When the European Court talks about affording a margin of appreciation to the assessment of the British government it assumes that its assessment will at the national level receive closer scrutiny.... [T]he fact that the European Court will accord a large margin of appreciation to the contracting states on the question whether the measures taken do not exceed those strictly required by the exigencies of the situation cannot be taken as the last word on the matter so far as the domestic courts are concerned.[60]

The 'closer scrutiny' on the domestic level advocated by Lord Hope logically entails different limits on the government's discretion depending on the national or international nature of the review. The difference between the international and national review is recognized when the Court's review is not 'taken as the last word on the matter so far as the domestic courts are concerned'. Similarly, the Norwegian Supreme Court has stated that while Norwegian courts must use the ECtHR's methods of interpretation,[61] they may in cases of interpretative doubt place emphasis on Norwegian values.[62] These national pluralistic approaches to the interpretation of the ECHR are a fact. The question is whether they are legitimate or illegitimate.

Legal pluralism as a legitimate fact

The key issue is whether the domestic interpretation and application of the ECHR may legitimately differ from the standards authoritatively applied by the Court in its subsidiary review.

A primary argument is found in the Preamble to the ECHR which is built on the 'maintenance and further realisation of human rights and fundamental freedoms'. The Preamble does not merely leave the rights to 'common understanding and observance' of human rights, but also to the 'effective political democracy'. The political democracies of the Contracting Parties should accordingly play the primary role in the development of the standards of the ECHR and domestic authorities should not await the Court's dynamic interpretation. This would, as the Court stated in *Stafford and Others*, entail a 'bar to reform or improvement'.[63]

---

[59] *A and others v Secretary of State for the Home Department; X and another v Secretary of State for the Home Department* [2004] UKHL 56, para 176 (16 December 2004).

[60] Ibid, para 131.

[61] See n 52 above.

[62] Decision of 24 June 2005 (HR-2005-01014-A) and L. Oftedal Broch, 'Skjønnsmarginen i nyere praksis fra Den europeiske menneskerettsdomstol', *Lov og rett* (2005), 282.

[63] *Stafford v United Kingdom* ECHR 2002-IV (2002), para 68.

Furthermore, Art 53 provides that nothing in the ECHR shall limit the rights and freedoms otherwise secured under domestic law. During the drafting of the ECHR, the focus was initially turned to the codification of domestic law and practice, but codification was soon supplemented by the collective guarantee of certain minimum standards. Article 53 is normally taken to mean that the Contracting Parties may voluntarily provide a high standard of protection, except where conflicting considerations obligate States to limit human rights.[64] Yet, Art 53 at the same time prevents the Contracting Parties from diminishing or deviating from higher national and international standards. Since nothing in the ECHR can be invoked to limit the rights and freedoms guaranteed, the principle of subsidiarity cannot legitimately be invoked to strike a fair balance to the detriment of individual rights, just as the restricted access to international review after Protocol No 14 cannot be taken to reflect an absence of violations of the ECHR.

Article 53 is regularly considered an interpretative principle, but the Court has recognized the subjective nature of the right laid down in Art 53. In *Okyay and Others v Turkey* concerning the applicability of Art 6 to domestic proceedings challenging the lawfulness of a thermal power plant, the government argued that the applicant's alleged civil right fell beyond the scope of Art 6 as the applicants could not claim to be victims of a violation. The Court argued, however, that the autonomous requirement of a direct and not too remote link between the dispute and the applicants' rights 'cannot be construed as limiting an enforceable right in domestic law within the meaning of Article 53 of the Convention'.[65] The argument is well known from *Engel and Others v Netherlands*, in which the Court decided that the criminal limb of Art 6 applies where domestic authorities have designated an offence as criminal, even if the application of Art 6 is not otherwise called for.[66] The *renvoi* from Art 6 to the better protection under domestic law is thus derivable from Art 53.

Article 53 accordingly entails a subjective right that can be invoked by individuals in conjunction with a higher level of protection under national or international law. Or as the Court observed 'the Convention reinforces, in accordance with the principle of subsidiarity, the protection afforded at national level, but never limits it (Article 60 [now Art 53] of the Convention)'.[67]

A confirmation of this perception of the interaction between national and international review is provided by the Court in *A v United Kingdom* on the derogation case discussed above.[68] The government argued in that case that the majority of the then House of Lords should have afforded 'a much wider margin of appreciation to the executive and Parliament'. This contention could be read either as addressing the breadth of the national discretion under Art 15 or as addressing the difference between the *international* review normally conducted in Strasbourg

---

[64] See n 48 above, para 54.
[65] *Okyay and Others v Turkey* Appl no 36220/97 (2005), paras 61–8.
[66] *Engel and Others v Netherlands* Series A no 22 (1976), para 81.
[67] *United Communist Party of Turkey and Others v Turkey* Reports 1998-I (1998), para 28.
[68] See n 59 above.

and the *national* review conducted in London. The Court approached the contention from the latter perspective thus recognizing the distinction between national and international review under the ECHR. The Court recognized the wide margin of appreciation allowed to national authorities and added:

The doctrine of the margin of appreciation has always been meant as a tool to define relations between the domestic authorities and the Court. It cannot have the same application to the relations between the organs of State at the domestic level. As the House of Lords held, the question of proportionality is ultimately a judicial decision, particularly in a case such as the present where the applicants were deprived of their fundamental right to liberty over a long period of time. In any event, having regard to the careful way in which the House of Lords approached the issues, it cannot be said that inadequate weight was given to the views of the executive or of Parliament.[69]

Accordingly, the Court explicitly recognized the difference between the subsidiary international review and the primary national review, just at it found that the House of Lords had not transgressed the borders of the scope of its primary review under the ECHR.

Domestic authorities can thus be considered not only empowered, but even obligated to interpret and apply the ECHR in good faith and in accordance with international standards without taking advantage of the subsidiary nature of the *international* review under the ECHR. The domestic authority should therefore perform a primary, national review and strike the balance that it would have struck had it not been for the enlarged discretion afforded to them as a consequence of the subsidiary nature of the Court's international review.

The legitimacy of pluralism is accordingly supported by strong arguments, but the concurrent legitimacy of conflicting interpretations remains to be addressed. The legitimacy of law is really a matter of legal philosophy, but I will nonetheless briefly address the issue to indicate how the concurrent legitimacy of multiple standards might be recognized.

The legitimacy of any doctrine of single or multiple standards hinges on one's definition of law. The legal philosophical implications attaching to different constructions of legitimacy—including the epistemological problem linked to obtaining knowledge of a 'right' answer and the ontological problems flowing from our restricted ability to describe the law—need not be addressed here. Because of the axiological nature of the definition of law, empirical evidence cannot be provided in the field of legitimacy.

Any reference to empirical evidence in order to establish legitimacy carries in its train an essentially positivist flaw; law is law if and to the extent that it materializes in a particular practice. And the legitimacy derives from this practice.[70] The determination of the legitimacy of a legal norm is empirically impossible, because a process of infinite regress is set in motion by a continuous search for the content

---

[69] *A v United Kingdom* Appl no 3455/05 (2009) para 184.
[70] F. Schauer, 'Amending the Presupposition of a Constitution' in S. Levinson (ed), *Responding to Imperfection: The Theory and Practice of Constitutional Amendment* (Ewing: Princeton University Press, 1995).

and legitimacy of the meta-norm, the meta-meta-norm etc. The legitimacy of various interpretations and applications of the ECHR may be accepted or rejected depending on individual perceptions of the nature of law.

The legitimacy of law hinges on definitions of law. It is but a claim to claim that States are (or are not) obligated to depart from the Court's practice and adopt a different standard of protection, if this departure is viable within the standard of protection of the ECHR, all things considered. Nothing per se contradicts (or dictates) the view that States must depart from the Court's practice in order fully to respect and implement the ECHR. At the end of the day, it all boils down to a question of legitimacy; the key question is whether authority attaches to the decision-maker or to the decision.[71] Or as Hart put it, 'it cannot be *demonstrated* that a decision is uniquely correct: but it may be acceptable as the reasoned product of informed impartial choice'.[72] And the informed choice may not be the same at the national and international level. The institutional setting of the national/ international reviewer may change the picture.

The Court's dependence on national independence

The proposition developed here is not nearly as exotic as it may appear to be. It may be that we are not accustomed openly to recognize and accept the pluralistic nature of the ECHR and its enforcement machinery, but the fact of the matter is that the Court relies heavily on national authorities to make independent and well-founded appreciations of human rights within their jurisdiction.

In legal literature and discourse, constructive debate has been prevented by the confusion surrounding the margin of appreciation doctrine which became a prominent issue in legal doctrine in the 1970s when the Court departed from the more textually oriented interpretations in favour of the search for a fair balance. Here, I will merely point out that the Court's practice provides many examples of judgments relying heavily on (formal) arguments concerning the domestic decision-making procedure and legitimacy rather than, or in addition to, (substantive) arguments going to the merits of the matter. If this subsidiary— or second order—review is to be meaningful, it must be counterbalanced by a non-subsidiary—or first order—review.

Some examples may demonstrate the nature of the argument. In *Hirst v United Kingdom (No 2)* concerning the bar on the applicant's right to vote as a result of being sentenced to life imprisonment for manslaughter, the majority would not accept automatic disenfranchisement 'based purely on what might offend public opinion'[73] and found the 'general, automatic and indiscriminate restriction on a vitally important Convention right' incompatible with Art 3 of Protocol No 1.[74]

---

[71] J. J. Shestack, 'The Philosophical Foundations of Human Rights' in J. Symonides (ed), *Human Rights: Concept and Standards* (Dartmouth: Ashgate, 2000), 43.
[72] H. L. A. Hart, *The Concept of Law* (Oxford: Clarendon Press, 1961), 200.
[73] *Hirst v United Kingdom (No 2)* ECHR 2005-IX (2005), para 70.
[74] Ibid, paras 80–1.

Interestingly, the majority of the Grand Chamber focused on the absence of parliamentary assessment of 'the proportionality of a blanket ban on the right of a convicted prisoner to vote' and the lack of 'any substantive debate by members of the legislature on the continued justification in light of modern day penal policy and of current human rights standards for maintaining such a general restriction on the right of prisoners to vote'.[75] Moreover, the domestic court did not undertake any assessment of the proportionality of the measure seeing that as a matter for Parliament and not for the national courts.[76] The majority thus indicated that the substantive balance might have been struck differently, provided the measure had been more firmly rooted in the domestic, democratic process.

Dissenting Judges Wildhaber, Costa, Lorenzen, Kovler, and Jebens disagreed arguing on the basis of substantive arguments[77] and dissenting Judges Tulkens and Zagrebelsky added:

> we note that the discussion about proportionality has led the Court to evaluate not only the law and its consequences, but also the parliamentary debate...This is an area in which two sources of legitimacy meet, the Court on the one hand and the national parliament on the other. This is a difficult and slippery terrain for the Court in view of the nature of its role, especially when it itself accepts that a wide margin of appreciation must be given to the Contracting States.[78]

The Court placed similar weight on the domestic authorities' view in *Ždanoka v Latvia* concerning the exclusion of communists from the right to stand for national elections after Latvia's independence. The Court accepted the restriction arguing, inter alia, that the domestic authorities are better placed to assess the difficulties faced in establishing and safeguarding the newly established democratic order and should be left sufficient latitude to assess the needs of their society in building confidence in the new democratic institutions 'provided that the Court has found nothing arbitrary or disproportionate in such an assessment'. Immediately thereafter the Court stated:

> In this respect, the Court also attaches weight to the fact that the Latvian Parliament has periodically reviewed section 5(6) of the 1995 Act, most recently in 2004. Even more importantly, the Constitutional Court has carefully examined, in its decision of 30 August 2000, the historical and political circumstances which gave rise to the enactment of the law in Latvia, finding the restriction to be neither arbitrary nor disproportionate at that point in time, i.e. nine years after the events in question.[79]

The Court, in other words, attached significant weight to the assessment of the legislature and in particular the domestic judiciary in accepting the impugned measure, which should, however, be kept under review with a view to bringing it to an early end.[80]

---

[75] Ibid, para 79.   [76] Ibid, para 80.

[77] Joint dissenting opinion of Judges Wildhaber, Costa, Lorenzen, Kovler, and Jebens in ibid, para 7.

[78] Joint concurring opinion of Judges Tulkens and Zagrebelsky in ibid, para 7.

[79] *Ždanoka v Latvia* Appl no 58278/00 (2006), para 134.

[80] Ibid, para 135. See similarly eg *Dickson v United Kingdom* Appl no 44362 (2007), and *B and L v United Kingdom* Appl no 36536/02 (2005).

The Court's practice accordingly supports the view that it makes a difference whether the Court faces a measure adopted by the domestic legislature, the domestic courts, and/or domestic administrative authorities. The Court at times focuses more on the role of the domestic authorities than on the substance of the case, and it seems difficult to deny the relevance of the nature of the domestic authority responsible for the decision, which is the object of the Court's review. The distinction drawn in *Ždanoka v Latvia* between the Parliament and the judiciary is telling.

Conclusion

It is impossible to escape the conclusion that the Court attaches importance to the role of the particular domestic authority. The Court's balancing of interests depends not only on the greater or lesser weight of the substantive—normally public and individual—interests, but also on the Court's subsidiarity approach and the ensuing respect of the domestic decision-maker. If the Court's decreasing review is not to lead to a devaluation of European human rights standards (and this was *not* an intention behind Protocol No 14), domestic authorities will need to fill the vacuum left by the Court's partial withdrawal from the scene of human rights adjudication.

It cannot be empirically proven that national authorities may and must act independently of the Court. Any concept of law depends essentially on unwritten, conventional assumptions concerning the definition of law. In my view, the key question is fairly simple: why should domestic authorities not act independently and strike a better substantive balance than the Court? The Court's practice is in fact restricted by the principle of subsidiarity, just as the Court is in fact a largely inaccessible human rights remedy. The Court's increasingly restricted capacity will continue to hinder effective access to individual relief as well as to continued development of the standards of the ECHR, unless the domestic authorities take their independent obligation seriously and implement the ECHR in good faith and in light of international standards.

V. Conclusion

The institutional balance is currently flowing away from the Court. The Court's role is decreasing as a result of its caseload burden. The changing institutional balance is likely to pose the greatest challenge to the further development of international human rights law in the Council of Europe—unless the role of national authorities changes to make up for the weakened position of the Court.

Even if we disregard the current caseload challenge, there are severe restrictions on the Court's role as an institution granting individual relief, just as there are serious limits on the Court's scope for developing a constitutional role. The Court's room for manoeuvre is very limited and there are no reasonable prospects of fundamentally changing the foundation of the Court's work. The key to developing the system lies with other actors.

The changing role of the Court should rub off on the role of national authorities. National authorities should understand the new dynamics of the interaction between national and international institutions and accept that the Court's review cannot always be taken to reflect the appropriate international standard of protection. If, and to the extent that, the Court is barred from applying the proper standard of the ECHR, the national authorities must assume the responsibility resting on the Contracting States and undertake a proper and independent review pursuant to international standards.

We have to ground the ECHR in national law and secure national ownership of international human rights law. We have to empower national authorities to take the lead on human rights issues. We have to secure popular participation in the development of human rights. We have to secure that the most vulnerable, including minorities and the disempowered, are recognized and protected. And we have to strengthen systems holding States accountable to international human rights standards. None of this can be done under the current system.

The time has come to change the dynamics of the ECHR. The time has come for political leadership in the field of human rights. The time has come, but who is prepared to take up the challenge?

11

Rethinking the European Court of Human Rights

*Luzius Wildhaber**

The European Convention on Human Rights (ECHR) originated in 1949/50, the European Commission of Human Rights (ECommHR) began its work in 1954, the European Court of Human Rights (ECtHR) in 1959. There can be little doubt that the edifice and the instruments launched some 50 to 60 years ago had a profound impact on subsequent developments. I shall discuss some of the most important aspects of these developments.

In a first section, I shall point out what I consider to be some signal achievements of the ECHR and the European Court of Human Rights (Section I). In a second section, I distinguish between five functions of the ECtHR: filtering and wailing wall, routine adjudication, borderline fine-tuning, grave human rights breaches, and structural and systemic problems (Section II). In a third section, I address the evolutive interpretation of the ECHR (Section III). The fourth section takes up issues of defective legislation or practice and asks whether and to what extent the ECtHR has ordered general measures and has considered such laws as incompatible with the Convention (Section IV). In a fifth section, on the overload of the ECHR system, I go beyond what I call 'incrementalism and tinkering' and sketch a reformed system, one which in my view would provide for more stability, predictability, transparency, and honesty (Section V). In a last section, I try to define and evaluate issues of individual, constitutional, and administrative justice (Section VI).

I. Some Achievements of the ECHR

Binding judgments of an international human rights court

The ECHR is a product of realistic idealism. It is a direct reaction to the atrocities of the 1930s and 1940s.[1] It is anchored in the belief that democratic regimes,

---

* Revised and amplified text of a Keynote Address delivered on 21 March 2009 at the University of Copenhagen. Sections V and VI are based on lectures at the University of Bristol (on 6 May 2009) and at Yale Law School (on 24 April 2009).

[1] D. Nicol, 'Original Intent and the ECHR', *Public Law* (2005), 152–72; A. W. Brian Simpson, *Human Rights and the End of Empire* (Oxford: Oxford University Press, 2001).

respectful of fundamental rights, do not go to war with one other, and that it can therefore no longer be an issue of purely domestic jurisdiction whether democracies relapse into dictatorships.

As it has turned out, the ECHR may be said to constitute the most successful attempt to implement the Universal Declaration of Human Rights through binding court decisions to which the Member States undertake to abide, rather than through recommendations, reports, information, exhortations, or lamentations. In putting matters this way, one distinguishes between binding legal obligations and non-binding soft law. One characterizes issues of the implementation of UN-based human rights law as largely soft law and of a political nature, and suggests that the effect of judgments of the ECtHR should go beyond that.

Of course, such a methodological approach might be qualified as somewhat old fashioned and as an oversimplification of issues of considerable complexity.[2] However, the ground on which international human rights are built is slippery enough. The risk that some States might feel tempted to consider all human rights of the ECHR as soft law and as subject to the 'sovereignty veto' of their governments exists. Indeed the Court has repeatedly been reviled for ignoring the boundaries between law and politics. For example, the Russian government called the *Ilaşcu v Moldova and Russia* judgment 'incoherent, controversial, subjective, political and based on double standards', and it further added that the *Ždanoka v Latvia* judgment 'ignored objective historical facts'.[3] While I do not believe that these insults are pertinent (or even proper), I nevertheless tend to think that the Court would be well advised to stay on safe ground.

In the recent case of *Demir and Baykara v Turkey*, the ECtHR departed from its earlier case law and considered the right of trade unions to bargain collectively as an essential element of Art 11 of the ECHR.[4] Relying on the doctrine of the 'living' nature of the Convention,[5] the Court stated that it:

can and must take into account elements of international law other than the Convention, the interpretation of such elements by competent organs, and the (consensus emerging from) the practice of European States reflecting their common values.[6]

And it added a remark which must come as a big but unwelcome surprise from the perspective of international law, noting:

that in searching for common ground among the norms of international law it has never distinguished between sources of law according to whether or not they have been signed or ratified by the respondent State.[7]

---

[2] D. Thürer, 'Soft Law—Norms in the Twilight between Law and Politics' in D. Thürer, *Völkerrecht als Fortschritt und Chance* (Zurich: Nomos, 2009), 159–78.

[3] Press Release no 1569 of 8 July 2004 of the Russian Ministry of Foreign Affairs. Cf *Ilaşcu and others v Moldova and Russia* Appl no 48787/99 (2004), ECHR 2004-VII (n 13 below); *Ždanoka v Latvia* Appl no 58278/00 (2006), ECHR 2006-IV.

[4] *Demir and Baykara v Turkey* Appl no 34503/97 (2008), paras 153–4 and concurring opinion of Judge Zagrebelsky.

[5] Ibid, para 68.   [6] Ibid, para 85.   [7] Ibid, para 78.

Jean-François Flauss has pointedly criticized the methodology of this judgment, remarking that the Court, by extending its 'consensual' method in all directions, adhered to a system of 'pick and choose'. He has qualified this system as shattering, alarming, presumptuous, and iconoclastic.[8]

Extension of the Convention to the whole of Europe

The second achievement I wish to emphasize is that the Convention was conceived in 1949/50 as an instrument to prevent democracies from relapsing into dictatorships, but was then extended to the whole continent of Europe. In a first step, it was gradually accepted by the whole of Western Europe. Not only was the Convention as such ratified, but over time the States also acceded to the optional clauses (individual applications to the ECommHR and compulsory jurisdiction of the ECtHR).[9]

In a second step, the Convention was extended, after the fall of the Iron Curtain, to practically all countries of Central and Eastern Europe, democratic or not so democratic, willing or not so willing, as one of the most visible signs of an attempted change in their systems of government. Future historians may well write that one of the main merits of the Convention and the Court's case law was simply to be there after the fall of the Iron Curtain, at the right time and the right place, as a credible model for those States which intended to demonstrate their commitment to democracy, the rule of law, and human rights. The changes which the ECHR brought about or supported in Central Europe have been praiseworthy and have not only benefitted individuals, but also the national courts and ultimately the separation of powers.

As a result, the ECHR is the only regional human rights catalogue which is binding on practically a whole continent.

An instrument of European public order

In a few important cases, the ECtHR has emphasized 'the Convention's special character as a human rights treaty'[10] and as an 'instrument of European public order (ordre public) for the protection of individual human beings',[11] as well as the 'objective obligations' and the 'collective enforcement' of the ECHR guarantees.[12]

---

[8] J.-F. Flauss, 'Actualité de la Convention européenne des droits de l'homme', *Actualité juridique droit administratif* (2009), 872–84. See also the less lofty, but nevertheless cautious comments by R. Nordeide in 103 *American Journal of International Law* (2009), 567–74.

[9] L. Wildhaber, 'Changing Ideas about the Tasks of the ECtHR' in L. Wildhaber, *The ECtHR 1998–2006: History, Achievements, Reform* (Strasbourg, Kehl: N. P. Engel, 2006), 138–43.

[10] *Al-Adsani v United Kingdom* Appl no 35763/97 (2001), ECHR 2001-XI, para 55.

[11] *Loizidou v Turkey* (Preliminary Objections) Series A no 310 (1995), ECHR A/310, paras 75 and 93; *Banković v Belgium et al* Appl no 52207/99 (2001), ECHR 2001-XII, para 80; *Bosphorus Hava Yollari Turizm ve Tikaret Anonim Şirketi v Ireland* Appl no 45036/98 (2005), ECHR 2005-VI, para 156.

[12] *Ireland v United Kingdom* Series A no 25 (1978), para 239; *Loizidou* (Preliminary Objections), n 11 above, para 70; *Mamatkulov and Askarov v Turkey* Appl nos 46827/99, 46951/99 (2005), ECHR 2005-I, para 100.

These formulations could be interpreted in different ways as claims:

(a) to achieve effective application of the ECHR in all territories of all Member States (this view would explain why the ECtHR decided it had jurisdiction in the *Loizidou* and the *Ilaşcu* cases, but not in the *Banković* case);[13] or

(b) to a special, constitutional character of the ECHR, which should be given primacy over national law, being an instrument of both international law and the municipal legal systems of the Member States (either in all its aspects or with respect solely to its core principles); or

(c) to a special, constitutional character of each specific judgment or decision of the ECtHR (since according to Art 46(1) the States 'undertake to abide by the final judgment of the Court in any case to which they are parties', judgments to which other States are parties will ordinarily be observed as precedents).[14] There is in my view no specific need to regard every judgment as an instrument of a pan-European public order.[15]

Without analysing these claims in more detail, it could at any rate be maintained that the core content of the triad of democracy, rule of law, and human rights has become indispensable for any contemporaneous, value-oriented understanding of a European Constitution.[16] In the same vein, the European Court of Justice in its early leading cases emphasized that human rights constituted general principles of Community law and were inspired by constitutional traditions common to the Member States, so that they could 'supply guidelines which should be followed'.[17]

Confirmation of the right of individual application

As a fourth achievement I would stress that the Convention has become a living illustration and confirmation of the right of individual application. Along with this has come an enormous workload and backlog.[18]

The ECHR was launched in the 1950s with an optional right to bring individual applications before the ECommHR, whose reports were authoritative but not binding. Proposals to give the Court the power to declare null and void national legislation and court decisions which violated the Convention were rejected. Only in 1994 did the 9th Additional Protocol give individuals direct access to the Court, and even that access was subject to leave given by the Court. The 11th Additional

---

[13] *Loizidou* (Preliminary Objections), n 11 above, *Loizidou v Turkey* (Merits) Appl no 15318/89 (1996), ECHR 1996-VI; *Ilaşcu et al v Moldova and Russia* Appl no 48787/99 (2004), ECHR 2004-VII; *Banković*, n 11 above.

[14] See n 81 below.

[15] If such a need were asserted, it would be indispensable to define what elements of a judgment would be binding, on the basis of what facts. It would also be necessary to agree whether only Grand Chamber judgments would be binding or also Chamber judgments (and, if so, under what conditions).

[16] By European Constitution I obviously refer to a wider notion than that of a constitution of the European Union.

[17] Case 4/73 *Nold* (1974) ECR 491; and see Case 29/69 *Stauder* (1969) ECR 419; Case 11/70 *Internationale Handelsgesellschaft* (1970) ECR 1125.

[18] I shall address this point under Section V.

Protocol then merged the ECommHR and the ECtHR in 1998, rendered the optional clauses obligatory, and thus fully institutionalized the right of individual application to the Court.

Only a few words are needed to emphasize the imposing significance of individual applications in the edifice of the ECHR. Article 34 ECHR does not provide for an *actio popularis*, but the Court may receive applications from any person, NGO, or group of individuals claiming to be the victim of a Convention violation. Individual applications are the Court's daily bread. Interstate cases are few and far between. Only 22 interstate applications have reached the Court, the most recent ones being the two pending cases of *Georgia v Russia*. Not all conflicts between States are submitted to the Court in the form of an interstate application. For instance, there have been no interstate cases concerning the dissolution of the former Yugoslavia or the conflicts and secession or autonomy claims of Chechnya or Nagorno-Karabach. Over time most conflicts reach the Court anyway by means of individual applications. Advisory opinions play a very negligible role before the Court. And as is well known, the ECHR does not provide for national filter systems or for preliminary rulings, or for writs of certiorari or leave-to-appeal systems.

For someone reflecting over the merits of different human rights protections systems,[19] the delivery of individual justice might seem the obvious answer. Quantitatively, such a system will soon attract applicants, at least if governments do not hinder the effective exercise of the right of petition. From the standpoint of autonomy, individuals choose themselves whether they want to complain, and no State or third party will be given this choice instead. Difficult cases and issues embarrassing for a government can readily be brought by individuals, whereas report systems are in the hands of the States and therefore reveal an amount of shadow-boxing and endeavours to gloss over real problems. Even a system of preliminary rulings initiated by national tribunals as it exists in the European Court of Justice may in some Council of Europe States be exposed to governmental pressures or excessive self-restraint on the part of the national tribunals. Last but not least, recourse to an international court seems to hold out the promise of a remedy to victims of human rights violations, although admittedly the Convention itself guarantees only declaratory, pecuniary, and procedural (and no substantive) remedies.

To sum up, if you want to launch an effective human rights protection procedure, a system of individual applications leading to binding judgments of an independent international court looks pretty good. This is, of course, what the human rights advocacy groups have emphasized all along, irrespective of the Court's overload, procedural delay, and loss of credibility, which constitute the main drawbacks of an individual application.[20]

---

[19] As Steven Greer has remarked aptly, a full and coherent argument that the systematic delivery of individual justice should be the key objective, has yet to be articulated: S. Greer, *The ECHR: Achievements, Problems and Prospects* (Cambridge: Cambridge University Press, 2006), 167.

[20] A typical illustration would be the article of P. Leach, 'Access to the ECtHR—From a Legal Entitlement to a Lottery?', 27 *Human Rights Law Journal* (2006), 11–25, who sees the right of applicants to an individualized adjudication as almost unconditional, but has no helpful proposals for the Court's overload problem.

II. Functions of the ECtHR

Premises

Courts should decide analogous facts according to the same rules. They should therefore normally follow precedent, unless significant changes of societal values and ideas or of living conditions require an overruling of prior judgments.[21] This follows from the core principles of predictability of the law, avoidance of arbitrariness, and equality before the law. Moreover, it is particularly important, but at the same time difficult, for international courts to avoid double standards, given the wide, sometimes obvious divergences between the Member States. In homogeneous national societies it may well be easier for courts to achieve a higher degree of coherence in their case law.

Let us inquire in the light of these premises which tasks and functions the ECtHR has to fulfil. Five categories may be distinguished.

Filtering and wailing wall

Individual applications must first be ruled admissible; in fact some 96 per cent of all applications do not reach that stage. Once they are declared admissible, however, the Court will find one or more violations in more than 90 per cent of all cases. To formulate matters somewhat differently, in practice the right of individual application is a right of access to the ECtHR, but cannot guarantee a specific treatment. Different categories of cases call for judicial treatment of varying scope. Taking into account the massive overload of the Court, it is just not possible to have a generalized guarantee for every applicant to have his or her case declared admissible or to have it debated at a public hearing or to have it submitted to the Grand Chamber.

Routine adjudication

Among the admissible applications, I classify some as falling into special categories: some concern grave breaches of human rights, some result from structural or systemic problems, some may be qualified as 'borderline fine-tuning'.

The ECtHR's database classifies cases by level. In early 2009, there were 1,361 (13 per cent) Level 1 ('most significant') cases, 1,725 (16 per cent) Level 2 ('significant contribution'), and 7,656 (71 per cent) Level 3 ('little legal interest') cases.[22] A sizeable number of the 'not so significant' cases are more or less routine judgments, whether or not the Court finds violations.

---

[21] See the authors quoted n 81 below.
[22] R. C. A. White and I. Boussiakou, 'Voices from the ECtHR', 27 *Netherlands Quarterly of Human Rights* (2009), 168–9.

Borderline fine-tuning

The ECtHR takes pride in its evolutive interpretation of the ECHR in light of changing societal values or changing needs of individuals. I leave aside for the moment the possibility that societal values might change in the sense that more restrictive approaches are advocated (for example with respect to terrorism or sexual abusers).[23] Undoubtedly, however, a good many judges of the Court see themselves more or less at the forefront of those courts that are active in further developing, evolving, and fine-tuning human rights.[24]

Grave breaches of human rights

The ECHR does not operate with the notions of core guarantees or kernels of fundamental freedoms. Even the Court's case law only rarely uses such terms. Nevertheless, unfortunately, clear cases of grave and massive human rights breaches have reached the ECtHR: random killings and torture, disappearances of persons, mass rapes, but also prolonged illegal detention, thoroughly unfair or arbitrary proceedings, or systematic elimination of effective political opposition would fall into this category. There is little doubt that it is an obvious task of a human rights court to sanction such grave breaches, even though the respective governments will resent the Court's judgments and will try to qualify them as political rather than legal.[25]

Structural or systemic problems

One of the biggest problems facing the Convention system is how to deal with large numbers of well-founded applications deriving from structural or systemic problems existing in the Contracting States, the so-called repetitive cases or mass claims. The best-known examples are the excessive length of court proceedings and the failure to execute final court judgments, problems which have existed or continue to exist in about half the Member States.[26]

I have been told that no matter how many cases concerning these problems arrive in the ECtHR, each applicant is equally aggrieved. This implicitly suggests that the Court should look at each case with equal care. If this is to be the task of a European Court with over 100,000 pending cases, one must be forgiven for questioning how

---

[23] In essence this possibility raises two fundamental problems, whether human rights necessarily prevail over democratic decision-making, and whether there is a human rights *acquis* that is irreversible. See Section III below.

[24] Very tentatively, with some trepidation and keeping in mind linguistic limits, the following courts outside Europe (but including the European Union) might deserve mention: Inter-American Court of Human Rights, European Court of Justice, Supreme Courts of Canada, USA, Israel, and India, Constitutional Court of South Africa.

[25] See text at n 3 above.

[26] For these and other illustrations, see Wildhaber, n 9 above, 121; L. Wildhaber, 'Europäischer Grundrechtsschutz aus der Sicht des Europäischen Gerichtshofs für Menschenrechte', 32 *Europäische Grundrechte Zeitschrift* (2005), 689–92.

this should happen. I grant that the lobby of NGOs, professors, and even judges who warn against what they consider to be restrictions on the right of individual application has been noisy and effective, and that there is virtually no lobby advocating effective reform. Before we look at the excessive workload of the ECtHR, I first take up the question of whether the differing functions of the Court can be reconciled.

On harmonizing the differing functions

The ECtHR has, first, the inevitable wailing wall-filter function for sifting out the large majority of applications which will not be decided on their merits.[27] An important part of all complaints will fail on formal grounds (for example, non-exhaustion of domestic remedies); others on mixed grounds (for example, being incompatible with the Convention); still others on substantive grounds (for example, being 'manifestly ill-founded'). There may be a 'spectrum of standards' concerning the notion of a 'manifestly ill-founded' application, 'ranging from totally unmeritorious to no *prima facie* breach'.[28] Indeed, given the impossible workload situation, it would be in the interest of honesty and transparency to concede that the Court cannot handle all applications; to continue to insist on admissibility conditions; however (going beyond these conditions), also to acknowledge that many applications cannot be examined, whether or not they are admissible (for example when the applicants have suffered no substantial disadvantage or when a case has no 'general repercussion in society').[29]

The ECtHR will, secondly, have to handle claims alleging grave breaches of human rights, since human rights courts cannot elude this task. If they tried to elude it, they would lose not only their credibility, but also their soul and their right to exist.

Thirdly, the Court must decide what should be the guiding principles with respect to structural or systemic problems. The details of the execution of the guiding principles should in my view be entrusted to the national authorities, but the ECtHR should have ways and means of controlling the national execution periodically in individual cases. Given the overload of the ECtHR, it is in my view simply not feasible to rely throughout on a case-by-case control by the Court. It is,

---

[27] Under Art 35 ECHR, applications are admissible:
- (a) after exhaustion of all domestic remedies, provided they are adequate and effective;
- (b) within a period of six months from the date of the final domestic decision;
- (c) if they are not anonymous;
- (d) if the complaint is not substantially the same as a matter already examined by the Court or another procedure of international investigation or settlement;
- (e) if they are not abusive, a condition which the Court interprets quite restrictively;
- (f) if they are not 'manifestly ill-founded', a condition which the Court handles with more discretion, all the way endeavouring not to make this criterion appear too intimately linked to issues of policy or management; and finally
- (g) if they are not incompatible with the Convention.

[28] D. J. Harris, M. O'Boyle, E. P. Bates, and C. M. Buckley, *Law of the ECHR* (2nd edn, Oxford: Oxford University Press, 2009), 785.

[29] This criterion was introduced in Brazil's Supreme Federal Tribunal, which was so overburdened that it was 'overstretched to the point of mutiny', *The Economist*, 23 May 2009, p 53.

furthermore, open to doubt whether a European Court can on its own discipline national systems which simply do not have the will to play by the rules of the game.

As to routine adjudication and fine-tuning in an open society, attitudes will necessarily oscillate between more activist and more self-restrained approaches.[30] Why is it that such a large number of controversial Grand Chamber judgments are accompanied by dissenting and separate opinions? Because agendas and perceptions differ, and because there are various ways of safeguarding human rights. There is on the whole nothing wrong with such divergences. Open and pluralistic societies must try to tolerate them. My own preference is for an ECtHR which develops an acute sense for effectivity and priorities and a realistic sense for what should be secondary, which takes the principle of subsidiarity seriously and which can accept that in many respects the reality of human rights is and will continue to be decentralized.

It is almost self-evident that the ECtHR will work hard to harmonize and reconcile the various functions assigned to it. Yet, objectively, such harmonization is delicate and dependent on the standpoints and agendas of the various players. 'Judicial activists' and 'perfectionists' will consider the Court's agenda to be, first, the steady expansion of human rights on a widening front; secondly, the abandonment of notions such as subsidiarity and margin of appreciation in favour of ambitious standard-setting; and consequently, thirdly, the lack of the distinctions advocated here such as 'routine adjudication', 'fine-tuning', and 'grave breaches', which would presumably be replaced by the simple concept of 'human rights violations writ large'. Advocates of 'judicial self-restraint', 'realism', and 'minimalism' might differ, but all would go less far; they would accept the ECHR's ineluctable and inexorable dependence on, and interconnectedness with, the various national courts, parliaments, and governments;[31] and they would insist on priorities and a sense of proportion in European human rights protection, so that the ECtHR would provide above all for inspiration, guidelines, minimal standards, and a programme of realistic idealism and idealistic realism.

This discussion leads us directly to issues of the evolutive interpretation and the overload and reform of the ECtHR.

---

[30] See F. J. Bruinsma and M. de Blois, 'Rules of Law from Westport to Wladiwostok: Separate Opinions in the ECtHR', 15 *Netherlands Quarterly of Human Rights* (1997), 175–86; P. Mahoney, 'Judicial Activism and Judicial Self-Restraint in the ECtHR: Two Sides of the Same Coin', 11 *Human Rights Law Journal* (1990), 60–88; F. Rivière, Les Opinions Séparées des Juges à la Cour européenne des droits de l'homme (2004), 366–427; E. Voeten, 'The Politics of International Judicial Appointments: Evidence from the ECtHR', 61 *International Organization* (2007), 699–701; R. C. A. White and I. Boussiakou, n 22 above.

[31] Cf. H. Keller and A. Stone Sweet (eds), *A Europe of Rights: The Impact of the ECHR on National Legal Systems* (Oxford: Oxford University Press, 2008); L. Garlicki, 'Some Observations on Relations between the ECtHR and the Domestic Jurisdictions' in J. Iliopoulos-Strangas (ed), Cours suprêmes nationales et cours européennes: concurrence ou collaboration, In Memoriam of Louis Favoreu (Brussels: Bruylant, 2007), 305–25; N. Krisch, 'The Open Architecture of European Human Rights Law', 71 *Modern Law Review* (2008), 183–216; S. Oeter, 'Rechtsprechungskonkurrenz zwischen nationalen Verfassungsgerichten, Europäischem Gerichtshof und Europäischem Gerichtshof für Menschenrechte', 66 *Vereinigung deutscher Staatsrechtslehrer* (2006), 361–91; C. Vedder, 'Integrierter Grundrechtsschutz in Europa—Görgülü und Bosphorus' in H. Bauer, D. Czybulka, W. Kahl, and A. Vosskuhle (eds), *Wirtschaft im offenen Verfassungsstaat, Festschrift Reiner Schmidt* (Munich: C. H. Beck, 2006), 179–203.

III. A Few Words on the Evolutive Interpretation of the ECHR

Where does evolutive interpretation lead?

The ECHR guarantees classical civil and political rights. As is the case with national catalogues of human rights, such guarantees cannot be interpreted like a Code of civil or criminal procedure or of taxation. The guarantees are more programmatic than normative formulations, open in time and into the future, to be unfolded and developed in light of changing conditions and societal values, a deteriorating environment, increasing global mobility, migration streams, rapid technological progress, and financial crises. Moreover, in my view, it is often hardly possible to demonstrate conclusively that a specific decision is uniquely correct. Tribunals can render their judgments acceptable if these appear as the reasoned product of informed impartial choice. The task of a judge, and in particular of a judge at an international human rights court, is doing justice and fairness through a vision of reasonableness.[32]

The ECtHR's hallmark has been the idea of a continuing development and the evolutive interpretation of the ECHR.[33] The notion of such an evolution may be evocative. But it is neither precise nor free of subjectivity. To a certain degree an evolution of human rights in the course of time is almost unavoidable.[34] Suffice it to invoke the irresistible expansion and generalization of the right to vote in the course of the past 220 years, the wide-ranging change of ideas and values concerning private and family life, the stigmatization of discrimination, and the profound changes in the underlying civil and criminal law in Europe in order to establish that an evolutive interpretation of human rights may often be rather self-evident, simply reflecting the course of history and modified philosophies, behaviour patterns, and beliefs.

So it will hardly come as a surprise that neither the Court as an institution nor I personally can really believe in historical interpretation and originalism. Far less than half the present 47 Member States of the ECHR had a say when the Convention was drafted. From a democratic standpoint it is not very satisfactory to

---

[32] J. Christoffersen, *Fair Balance: Proportionality, Subsidiarity and Primarity in the ECHR* (Leiden: Martinus Nijhoff, 2009), 198–204, 566–77.

[33] See Christoffersen, ibid, 44–68; Harris, O'Boyle, Bates, and Buckley, n 28 above, 5–18; O. Jacot-Guillarmod, 'Règles, méthodes et principes d'interprétation dans la jurisprudence de la Cour européenne des droits de l'homme' in L. E. Pettiti, E. Decaux, and P. H. Imbert (eds), *La Convention européenne des droits de l'homme* (2nd edn, Paris: PUF, 1999), 41–63; G. Letsas, *A Theory of Interpretation of the ECHR* (Oxford: Oxford University Press, 2007); S. C. Prebensen, 'Evolutive Interpretation of the ECHR' in P. Mahoney, F. Matscher, H. Petzold, and L. Wildhaber (eds), *Protecting Human Rights: The European Perspective, Mélanges Rolv Ryssdal* (Cologne: Carl Heymanns Verlag, 2000), 1123–37; Rivière, n 30 above, 323–421; C. Tomuschat, 'Das Europa der Richter' in J. Bröhmer, R. Bieber, C. Calliess, C. Langenfeld, S. Weber, and J. Wolf (eds), *Festschrift Georg Ress* (Cologne: Carl Heymanns Verlag, 2005), 867–8.

[34] In the same sense R. Bernhardt, 'Rechtsfortbildung durch den Europäischen Gerichtshof für Menschenrechte' in S. Breitenmoser, B. Ehrenzeller, M. Sassòli, W. Stoffel, and B. Wagner Pfeifer (eds), *Human Rights, Democracy and the Rule of Law, Liber amicorum Luzius Wildhaber* (Zurich: Dike, 2007), 91–101.

consider all newcomers bound to rules which they did not shape. This is why the 1969 Vienna Convention on the Law of Treaties (which expresses customary law in this respect) considers historical interpretation as only a 'supplementary means of interpretation'.[35] We must therefore never forget that it is a Convention we are expounding.[36]

Undoubtedly the autonomous and evolutive interpretation of ECHR concepts, and the desire to regard the Convention guarantees as something more than illusory and empty rhetoric and make them effective and tangible, aspire to establish more than minimal standards of protection.[37] In terms of the functions of the ECtHR, the ambition would seem to be to reach beyond 'routine adjudication' into the realm of 'borderline fine-tuning'. For some, evolutive interpretation would seem to encourage judicial activism to the detriment of judicial self-restraint.[38] The notion of evolutive interpretation certainly does not offer an easy recipe. It rather leads into the thicket of controversies.

A few illustrations may be helpful. Although Art 6 ECHR, the due-process guarantee of the Convention, does not expressly mention a right of access to a court, the ECtHR recognized such a right in the *Golder* case, saying that the 'fair, public and expeditious characteristics of judicial proceedings are of no value at all if there are no judicial proceedings'.[39] Along the same lines, the ECtHR noted in the *Hornsby v Greece* case that the right of access to a court 'would be illusory if a Contracting State's domestic legal system allowed a final, binding judicial decision to remain inoperative to the detriment of one party'.[40] The obligation to protect the right to life and the prohibition of torture require, in the ECtHR's view, by implication that there should be an effective official investigation when individuals have been killed as a result of the use of force or have disappeared or credibly assert that they have been tortured.[41] The discrimination of homosexuals and transsexuals

---

[35] Arts 32 and 31(1) and (3).

[36] Borrowed and paraphrased from Chief Justice Marshall in *McCulloch v State of Maryland* 17 US (4 Wheaton) 306 at 405–7, 415 (1819).

[37] See the authors quoted n 33 above; and see *Tyrer v United Kingdom* Series A no 26 (1978), para 31; *Marckx v Belgium* Series A no 31 (1979), para 41; *Selmouni v France* Appl no 25803/94 (1999), ECHR 1999-V, para 101; *Stafford v United Kingdom* Appl no 46295 (2002), ECHR 2002-IV, para 68; *Christine Goodwin v United Kingdom* Appl no 28957/95 (2002), ECHR 2002-VI, para 74; *Mamatkulov and Askarov v Turkey* Appl nos 46827/99, 46951/99 (2005), ECHR 2005-I, paras 101 and 121.

[38] Lord Hoffmann, 'The Universality of Human Rights, 125 *Law Quarterly Review* (2009), 428: 'The proposition that the Convention is a "living instrument" is the banner under which the Strasbourg Court has assumed power to legislate what they consider to be required by European public order'. And see at 431: 'The problem is the Court; and the right of individual petition, which enables it to intervene in the details and nuances of the domestic laws of Member States'. Similar expressions have emerged in France, see B. Edelmann, 'La Cour européenne des droits de l'homme: Une juridiction tyrannique?', *Recueil Dalloz* (2008), 1946; Flauss (text at nn 7–8 above); L. Gannagé, 'A propos de l' "absolutisme" des droits fondamentaux' in *Vers de nouveaux équilibres entre ordres juridiques: Liber amicorum Hélène Gaudemet-Tallon* (Paris: Dalloz, 2008), 265–84; Y. Lequette, 'Des juges littérale-ment irresponsables' in L. Cadiet, P. Callé, T. le Bars, and P. Mayer (eds), *Mélanges dédiés à la mémoire du doyen Jacques Héron* (Paris: LGDJ, 2008), 309–30.

[39] *Golder v United Kingdom* Series A no 18 (1975), para 35.

[40] *Hornsby v Greece* Appl no 18357/91 (1997), Reports 1997-II, para 40.

[41] *McCann v United Kingdom* Series A no 324 (1975), para 161; *Kaya v Turkey* Appl no 22729/93 (1998), Reports 1998-I, para 105; *Assenov v Bulgaria* Appl no 24760/94 (1998), Reports 1998-VIII,

was treated by the ECtHR as an issue of disproportionate interference with private life under Art 8 ECHR;[42] in the last analysis, I believe, these are issues of each person's freedom to choose himself or herself the aim, the sense, and the direction of his or her life. In the case of *Marckx v Belgium*, the discrimination of illegitimate children was found to constitute violations of Arts 8 and 14 ECHR and of Art 1 of Protocol No 1 and to lack objective and reasonable justification.[43] In the case of *MC v Bulgaria*, the Court considered that 'States have a positive obligation inherent in Arts 3 and 8 of the Convention to enact criminal-law provisions effectively punishing rape and to apply them in practice through effective investigation and prosecution'.[44] And since the Court found a clear and steady trend in Europe towards no longer requiring physical resistance as an element of the offence of rape,[45] Bulgaria's legislation which failed to reflect this trend was found to be in violation of Arts 3 and 8 ECHR. Similarly in the case of *Opuz v Turkey*, the lacking protection of Turkish women from domestic violence led to the finding of violations of Arts 2, 3, and 14 ECHR.[46]

I admit that these are some of my favourite examples of an evolutive interpretation. Other persons prefer other cases. Some would like to see even more of such cases, some less.

The one-way-street theory

In his partly dissenting opinion in the recent case of *Gorou v Greece (No 2)*, Judge Casadevall advocated a theory which he called the 'standstill' or 'cogwheel' technique and which I would propose to call the 'one-way-street theory'. This is how he put it:

Once the Court 'has decided to extend individuals' rights in a particular aspect of the right to a fair hearing, it should not—unless there has been a manifest mistake—reverse its decision. Acquired rights in the cause of human rights are at least as precious as acquired rights in other branches of the law and therefore the principle of non-regression must prevail.[47]

para 102; *Tanrikulu v Turkey* Appl no 23763/94 (1999), ECHR 1999-IV, para 101; *Nachova v Bulgaria* Appl no 42577/98 (2005), ECHR 2005-VII, paras 110–13; *Isayeva v Russia* Appl no 57950/00 (2005), EuGRZ 2006 32, 37–8, paras 208–13.

[42] *Dudgeon v United Kingdom* Series A no 45 (1981), paras 60–1; *Norris v Ireland* Series A no 142 (1988), para 46; *Modinos v Cyprus* Series A no 259 (1993), para 25; *Christine Goodwin v United Kingdom*, n 37 above; *Karner v Austria* Appl no 40016/98 (2003), ECHR 2003-IX, para 26; *EB v France* Appl no 43546/02 (2008).

[43] *Marckx*, n 37 above, paras 31–4.

[44] *MC v Bulgaria* Appl no 39272/98 (2003), ECHR 2003-XII, para 153.

[45] Ibid, paras 156–66.

[46] *Opuz v Turkey* Appl no 33401/02 (2009).

[47] *Gorou v Greece (No 2)* Appl no 12686/03 (2009), partly dissenting opinion of Judge Casadevall, para 8. Similar ideas can be found in an early contribution by (Judge) W. Ganshoff van der Meersch, 'Le caractère "autonome" des termes et la "marge d'appréciation" des gouvernements dans l'interprétation de la Convention européenne des droits de l'homme' in F. Matscher and H. Petzold (eds), *Protecting Human Rights: The European Dimension—Studies in Honour of Gerard Wiarda* (The Hague: Kluwer Law International, 1988), 201–2. And see P. Mahoney, n 30 above, 62–6.

This theory is in my view flawed in several ways. First of all, since human wisdom has its limits, courts may be wrong and should be allowed to make amends.[48] Secondly, the world of human rights not only takes place in the relationship between State and applicants, but in a comprehensive context with many actors who may have very different interests, all of which deserve consideration: victims and witnesses in criminal proceedings, spouses and children in family quarrels, media and the persons about whom they report, terrorists and the persons they threaten, to mention just a few examples. Thirdly, democratic societies may change their values and laws. Their views, if expressed in democratic decisions, deserve respect, even deference.[49] This is the more so because it is clearly more difficult to amend the substantive guarantees of the ECHR than municipal rights guarantees. Fourthly, the weighing and balancing of all sorts of public and private interests is at the centre of the ECtHR's activities. A truncated, lopsided, and ultimately formalistic version of such balancing would serve neither the cause of the Court nor that of human rights. As the Court has stated as early as in the *Belgian Linguistic* case, the Convention 'implies a just balance between the protection of the general interest of the community and the respect due to fundamental human rights, while attaching particular importance to the latter'.[50] And as Jonas Christoffersen expressed it:

The Court's use of the fair balance-test in widely different areas of case-law reflects the inherent and unavoidable resolution of conflicting interests flowing from the complex nature of the cases put before the Court as well as the flexibility of the norms of the ECHR.[51]

Fifthly, and finally, in the *Gorou (No 2)* case the judges of the Grand Chamber did not agree about the extent to which the Chamber had established a clear practice. As a matter of the Court's internal decision-making, it is not judicious to impose one Section's tentative practice on all other Sections in the name of an alleged 'human rights *acquis*'.

IV. Defective Legislation or Practice

Judgments on the facts of individual cases

As a rule the ECtHR refrains from attacking domestic statutes as such, both out of respect for democratic decision-making and because the ECHR does not give it that power, at least not expressly. A sort of a corollary of the right of individual petition

---

[48] A. Guiterman, *Poet's Proverbs* (1924), 38 quoted by E. H. Wilson, 'Stare Decisis, Quo Vadis? The Orphaned Doctrine in the Supreme Court', 33 *Georgetown Law Journal* (1945), 251 at 254: 'You're sure that you are Right? How fine and strong! But were you never just as sure—and Wrong?'

[49] Cf L. Wildhaber, 'Glossen zum Verhältnis von Demokratie und Europäischer Menschenrechtskonvention' in A. Fischer-Lescano, H. P. Gasser, T. Marauhn, and N. Ronzitti (eds), *Frieden in Freiheit: Festschrift Michael Bothe zum 70. Geburtstag* (Baden-Baden: Nomos, 2008), 1243–51.

[50] *Belgian Linguistic* case, Series A no 6 (1968), 32, para 5. See also *Klass v Germany* Series A no 28 (1978), para 59; *Sporrong and Lönnroth v Sweden* Series A no 52 (1982), para 69.

[51] Christoffersen, n 32 above, 203.

is therefore the Court's constant jurisprudence that it decides individual cases on the facts of each case. However, this has never been as clear as it appeared to be. In the 1978 judgment in the interstate case of *Ireland v United Kingdom*, the Court stated that its 'judgments in fact serve not only to decide those cases brought before the Court but, more generally, to elucidate, safeguard and develop the rules instituted by the Convention, thereby contributing to the observance by the States of the engagements undertaken by them as Contracting Parties'.[52] In varying shades and formulations, this idea was taken up later on and manifested itself also when the possibilities of issuing so-called 'judgments of principle' or of an '*erga omnes* effect' of the Court's judgments or of new ways of handling mass claims were discussed. In the *Karner v Austria* case of 2003, the Court affirmed that while

the primary purpose of the Convention system is to provide individual relief, its mission is also to determine issues on public-policy grounds in the common interest, thereby raising the general standards of protection of human rights and extending human rights jurisprudence throughout the community of Convention States.[53]

Can the Court state general rules irrespective of the facts of each case?

Three recent cases of the Court's Grand Chamber demonstrate striking disagreements among the judges as to what the role of the Court should be.

In the well-known *Hirst* case,[54] the ECtHR was confronted with a domestic legislation which provided for a general and automatic disenfranchisement of convicted prisoners from voting in parliamentary and local elections. Hirst was serving a sentence of discretionary life imprisonment for manslaughter. He complained of a disproportionate interference with his right to vote under Art 3 of Protocol No 1. The Court found a violation, although it reaffirmed that under its case law States enjoyed a wide margin of appreciation.[55] It did not give the UK government detailed guidance, beyond commenting that individuals who had 'seriously abused a public position or whose conduct threatened to undermine the rule of law or democratic foundations' could be deprived of their electoral rights.[56]

Judges Tulkens and Zagrebelsky wrote in their concurring opinion that the 'fact that by law a convicted person's imprisonment is the ground for his or her disenfranchisement [was] . . . conclusive'.[57] Apparently in their view any statute providing for a general disenfranchisement of prisoners is incompatible with the ECHR; restrictions of the right to vote must respect the 'principle of universal suffrage'.[58]

---

[52] *Ireland v United Kingdom*, n 12 above, para 154.
[53] *Karner v Austria*, n 42 above, para 26.
[54] *Hirst v United Kingdom (No 2)* Appl no 74025/01 (2005), ECHR 2005-IX.
[55] Ibid, paras 60–2 and 82.
[56] Ibid, para 71.
[57] Ibid, p 226.
[58] Ibid, para 62 (in the wording of the Court's majority).

This sort of creative law-making led to the protest in the joint dissenting opinion of Judges Wildhaber, Costa, Lorenzen, Kovler, and Jebens 'that the Court is not a legislator and should be careful not to assume legislative functions'.[59] They further added that in the instant case it was hard to see how the UK legislation was incompatible with the ECHR: 'Since restrictions on the right to vote continue to be compatible, it would seem obvious that the deprivation of the right to vote for the most serious offences such as murder or manslaughter, is not excluded in the future'.[60]

In the case of *DH v Czech Republic*[61] the Court found a violation of Art 14 ECHR in conjunction with the right of education under Art 2 of Protocol No 1, on account of the disproportionately high number of Roma children in Czech special schools. The majority of the Grand Chamber summarized its approach as follows:

since it has been established that the relevant legislation as applied in practice at the material time had a disproportionately prejudicial effect on the Roma community, the Court considers that the applicants as members of that community necessarily suffered the same discriminatory treatment. Accordingly, it does not need to examine their individual cases.[62]

As was pointed out by one of the dissenters, the question of consent by the parents and other factors would have necessitated a more thorough inquiry into the facts of each individual case.[63]

In the case of *EB v France*,[64] the French authorities and courts refused the request of a lesbian to adopt a child on two grounds: the lack of a paternal referent and the ambivalence of the applicant's partner's commitment to her adoption plans. The majority of the Grand Chamber considered that the reference to the lack of a paternal referent was tantamount to a reference to the applicant's homosexuality, which was 'if not explicit, at least implicit'.[65] They concluded that 'the illegitimacy of one of the grounds [had] the effect of contaminating the entire decision'.[66] Most of the dissenting judges accepted that refusals to adopt a child 'could not be based on homosexuality without violating Art. 14 and 8',[67] and would have been willing to state that much, in the abstract. Yet in their view, the contamination theory was wrong in the instant case because it was not the applicant's homosexuality, but rather the grounds indicated by the French courts (and specifically the ambivalence of the applicant's partner), that had prevented her from obtaining the authorization.

One could perhaps sum up by saying that the majority in all three cases wanted to formulate a general principle and took the liberty of considering the facts of the individual cases as of secondary importance. Put differently, it is not always so that

---

[59] Ibid, para 6 at 230.   [60] Ibid, para 8 at 231.
[61] *DH v Czech Republic* Appl no 57325/00 (2007).
[62] Ibid, para 209.
[63] Ibid, dissenting opinion of Judge Borrego Borrego.
[64] *EB v France*, n 42 above.
[65] Ibid, para 89.
[66] Ibid, para 80.
[67] Ibid, dissenting opinion of Judge Costa, joined by Judges Türmen, Ugrekhelidze, and Jočienė.

the Court decides individual cases exclusively on the facts of each case. Especially in recent years, it would seem that a majority insists on formulating general jurisprudential rules underlying the judgments, some rather abstract, some more narrow. While I think that this is quite understandable, in my view the facts of individual cases should always square with the jurisprudential rules, because, if they do not, either the jurisprudential rules should have been drafted differently, or the individual case should have been decided differently.

The Committee of Ministers as supervisory organ in charge of executing the Court's judgments has repeatedly tried to induce the States concerned to change their legislation and practices.[68] The ECtHR has imposed on States a duty to take remedial measures, which went beyond granting reparation for past prejudice.[69] In pilot judgments, it has furthermore indicated legislative measures in order to overcome structural problems. However, as the following discussion will show, the Court still does not declare national laws per se null and void. It finds violations in respect of certain applicants and, by following its (new) case law, hopes to achieve legislative changes over time.

The question of general rules in the *Marckx* and the *Vermeire* cases

Cases insisting on the principle of non-discrimination in a general way (for example the cases concerning illegitimate children such as *Marckx*, *Vermeire*, or *Mazurek*,[70] or transsexuals such as *Christine Goodwin*,[71] or homosexuals such as *Dudgeon*, *Norris*, *Modinos*, *Smith and Grady*, or *Karner*)[72] are usually meant to be extended to all Member States. In the famous *Marckx* case of 1979, the Belgian government defended its legislation containing discriminatory provisions against children born out of wedlock, claiming that it was 'not the Court's function to rule *in abstracto* on the compatibility with the Convention of certain legal rules'.[73] The Court flatly

---

[68] R. Bernhardt, 'Judgments of International Human Rights Courts and Their Effects in the Internal Legal Order of States' in *Studi di diritto internazionale in onore di Gaetano Arangio-Ruiz* (Naples: Editoriale Scientifica, 2004), 435; Garlicki, n 31 above, 319–24; P. Mahoney, 'Judgments of International and Supranational Courts: Effect, Non-Compliance and Enforcement. The ECtHR as a Case Study', Manuscript of a conference at the University of St Gallen, 2–3 October 2008, 6–11.

[69] *Papamichalopoulos v Greece* (Just Satisfaction), Series A no 330-B (1995), para 34; *Scozzari and Giunta v Italy* Appl no 39221/98 (2000), ECHR 2000-VIII, para 249; *Maestri v Italy* Appl no 39748/98 (2004), ECHR 2004-I, para 47; *Assanidze v Georgia* Appl no 71503/01 (2004), ECHR 2004-II, paras 198, 202–3; *Ilaşcu v Moldova and Russia* Appl no 48787/99 (2004), ECHR 2004-VII, paras 487 and 490; *Öcalan v Turkey* Appl no 46221/99 (2005), ECHR 2005-IV, para 210. And see L. Caflisch, 'La mise en œuvre des arrêts de la Cour: nouvelles tendances' in F. Salerno (ed), *La nouvelle procédure devant la Cour européenne des droits de l'homme après le Protocole no 14* (actes du Colloque de Ferrara) (Brussels: Bruylant, 2007), 157–74; L. Wildhaber, 'The Execution of Judgments of the ECtHR: Recent Developments' in P.-M. Dupuy, B. Fassbender, M. N. Shaw, and K. P. Sommermann (eds), *Essays in Honour of Christian Tomuschat* (Kehl: N. P. Engel, 2006), 671–80.

[70] *Marckx v Belgium*, n 37 above; *Vermeire v Belgium* Series A no 214-C (1991); *Mazurek v France* Appl no 34406/97 (2000), ECHR 2000-II.

[71] *Christine Goodwin v United Kingdom*, n 37 above.

[72] *Dudgeon v United Kingdom*, n 42 above; *Norris v Ireland*, n 42 above; *Modinos v Cyprus* Series A no 259 (1993); *Smith and Grady v United Kingdom* Appl no 33985/96 (1999), ECHR 1999-VI; *Karner v Austria*, n 42 above.

[73] *Marckx*, n 37 above, para 26.

rejected this argument, however, stating that 'Article 25 of the Convention entitles individuals to contend that a law violates their rights by itself, in the absence of an individual measure of implementation, if they run the risk of being directly affected by it'.[74]

It is of course correct to explain these passages of the *Marckx* judgment as extensions of the victim status, allowing certain victims of violations of Convention guarantees—in rather exceptional situations—to attack national legislation direct-ly.[75] But one could also broaden the scope of inquiry (as Wojciech Sadurski and Lech Garlicki have done recently)[76] and ask how one should analyse the powers of the ECtHR where a widespread practice or a law or statute fails to match the Convention standards. As I have explained, traditionally the Court's role was restricted to the consideration of fact-specific, concrete acts and decisions rather than to the law underlying the concrete acts. As a consequence, the Court's finding of a Convention violation was expressed in the operative part of the judgment as a finding that the impugned concrete act was incompatible with Convention stan-dards, 'with respect to the applicants', as the Court put it in the *Marckx* judgment of 1979.[77] Certainly, the reasoning of the *Marckx* judgment made it clear that the challenged acts or decisions were taken on the basis of a law, and the Court's scrutiny inevitably involved a critical analysis of the flawed law itself.[78] The finding of Convention violations in the *Marckx* judgment in reality resulted from the discriminatory content of the Belgian legislation and not from an allegedly incor-rect application of that legislation by municipal courts or administrative agencies. In effect, the Court left the problem of the execution of its judgments largely to the Committee of Ministers,[79] which had to decide whether a judgment of the Court called for a change of legislation. Sadurski calls this approach inadequate and hypocritical.[80] This would seem a somewhat harsh criticism. Since the ECtHR normally follows its own precedents, it will become clear over time anyway that in each case of reliance on flawed legislation the Court will find a Convention violation.[81]

---

[74] Ibid, para 27.

[75] Cf L. Wildhaber, 'Internationaler Kommentar zur Europäischen Menschenrechtskonvention, Art 8' in H. Golsong, W. Karl, H. Miehsler, E. Riedel, K. Rogge, T. Vogler, L. Wildhaber, and S. Breitenmoser (eds), *Internationaler Kommentar zur Europäischen Menschenrechtskonvention* (Cologne: Carl Heymanns Verlag, 1992), 28–9, nos 47–50.

[76] W. Sadurski, 'Partnering with Strasbourg: Constitutionalisation of the ECtHR, the Accession of Central and East European States to the Council of Europe, and the Idea of Pilot Judgments', 9 *Human Rights Law Review* (2009), 397–453; L. Garlicki, 'Broniowski and After: On the Dual Nature of "Pilot Judgments"' in L. Caflisch, J. Callewaert, R. Liddell, P. Mahoney, and M. Villiger (eds), *Human Rights— Strasbourg Views: Liber Amicorum Luzius Wildhaber* (Kehl: N. P. Engel, 2007), 182–3.

[77] *Marckx*, n 37 above, paras 29–30.

[78] Characteristically, the sharp criticism of the *Marckx* judgment by François Rigaux carries the title 'La loi condamnée', 94 *Journal des Tribunaux* (1979), 513–24. Rigaux did not doubt that the ECtHR had undermined the Belgian legislation as such.

[79] Under Art 46 (2) ECHR.

[80] Sadurski, n 76 above, 413–14.

[81] See generally R. Post (ed), 'Global Constitutionalism' (Yale Law School Seminar, 2009), V-1-85; with respect to the ECtHR: K. Lucas-Alberni, *Le revirement de jurisprudence de la Cour européenne des droits de l'homme* (Brussels: Bruylant, 2008); A. Mowbray, 'An Examination of the ECtHR's Approach

And this is precisely what happened. In the *Vermeire* case of 1991,[82] the Court followed the *Marckx* judgment of 1979. It had taken Belgium until 1987, that is to say eight years, to modify its legislation to take into account the *Marckx* judgment. The Court in *Vermeire* did not accept this delay and commented ungraciously that there had been 'nothing imprecise or incomplete about the rule which prohibited discrimination' against illegitimate children.[83] And it added:

The freedom of choice allowed to a State as to the means of fulfilling its obligation under Article 53 cannot allow it to suspend the application of the Convention while waiting for such a reform to be completed, to the extent of compelling the Court to reject in 1991, with respect to a succession which took effect [in] 1980, complaints identical to those which it upheld [in] 1979.[84]

This sequence from the *Marckx* to the *Vermeire* judgments anticipates to a certain extent the modern pilot judgment procedure, introduced in the *Broniowski* and *Hutten-Czapska* cases of 2004 and 2005.[85] Already in the early Belgian cases, not much was left of fact-specificity, except for the operative part of the judgments. Apart from that, the Court's insistence on a modification of the Belgian legislation became quite clear.

Pilot judgment procedures

The boldest attempt to tackle the problem of defective national legislation or practice has undoubtedly been the development of the so-called pilot judgment procedure.[86] The Committee of Ministers of the Council of Europe invited the Court in 2004

to identify, in its judgments finding a violation of the Convention, what it considers to be an underlying system problem and the source of this problem, in particular when it is likely to give rise to numerous applications, so as to assist States in finding the appropriate solution and the Committee of Ministers in supervising the execution of judgments.[87]

---

to Overruling its Previous Case Law', 9 *Human Rights Law Review* (2009), 179–201; G. Ress, 'Aspekte der Stabilität der Rechtsprechung des Europäischen Gerichtshofs für Menschenrechte' in A. Epiney, M. Haag, and A. Heinemann (eds), *Die Herausforderung von Grenzen, Festschrift Roland Bieber* (2006); L. Wildhaber, 'Precedent in the ECtHR' in P. Mahoney, F. Matscher, H. Petzold, and L. Wildhaber (eds), Protecting Human Rights: The European Perspective, Studies in Memory of Rolv Ryssdal (Cologne: Carl Heymanns Verlag, 2000), 1529–45, reproduced in L. Wildhaber, 'Changing Ideas about the Tasks of the ECtHR' in L. Wildhaber, n 9 above, 154–73.

[82] *Vermeire v Belgium*, n 70 above.
[83] Ibid, para 25.
[84] Ibid, para 26.
[85] See W. Sadurski, 'Partnering with Strasbourg: Constitutionalisation of the ECtHR, the Accession of Central and East European States to the Council of Europe, and the Idea of Pilot Judgments', 9 *Human Rights Law Review* (2009), 412–26.
[86] See L. Garlicki, 'Some Observations on Relations between the ECtHR and the Domestic Jurisdictions' in J. Iliopoulos-Strangas (ed), n 31 above; V. Zagrebelsky, 'Questions autour de Broniowski' in *Human Rights*, n 76 above, 521–35; L. Wildhaber, 'Pilot Judgments in Cases of Structural or Systemic Problems on the National Level' in R. Wolfrum and U. Deutsch (eds), *The ECtHR Overwhelmed by Applications: Problems and Possible Solutions* (Berlin: Springer, 2009), 69–75 and the discussion at 77–92.
[87] Res (2004) 3.

Ever since, the Court has been feeling its way as regards recourse to the pilot judgment procedure. There appear to be several variants, and this may recognize the flexibility needed to accommodate the range of different situations with which the Court is confronted. In what we might call the classical or the enriched version of pilot judgments of the *Broniowski* and the *Hutten-Czapska* type,[88] the Court will specify the type of general measures required to bring the domestic law within the Convention, will include its recommendation as to general measures in the operative part of the judgment, and will adjourn consideration of all similar applications. The *Broniowski* and the *Hutten-Czapska* judgments were based on judgments of the Polish Constitutional Court and amounted to a sort of a dialogue with the national judiciary. They served less to reduce the number of pending applications, but rather helped to deflect future potential applications from the Court.

It remains to be seen whether pilot judgments can be similarly successful if they go against the national judiciary and encounter a recalcitrant government. The pending case of *Burdov v Russia (No 2)* will constitute an important landmark in that respect.[89] This is a case of a rescue worker who had been exposed, in the nuclear reactor incident at Chernobyl in 1986, to massive radioactivity. Several Russian court judgments concerning his pension and insurance benefits were left unexecuted; one for three years, one for two years and only half of the sum allotted to him in the third judgment was paid promptly. The Court found violations of the guarantee of fair procedure (Art 6), of an effective national remedy (Art 13), and of the right to property (Art 1, Protocol No 1).

But given the fact that it had found in more than 200 cases that final Russian court judgments had been left unexecuted for too long, it decided to launch a pilot judgment procedure. It did not indicate specific general measures which Russia should take, apart from the fact that an effective national remedy should be introduced within six months. In addition, it suspended the handling of all new applications until one year after the final judgment in the *Burdov* procedure. With respect to cases already pending, Russia was told that it must pay adequate compensation to all applicants within one year after the final judgment in the *Burdov* procedure. It should be clear that the introduction of a new national remedy is based on the understanding that the new remedy must be effective and non-arbitrary in practice. Since the ECtHR has encountered at least as much defective practice as defective legislation in Russian cases, neither the *Burdov (No 2)* judgment nor the new Russian remedy may constitute the last word on the problem.

---

[88] *Broniowski v Poland* Appl no 31443/96 (2004), ECHR 2004-V (GC); (2005) ECHR 2005-IX (friendly settlement); *Hutten-Czapska v Poland* Appl no 35014/97 (2006) (GC), (2008) (friendly settlement).

[89] *Burdov v Russia (No 2)* Appl no 33509/04 (2009).

V. Overload and Reform of the ECtHR

Some essential figures

Whereas in the 1960s, the ECtHR proclaimed one or two cases per year, since the entry into force of Protocol No 11 on 1 November 1998, the Court has handed down some 188,000 inadmissibility decisions and some 10,000 judgments on the merits.[90] In 1999 8,400 new applications were submitted, in 2008 some 50,000.[91] More than 100,000 cases are pending before the Court.[92]

Incrementalism and tinkering

The Court has responded to this avalanche of applications by constantly simplifying, accelerating, re-evaluating, and modernizing its procedures. It has vastly improved its case management and statistics, extended its research facilities, has more and more decided on admissibility and merits together, created a Fifth Section, admitted unilateral declarations on ECHR violations, introduced pilot judgment procedures, simplified the drafting of judgments, and endeavoured to clarify the order in which cases are handled. It has almost continuously tried to improve a very difficult workload situation.[93]

One feels tempted to call the past decade a period of 'tinkering' and of 'muddling through'. Owing to the Court's will to renovate and reappraise ceaselessly, the overall picture is less gloomy than it would otherwise be. Nevertheless, and despite the Court's efforts, in all these years the number of new applications reaching the Court has mercilessly surpassed the number of decisions rendered by the Court.[94]

The tinkering system (or lack of a system) is minimalist and consensual in the sense that it has helped the Court to stay together. It has expressed the political reality that the lobby of those resisting change (which often consisted of groups otherwise supporting the ECHR) has been more effective than those advocating reform. But, over time, delays and tinkering are bound to undermine the credibility of the ECtHR. Paul Mahoney, the former Registrar of the Court, has termed the caseload 'unmanageable';[95] Steven Greer and Andrew Williams have called the systematic delivery of individual justice a 'doomed quest';[96] Jonas Christoffersen

---

[90] 'Mémorandum du Président de la Cour européenne des droits de l'homme aux Etats en vue de la Conférence d'Interlaken du 3 juillet 2009', section I, available at: <http://www.echr.coe.int/NR/rdonlyres/D61B67EF-07E6-49E5-BD26-ED8588E01C10/2791/03072009_Memo_Interlaken_fran%C3%A7ais.pdf>.

[91] Ibid, II, para 1.

[92] Ibid.

[93] Ibid, II, para 2.

[94] Wildhaber, n 9 above, 138–45.

[95] P. Mahoney, 'Thinking a Small Unthinkable: Repatriating Reparation from the ECtHR to the National Legal Order' in *Human Rights*, n 76 above, p 266.

[96] S. Greer and A. Williams, 'Human Rights in the Council of Europe and the EU: Towards "Individual," "Constitutional" or "Institutional" Justice?' 15 *European Law Journal* (2009), 469–70.

speaks of the 'Court's increasingly restricted capacity';[97] and I have said that 'the inexorable accumulation of... both inadmissible and substantial cases will increasingly asphyxiate the system so as to deprive the great majority of... cases... of any practical effect'.[98]

The ECtHR's responsibilities

Much has been said, written, and done about the reform of the ECHR system, which I need not repeat here. If all constructive proposals were lumped together, if some of the ideas contained in the Management Report of Lord Woolf of Barnes were added, if class actions were handled collectively, and if repetitive matters were sent directly to the Committee of Ministers and/or the States (as President Costa suggests in his Memorandum of 3 July 2009[99]), matters would definitely look more hopeful. However, the problem of the Court's overload would only move closer to a permanent solution, if (and that is a big 'if') the judges of the ECtHR could be persuaded that it is their responsibility not only to render the Convention guarantees effective and real, but also and just as much to make the ECHR system effective and real, too. The priorities and the management of the ECHR system should be reappraised and insofar as necessary re-ordered; the inevitable conclusion that the ECtHR cannot cope with its workload should lead to a more restrictive practice with respect to both admissibility and merits; and a new modesty should allow the recognition that the ECHR can continue to make effective and real, rather than illusory, progress, but only provided it functions properly.

For the benefit of those who might believe that these arguments shift all the blame to the Court, I wish to add that this is not how I would look at matters. To the contrary, most political actors—in the understandable, though heady, optimism of the period after the fall of the Iron Curtain—have underestimated the difficulties and overestimated the real possibilities of the ECtHR to change national judicial and political systems. And they have failed to evaluate the changed situation comprehensively and to draw consequences from it.

A realistic Court system at last

Since incrementalism and tinkering could not resolve the ECtHR's workload problem in the long run, the access of individuals to the Court is today in fact restricted. Once this is recognized, it would be worthwhile to look beyond, even if this requires an amendment of the ECHR. Without discussing alternatives or indulging in wishful thinking, I would propose a threefold approach which should at least be pondered seriously:

---

[97] Christoffersen, n 32 above, 577.
[98] Wildhaber, n 9 above, 50 (speech at the Opening of the Judicial Year, 22.1.2004).
[99] 'Mémorandum', n 90 above, IIIB.2, para 3.

1. On the level of sifting out cases, we should probably give up thinking in terms of 'admissible' applications. Instead we should distinguish between cases which the Court should handle and those which it cannot handle. Time and again judges will encounter national judgments which they would have decided differently. The issue is not, however, what are the judges' predilections, but what will promote the reality of human rights in the whole of Europe. Applications which are manifestly ill-founded, incompatible with the Convention, trivial, or in which applicants suffered no significant disadvantage should not be handled.

2. Certain categories of cases should automatically be decided on the merits, provided they are admissible.[100] These could include:

(a) right to life, prohibition of torture, prohibition of slavery;
(b) long periods of illegal detention;
(c) wholly arbitrary and unfair procedures;
(d) overruling of well-established ECtHR precedents;
(e) issues gravely affecting national constitutions;
(f) issues vital to the survival of a democracy and a democracy's right to defend itself against its enemies;
(g) guidelines for structural and systemic problems;[101]
(h) pilot judgments;
(i) interstate applications.

3. The ECtHR is overloaded with both admissible and inadmissible applications. Lamentably, at present 29 per cent of the cases which will be decided in Chambers constitute backlog, that is to say, they have been pending for more than three years,[102] a duration which the ECtHR would consider as a Convention violation if it occurred in national courts. We should therefore abandon the idea of an unrestricted individual petition in favour of a system with manageable priorities, in which the Court would decide itself, within the framework of a leave-to-appeal system, which cases it should handle. Since the Court can hardly adjudicate more than 2,000 applications per year, and since there is a sizeable number of cases which the Court must handle automatically, a good solution would be to let the Court select a number of some 1,000 cases per year which would be adjudicated, whereas the other cases would not be handled.

These proposals look radical. However, the end result would be surprisingly similar to the system presently in force. In 2008, the ECtHR handed down 1,543 judgments, that is, approximately the same number it would decide under the system which I have sketched.[103] Instead of disposing of thousands of cases administratively, losing

---

[100] In this category, cases would be decided in the traditional way, first being examined with respect to admissibility, then being decided on the merits.

[101] Structural problems should first be scrutinized in this category of cases. They should in other words be handled automatically. The follow-up cases should be assigned to the domestic level, but some cases should be re-appraised periodically by the ECtHR in the leave-to-appeal procedure.

[102] ECtHR, 'Analysis of Statistics 2008' (2009), 11.

[103] ECtHR, *Some Facts and Figures 1959–2009* (2009), 5.

thousands of applicants who realize that years will pass by before their turn has come, declaring cases manifestly ill-founded which may not be manifestly ill-founded, the new system would bring more predictability, transparency, and honesty, would concentrate on real priorities, and would therefore serve the overall effectiveness of human rights better. I realize that these proposals will be harshly criticized. I myself see some factors which are left without answers. If I nevertheless formulated these proposals, it is because I feel that the cause of human rights would be much better served if the period of tinkering came to an end and clear and more honest priorities became visible again.

Paul Mahoney and Jonathan Sharpe have taken up the ideas of Judge Carlo Russo and Frédéric Sudre and have submitted a proposal to create a new Supreme European Court of Human Rights.[104] This Court would be permanent, be composed of 15 judges and would more or less take the place of the Grand Chamber of the present Court. Instead of creating a purely filtering body below the present ECtHR, the two authors would create a Supreme Court above the present Court, endeavouring to concentrate and focus the case law and improve its quality. Such a two-tier system is obviously reminiscent of the pre-Protocol No 11 system with Commission and Court. Since, however, not all Member States would be represented in the Supreme Court, it is easy to foresee opposition to this proposal. Nonetheless my ideas about Court reform would also necessitate an amendment to the ECHR, and the proposal for a Supreme European Court of Human Rights might well be considered in such a context.

VI. Individual, Constitutional, and Administrative Justice

Recent years have witnessed a discussion about the so-called 'constitutional justice' of the ECtHR. Such a discussion may be an attempt to save the Court from its chronic overload, but also an attempt to redefine the role and the priorities of the Court. I shall submit various interpretations of what could be meant by 'constitutional justice'.

Although the intention of the founders of the Convention to avert totalitarianism and to preserve democracy is still a very legitimate aim of the ECHR, this is hardly how the system looks 60 years later. While there have been many important cases, only a few have been so exceptional as to influence, per se, the fate of a European democracy. The *Greek military junta* case may qualify,[105] perhaps also the cases which recognized the existence of a democracy's right to defend itself against its enemies, such as *Rekvényi, Refah Partisi*, or *Ždanoka*.[106] The founders of

---

[104] P. Mahoney and J. Sharpe, 'The Legacy of Carlo Russo: Creation of a Supreme European Court of Human Rights' in M. Romeris (ed), *Liber amicorum Pranas Kūris* (Vilnius: University Vilnius Press, 2008), 281–94.

[105] G. Nolte and S. Oeter in R. Bernhardt (ed), *Encyclopaedia of Public International Law* (2nd edn, Amsterdam: North Holland, 1995), 146–8.

[106] *Rekvényi v Hungary* Appl no 25390/94 (1999), ECHR 1999-III; *Refah Partisi* Appl nos 41340/98, 41342/98, ECHR 2003-II; *Ždanoka v Latvia*, n 3 above.

the Convention had intended to contribute to the prevention of war in Western and perhaps even in the whole of Europe. The 50 years of the ECtHR's existence have, however, witnessed much more normalcy than exeptionalism. To a large extent, the ECtHR has decided the same kind of issues as a domestic Supreme or Constitutional Court, according to similar principles, exploring whether the aims invoked to restrict human rights are legitimate, whether the restrictions are grounded in a sufficient legal basis, and whether they are proportionate and necessary in a democratic society.[107] Because of that similarity the ECtHR has been qualified as a quasi-Constitutional Court *sui generis*.[108] Despite the similarity, the ECtHR remains of course an international tribunal. This is why it operates in the fragmented and less-developed context of the international legal order,[109] with doctrines such as subsidiarity and margin of appreciation, and why its judgments are only declaratory and are not directly executory in municipal law, unlike those of the European Court of Justice.

I realize that those who take up the discussion among international law scholars about the so-called constitutionalization of international law might be warned (as Anne Peters puts it graphically) that the 'danger of blowing up an academic paper tiger is very real'.[110] Without wishing to speculate about the pleasures of 'a ride on a tiger', in my view democracy and human rights should be counted among the formative principles of contemporary international law. Also in that (second) sense the ECtHR could be classified as a 'quasi-Constitutional Court', and the ECHR is an important part of the constitution of Europe.

There are authors like Steven Greer who have still another (third) approach.[111] They speak of the constitutionalization of the ECtHR, meaning that only the most essential and grave issues should be submitted to it. This could be understood as a device to respond to the insoluble workload problem, which in turn leads to an insidious undermining of the credibility of the Court. It could also be understood as an attempt to distinguish between more or less absolute Convention guarantees, irrespective of workload issues, in an attempt to prevent the Court from encroaching on too many aspects of local concern only.

To complicate matters even more, complaints alleging administrative and governmental partiality and arbitrariness have led to a steady increase of right to

---

[107] Alec Stone Sweet and Jud Matthews speak in that context of 'Proportionality Balancing and Global Constitutionalism', 47 *Columbia Journal of Transnational Law* (2008), 27.

[108] Wildhaber, n 9 above, 113. And see S. Greer, n 19 above, 7: the ECtHR 'is already "the Constitutional Court for Europe," in the sense that it is the final authoritative judicial tribunal in the only pan-European constitutional system there is'.

[109] See for a general discussion, P. Mahoney, 'The International Judiciary—Independence and Accountability', 7 *Law and Practice of International Courts and Tribunals* (2008), 313–49; for a discussion which is more focused on the ECtHR, P. Mahoney, 'Separation of Powers in the Council of Europe: The Status of the ECtHR vis-à-vis the Authorities of the Council of Europe', 24 *Human Rights Law Journal* (2003), 152–61; Wildhaber, n 9 above, 113–35, 196–211, and passim. And see Judge Ziemele's dissenting opinion in *Andrejeva v Latvia*, 18.2.2009, no 55707/00.

[110] J. Klabbers, A. Peters, and G. Ulfstein, *The Constitutionalization of International Law* (Oxford: Oxford University Press, 2009), 343 (quoted from Anne Peters' Conclusions).

[111] S. Greer, 'Constitutionalizing Adjudication under the ECHR', 23 *Oxford Journal of Legal Studies* (2003), 405–33.

property cases before the ECtHR. At present 17 per cent of all applications are right to property cases.[112] If the Court were able to cope with its workload of more than 50,000 applications per year, then it would contribute not only to the protection of property, but also to the reduction of arbitrariness. Looking at recent complaints about inadequate compensation for expropriations, or about hidden or de facto expropriations, or about excessively high fines or fees, one should probably ask whether the ECtHR is in the process of becoming not only a quasi-Constitutional Court of Europe, but even (in a fourth sense) a 'quasi-Supreme Administrative Court of Europe', in charge of standing up against arbitrariness and excesses of State authorities.[113] In essence, there seems to be a development to treat the notion of arbitrariness as identical with the violation of human rights guarantees under the ECHR.[114] The described trend would confirm the idea advocated by some human rights lawyers that international human rights law is all-inclusive and therefore leaves no human rights free zones.[115] Indeed it would constitute an enormous success if the ECtHR could tame the arbitrariness of some State administrations and tribunals. There remains the anxious question of what would happen if the workload of the Court further exploded, and since such an explosion seems plausible enough that must of course be a very anxious question indeed, because a further explosion would further undermine the credibility of the Court.[116] In an imperfect world, the Court is flatly incapable of resolving all problems. As I have written elsewhere, 'If it suffices to say—as does the *Mamidakis v. Greece* judgment—that a fine constitutes "an element of property,"[117] then any amount of applications complaining about fines, fees, taxes or the like might reach the Court'.[118]

Elaborating on this last consideration about arbitrariness, a word of warning is needed. The notion of constitutional justice according to my firm conviction does not have a fifth sense and does not mean that all Member States have agreed to unleash a subsidiary international court from its fetters and to let it operate without any subsidiarity, without any margin of appreciation, and at the same time without any accountability.

VII. Conclusion

The ECHR has been qualified as 'the most effective human rights regime in the world'.[119] Of course, this cannot mean that it has not encountered major

---

[112] ECtHR, *Some Facts and Figures* (January 2008).
[113] Cf L. Wildhaber and I. Wildhaber, 'Recent Case Law on the Protection of Property in the ECHR' in C. Binder, U. Kriebaum, A. Reinisch, and S. Wittich (eds), *International Investment Law for the 21st Century: Essays in Honour of Christoph Schreuer* (Oxford: Oxford University Press, 2009), 674–6.
[114] The question arises whether the production of arbitrary judgments by a national system amounts to a structural problem.
[115] J. Viljanen, The ECtHR as a Developer of the General Doctrines of Human Rights Law (Tampere: Tampere University Press, 2003), 25.
[116] See Section V above.
[117] *Mamidakis v Greece* Appl no 35533/04 (2007).
[118] See n 113 above, 676.
[119] H. Keller, and A. Stone Sweet, n 31 above, 3.

challenges. The overload is the most obvious one. But to find a proper long-term perspective and balance, to identify lasting and new problems, without neglecting the necessary willingness of the national instances and particularly tribunals, remains an ongoing challenge. The ECHR system and especially the right of individual application has many merits. But it should not be understood as untouchable. Otherwise—alluding to the expression that the Court is a victim of its own success—the Court might indeed one day become a victim. And that would surely not help the right of individual petition, which would become a victim, too.

Index

Index